The Economics and Politics of European Integration

The Economics and Politics of European Integration offers a comprehensive history of European integration, from the conceptualization of a United States of Europe, to the present day. The special role of the United States in this process of integration, and the expansion and evolution of the European Union, is critically analyzed. The book also thoroughly discusses the current view of the EU and the complex crises emerging from the COVID-19 pandemic.

While the book focuses primarily on Europe, the role of other countries is also examined. The rise of hostile enemies from Turkey, Russia, the US and China is explored, and the history and outcome of Brexit also receives unique focus. Maps are used throughout to clearly depict the enlargement process.

This illuminating text will be valuable reading for students and researchers across international economics, economic history, political economy and European studies.

Ivan T. Berend has been Distinguished Research Professor at UCLA since 1990. He was born in Budapest, Hungary, and studied at the Budapest University of Economics and Lorand Eötvös University. He worked as an assistant professor at the University of Economics (1953), as an associate and full professor (1963) and as Distinguished Professor of History at the University of California History Department (1960–1985) before taking up his current post.

The Economics and Politics of European Integration

Populism, Nationalism and the History of the EU

Ivan T. Berend

LONDON AND NEW YORK

First published 2021
by Routledge
2 Park Square, Milton Park, Abingdon, Oxon OX14 4RN

and by Routledge
52 Vanderbilt Avenue, New York, NY 10017

Routledge is an imprint of the Taylor & Francis Group, an informa business

© 2021 Ivan T. Berend

British Library Cataloguing-in-Publication Data
A catalogue record for this book is available from the British Library

Library of Congress Cataloging-in-Publication Data
A catalog record for this book has been requested

ISBN: 978-0-367-55842-0 (hbk)
ISBN: 978-0-367-55831-4 (pbk)
ISBN: 978-1-003-09537-8 (ebk)

Typeset in Galliard
by Apex CoVantage, LLC

To my late friend, Alan Milward, the best historian of European integration

Contents

Illustrations

Boxes

Tables

Maps

A personal introductory note

I have to start with a confession: I am a convinced believer in the historical importance of European integration. As a historian of modern Europe, my life-long study of Europe has shown me that the integration of Europe through the formation of the European Union is one of the greatest historical events in the entire history of the old Continent. Aside from my academic study of this topic, my personal involvements in the tumults of the last century have also poignantly led me to this conclusion.

I was born in the wrong place at the wrong time: during the middle of history's deepest economic crisis, the Great Depression, and in an authoritarian Central European country that was the intimate ally of Benito Mussolini's fascist Italy that would, in a few years, become a close friend of Hitler's Nazi Germany. At the time, I was too young to understand the significance of these events. I was still not yet 10 years old when history's most devastating war, World War II, began. For me, Europe was only a map where my father – when he was still at home, before he was taken away – showed me the moving fronts. I was too young to fully understand what the war meant, and I enjoyed the long "coal breaks" from school that occurred because they were unable to heat the classrooms in the winter.

Soon I learned the real meanings of war and fascism when they decimated my family. At 14 years old in a Hungarian prison cell, I first experienced the horror of fascist Hungary, and soon after, the brutality of Nazi Germany. I survived and returned to Hungary. I hoped and enthusiastically believed in a changed world, but in a couple of years' time, the country became part of the Soviet Bloc and hermetically closed. Europe was divided, the two parts separated; the real Europe was far away for me, unknown and unapproachable. Mass tourism emerged in the West, but I was closed off in Hungary, unable to visit even the next neighboring countries. I studied economics and history at university during the worst Stalinist period in Hungary, without learning or even knowing about modern economics and the true historical record. I was in my 20s and already an assistant professor when I participated at a huge demonstration with a large group of my students that came to change the course of history. As we stood in the square in front of the Parliament building in Budapest, named after the mid-nineteenth-century revolutionary freedom fighter Lajos Kossuth, the 1956 revolution began and wanted to change the country.

I was 30 years old when I was finally able to travel to the West and see what felt like the "real" Europe for the first time – unlike the Europe I knew, it was rich, safe, democratic and already on the road towards integration. This trip was actually my second journey across the Continent. The first occurred in the summer of 1945, when I returned from a Nazi prison camp amidst a Europe in ruin; now, fifteen years later during my second trip in 1960, it was already flourishing. The European Economic Community seemed to like a miracle – it offered the greatest promise of peace for a war-ridden Europe. Two hundred of Europe's 400-year history had seen major recurring wars between its countries. Countries launched wars again and again, breeding political instability and destruction. I learned this history through my own life experiences, and became an historian of modern Europe to study its causes. The European Union, although I never lived within its territory, became a very personal issue for me.

During the last third of my life, as Professor of History at the University of California, Los Angeles, I passionately researched and taught the history of modern Europe, especially the economic history of the nineteenth and twentieth centuries, the complex story of Central and Eastern Europe and last but not least, the history of the European Union. I spent the first decade of the twenty-first century searching archives, reading tons of studies and burying myself in statistical volumes. These efforts led me to publish four books on the various historical problems of the EU over the course of the 2010s.

As I write this study at the beginning of the next decade, nationalist-populist parties are viciously attacking the integrated Union from within. Authoritarian rule and many of the ugly elements of the past have returned to some countries in Europe. These developments are examples of the phenomenon that the French Annales School of History dubbed "path dependence" and that the writer Thomas Mann artistically called the "renewal of the past in the present."[1] The regeneration of such forces exemplifies a tragic historical phenomenon and represents an immense danger for integration. It is also a painful personal experience for me. Britain has already stepped out of the European Union, which is surrounded by hostile enemies in the east and southeast; Russia and China are attempting to divide the member countries and gain greater spheres of interest in Europe; and America, having launched tariff wars against the bloc, is no longer a firm ally. The European Union has declined into crisis.

While this situation is very bad, it also represents an opportunity. This moment may be a crucial turning point in which the future will be hammered out. As Jean Monnet, one of the founding fathers of the EU wisely recognized and noted in his oft-quoted memoir line, "Europe will be forged in crises, and will be the sum of the solutions adopted for those crises."[2] In this moment of crucial transition, I have decided to sum up everything I have learned and previously published about European integration, adding information that my most recent years of research and continued reflections on my historical experience have produced.

I have learned from both my studies and personal experiences that the project of European integration and, indeed, the history of Europe are not comprehensible without an understanding of the entire worldwide economic and political environment or without an appreciation of the impact of the international capitalist economic regime and the influence of global political order. The isolationist economic nationalism and wartime command economy during the first half of the twentieth century had a devastating effect on the Continent. After World War II, the reestablishment of the capitalist free market and trade system became a must for the United States, Europe and the world. Without this crucially important incentive, European integration would probably not have happened. It definitely would not have occurred without the influence of a second international factor, the ascendancy of a parallel Cold War world political order, which made the project of developing a united Western world compulsory. The United States, the unquestionable leader of the postwar West, consequently pushed Western Europe to integrate. This American influence started with the Marshall Plan and dominated throughout the 1950s and 1960s. Thus, postwar crisis led to renewal.

In the 1970–1980s, globalization became another major incentive for further European integration. Europe lost a great part of its own market to rivals – the United States, Japan and the "Small Asian Tigers." This critical international challenge forced Europe to further integrate via regionalizing the European market by introducing the Single Market between 1985 and 1992 and the common currency, the euro, at the turn of the millennium. Today, the "Trump factor" has weakened the NATO alliance and destabilized the American security umbrella that had offered comfortable, stable security to Europe for half a century. Rivals and enemies continue to throng, trying to divide Europe. Europe has to speak with one voice. Stable and safe defense for Europe must be taken into European hands. Consequently, after the decades-long resistance of some of the nation-states, the European Union has already taken the first steps towards the establishment of a joint European army.

As I have stated, these examples amply demonstrate why one cannot begin to understand European integration without contextualizing it within the global economic and political environment. And as I alluded to, I also learned this historical lesson as a result of my life experiences during the major conflicts of the twentieth century. What happened to my family in Hungary when I was a teenager could not have happened without the events that unfolded in Germany. But by the same token, I would not have survived Nazism if the Russian army did not storm Hitler's bunker in Berlin, if America did not enter the war or if the American army did not liberate me near Munich.

***

I offer this volume to my readers as a record of all that I have learned. I present the history of the European Union from its genesis as a mere idea (now already a century ago), through its realization, and to its present-day crisis. Along the way, I introduce the proponents – idealist dreamers and calculating, pragmatist integrationist politicians – who played decisive roles in building Europe, as well as some of the short-sighted, power-hungry, selfish, nationalist-populist enemies of integration, who wanted to stop the project and sought to undermine it. I present the full history of modern European integration from the beginning, through successful and crisis-ridden periods, in often troubled, but always pressing international environments. This book gives the account of what I have seen as a first-hand witness, and what I have researched as a committed historian.

Ivan T. Berend, Los Angeles, 8 April 2020

Notes

1 Thomas Mann, "Freud and the Future," *Daedalus* 88, no. 2 (1959): 376–378.
2 Jean Monnet, *Memoirs*, trans. Richard Mayne (Garden City, NY: Doubleday, 1978), 417.

1 The new postwar economic and political world order

The ground paved for European integration

War devastation

World War II left the global capitalist economy in an extremely troubled state, especially with regard to the European arena. First of all, the most devastating war in history – which 30 countries participated in between 1939 and 1945 – left Europe (but also some other parts of the world) in ruins, and decimated the global population. About 70–85 million people, or 4 percent of the world's population, were killed by military (or military-related) attacks or hunger. China lost about 20 million people; the entire Pacific region lost roughly 30 million people. Europe's share was overwhelming: 40 million deaths, or roughly 10 percent of the continent's population. In some countries such as Poland (5 million), the losses amounted to 15 percent of the total prewar population. The Soviet Union lost about 27 million people; Germany 9 million; Yugoslavia 1 million; France and Britain together more than 1 million; and Romania, Hungary and Italy together more than 2 million. The Holocaust killed 6 million Jewish victims in Europe.

After the war, fascist countries and the courts in formerly occupied countries tried many criminals and Nazi collaborators. Some were imprisoned and even hanged, while many more were dismissed from their previous jobs. Millions were expelled from several countries, and tens of thousands were punished by local communities without due legal process. In France and Italy, for example, between 10,000 and 11,000 people were lynched.

The war did not fully stop after it officially ended on 8 May 1945 in Europe, nor on 2 September 1945 after the Japanese surrender. Revolutionary wars in Asia and Africa continued, and Europe also experienced civil war in Greece, bloody revenge in France and Italy, ethnic cleansing that expelled millions in most of Central and Eastern Europe, and uncontrollable criminal activities and famine all over the continent. These struggles caused hundreds of thousands of additional deaths until stability gradually returned in the 1950s.

Millions of "displaced persons" – an important new phenomenon – flooded Europe. About 13 million Germans escaped or were expelled from central and eastern Europe and moved to Germany. The Soviet Union expelled 2 million Poles from the newly acquired territories of former eastern Poland, east of the famous Curzon Line that became part of the Soviet Union. Hungarians were expelled from Czechoslovakia. Anti-Jewish pogroms in Poland and Hungary after the war pushed about 1 million Jewish survivors of the Holocaust to leave Europe. Prisoners of war, forced laborers and survivors of Nazi concentration camps ("Häftlingen") from several countries – 5 million Russians among them, in addition to millions of Germans, French, Italians, Hungarians and others – were gradually released. About 21 million displaced peoples flooded roads across Europe and started wandering home. About 10 million demobilized servicemen from nations across the world also returned to their home countries and began looking for jobs. Millions of orphans, unaccompanied children, "tired, wan, broken little old men and women, who had forgotten – or never knew – how to play," (in Yugoslavia alone, for example, 300,000 such individuals) – needed some placement. Millions suffered from starvation and survived on less than 1,000 calories per day.[1] In Poland, for example, the average daily caloric intake was only approximately 930 calories, hardly enough to survive. In the winter of 1944–1945, 20,000 Dutch people died due to the severe hunger crisis. Hunger continued to hit the continent into 1945–1946. In the spring of 1945, the media reported about widespread famine and "critical situation" in Germany, Austria, Italy, Spain, Poland and Portugal. "Hungry nations," reported the *New York Times* in April 1945, "have 11–12 million tons of wheat instead of the 20 million, needed."[2]

By the end of 1945, the high death toll and sharply declined wartime birth rates produced a population deficit of roughly 110–120 million. The total number of those wounded and crippled is not exactly known, but it is estimated that four to five times more people were injured by military actions than those who were killed, so altogether it is likely that the true total highly surpasses these numbers. As British historian Keith Lowe describes in the introduction to his *Savage Continent: Europe in the Immediate Aftermath of World War II* (2012):

> Imagine a world without institutions. There are no governments . . . no school or universities . . . no access to any information whatsoever. . . . There are no banks, because money no longer has any worth. There are no shops, because no one has anything to sell. . . . Law and order are virtually non-existent because there is no police force and no judiciary. . . . Men with weapons roam the streets, taking what they want and threatening anyone who gets in their way. Women of all classes and ages prostitute themselves for food and protection.[3]

The physical destruction was also unbelievable. In the Soviet Union, 1,700 towns and 70,000 villages were devastated. Germany lost about 70 percent of its housing. In the 49 largest cities, most of the downtown centers were eliminated, and nearly 40 percent of the dwelling units were destroyed or seriously damaged. Britain lost 30 percent of the countries' dwellings; France, Belgium and the Netherlands all lost between 20–20 percent each. Transportation was totally paralyzed: huge parts of the railway tracks, bridges, locomotives and even wagons were destroyed. Half of both the European railroad capacity and the continent's industrial infrastructure were eliminated. Significant parts of the land remained uncultivated in 1944–1945 due to military movements, a labor-force shortage and the destruction of animal stock and instruments. France was robbed by Nazi Germany and Britain was crippled by shouldering the tremendous burden of the war. On the Axis side, the Paris Peace Treaty demanded huge reparation payments. Germany lost about $10 billion (in today's value, $131 billion) in patents and know-how as a part of "intellectual reparation"; furthermore, the Allies took over more than 700 German industrial plants. Italy had to pay $360 million (about 4.3 billion today) to Yugoslavia, Greece, Albania, Ethiopia and the Soviet Union. Most of the European countries suffered a loss of value equal to two to three years of their prewar annual national income. The destruction was especially catastrophic in the eastern half of the continent. Poland lost 30 percent of its buildings, agricultural properties, industrial and electric power facilities and mines. Yugoslavia lost 21 percent of dwellings. All of Hungary's spectacular Danube bridges were underwater. High inflation hit several countries and Hungary suffered world history's highest inflation when in the summer of 1946, in one single month the Hungarian pengő (the currency unit) had a monthly inflation rate of 42 quadrillion percent and, the currency, at the peak of inflation lost more than 10 percent of its value per hour, thus no one accepted money any longer, but jewelry, closing and furniture, thus the country returned to the ancient trade in kind. In July 1946, one US dollar was equivalent with the astronomical number of 460 trillion-trillion pengő.[4]

As Table 1.1 shows, Austria and Germany's per capita national income dropped to less than half. At the end of World War II, the GDP per capita in France, Italy and the Netherlands had sunk to somewhat more than half of the prewar level. However, most of the countries in Western Europe had returned to their prewar (1938) economic levels by 1948.

The collapse of colonial empires

These immense losses weakened the former European colonial great powers – Britain, France, Holland and Belgium – who were unable to continue ruling their former empires after the war ended. In Asia, several European powers lost control of their colonies during Japanese occupation, and did not regain them after the conflict ended. More importantly, strong, well-armed national liberation movements emerged in Asia and Africa at the end of the war and fought against their former rulers. The Vietnamese resistance against Japanese occupation that Ho Chi Minh lead during the war transformed into armed resistance against French

Table 1.1 Drop in per capita GDP (in 1990 USD): the postwar years compared to 1938[5]

Year	Austria	Denmark	France	Germany	Italy	Holland	Britain	US
1938	3,583	5,544	4,424	5,129	3,244	5,122	5,938	6,134
1945	1,736	4,874	2,549	4,326	1,880	2,621	6,737	11,722
1946	1,969	5,577	3,818	2,503	2,448	4,348	6,440	9,207
1947	2,181	5,806	4,099	2,763	2,856	4,357	6,306	8,896

colonial rule afterwards. France launched a series of years-long colonial wars to preserve its empire. They fought against independence movements in Indochina between late 1946 and the spring of 1954 and in North Africa against the Algerian National Liberation Front between 1954 and 1962, but lost all of those wars on both continents. The Netherlands confronted an Indonesian independence revolt followed by the Proclamation of Indonesian Independence in 1945. After military confrontations, the Netherlands recognized Indonesia's independence at the end of 1949. In India, Britain faced the revival of nationalist forces and the reemergence of the fight for independence that had destabilized its control of the region in the nineteenth century. This push for independence gained strength from the non-violent resistance efforts led by Mahatma Gandhi. During World War II, Britain needed Indian assistance for their war efforts. As a result, after the war the British issued the Indian Independence Act in 1947 without military confrontation. India remained a Dominion until January 1950, but then became an independent country and Britain lost its crown-jewel colony.[6]

The mighty British colonial empire started to melt down after the war, and by 1960 – only one and a half decades later – the territorial gains it had assumed over the previous 400 years had vanished. The African colonies became independent one after another during the 1950s and early 1960s. With very little exceptions, the world colonial system spectacularly collapsed. All of the rich Western European countries lost their colonies; as a result, about 150 new independent countries emerged.[7]

A return to normalcy?

The task of coping with wartime devastation and encouraging postwar recovery posed more than enough challenges by itself. Unfortunately, the capitalist economic system itself also had deep longstanding wounds that needed to be cured. During the first half of the twentieth century – and especially in the interwar decades – the world economy was not in a normal state. Harsh protectionism and nationalist economic isolation had created deadly rivalries among nations even during peacetime. The free trade system that had dominated the global economic scene for the latter half of the nineteenth century was eliminated. The United States gradually turned to protectionism. The origins of this policy shift date from the introduction of the first tariffs in 1816, soon followed by higher ones in 1824, 1862 and 1864. The two real turning points, however, were the introductions of the McKinley Act in 1890 and the Dingley Tariff in 1897. After this last measure, the defensive tariff reached 57 percent of the value of imported goods. The United States entered the twentieth century under an economic regime of high protectionism.

United Germany followed. In 1879, the country introduced a rather moderate tariff, but subsequently increased the rate by introducing higher tariffs in 1885, 1888 and 1902. These last general tariffs introduced high protections for finished industrial and agricultural products. This policy shift was not restricted to Germany: the laissez-faire system came under attack all over Europe at the turn of the century, with Russia leading the charge. The country first introduced tariffs in 1868 and significantly increased them in 1891, 1893 and 1900 in order to defend its infant industry. Switzerland introduced tariffs in 1884 and significantly increased them in 1906, Italy followed suit in 1887, and France likewise introduced tariffs in 1892 and raised them in 1910. By the start of World War I, only Britain, the Netherlands and Denmark had preserved the free trade system.

Nevertheless, World War I became a real turning point. Even Britain, the originator of free trade system, turned to protectionism. France and virtually all other European countries followed. Italy and Germany put in place agricultural tariffs of 66 percent and 83 percent, respectively. At their peaks, protective tariffs across Europe were as high as 40–50 percent of the value of imported products. In some cases the industrial consumer goods tariffs reached 70 percent – 170 percent of the original goods' value. Most of the countries used tariffs *de combat*, instituting extremely high tariffs as bargaining weapons to force their partners to compromise. By the second half of the 1920s, Europe was already fighting a bitter trade war. Many of the Central and Eastern European countries, some of which had been newly created after World War I, also introduced high tariffs during this period: Bulgaria did so in 1922 and 1924; Romania in 1924 and 1927; Austria, Hungary and Yugoslavia in 1925; and Czechoslovakia in 1926.

By 1924, the situation had escalated so far that John Maynard Keynes proclaimed "The End of Laissez-faire" in his eponymous Sidney Ball Lecture at Oxford University. However, this moment did not yet mark the end. France pioneered a new import quota system, and by 1939 already 19 countries had adopted it. The widespread introduction of this system further damaged the global capitalist system: "Import quotas were even more damaging to international trade than tariffs, since a quota limits the level of possible imports [in fixed quantities] and thus operates independently of the price mechanism."[8]

The interwar years saw the worst economic crisis of modern times. The events of the early twentieth century – the catastrophic Great Depression, closely sandwiched between two highly counterproductive economic periods produced by ultranationalist policies and two devastating world wars – pushed the capitalist world economic system to the brink.

Post-World War I European economic development was rather slow. While Western Europe increased its GDP by 76 percent between 1870 and 1913, it's GDP only increased by 27 percent between 1913 and 1938. In southern Europe, the rates of economic growth during the same periods were 58 percent

Table 1.2 Economic growth measured by GDP per capita before and after World War I (in 1990 USD)[9]

Year	Western Europe		Southern Europe		Eastern Europe	
1870	2,110	57%	1,111	63%	1,030	66%
1913	3,704	100%	1,753	100%	1,557	100%
1938	4,719	127%	1,931	110%	2,083	142%

and 10 percent, respectively. Eastern Europe was the only exception: the growth performances during the pre- and postwar periods were very similar: 51 percent and 42 percent. This similarity was mainly caused by the unique Soviet growth rate of 50 percent.

More importantly, the southern and eastern peripheries did not experience economic breakthroughs leading to a modern restructuring of their economies. While industrial economies had emerged in the West during the nineteenth century, agriculture remained the leading sector in the peripheral regions of Europe until the mid-twentieth century. While agriculture employed only 13 percent of the labor force in the West, during the same period this sector employed 41 percent of the population in southern Europe and more than 50 percent in Eastern Europe. At this time modern services had barely been developed in these regions. The prevalence of import-substituting industrialization policies in this part of Europe led to the development of foundational consumer-goods industries, in areas such as textile. While these industries were already declining in the West, these sectors between doubled and quadrupled increased their outputs in Europe's peripheral regions.

Moreover, the Russian communist revolution and emergence of the Soviet Union – with its state-owned, forced industrialization economic regime – posed a serious ideological challenge to the traditional liberal capitalist world economic system. After World War II, this challenge became even more dangerous because communism was on the rise: it was introduced into the eastern half of Europe by a series of postwar Soviet occupations that culminated in the creation of the Soviet Bloc. It became successful in China and Vietnam; and despite the efforts of the Truman Doctrine, it even spread over to Latin America and post-colonial Africa.

This communist challenge precipitated economic rivalries and galvanized major reforms within the capitalist world economic system. In many ways the resultant situation reprised many of the challenges of the war, which had likewise required social solidarity within belligerent countries and generated widespread economic transformation, such as the rise of welfare capitalism and the move towards more equalized income distribution. Overall, Europe was in ruins after enduring wars that decimated the population of the continent. Isolated Europe remained behind the renewed technology of America that had emerged before and during the war years.

The economic forecasts for postwar Europe generated by the world's best economists were very dark. Writing in 1943, Paul Samuelson prophesized,

> When this war comes to an end. . . . We shall have to face a difficult reconversion period during which current goods cannot be produced and layoffs may be great. . . . The final conclusion to be drawn from our experience at the end of the last war is inescapable. . . . *Were the war to end suddenly in the next 6 months . . . there would be ushered in the greatest period of unemployment and industrial dislocation which any economy has ever faced.*[10]

Likewise, Gunnar Myrdal's 1944 *Atlantic Monthly* article "Is American Business Deluding Itself?" also predicted "a high degree of economic unrest" and even an "epidemic of violence" after the war.[11]

Transforming the wartime economic regimes into peacetime ones and rebuilding the destroyed Europe were already tremendous enterprises. The necessary host of postwar undertakings seems almost Sisyphean when one considers the concurrent imperatives faced by countries around the world: the creation of expensive new welfare regimes, the return from isolated national economies to free trade systems, and the integration of these systems into a transforming and newly globalizing world economic system.

Europe's situation was especially grim because it had fallen from its status as a conglomerate of world powers. The continent became extremely dependent upon the rapidly elevating United States. In 1900, the US had a $4,096 per capita GDP, less than that of Britain or the Netherlands. Just a little over a decade later, by 1913, America's per capita GDP rose to $5,307, surpassing that of Britain ($5,032) and outpacing the average per capita GDP of Western Europe ($3,704) by 43 percent. By 1938, the American average reached $6,134; in 1945, it had soared to $11,722; and by 1950, the average income level had surpassed the average West European level by nearly double (189 percent). The number of scientific workers in America's industry was quintuple that of Britain. On top of these defeats, Europe also lost its role as a major powerhouse of international banking, as by mid-century three-quarters of the world's gold reserves were in American hands. Europe could no longer pose as a serious capitalist competitor to the United States; the continent became dependent on American credits and technology exports. Western Europe received $17 billion in resources from the US via the Marshall Plan – equal to 1.8 percent of the American GDP between 1948 and 1952 – to rebuild and modernize. The United States became the pioneer of modern technology and the monopolist of nuclear energy, producing revolutionary inventions as varied as penicillin, microwaves, microchips and computers. Whereas decimated Europe produced an annual average population growth of 0.6 percent, the US population increased by 50 percent between 1913 and 1950. In the same period, Europe's share in producing the world's total GDP dropped from one-third to one-quarter, while its share of world exports dropped from 60 percent to 41 percent. Western Europe's post-WWII productivity level was 46 percent of the American productivity level; that of the Mediterranean region and Eastern Europe was only 24 percent.

While American economic development was based on the *intensive* development model, which valorized innovation and productivity increases, from the postwar decades until the 1960s Europe relied upon an *extensive* development model, using imported technology and increasing labor input to generate economic growth. In other words, Europe's economy became a follower of, and dependent upon, on the United States.

The capitalist world economy had to be radically rebuilt. Luckily, as its entire history has proved, this system has the capacity for renewal. As the Austrian-American economist Joseph Schumpeter noted, the capitalism of the British Industrial Revolution – including, we should add, the capitalism of interwar Europe – and the capitalism after World War II, should hardly be called by the same name, as they exhibit such markedly different characteristics. Ultimately, rebuilding the capitalist economic regime occurred in two main veins after the war: the intro-duction of welfare capitalism, and the return to the international division of labor and the free trade system.

Rebuilding the postwar capitalist economic regime: welfare capitalism

The capitalist economic regime required a major renewal during the exception-ally deep economic crisis of the Great Depression and the war years, which necessitated maximum countrywide efforts and thus national solidarity. The first steps towards a European welfare state were taken in Sweden during the mid-dle of the Great Depression after the Social Democratic Party gained power in 1932. In the worst year of crisis, Swedish socialists opened a new chapter in the history of capitalism. Their example became increasingly important during the war, when solidarity became a central demand and then a requirement. Noth-ing exemplifies this trend better than Winston Churchill's wartime coalition government in Britain, which appointed a committee led by economist William Beveridge to analyze the existing social insurance and service system and make recommendations. Beveridge presented his report in 1942 and proposed the introduction of a comprehensive social welfare system to eliminate the "five giant evils": want, disease, ignorance, squalor and idleness. The report presented a complex program. Among other goals, it stated that "Medical treatment cov-ering all requirements will be provided for all citizens . . . where needed without contribution conditions in any individual case." It also suggested providing a children's allowance; unemployment, disability, and training benefits; and pen-sion for everyone above 60 or 65 years of age for women and men respectively, regardless of previous income.[12]

This report became the basis for postwar reforms by the Clement Atlee Labor government after its victory in the first postwar elections of 1945 – to care for people "from the cradle to the grave." Fueled by this zeitgeist, Britain introduced the National Insurance Act and the National Assistance Act, and established the National Health Service.

This idea spread like wildfire throughout Europe. Austria initiated the *Sozial-partnerschaft*, a pact among the trade unions, entrepreneurs, and the government in 1947, followed by second, third, fourth, and fifth agreements. Price and wage controls were introduced. Swedish Socialists, conservative French Gaullists, and German and Italian Christian Democrats all adopted the same policy. The new French Constitution of 1946 declared: "Every worker may participate through his delegates in the collective determination of working conditions. . . . These committees . . . were involved with social welfare programs within the com-pany."[13] Germany introduced the *soziale Marktwirtschaft*, or social capitalism, a form of free market capitalism bolstered by widespread welfare-state social poli-cies. In 1950 they also enacted the *Wohnungsbaugesetz* to build 1.8 million new apartments in six years to offer affordable housing.[14] Although differences existed between countries, overall the new postwar European welfare capitalism offered free social and health services, free schooling at all levels, targeted full employment, stable prices, and an increased average income.

Building the free trade system and international institutions

Just as social cooperation became the rule on the national level, cooperation among countries once again became the rule in the international arena. This shift first required the total elimination of the interwar policies of self-sufficiency, protectionism and tariff wars and necessitated a return to the free trade system that had predominated in the nineteenth century. Two wars and the interwar economic warfare – which, as Sidney Pollard phrased it, produced "decisive traumatic effects on the whole of Europe" – taught an unforgettable lesson. The Western countries showed "a determination not to repeat the mistakes . . . and deliberately set about their task of formulating an international political and economic order" based on cooperation and international regulations.[15]

United States, the ultimate winner of the war and the benign hegemon of the western world, led the enactment of this policy. The US started building a coordinated and cooperative international regime. Two key institutions were established to serve this new order. The first targeted a well-working international monetary system. Before the end of the war in July 1944, the representatives of 44 nations gathered in Bretton Woods, New Hampshire to establish the International Monetary Fund (IMF); a multilateral payment system was introduced based on stable exchange rates and convertible currencies. The Fund could offer financial assistance to member countries from its reserves if they experienced payment difficulties. In the event of monetary troubles, the IMF would help the world monetary system return to normalcy. The member countries agreed not to use exchange restrictions and discriminatory measures until 1952. They all contributed to create the financial basis for the Fund through payments. Their contributions were based on a quota system due determined by their economic strength, and they agreed to voting rights based on contributions. The US's share was by far the biggest at $2.8 billion, followed by Britain's $1.3 billion; France and India's contributions were $450 million and $400 million, respectively. America, consequently, became the virtual leader of the world new monetary order. Through the new international financial institutions, meanwhile, the United States took responsibility for the budget deficits of other capitalist countries. The Bretton Woods Agreement also established the International Bank for Reconstruction and Development, commonly called the World Bank, via $10 billion in capital that was gradually increased to $21 billion. The World Bank's function was to give loans for reconstruction and assist development projects.

The other key institution of the new cooperative economic order was the General Agreement on Tariffs and Trade (GATT), established in Geneva in 1947 by 23 countries. They agreed to curb tariff barriers and import quotas in order to eliminate the economic nationalism that had flourished during the interwar period. In less than one and a half decades after its founding, the number of

GATT member countries increased to 70, which represented 80 percent of the world's trade. In less than a half a century, 123 countries (a number that has since grown to 164 countries) joined the renamed and much more efficient iteration of this institution, the World Trade Organization (WTO). When GATT was established, the average tariff level for participant countries was about 22 percent of value, but by 1999 this amount had dropped to 5 percent.

There are no doubt that all these postwar American initiatives served well-recognized, evident American self-interests. As a military and nuclear superpower, the United States significantly strengthened its economic standing to become the unquestioned world-dominant economic and financial power, ultimately establishing itself as the "leader of the free world" (meaning, of course, the world minus the gradually enlarging Soviet sphere of interest). The United States became highly interested in increasing its economic activities, conquering new markets, catalyzing trade, establishing companies and fostering subsidiaries by investments throughout the world. The free-trade system and the emerging globalization that started in the postwar years served American interests and further strengthened the influence of the United States.

Nevertheless, free trade and financial stability were also world interests *par excellence*, in that they reestablished a cooperative and peaceful world economy. Moreover, reestablishing these economic structures was the most important and urgent interest for war-devastated Europe. Peaceful cooperation and strengthened economic ties between winner and loser countries – in other words, the reestablishment of a peaceful continent and the reintegration of Germany into Europe – were vital goals for countries on the continent. Enacting this goal required the formulation of a new positive solution to the so-called "German Question," that would create assurances and avoid the possibility of a new war.

Immediately after the war, the first American, British and French solutions to the German Question called for deindustrialization, the overall weakening of Germany, and the dissolving of the territorial unity established in 1871. However, it was soon recognized that successful European reconstruction and the galvanization of a badly needed economic boom that would spark fast development in Europe would hardly be possible without Germany, which had been the engine of the European economy since late nineteenth century.

In the so-called Western world (including the entire western half of Europe), American-led international institutions bound countries together and opened a new chapter in the history of the capitalist economic regime. The economic ground for European cooperation was not only prepared in the postwar years, but elemental self-interests pushed war-ridden countries to cooperate and even somewhat integrate with each other economically. Pushing and assisting integration in the face of the rising Cold War confrontation became a definitive core of American policy.

American assistance to Europe

The United States, the victorious superpower, embarked upon a new road of foreign policy by assisting Europe. American assistance to save Europe began almost immediately after the war. By the spring of 1947, the United States had already given $11 billion to the liberated Western countries in the form of loans, food deliveries, and various kinds of shipments. Two years after the war, on 12 March 1947, President Truman addressed the US Congress: "The seeds of totalitarian regimes," he stated, "are nurtured by misery and want. They reach their full growth when the hope of a people for a better life has died. We must keep that hope alive." Economic and financial aid can assure "economic stability and orderly political processes."[16]

This speech established the political groundwork for major American aid to Europe. Shortly thereafter, Congress embarked upon a brand-new American foreign policy by approving $400 million in aid to Greece and Turkey. However, that was only the prologue. Less than three months later, on 5 June 1947, Secretary of State George Marshall delivered his famous speech at Harvard University, in which he announced a major new American aid program for Europe:

> In considering the requirements for the rehabilitation of Europe the physical loss of life, the visible destruction of cities, factories, mines and railroads was correctly estimated, but . . . this visible destruction was probably less serious than the dislocation of the entire fabric of European economy. . . . Long-standing commercial ties, private institutions, banks, insurance companies and shipping companies disappeared, through loss of capital, absorption through nationalization or by simple destruction. . . . Europe's requirements for the next three or four years of foreign food and other essential products – principally from America – are so much greater than her present ability to pay that she must have substantial additional help. . . . The modern system of the division of labor upon which the exchange of products is based is in danger of breaking down. . . . It is already evident that . . . the United States Government. . . [has to assist] the European world on its way to recovery. . . . It would be neither fitting nor efficacious for this Government to undertake to draw up unilaterally a program designed to place Europe on its feet economically. This is the business of the Europeans. The initiative, I think, must come from Europe. The role of this country should consist of friendly aid in the drafting of a European program and of later support of such a program.[17]

A day after the speech, British Foreign Minister Ernest Bevin contacted French Foreign Minister Georges Bidault and arranged a conference in Paris to define the nature of the economic problems and discuss what was needed from the US. On 12 July 1947, representatives of 17 nations (the Committee of European Economic Cooperation) began meeting to discuss the issues. The Committee reported on 12 September 1947 that the 17 nations needed $29 billion for the period of 1948–1951. The State Department scaled down this amount to $22 billion. On December 19, Truman submitted the European Recovery Program Bill to Congress, requesting $17 billion over the next four years (in the 2020 dollar value, this amount is more than one hundred times higher: about $180 billion). The Congress approved $13 billion (today roughly $130 billion). The program became law on 8 April 1948.

The Marshall Aid Program consumed 2.1 percent of the American GDP in 1948 and 2.4 percent in 1949; altogether, 1.8 percent of the American national income. The biggest receivers were Britain and France with 23 percent and 20.6 percent of the total aid, respectively. In the crucial first years of 1948–1949, the program contributed 14 percent, 10.9 percent and 5.3 percent to the Austrian, Dutch and Italian GDPs, respectively. During the entire aid period, its share equaled 2 percent of the recipients' GDPs. It helped to cover the huge trade deficits that those countries had accumulated during and after the war. These funds also contributed to an increase of recipients' capital formation during the first two years by roughly 10 percent (in the case of Germany, this influx was responsible for an increase of capital formation between 31 percent and 22 percent). Investment goods represented 20–37 percent for Belgium, Norway, France and Italy. This influx of capital helped the increase of recipients' industrial output by more than one-third.[18]

Beside the major financial assistance, the central goal of the Marshall Plan – as clearly described by the Harvard speech – was to force the European countries to work and make the decisions together. This cooperation was organized in 1947 by a newly established committee, which became the Organization for European Economic Cooperation (OEEC) in April 1948. The Committee worked out the reconstruction plans, including the distribution and uses of American aid. They also decided the terms of trade liberalization and the enacted the formation of the European Payment Union (EPU), which was officially formed in July 1950. Countries within the Union turned from bilateral to multilateral payments and trades and eliminated discriminatory trade measures. Trade within the EPU more than doubled during its existence until the end of 1958. As Derek Urwin correctly summed up in his book, the Marshall Plan was the "first lesson in economic cooperation."[19] Alan Milward, the preeminent expert of the Marshall Plan's history, rightly went much further when he called its organizations "a West European government in embryo."[20] As one of the best-informed American politicians during that time, Allen W. Dulles – who ran the Office of Strategic Services (OSS), which later became the Central Intelligence Agency (CIA), during the war – stated in his 1948 booklet *The Marshall Plan*, it was

> not a philanthropic enterprise. . . . The United States is the only country . . . which can really help to bring the European states together in a union. . . . [The idea of] a United States of Europe is not a project of mere dreamers.[21]

Rebuilding the capitalist economic world system by returning to free trade and international cooperation was at the center of postwar American policy. With its unique aid policy and overwhelming political and military power, the United States virtually forced its West European allies to cooperate and start integrating their economies. Such a development was not only highly favorable for the West European countries, but also created a better economic environment for rebuilding and maintaining strengthened alliances with the United States.

Rearranging the postwar world: the rising Cold War regime

Coercing West European integration was, however, not just one component of the larger American goal of rebuilding the international capitalist economic system. It was also – or, it would even be better to say, foremost – part and parcel of the new American policy to establish a new American-led world political order. Allen Dulles, in his earlier-quoted booklet about the Marshall Plan, clearly expressed that aiding Western Europe "is the only peaceful course now open to us, which may answer the communist challenge."[22]

As at the end of World War I, when the seeds of World War II had already been sown, clouds of deadly new conflict started to gather and threaten the possibility of World War III even before the guns had muted in 1945. This time two wartime allies, the United States and the Soviet Union, turned against each other in a frightening Cold War confrontation.

During the war against Hitler, the alliance composed of United States, Britain, and the Soviet Union carried the greatest burden and sacrificed the most people in the war. At that time, of course, these western and eastern allies had a basic common interest. To realize it, they accepted and even helped to realize their allies' interests. Two famous episodes clearly prove it. The firs happened in October 1944, when Winston Churchill visited Stalin in Moscow. As Churchill himself described, after his arrival from the airport to the Kremlin, he turned to Stalin before they set down for dinner and said,

> Let us settle about our affairs in the Balkans. . . . How would it do for you to have 90 percent predominance in Romania, for us to have 90 percent of the say in Greece and so fifty-fifty about Yugoslavia?

Churchill also offered 75 percent Russian dominance in Bulgaria and 50 percent in Hungary.[23] Stalin immediately accepted this share of influence and certainly believed it to be a base for a postwar sphere-of-influence arrangement. As Evan Luard, a French historian of the Cold War, stated, "Stalin interpreted his wartime discussions with the Western allies as implying that he would have a predominant influence in Eastern Europe in exchange for American and British influence in Western Europe."[24]

The second noteworthy episode happened in December 1944 after the Red Army liberated Poland. The Big Three–Roosevelt, Stalin and Churchill – had already discussed the postwar Soviet-Polish border question in their Teheran meeting, and finalized the agreement at the Yalta Conference in February 1945. Roosevelt and Churchill basically accepted and agreed with Stalin's argument that the Soviets' security interests necessitated the redrawing the borders between the Soviet Union and Poland by literary shifting Poland to the west and giving the former eastern Polish territories (east from the so-called Curzon Line[25]) to the Soviet Union. In return, Poland would be compensated with confiscated eastern territories from Germany.

Nevertheless, suspicion and conflict between the allies also accompanied the entire wartime period of alliance. Both sides wanted long-term guarantees for their own securities – sometimes at the expense of the alliance. Furthermore, the old ideological political differences, suspicion and conflict never ceased; these tensions sharpened as the war neared its end. For example, in February 1945, Stalin received a military intelligence report about a secret American-British and Nazi German meeting in neutral Switzerland, initiated by Karl Wolf, the commander of the German SS forces in Italy, about the German surrender. Stalin immediately angrily complained to Roosevelt that the Western allies had not informed or included Russia in this meeting. Moreover, he stated that he had knowledge about an American-British agreement with Marshal Kesselring "to open the front and permit the Anglo-American troops to advance to the East."[26] Stalin was convinced that he had been betrayed.

Other episodes strengthened his resentment. In May 1945, the Soviets asked for a $6 billion wartime American Lend-Lease loan to promote reconstruction, but President Truman – who assumed the presidency after the death of Roosevelt in April 1945 – rejected this request.[27] Meanwhile, however, Truman continued the wartime Lend-Lease loan program for Britain. Furthermore, the United States forgave the repayment of American wartime loans for Britain, but not for the Soviets. Lastly, an even more frightening event occurred on July 1945, when the first American atomic bomb was tested and detonated in Alamogordo, New Mexico. For Stalin this testing made clear that the US had a new superweapon that they had kept secret from Stalin (which, in fact, they had – Roosevelt and Churchill agreed to do so in a September 1944 meeting at Roosevelt's Hyde Park home).

On the other hand, various Soviet steps had irritated and frightened the Western allies. In December 1944, when the Red Army liberated Poland, Stalin appointed a Polish provisional government from the Lublin Committee, which had been formed by him from his circle of Polish communist friends. This choice was a clear sign that Stalin was going to create a satellite country in Poland. After the other allies expressed outraged, Stalin tried to win over Roosevelt, explaining that

> the Soviet Union is interested [in Poland] more than any other power . . . because Poland is a border state with the Soviet Union and the problem of Poland is inseparable from the problem of security of the Soviet Union.[28]

Roosevelt did not accept this explanation, replying, "I am disturbed and deeply disappointed over your message on December 27 in regard to Poland."[29] Another expression of Stalin's expansionist plans manifested in Iran. In 1941, the Allies decided to invade and occupy Iran in order to protect their wartime supply chains to Russia and gain necessary supplies. However, they agreed that they would all withdraw their troops from the country six months after the end of the war. However, when this deadline expired in early 1946, Stalin refused to withdraw and instead supported his separatist Iranian allies. Actually, this was the very first Cold War crisis; it only ended with Soviet withdrawal after very serious Western warnings.

Although Roosevelt's attitude towards the Soviet Union had already started to change during the final part of the war, it was President Truman who ended the friendly relations that his predecessor President Roosevelt had built with the Soviet Union. Against the warnings of two of his cabinet ministers – Henry L. Stimson, the secretary of war since 1940, and Henry A. Wilson, Roosevelt's former vice president and currently the secretary of commerce – Truman decided to distance the United States from the Soviets. He decided not to share atomic secrets with the Soviets, as had Stimson recommended, and not to build shared international military bases, as Wilson had warned were important for maintaining friendly relations with Stalin. Instead, both secretaries were dismissed from Truman's government. The warnings, of course, had solid bases, and Truman's rejections of both men's suggestions naturally generated suspicion on the Soviet side.

Stalin felt a sense of rivalry with newly strengthened America. As a result, he naturally returned to the old Russian military defense strategy that had generated historical successes since the Napoleonic offensive: securing the country's western borders by building a large buffer zone to guard against any possible military attacks that might come from the West. Stalin began instituting this policy in Poland even before America had started establishing its system of worldwide military bases. When the competition became manifest, Stalin enlarged the buffer zone by gradually incorporating the liberated-occupied region of central Europe and the Balkans, crowning it by incorporating Hungary and Czechoslovakia into the Soviet Bloc and creating the German Democratic Republic from the Soviet-occupied east German territories between 1947 and 1949.

The bomb and the nuclear arms race

Truman, who considered Roosevelt's Soviet policy naïve, rejected the possibility of an alliance and turned instead to open hostility against the Soviet Union. Even at the first meeting of the victorious powers after the end of the European war in Potsdam in July 1945, serious differences began to emerge despite the veneer of politeness. Major tensions arose regarding Germany, especially over the amount of German reparations to the Soviet Union. At this meeting, Truman informed Stalin about his "new weapon of unusual destructive force."[30] During his way back to Washington, Truman received the news that on 6 August 1945, the first atomic bomb had been dropped on Hiroshima; three days later, the second was dropped on Nagasaki, killing 300,000 people altogether. In the meantime, as a result of the agreement by the great powers, the Soviet troops invaded Japanese-occupied Manchuria on 8 August. Emperor Hirohito announced Japan's unconditional surrender on 15 August. World War II ended.

Truman and his supporters justified the use of the atomic bomb by pointing out that this method saved more than 100,000 American lives by avoiding an invasion of Japan. Beside this official American explanation for the bomb's usage, there was another reason as well. The bomb served as a spectacular and frightening warning to the Soviet Union. Many historians and political scientists have weighed in on which of these reasons was truly behind Truman's decision.

Among others, Campbell Craig and Sergey Radchenko examined this question in detail in their 2008 study *The Atomic Bomb and the Origins of the Cold War*.[31] Of course, one can only guess at Truman's true motives, but it is an unquestionable fact that the bomb definitely pushed the two victorious great powers to a deadly arms race. This confrontation could very easily have led (even by accident) to the explosion of a World War III, which would very likely have been the bloodiest war yet. As John Mueller rightly concluded, the ensuing Cold War was the "functional equivalent of World War III."[32]

Joseph Stalin, paranoid enough to see enemies everywhere, was certainly convinced that the real target of this new deadly weapon was the Soviet Union. His spies at the Manhattan Program provided nuclear secrets to the Soviets, and by August 1949, the Soviet Union had also successfully tested its first nuclear bomb. The nuclear arms race that would span the entire four decades of the Cold War began.

Thus, as I have shown, the Cold War was already taking shape before the hot war finally drew to the close. It became manifest in less than a year, in early 1946. One of the first individuals to openly declare its existence was Winston Churchill. On 5 March 1946, Churchill delivered his famous "Iron Curtain speech" at Fulton College, Missouri, with President Truman in the audience:

> From Stettin in the Baltic to Trieste in the Adriatic an iron curtain has descended across the Continent. Behind that line lie[s] . . . the Soviet sphere. . . . The Communist parties . . . are seeking everywhere "to obtain totalitarian control" and represent "a growing challenge and peril to Christian civilization."[33]

In response, Stalin answered in the Russian newspaper *Pravda*:

> I do not know if Mr. Churchill and his friends will succeed in organizing after the Second World War a new military campaign against eastern Europe. But if they succeed . . . then one man confidently says that they will be beaten, just as they were beaten twenty-six years ago.[34]

Churchill went to the podium again in September 1946 in Zurich to warn that the Dark Age might return; against it, he remonstrated, "the European family" must be recreated: "We must build a kind of United States of Europe."[35]

Cold war crises of 1948–1950: close to a World War III

In the summer of 1948, the emergence of the first major confrontation pushed the Cold War conflict to the threshold of hot war. That June, the United States unilaterally decided to introduce a separate West German currency, the new Deutsch Mark. This currency heralded the creation of an independent West German state. The Soviet Union answered in a very hostile way, immediately closing all surface transport connections between the western occupation zones and

Berlin, which was located in Germany's Soviet occupation zone but was also divided into western and Soviet zones. Beginning in June 1948, all supplies for about 2 million Berliners – from coal to everyday food stores – had to be delivered by air from the western zone. The Soviets continued the blockade until May 1949: thus Western air forces continued for a year, altogether flying 92 million miles to deliver 4–5,000 tons of goods every day. Even one accident, like the accidental shooting of even one American or British airplane – could produce an explosive military confrontation.

Two years later, the first real war exploded between the two blocs in Korea. The Korean peninsula, which had been occupied by Japan during World War II, was liberated by the Soviet and American armies in August 1945. Similar to Europe, Korea was divided into occupation zones at the 38th parallel to create a Soviet zone in the north and an American one in the south. The two zones soon became two independent states: the Soviet zone became communist North Korea, while the American zone transformed into the democratic-capitalist country South Korea. In June 1950, North Korea invaded the South and the two great powers immediately became involved. The North was assisted by the Soviet Union and by communist China, which sent a huge army. The South was aided by the United States and – after the US-led United Nations also became involved – by 21 other countries, who sent military contributions and even troops; however, American participation represented about 90 percent of South Korea's aid. As Konrad Adenauer, the new Chancellor of the Federal Republic of Germany, suggested, the Korean War was a kind of dress rehearsal for another European war between the two rival superpowers. Adenauer told the American envoy, John McCloy:

> The fate of the world will not be decided in Korea but in the heart of Europe. I am convinced that Stalin has the same plan for Europe as for Korea. What is happening there is a dress-rehearsal for what is in store for us here.[36]

The war continued until July 1953. During those three years, about 3 million people died. This war became the first military conflict between the two Cold War camps, pushing the world to the brink of World War III. Europe was shocked.

Forming the new Cold War political world order

The Cold War, including those two first major crises, rearranged the world order. The new postwar political order was shaped both by the realities of the Cold War struggle and by the continued possibility of a new world war. This specter had already started to take shape at the end of wartime alliance before Churchill made it a well-known public commonplace in his 1946 speech.

George F. Kennan, the Moscow-based *chargé d'affaires* for Secretary of State George Marshall and one of the best Soviet Union experts in the American government, sent his "Long Telegram" to Washington in February 1946. In this document, he analyzed the reigning Soviet ideology and foreign policy, suggesting ways of countering it. The containment strategy that he recommended became the official policy of the Truman administration, and, indeed, the primary American foreign policy for four decades. Let me quote the essence of Kennan's analysis at length. Stalin believes, Kennan's telegram stated, that

> the USSR still lives in antagonistic "capitalist encirclement" with which in the long run there can be no permanent peaceful coexistence. . . . Capitalist world is beset with internal conflicts . . . insoluble [*sic.*] by means of peaceful compromise. . . . As stated by Stalin in 1927 to a delegation of American workers: "In course of further development of international revolution there will emerge two centers of world significance: a socialist center . . . and a capitalist center . . . Battle between these two centers for command of world economy will decide fate of capitalism and of communism in entire world." [The Soviets believes that] everything must be done to advance relative strength of USSR. . . . Soviet efforts, and those of Russia's friends abroad, must be directed toward deepening and exploiting of differences and conflicts between capitalist powers. If these eventually deepen into an "imperialist" war, this war must be turned into revolutionary upheavals within the various capitalist countries." [The Russians] seek security only in patient by deadly struggle for total destruction of rival power. . . . Soviet power . . . does not take unnecessary risks . . . it is highly sensitive to logic of force. . . . [I]t can easily withdraw – and usually does – when strong resistance is encountered.[37]

Kennan concluded that the best response would be for the United States to prevent any advances of communism at any place in the world. In another memorandum from 1 April 1946, he also suggested that America should promote the integrate of its Western European allies, explicitly stating that Russia wanted to keep Western Europe unintegrated and would try to oppose those who were "capable of pulling Western European countries together into an effective regional society."[38]

Undersecretary of State Dean Acheson further developed this containment policy through his concept of the Soviet "falling domino" principle. Acheson maintained that if one country fell to communist rule, it would generate further falls; thus the Western world must not allow any country to fall.[39] During the Korean War in 1950, Churchill went even further when he stated "What the Communists have begun in Korea should not end in their triumph. If that were to happen a third world war . . . would certainly be forced upon us."[40] The Brooking Institution, a think tank in Washington DC, had already spoken about the possibility of a "piecemeal or wholesale absorption [of Western Europe] by the Soviet Union."[41] Accelerated fear and even hysteria about the possibility of a Soviet invasion of Europe emerged.[42]

In the spring of 1947, the new American containment policy was officially declared in Truman's speech, quoted earlier, before a joint session of the Congress on 12 March 1947. The President outlined his policy of assisting countries that were endangered by communist "armed minorities or by outside pressures."[43] The policy, called the Truman Doctrine, clearly expressed the goal of not allowing any advances in communism across the world. That policy was behind the United States' decision to give aid to Turkey and Greece in 1947 and to Western Europe through the Marshall Plan. In the spring of 1947, the United States pushed West European countries ruled by coalition governments that included communist party members, namely France and Italy, to get rid of the communists. The United States amply rewarded countries who complied: just a few hours after France's purge of communists from its coalition government, for example, the World Bank announced a loan for France.

A new solution to the "German Question"

As part of its efforts to build a strong West European alliance, America radically changed its policy towards Germany. The first plans were drafted in a memorandum before the end of the war by Roosevelt's Treasury Secretary Henry Morgenthau. Along with Morgenthau, Roosevelt and Churchill discussed these ideas at the Quebec Conference in mid-September 1944. Although Churchill first opposed the American position, he later accepted it. Morgenthau's memorandum called for "eliminating the war-making industries in the Ruhr and the Saar. . . [and] converting Germany into a country primarily agricultural and pastoral in its character."[44] The Roosevelt administration's plan called for deindustrializing and mutilating Germany by cutting off the country's most important industrial zones. East Prussia and the southern part of Silesia would be given partly to Poland but mostly to the Soviet Union. France would receive the Saar region, while the Ruhr area would put under international administration. The remaining parts of Germany would be divided into independent northern and southern states. As Roosevelt stated in a letter from 26 August 1944:

> There are two schools of thought, those who would be altruistic in regard to the Germans, hoping by loving kindness to make them Christians again – and those who would adopt a much "tougher" attitude. Most decidedly I belong to the latter school, for though I am not bloodthirsty, I want the Germans to know that this time at least they have definitely lost the war.[45]

France, led by Charles de Gaulle, wanted to go even further. Since 1870, France had been attacked by Germany three times in seven decades. As such, they wanted to maintain an unlimited occupation of Germany and permanently dismember their rival by recreating the pre-unification (1871) situation, when 35 German states had existed. Soon after the liberation of France on 11 April 1945, General de Gaulle invited several top American representatives–John McCloy, the assistant secretary of war; General Ralph Smith, a military attaché at the American Embassy in Paris; and ambassador Jefferson Caffery – to dinner. As Caffery reported to the Secretary of State in Washington, de Gaulle argued that in the interests of French security, all German land on the left side of River

Rheine "from Cologne to the Swiss frontiers" should be broken into small, semi-independent states under French control. As for the Ruhr area, the heartland of German heavy industry, "its mines and industries would be operated for the benefit of all Western European countries" under international administration.[46] This French position turned out to be adamantine; as late as the summer of 1947 they even prepared a "Saar constitution" that stated the need of the "Saar's organic integration within the economic sphere of France."[47] Around the end of the war, US State Department basically agreed with all essential demands of France, including the 'annexation' of the Saarland, and reaffirmed it several times.[48]

Although the official American policy ended up being somewhat more moderate than the Morgenthau plan – it did not express the desire for the "re-agrarization and pastorization" of Germany – the United States did not initially seek to promote economic rebuilding in Germany. Two days after the European war ended on 10 May 1945, the new president, Harry Truman, revised Roosevelt's policy. He approved the Joint Chiefs of Staff #1067 directive, issued to General Eisenhower, which ordered the US occupation forces in Germany to "take no steps looking toward the economic rehabilitation of Germany, [nor steps] designed to maintain or strengthen the German economy." The first American "level of industry" plan of 1946 also stated that German heavy industry was to be lowered to 50 percent of its 1938 level by closing 1,500 industrial plants.

Together with deindustrialization, a harsh plan of *denazification* also ensued. According to the official American policy, all those who had more than nominal participation in the Third Reich, the Nazi party or its military organizations were to be "excluded from public office and from positions of importance in quasi-public and private enterprises." Under the denazification law of March 1946, all adult Germans were screened under the supervision of the Allied military authorities. That screening categorized the Germans in five groups from "major offenders" to "followers" categories. In the American occupation zone, 25 percent of Germans belonged to one of those categories.[49] Investigations of individuals sometimes took several years, and during the time of the investigation, old-age pensions were not payed. As US Consul Maurice Altaffer reported to the State Department in December 1946, "the present state of denazification has become unbearable for all concerned."[50] More importantly, American officials started to recognize that their deindustrialization and denazification policies might alienate the Germans and instead work to the advantage of the Left and therefore the Russians.

Konrad Adenauer, president of the Christian Democratic Union (CDU) in the British occupation zone, outlined view most clearly. In a memorandum to the military governors in December 1946, he called for "a complete cessation of any further dismantling of factories." Adenauer also met several times with American officials and consuls to complain about the dismantling of German industry. He also denounced the political echo chamber produced by the American denazification policy (among other consequences) and argued for a general amnesty; otherwise, he remonstrated, the Germans would be pushed into the arms of Russia. In his opening speech at the Congress of CDU in September 1948, Adenauer went so far as to portray the American Morgenthau Plan as "a crime against humanity which could well compare with National Socialist crimes."[51]

Adenauer did not hesitate to play the Soviet card as well. American Consul Altaffer reported to Washington in 1947 that Adenauer had

> informed me that representatives of Soviet Russian government approached him. . . [as well that called the attention to the fact that there is] a school of thought [in Germany] favoring close relations . . . between Germany and Russia.[52]

On another occasion, Adenauer expressed that due to the harsh Western policy towards Germany, he "feared that the communists would go a long way towards the achievement of their objectives."[53] The top American official in Germany, John McCloy, reported:

> Adenauer stated he did not want to gain the reputation that he was black-mailing . . . on the basis of Soviet moves, but that if actions were not taken along the lines he suggested, all of Western Europe would fall in Soviet orbit. . . . The dismantling program was speeded up [in the French and British zones] and that he could not be responsible for the consequences in term of public distrust.[54]

In a secret cable sent to Washington on 19 July 1946, General Lucius D. Clay, the US military administrator of Germany, cited these popular German views in his recommendation that the Truman administration break with the restriction policy.

Consequently, as Cold War emerged, America's deindustrialization and denazification policies also gradually halted. As an American consular report stated in October 1947, the first step was transferring the task of screening and punishing Nazi sympathizers from the occupying authorities to the German ones. It was also ordered that "after December 31 no more persons shall be removed from their posts except in quite exceptional cases."[55] The outcome was dramatic. In Austria, for example,

> there was scarcely a sitting judge who had not belonged to the Nazi Party. . . . West German courts, mostly presided over former Nazis, were reluctant to act. . . . West German authorities made sure that the prisoners would soon be released.[56]

Some American consuls sent alarming reports to Washington on the consequences of this transfer of jurisdictional power: "The failure of the program of denazification led to an evident renazification in many fields of Bavarian life . . . 30 percent of top civil servants are former Nazis." Another consul reported that the:

> Spruchkammer trials . . . qualifying persons for employment and other activities on all levels . . . beside serving as a more rapid rehabilitation . . . also served to make possible the re-entry into influential positions of ex-Nazis.

This phenomena "would be reversing a trend which Military Government itself has supported in the past year and one half." In November 1949, an American consul sent a 44-page report about appointing and electing "big Nazis [to] influential positions."[57]

The new policy led to the bizarre consequence that, it the end, the Netherland, Norway, Denmark, France, and Italy punished significantly more of Hitler's collaborators than postwar Germany and Austria punished actual German war criminals.

> Amazingly, the harshest sentences were produced in Norway, Denmark and the Netherlands. . . . In Norway more than 90,000 people were tried after the war, nearly 4 percent of the population. . . . Nearly similar proportions existed in Denmark, while in the Netherlands 150,000 people were detained.[58]

In France and Italy, 10,000–11,000 people were lynched by fellow citizens without any legal procedure. In his *Europe on Trial: The Story of Collaboration, Resistance, and Retribution During World War II*, István Deák concludes:

> Aside from the seventy-odd Nazis executed under orders of the Nuremberg Tribunal and other American-dominated courts during the first years after the war [and just a handful of Nazi war criminals in prisons], all other Germans tried and sentenced by the Allies in West Germany were released. Their properties were restituted, and they were given good jobs and pensions.[59]

Despite these alarming reports, American authorities were ordered to follow this new policy line and top officials continued to argue for it because of the "Soviet danger." On this basis, American officials sharply criticized the French policy, which remained unchanged:

> Western powers had attained impressive 'lead' over Soviet Communist rivals in Germany; and it would be tragic if Kremlin forged ahead now due to continued French conception of their German policy. . . . Continued French intransigency toward German people will advance Soviet design.[60]

All in all, American attitudes and policies towards Germany gradually changed between 1945 and 1947 as the Truman administration gave up its deindustrialization and denazification policies step by step. As the initiation of the Cold War became evident, the new American policy also became manifest. On 6 September 1946, half a year before President Truman announced the Truman Doctrine, Secretary of State James F. Byrnes delivered his famous "Restatement of Policy on Germany" speech in Stuttgart:

> We have learned, whether we like it or not, that we live in one world, from which world we cannot isolate ourselves. We have learned that peace and

well-being are indivisible and that our peace and well-being cannot be purchased at the price of . . . the well-being of any other country. . . . The basis of
the Potsdam Agreement was that, as part of a combined program of demili-
tarization and reparations, Germany's war potential should be reduced by
elimination and removal of her war industries and the reduction and removal
of heavy industrial plants.

The United States is firmly of the belief that Germany should be admin-
istered as an economic unit. . . . Germany must be enabled to use her skills
and her energies to increase her industrial production. . . . Germany is a part
of Europe and recovery in Europe, and particularly in the states adjoining
Germany, will be slow indeed if Germany with her great resources of iron
and coal is turned into a poorhouse. . . . The American people want to return
the government of Germany to the German people. . . [and] help the German people to win their way back to an honorable place among the free and
peace-loving nations of the world.[61]

Two weeks later on 19 September 1946, Winston Churchill went to Zurich,
Switzerland and delivered a rather similar speech:

We must all turn our backs upon the horrors of the past and look to the
future. We cannot afford to drag forward across the years to come hatreds
and revenges. . . . If Europe is to be saved from infinite misery, and indeed
from final doom, there must be this act of faith in the European family. . . .
I am now going to say something that will astonish you. The first step in the
re-creation of the European family must be a partnership between France
and Germany. . . . There can be no revival of Europe without [France and
Germany]. . . . Germany, freely joined for mutual convenience in a federal
system. . . . But I must give you warning, time may be short. . . . If we are
to form a United States of Europe, or whatever name it may take, we must
begin now. In these present days we [are] . . . under the . . . protection, of
the atomic bomb.[62]

The Morgenthau Plan was dead. Truman replaced the highly punitive Joint
Chiefs of Staff Directive #1067 with JCS Directive #1779, which stressed that
"an orderly, prosperous Europe requires the economic contributions of a stable
and productive Germany."[63]

As a 1948 State Department document stated:

It has become a paramount objective of US foreign policy to endeavor to
reinforce Western Europe through the integration with it of a democratic
Germany. . . . [It is] important that the US Government not . . . count itself
[sic] to any permanent economic and political restriction upon the prospec-
tive German government which will make it impossible to carry out the
economic and political rehabilitation of Germany.[64]

A 1956 Commission of the European Community document retrospectively summed up the American policy:

> One of the most consistent aspects of postwar United States foreign policy has been steadfast support of economic and political integration . . . of Europe. This policy took shape soon after the war and has continued until the present day . . . European integration within the framework of an expanded Atlantic Community remains the cornerstone of its [American] Western European policy.[65]

Indeed, a new world political order emerged after World War II. In the nineteenth-century world, the dominant European colonial empires had confronted each other and dominated the world. In the interwar years, the world order was characterized by a struggle between the Axis (Germany, Italy, Japan and their allies) and the Allied powers (Britain, France, the United States, and their allies, including Bolshevik Russia). The former side was composed of fascist totalitarians, Nazis and anti-democratic new-imperialist conquering powers, while the latter (aside from Russia) represented democracy.

When a new political world order emerged after the war, the powers of Western democracy – led by the United States in close alliance with Western Europe – confronted the Soviet Union and the enlarging communist world. In this world order, the United States of America became the unquestionable "leader of the West" with its enormous economic, political and military strength and its newly developed nuclear power. Devastated, decimated and weakened Western Europe became highly dependent on the US. Likewise, the continued security of the United States depended upon a rebuilt, strong and united Western Europe. American interests dictated the integration of Western Europe – in other words, they shaped the creation of an integrated Western community. Western Europe, at the same time, badly needed American assistance and an American guarantor of their security and defense. Thus, they enthusiastically accepted America's leadership.

The plan for a joint Western European army

Besides assisting recovery efforts, forcing cooperation and encouraging integration between the Western European countries – former allies and enemies alike – through the Marshall Plan, the United States also initiated the formation of a joint West European army as part of its plan to push its western allies into a federal state. At the German Desk of the State Department, Henry Byroade prepared a memorandum entitled "An Approach to the Formation of a European Army" in 1950. He sent it over to John McCloy (Eyes only for McCloy), although Secretary of State Dean Acheson was also informed. After exchanging a few cable messages with Byroade, McCloy immediately set up a meeting with his influential French friend Jean Monnet to discuss the possibility of France's adoption of the American plan. As Monnet later explained, he met with McCloy in his country house in Houjarray, not far from Paris, where they discussed Byroade's approach to the issue and agreed upon it. As Monnet phrased it, based on Byroade plan "the eventual framework of the European Defense Community was conceptualized." The creation of this plan required nothing more than Monnet's translation of the American plan into a French one. When he was ready, he presented the plan to the new French Prime Minister, René Pleven. The "Pleven Plan," as it was called, contained the complete fusion of the European armed forces (with German participation under a European Minister of Defense; and a supra-national command, a budget, and general staff. While in the postwar years France had strongly opposed the rearmament of Germany, the Pleven Plan proposed allowing it in the context of this all-West European framework.[66]

At the North Atlantic Council meeting in December 1953, US Secretary of State John Foster Dulles, delivered a frightening speech warning the European allies that if "the European Defense Community should not become effective . . . there would be grave doubt whether continental Europe could be made a place of safety." Dulles even tried blackmailing the European allies by saying that the failure of the plan "would compel an agonizing reappraisal of basic United States policy" and would cause America to remove its forces from Europe. In his words, if they "decide[d] to commit suicide, they may have to commit it alone." Furthermore, he added, if Western Europe "cannot integrate in freedom, it might be that Western Europe would be unified, as Eastern Europe has been unified in defeat and servitude."[67]

Although the Pleven Plan received primary approval at the French National Assembly in October 1950, it was rejected by the same Parliament in August 1954. The American idea of a joint west-European army has not been realized until now.

* * *

At that time, military unification would certainly have been too premature and too drastic: it was too big of a step forward for France and the other countries. Nevertheless, the United States wanted to create a Western political-military system similar to the way that it had spearheaded the creation of international economic organizations. In June 1948, the American Congress adopted a resolution recommending that the United States join the West European countries in a defense pact. For the first time since 1778, the United States established a peacetime military alliance, the North Atlantic Treaty Organization (NATO). In the beginning, twelve countries – the United States, Canada, Britain, France, Italy, the Netherlands, Denmark, Norway, Iceland, Portugal and Luxembourg – joined. More were added later on: Greece and Turkey in 1952, the Federal Republic of Germany in 1955, and Spain in 1982. In October 1949, the American Congress authorized $1.3 billion in military aid for the new alliance.

Eager to regaining strength and power, the Western European countries expressed high interest in cooperating with each other and in accepting American leadership, military assistance and policy initiatives. In the new world political order, the realization of west European integration became the most important requirement for both America and Western Europe. In building this new world order, the United States and the Soviet Union both were crafting and enlarging their alliance systems. In other words, the new political world order, together with the rebuilding of the world capitalist economic regime (as previously discussed), prepared the soil and provided the incentives for European integration.

Notes

1 See Tony Judt, *A History of Europe since 1945* (London: Penguin Group, 2005); Tony Judt (with Timothy Snyder), *Thinking the Twentieth Century* (London: Penguin Books, 2012); Mark Mazover, *Dark Continent: Europe's Twentieth Century* (London: Allen Lane Publisher, 1995), 5; Tara Zahra, *The Lost Children* (Cambridge, MA and London: Harvard University Press, 2011), 9.

2 *Fortune Magazine*, May 1945, Vol. XXXI #5, Food Scandal; *The New York Times*, April 28. Cabell Philips Reports.

3 Keith Lowe, *Savage Continent: Europe in the Aftermath of World War II* (London: St. Martin Press, 2012), Introduction.

4 See Ivan T. Berend, *Ujjáépités és a nagytőke elleni harc Magyarországon, 1945–1948* [Reconstruction and the Fight against the Big Capital in Hungary] (Budapest: Közgazdasági és Jogi Könyvkiadó, 1962).

5 Angus Maddison, *Monitoring the World Economy, 1820–1992* (Paris: Development Centre of the Organisation for Economic Co-operation and Development, 1995), 195, 197.

6 The British partitioned India in 1947 to create Pakistan, which remained a dominion until 1956. In 1971, Bangladesh separated to become an independent country.

7 Here are some of the most recent contributions to a huge body of scholarship on the topic: James R. Akerman, ed., *Decolonizing the Map: Cartography from Colony to Nation* (Chicago, IL: University of Chicago Press, 2017); Walter Mignolo, *The Darker Side of Western Modernity: Global Futures, Decolonial Options* (Durham, NC: Duke University Press, 2011); Elizabeth Schmidt, *Cold War and Decolonization in Guinea, 1946–1958* (Athens, OH: Ohio University Press, 2007); Gary Wilder, *Freedom Time: Negritude, Decolonization, and the Future of the World* (Durham, NC: Duke University Press, 2015); Christopher J. Lee, ed., *Making a World after Empire: The Bandung Moment and Its Political Afterlives* (Athens, OH: Ohio University Press, 2010); Kara Moskowitz, *Seeing like a Citizen: Decolonization, Development, and the Making of Kenya, 1945–1980* (Athens, OH: Ohio University Press, 2019).

8 A. G. Kenwood and A. L. Lougheed, *The Growth of the International Economy, 1820–1960* (Albany, NY: SUNY Press, 1971), 216–217.

9 Maddison, *Monitoring the World Economy, 1820–1992*, 212.

10 Paul A. Samuelson, "Full Employment after the War," in *Postwar Economic Problems*, ed. Seymour Harris (New York and London: McGraw-Hill, 1943), 51.

11 Gunnar Myrdal, "Is American Business Deluding Itself?," *The Atlantic Monthly* 174 (November 1944): 51.

12 William Henry Beveridge, *Social Insurance and Allied Services* ["The Beveridge Report"] (London: H.M. Stationery Office, 1942).

13 Warren C. Baum, *French Economy and the State* (Princeton, NJ: Princeton University Press, 1958), 181–182, 274–275.

14 Hanns M. Sauter, Arno Hartman, and Tarja Katz, Die Wohnungsbaugesetze und der Soziale Wohnungsbau, https://link.springer.com/chapter/10.1007/978-3-8348-8212-7_11, accessed September 23, 2019.

15 Sydney Pollard, *Peaceful Conquest: The Industrialization of Europe, 1760–1970* (Oxford: Oxford University Press, 1986), 728–730.

16 Harry S. Truman, *Memoires*, vol. 2 (New York: Doubleday, 1955–1956), 106.

17　George C. Marshall, "Marshall Plan Speech" (Speech, Harvard University Commencement, Cambridge, MA, June 5, 1947), www.marshallfoundation.org/library/digital-archive/marshall-plan-speech-original/, accessed November 3, 2019.

18　Alan S. Milward, *The Reconstruction of Western Europe, 1945–51* (Oxon: Routledge, 1984), 94, 96, 101.

19　Derek Urwin, *The Community of Europe: A History of European Integration since 1945*, 2nd ed. (Oxon and New York: Routledge, 1995), 43.

20　Milward, *The Reconstruction of Western Europe, 1945–51*, 70.

21　Allen Welsh Dulles, *The Marshall Plan* (Oxford: Berg, 1948), 11, 116.

22　Ibid., 111.

23　Winston Churchill, *The Second World War: Triumph and Tragedy*, vol. VI (Boston, MA: Houghton Mifflin, 1953), 227–228.

24　Evan Luard, *The Cold War: A Reappraisal* (London: Thames & Hudson, 1964), 52.

25　George Curzon, The British Foreign Secretary, suggested this line to demarcate the border between newly established Poland and the Soviet Union after World War I. It was not, however, realized until 1939, when the Ribbentrop-Molotov Pact divided Poland between the Soviet Union and Nazi Germany. See Sarah Meiklejohn Terry, *Poland's Place in Europe: General Sikorski and the Origin of the Oder-Neisse Line, 1939–1943* (Princeton, NJ: Princeton University Press, 1983), 121.

26　Joseph Stalin, "Telegram: 14 April 1945 to President Roosevelt," in *Churchill and Roosevelt, the Complete Correspondence: Alliance Declining, February 1944–April 1945*, ed. Warren F. Kimball, vol. III (Princeton, NJ: Princeton University Press, 1984), 610.

27　The Lend-Lease Act was accepted by the American Congress in March 1941 to lend or lease war supplies to a country "whose security was vital to the defense of the United States. See National Archive, Records of the US House of Representatives, HR-77 A-D13, Record Group 233, Stalin, "Telegram: 14 April 1945 to President Roosevelt," 610.

28　Kimball, *Churchill and Roosevelt*, 476.

29　Ibid., 482.

30　Harry S. Truman, *Year of Decisions* (Garden City, NY: Doubleday, 1955), 416.

31　Campbell Craig and Sergey S. Radchenko, *The Atomic Bomb and the Origins of the Cold War* (New Haven, CT and London: Yale University Press, 2008).

32　John Mueller, "Quiet Cataclysm: Some Afterthoughts about World War III," *Diplomatic History* 16, no. 1 (January 1992): 66–75, https://doi.org/10.1111/j.1467-7709.1992.tb00487.x, accessed October 6, 2019.

33　Winston Churchill, "The Sinews of Peace: A Speech to Westminster College" (Speech, Fulton, Missouri, March 5, 1946), in *Winston S. Churchill: His Complete Speeches, 1897–1963: 1897–1908*, ed. Robert Rhodes James, vol. VII (New York and London: Chelsea House Publishers, 1974), 7290–7292.

34　"Stalin Interview with Pravda on Churchill," *The New York Times*, March 14, 1946.

35　Winston Churchill, "The Tragedy of Europe" (Speech, University of Zurich, September 19, 1946), www.churchillarchive.com/explore/page?id=CHUR%205%2F8%2F145-162#image=0, accessed January 5, 2020.

36　Jean Monnet, *Memoirs*, trans. Richard Mayne (Garden City, NY: Doubleday, 1978), 337.

37　George Kennan, *The Chargé in the Soviet Union (Kennan) to the Secretary of State [The "Long Telegram"]* (Moscow: U.S. Department of State–Office of the Historian, February 22, 1946), https://history.state.gov/historicaldocuments/frus1946v06/d475, accessed October 3, 2019.

38　George Kennan, *George Kennan's Memorandum [NARA 711.51/4–146]*, Memorandum (Moscow: U.S. Department of State, April 1, 1946).

39　President Eisenhower discussed the "falling domino" principle at a press conference on the French war in Indochina on April 7, 1954. Neil H. Petersen, ed., "Editorial Note," in *Foreign Relations of the United States, 1952–1954, Indochina*, vol.

XIII, Part 1 (Washington, DC: U.S. Government Printing Office, 1982), Document 716, https://history.state.gov/historicaldocuments/frus1952-54v13p1/d716, accessed September 29, 2019.

40 Winston Churchill, "Speech at the Independence Day Dinner of the American Society in London–July 4, 1950," in *In the Balance: Speeches of 1949 and 1950 by Winston Churchill*, ed. Randolph Churchill (London: Cassell & Company Ltd, 1951), 312.

41 *The Brookings Institution, Major Problems of the United States Foreign Policy, 1949–50* (Washington, DC: The Brookings Institution, 1949), 406.

42 See Ivan T. Berend, *The History of European Integration: A New Perspective* (Oxon: Routledge, 2016), 21–23.

43 Harry Truman, "Address of the President to Congress, Recommending Assistance to Greece and Turkey" (Presidential Address, Joint Meeting of Congress, Washington, DC, March 12, 1947), www.trumanlibrary.gov/library/research-files/address-president-congress-recommending-assistance-greece-and-turkey, accessed October 18, 2019.

44 *Memorandum Initialed by President Roosevelt and Prime Minister Churchill [Document 283]* (Moscow: U.S. Department of State–Office of the Historian, September 15, 1944), Roosevelt Papers, https://history.state.gov/historicaldocuments/frus1944Quebec/d283, accessed October 24, 2019.

45 Franklin Delano Roosevelt, "Letter to George Stimson," August 26, 1944. In Anthony James Nicholls and John Wheeler-Bennett, *The Semblance of Peace: The Political Settlement after the Second World War* (London: Palgrave Macmillan, 1972), 175.

46 National Archive, "Confidential US State Department Central Files, France, Foreign Affairs, 1945–1949," 711.51/4–2045.

47 National Archive, "Ernest de W. Mayer US Consul's Report," October 10, 1947, 862.00/10–1047. The US Embassy report described the Saar policy as such: "Saar Constitution, December 15, 1947, independent from Germany, France takes over defense and foreign relations. French frank is the legal currency." National Archive, Embassy Report from Paris to Secretary of State, September 3, 1949, 862.00/9–349.

48 In a letter to Georges Bidault in September 1945, James F. Byrnes stated: "I shall be happy to support the position of the French government that certain immediate steps be taken toward integration the economy of the Saar with France." National Archive, James F. Byrnes, "Letter to George Bidault–against French Unilateral Action to Annex the Saarland," September 25, 1945, 862.014/9–2546. In December 1947 the acting Secretary of State telegrammed: "we approved French proposal on economic integration of Saar territory into that of France." National Archive, Acting Secretary of State Telegram," December 23, 1947, 862.00/12–1747.1.

49 National Archive, "The Evolution of US Denazification Policies in Germany." Report of the Political Advisor of the Military Government in Germany," May 5, 1948, 862.00/5–1148.

50 National Archive, "Consul Maurice W. Altaffer's Report on Denazification to Secretary of State," December 24, 1946, 862.00/12–2446.

51 National Archive, "Report of the American Consul in Bremen about the Congress of the Christian Democratic Union," September 8, 1948, 862.00/9–848.

52 National Archive, "Consul General Maurice W. Altaffer's Report on His Meeting with Adenauer, Bremen," January 5, 1947, 862.00/6–547.

53 National Archive, "Report of Consul Martin J. Hillenbrand, Attached to Consul General Altaffer's Letter," October 13, 1947, 862.00/10–1447.

54 National Archive, "McCloy Report on an Informal Meeting between the Federal Chancellor and the Council of the Allied High Commission," October 27, 1949, 862.00/9–2749.

55 National Archive, "Consul Altaffer's Report from Bremen," October 8, 1947, 862.00/10–847; National Archive, "Report of the US Consulate in Hamburg," January 13, 1948, 862.00/1–1348.

56 István Deák, *Europe on Trial: The Story of Collaboration, Resistance, and Retribution during World War II* (Boulder, CO: Westview Press, 2015), 111, 203, 213.
57 National Archive, "Some Aspect of Renazification in Bavaria, Clarens M. Bolds, Acting Land Commissioner, to J. McCloy, Munich," November 1, 1949, 862.00/11–149; National Archive, "Robert Murphy's Report to the Secretary of State," July 28, 1948, 862.00/8–648. As Consul General B. Tomlin Bailey reported: "In Landkreise, Krumbach, and Dinkelsbuehl, the percentage of reelected ex-Nazi bürgermeisters is 71 percent and 60 percent respectively . . . Nazis have returned to positions within government agencies throughout Bavaria." National Archive, "Consul General B. Tomlin Bailey's Report from Munich," August 16, 1948, 862.00/8–1648.
58 Deák, *Europe on Trial*, 204–205.
59 Ibid., 213.
60 National Archive, "Barbour's Message to Secretary of State," October 20, 1949, 862.00/10–2049.
61 J. F. Byrnes, "Address by Secretary of States Byrnes on United States Policy Regarding Germany, Stuttgart, September 6, 1946." In *Documents on Germany, 1944–1970* (Washington, DC: U.S. Government Printing Office, 1971), 62–63.
62 See: Churchill, "The Tragedy of Europe."
63 Dieter Waibel, "Von der wohlwollenden Despotie zur Herrschaft des Rechts: Entwicklungsstufen der amerikanischen Besatzung Deutschlands, 1944–1949," in *Beiträge zur Rechtsgeschichte des 20. Jahrhunderts*, ed. Thomas Duve et al. (Tübingen: Mohr Siebeck GmbH & Co., 1996), 373–384.
64 National Archive, "Proposal for Meeting Anglo-French Security Desires with Respect to Germany," December 9, 1948, 862.00/12–948.
65 "The Community's Relations with the Outside World," *Bulletin from the European Community for Coal and Steel*, no. 20 (December 1956): 3.
66 National Archive, "John J. McCloy, Telegram No. 962 for Acheson and Byroade," August 3, 1950, in record group 4666, Top Secret General Records, Box No. 2, File August 1950; J. J. McCloy Papers; Henry Byroade telegram No. 943, August 4, 1950. Both telegrams were cited in Manfred Görtemaker, "The Failure of EDC and European Integration," in *Crisis in European Integration: Challenges and Responses*, ed. Ludger Kühnhardt (New York: Berghahn Books, 2009), 38–39.
67 Allen Welsh Dulles, *Statement by the Secretary of State to the North Atlantic Council [Document 238]* (Paris: NATO Ministerial Meeting, December 14, 1953). In John Bernbaum, Lisle Rose and Charles Sampson, eds., *Foreign Relations of the United States, 1952–1954: Western European Security*, vol. V, Part 1 (Washington, DC: U.S. Government Printing Office, 1983), https://history.state.gov/historicaldocuments/frus1952-54v05p1/d238, accessed November 6, 2019.

2 Federalist dreamers and pragmatic integrationists

The conceptualization and first steps towards a United States of Europe

The idea of a United States of Europe

Europe had been divided since its early history. The conquests and gradual enlargement of the Roman Empire first divided the continent into two parts. The Roman Empire controlled the western portion as far as Britain; most of southern Europe; and parts of central Europe up to the *limes*, or the borderline of River Danube, plus Illyria and Dacia (modern-day Croatia and the Transylvanian region of Romania), until its fall in 476. The eastern half of Europe was ruled by "barbarian" tribes: Slavs, Huns, Avars and others. They arrived during the Great Migration from the east, settled on the borders of the empire, and formed short-lived empires of their own. Eventually, however, most of them disappeared.[1]

The Roman Empire established a kind of longstanding unity in the western half of the continent. Three centuries after the fall of Rome, Charlemagne looked to recreate this sense of unity, positioning the Carolingian Empire as its successor. This sense of unity reigned until the late ninth century, and then was reestablished during the thirteenth century by the *Sacrum Imperium Romanum*, or Holy Roman Empire. The Holy Roman Emperor was considered to be the King of Romans. Although it was not a centralized empire and its various parts became quite independent units, it was considered to be the heart of Christian (Catholic) Europe. In fact, it was not even called Europe but *Christianitas* or Christendom, the world of the Christians, in contrast with the Islamic and the Eastern Orthodox world. Thus the Holy Roman Empire, however increasingly frail it became, represented a concept of unity and togetherness of Western Europe until the beginning of the nineteenth century.

Those who dreamed of a peaceful and integrated Europe planted the seed of the future creation of a United States of Europe. Western Europe had a good soil for the growth and development of that tree because the continent's early history exemplified continent-wide unity; thus, Europe enjoyed a manifest cultural tradition of integration. More importantly, the Roman Empire also led to modern socioeconomic, legal and political similarities in the Western countries. The highly influential luminaries of the French Enlightenment clearly recognized and commented up this similitude. Montesquieu, who had travelled outside Europe, stated:

> A prince believes he will become greater through the ruin of a neighboring state. On the contrary! The condition of Europe is such that states depend

on each other: France has need of the wealth of Poland and Muscovy. . . .
Europe is a state composed of several provinces.

Voltaire expressed the same idea: "Christian Europe could be regarded as a single republic divided in several states." Later on, eighteenth-century political theorists continued to repeat their ideas. For example, Dublin-born political theorist Edmund Burke stated in 1796 that Europe was "virtually one great state, having the same basis in general law." A traveler in it "never felt himself quite abroad."[2]

These views, however, were soon buried when the nation-state was born at the turn of the nineteenth century out of the American and French revolutions. The nineteenth century was an age of nationhood and nationalism. In spite of this ethos, or perhaps because national conflicts and confrontations generated the natural longing to establish a peaceful and united continent, the idea of the United States of Europe was born during this century.

Bonaparte Napoleon also had the idea of uniting the continent of Europe, this time with Paris rather than Rome as its center. Napoleon represented a strange combination of views – liberal ideas inherited from the French Revolution intermingled with the domineering ideas of a military man. He was a born leader and conqueror who wanted to both liberate and occupy Europe by uniting it under his rule. Napoleon's self-identification as both liberator and conqueror was shared by a great number of Europeans. The German philosopher George Wilhelm Friedrich Hegel looked at him as the embodiment of the "world soul" (*Weltseele*). In a letter from Jena on 13 October 1806 – "the day the French occupied Jena and the Emperor Napoleon penetrated its walls" – he recorded in his famous letter to Niethammer:

> I saw the Emperor – this world-soul – riding out of the city on reconnaissance. It is indeed a wonderful sensation to see such an individual, who, concentrated here at a single point . . . reaches out over the world and masters it . . . such advances as occurred from Thursday to Monday are only possible for this extraordinary man, whom it is impossible not to admire.[3]

As a prisoner on the island of St. Helena, Napoleon, retrospectively expressed his goals to conquer and liberate:

> Europe thus divided into nationalities . . . peace between States would have become easier: the United States of Europe would become a possibility. . . . I wished to found a European system, a European Code of Laws, a European judiciary: there would be but one people in Europe.[4]

Although Napoleon failed to create a permanent physical empire that encapsulated all of Europe, his customs union, the Continental system, and the broadly adopted legal system of the Napoleonic Code were all achievements in the direction of unification.

The idea of creating a unified Europe as a peace program virtually always present during the nineteenth century. In France, socialists such as Claude Henri

Saint-Simon and Augustin Thierry wrote a long essay about the idea of a European parliamentary federation in 1814.[5] The United States of Europe concept was also presented by Polish thinker Wojciech Jastrzębowski's "About the Everlasting Peace Between the Nations," published in May 1831. Twelve years later in 1843, the Italian politician Giuseppe Mazzini called for the creation of a federation of European republics. In the mid-nineteenth century, as a reaction to the Napoleonic and later wars, seven peace conferences – in Paris, London, Brussels and Edinburgh, among other cities – were organized in Europe between 1843 and 1853. One of the most enthusiastic pacifists, the well-known French writer Victor Hugo, expressed his hopes for European unification at the Mazzini-organized Paris conference of 1849:

> A day will come when your arms will fall from your hands! A day will come when war will seem as absurd between Paris and London, between Petersburg and Berlin, between Vienna and Turin. . . . A day will come when . . . you all, nations of the continent, without losing your distinct qualities and your glorious individuality, will be merged closely within a superior unit and you will form the European brotherhood. . . . A day will come when the only fields of battle will be markets opening up to trade and minds opening up to ideas . . . and bombs will be replaced by votes, by . . . a great sovereign senate which will be to Europe what Parliament is to England. . . . A day will come when . . . the United States of America and the United States of Europe, stretching out their hands across the sea.[6]

Eighteen years later in 1867, Hugo sat down with the Italian freedom fighter Giuseppe Garibaldi, the British philosopher-economist John Stuart Mill, and the Russian revolutionary anarchist Mikhail Bakunin at a congress of the League of Peace and Freedom in Geneva. Bakunin stated "that in order to achieve the triumph of liberty, justice and peace in the international relations of Europe, and to render civil war impossible among the various peoples which make up the European family, only a single course lies open: to constitute the United States of Europe."[7] And finally, a century before modern unification became a reality, Polish writer Theodore de Korwin Szymanowski's treatise "The Future of Europe in Economic, Political and Social Terms" (1885) presented a practical program for unification. Szymanowski focused foremost on economic and monetary policy, proposed the introduction of customs union, and even suggested a common currency to unify Europe.[8]

After the tragic shock of World War I, dreamers reappeared and argued even more convincingly against the widespread destruction created by continual warfare in Europe. The only way to avoid it, they argued, was through the unification of Europe. Soon after the war, the young Austrian Richard von Coudenhove-Kalergi founded the Pan-Europa movement in 1923 and arranged the First Pan-Europe Congress in Vienna in 1926. The most celebrated intellectuals of the period joined, including Albert Einstein, Thomas Mann, Franz Werfel, Sigmund Freud and Benedetto Croce. In his Pan-Europe Memorandum, Kalergi warned of two imminent dangers: "Europe's policy is heading for a new war. . . . One crisis triggers another. This can be performed daily by an accident." He also called for unification against the danger posed by communist Russia: "Under the leadership of a red or white dictator" (meaning the Bolshevik Red Army or the counter-revolutionary White Army), Russia could endanger and conquer "the small states of Eastern Europe, Scandinavia and the Balkans nor disarmed Germany would then be able to repel the Russian rush. Against this danger there is only one salvation: the European union."[9]

2.1 Richard Coudenhove-Kalergi

Born in 1894, Richard Nikolaus Aoyama Eijiro, Count of Coudenhove-Kalergi, was a genuine all-European *par excellence*. His father, Heinrich, was a diplomat of the Austro-Hungarian monarchy who served all over the world, spoke 16 languages, and married in Japan during his service there. The von Coudenhove-Kalergis were a complex all-European family. The Coudenhove family branch was originally Flemish, but during the French Revolution they immigrated to Austria. The Kalergi side was originally a Greek Byzantine-Venetian aristocratic family, mixed with Polish, German, French, and Baltic families. Richard himself was born in Japan to a Japanese mother as an Austrian citizen, although he took Czechoslovak citizenship in 1919, during the troubled interwar years, after the dissolution of Austria-Hungary. Then, after the Nazi occupation of Czechoslovakia, he became a French citizen in 1939, and immigrated to the United States after the German occupation of France in 1940. In other words, he himself was a "melting pot," an all-European.

Coudenhove-Kalergi, indeed, became a dreamer of united Europe. In 1923, at 29 years old – during a time of extreme nationalism, the same year that Hitler first attempted to take over Germany in a failed coup d'état – he swum against stream by publishing his first book, *Pan-Europe*, and established an all-European movement. He wanted to mobilize people to block the road, as he later called it, towards "the most dangerous revolution in the history of the world – the revolution of the State against mankind. We are living through the most dangerous idolatry of all ages – the deification of the State."[10]

His entire life represented this idea, and he called consistently for the unification of Europe. To advocate for and spread the idea of "Paneuropa" he published his journal *Paneuropa*, and in 1926 his Pan-Europa movement held its first congress in Vienna with the participation of two thousand delegates, among them the top intellectuals of the age, including Albert Einstein, Thomas Mann, and Sigmund Freud. He was an utopist dreamer, but, as he noted in his book, "every great historical event began as a utopia and ended as a reality."[11]

> Coudenhove-Kalergi advocated for a common European market and currency; he was a forerunner of European integration his entire life. He was lucky enough to see the first steps of the realization of his "utopia," the foundation of the European Coal and Steel Community, and then the European Economic Community. In 1929 he suggested the triumphant music of the famous "Ode to Joy," based on Friedrich Schiller's poem from Beethoven's Ninth Symphony, as the Anthem of Europe; his ideas was later accepted by the European Community. When Coudenhove-Kalergi died in 1972, he was buried at Gruben in the Swiss Alps, and the simple phrase "*Pionnier des États-Unis d'Europe*" – "Pioneer of the United States of Europe" was written upon his gravestone.

France's political elite also promoted cooperation between Continental countries. Emil Borel, the head of the Radical Party, established a French Committee for European Cooperation in 1927. Twenty countries followed by setting up similar committees. Two years later, French Prime Minister Aristide Briand gave a speech at the League of Nations Assembly on 9 September 1929 in which he proposed a federation of European nations. In 1930, he presented a Memorandum on the Organization of a System of European Federal Union that provided more specific details on the structure of his proposed institution. Briand stressed the importance of cooperation in the economic arena. British economist John Maynard Keynes enthusiastically welcomed the suggestion. The next year Édouard Herriot (later prime minister of France) published a book entitled *The United States of Europe*.[12] Despite the enthusiasm among political intelligentsia about the possibility of a unified Europe, people were slow to learn. Europe increasingly shifted in the opposite direction, especially after Hitler gained power in Germany during the 1930s. Instead of forging ahead with cooperation, the continent's countries started preparing for war.

During the tragic years of World War II and immediately after, the idea of European unification reemerged stronger than ever before. For first time in modern history, the elimination of nation-states became a major widespread political agenda. Two political prisoners of Mussolini's fascist Italy, Altiero Spinelli and Ernesto Rossi, penned the famous Ventotene Manifesto in 1941 (named for the island of Ventotene where they were incarcerated). The treatise – one of the best-known radical federalist programs of the time – suggested the elimination of nation-states:

> The question which must first be resolved . . . is that of the abolition of the division of Europe into national, sovereign states. . . . The general spirit today is . . . a federal reorganization of Europe. . . . The multiple problems which poison international life on the continent . . . would find easy solution in the European federation . . . the single conceivable guarantee . . . of peaceful cooperation.[13]

2.2   Altiero Spinelli

Spinelli was born in 1907. A convinced anti-fascist, at the age of 17 Spinelli joined the Italian Communist Party to fight against Mussolini. Three years later, in 1927, he was arrested, imprisoned and spent over a decade in prison and internment until the end of the war in Italy in 1943. Sixteen years are a long time to think about communism, fascism and war. Spinelli used that time in a very intellectually productive way: he realized the true face of Stalinism and broke with the communist party in the 1930s. He also recognized the real cause of frequent warfare and found the medicine against it in the ideas of a federal Europe. This idea became his central guiding light during his entire life.

In Mussolini's prison island, Ventotene, he wrote – together with another prisoner, Ernesto Rossi – the *Ventotene Manifesto for a Free and United Europe* in 1941. They stated that the nation-state, an important force of human development, had become deformed. The state had become

> a divine entity, an organism that has to consider only its own existence . . . without the least regard for the damage this might cause to others. The absolute sovereignty of national states has given each the desire to dominate.

They concluded at the solution was the dissolution of the system: after the war, the nation-states should not be reestablished; they should be replaced by a European Federation that would solve "multiple problems which poison international life on the continent."[14]

After his liberation in 1943, Spinelli started struggling for the realization of his idea and continued to do so during his entire life. In 1943, he founded the *Movimento Federalista Europeo*, or Federalist Movement of Europe. His manifesto was circulated and mobilized several resistance movements in various countries. In 1944, the delegates of several resistance movements gathered in Geneva at a meeting attended by Spinelli, where they all voiced strong support for the federal idea, influencing postwar attitudes for integration. He became the political advisor to Alcide de Gasperi, Italy's first prime minister after the war, and strongly influenced him to be an advocate of federation.

Soon after the establishment of the European Economic Community, Spinelli became one of the commissioners of the European Commission responsible for internal policy between 1970 and 1976. In 1979, he was elected as a member of the European Parliament, where he effectively worked on the realization of his federalist vision. When the Parliament set up the Committee on Institutional Affairs in January 1982, Spinelli became the General Rapporteur and worked out a proposal, the Draft

Treaty Establishing the European Union (Spinelli Plan), which was adopted by the Parliament with an overwhelming majority in February 1984. The national parliaments, however, did not endorse the federalist treaty, and it was consequently shelved.

Altiero Spinelli died in 1986, a year after Jacques Delors became President of the European Commission. In the year of Spinelli's death, his plan was taken over by Delors, and the Spinelli Plan became the basis for the Single European Act of 1986 and the Maastricht Treaty of 1992. In 2010 a Spinelli Group was formed to reinvigorate the idea of federalization of the European Union, a concept that has subsequently been supported by people such Jacques Delors and Joschka Fischer. Spinelli, a federalist dreamer, played a crucially important role in the process of European integration and definitely became one of its founding fathers.

Across Europe, anti-Nazi resistance movements nurtured the idea of postwar unification throughout the war. The German historian Walter Lipgens collected 176 published manifestoes issued by Italian, French, Belgian, Dutch and German wartime resistance organizations, among other nationalities. These early dreamers' ideas of a federal Europe gained relatively widespread recognition during the war. In the spring of 1944, the French socialist resistance group *Libérer et Fédérer* published its federalist manifesto in its journal. Between the fall of 1943 and the spring of 1944, representatives of various resistance groups from several countries met three times in neutral Switzerland – in Geneva – to discuss the postwar future of Europe. On 20 May 1944 they agreed upon a federalist program, announcing in their Geneva Declaration:

> The peoples of Europe are united in the resistance to Nazi oppression. This common struggle has created among them solidarity and unity. . . . During the lifetime of one generation Europe has been twice the centre of a world conflict whose chief cause was the existence of thirty sovereign States in Europe. It is the most urgent task to end this international anarchy by creating a European Federal Union.[15]

Three months before the war ended several of these resistance movements established the Europeesche Actie at The Hague, with the goal of working towards European integration.

During the late 1930s and 1940s, even top British politicians welcomed the federalist idea. In November 1939, Clement Atlee, the head of the Labor Party (and the postwar prime minister) declared: "Europe must federate or perish." As Master of University College, Oxford, William Beveridge published a study entitled *Peace by Federation?* In 1940. The most influential British politician, Winston Churchill, was no exception. On 9 May 1938 he published an article that ran in both *The Saturday Evening Post* and *The News of the World with the title* "Why

Not 'The United States of Europe'?" The version printed in the working-class paper *John Bull* on the same day lauded Churchill's insight even more explicitly by running the article with the title "A Great Big Idea." Churchill concluded,

> The conception of a United States of Europe is right. Every step taken to that end which appeases the obsolete hatred and vanished oppressions, which make easier the traffic and reciprocal services of Europe, which encourages its nations to lay aside their precautionary panoply, is good in itself, is good for them and good for all.[16]

Churchill's enthusiasm for European integration was not just a prewar phenomenon. On 21 October 1942 he wrote to Anthony Eden, his Foreign Secretary, "Hard as it is to say now . . . I look forward to a United States of Europe, in which the barriers between the nations will be greatly minimised and unrestricted travel will be possible."[17]

Inter-European confrontation and war understandably pushed British politicians in this direction. As such, Churchill became one of the first to advocate European integration in the postwar years. To reiterate, as early as September 1946 he had advocated for a Franco-German reconciliation for this reason. In order to "to recreate the European family. . . . We must build a kind of United States of Europe."[18] As a first step, he initiated the foundation of a Council of Europe in 1948. Some politicians and historians, including EU scholar Jon Danzig, even call him one of the "founders of the European Union." Roy Jenkins–Churchill's biographer and an enthusiastic Europeanist who previously served as President of the European Commission – likewise believed Churchill's commitment to European integration. "Was he merely telling others to unite, or was he willing to do so too?" Jenkins queries. "The evidence is generally held to be against a Churchill commitment to full British participation. I find it conflicting." Recalling Churchill's speech in The Hague Conference, when he urged the formation of economic and military relationships among the western countries, Jenkins surmises, "It would have been difficult in these circumstances to add, or even to harbor the thought, but of course I am only talking for others and not for Britain's unique position outside."[19]

Churchill's wartime and even postwar advocacy for integration were clearly rooted in the necessity for unity during wartime – first during World War II and then during the Cold War period. It was vital for the Western European countries to stand together against Hitler and then against Stalin.

At the same time, when Churchill urged France and Germany to "take the lead together" in establishing a united Europe at the end of his Zurich speech in 1946, he clearly expressed the typical British view:

> we are with Europe, but not of it. We are linked, but not comprised. We are interested and associated, but not absorbed. . . . Great Britain, the British Commonwealth of Nations, mighty America . . . must be the friends and sponsors of the new Europe and must champion its right to live.[20]

On 28 November 1949, he gave a more detailed explanation:

> The French Foreign Minister, M. Schuman, declared in the French Parliament this week that 'without Britain there can be no Europe.' This is entirely true. But our friends on the Continent need have no misgivings. Britain is an integral part of Europe. . . . But Britain cannot be thought of as a single state in isolation. She is the founder and centre of a worldwide Empire and Commonwealth. We shall never do anything to weaken the ties of blood, of sentiment and tradition and common interest which unite us with the other members of the British family of nations.[21]

Speaking about the Schuman Plan of European integration in June 1950, he added, "Everyone knows that [the Empire and Commonwealth] stands first in all of our thoughts. First, there is the Empire and the Commonwealth, secondly, the fraternal association of the English-speaking world; and thirdly the revival of united Europe."[22]

All in all, Churchill, the "founder of the European Union," in reality recommended integration for *others* while simultaneously rejecting full participation within it. He consistently followed this policy. After all, instead of quoting some of his enthusiastic speeches about the need for unification, we must base our view on facts. Churchill rejected joining the integration process even after he returned to power and became prime minister again between 1951 and 1955, the crucial years that marked the beginning of European integration. Britain, with her old identity as a world power – which had actually survived the collapse of the British Empire – recommended European unification for the others. Actually, this attitude was quite common among Tories and Laborites alike. Churchill and Atlee, Eden and Bevin all shared the same feeling of British superiority. Meanwhile, the newly formed postwar governments in Belgium, the Netherlands and Italy – socialist and Christian democrat leaders alike – were all headed by federalist politicians. As one scholar puts it, "the Belgian government under Paul-Henri Spaak and the Italian government under Alcide de Gasperi had made proposals aiming at European unification. . . [that] had been rejected in London and Paris."[23] This series of circumstances occurred again and again.

2.3   Alcide de Gasperi

Alcide Amedeo Francesco De Gasperi was born the son of a policeman in 1881 in Trentino-Alto Adige (South Tyrol), which at that time was an Italian-populated part of the Habsburg Empire. In 1900, he joined the Faculty of Literature and Philosophy in Vienna, but soon turned to politics and was elected to the Austrian Reichsrat, or Parliament, in 1911 to represent Trentino; he served there for six years.

After the war, that part of the Habsburg Empire became part of Italy. De Gasperi co-founded the Italian People's Party in 1919 and became a member of the Italian Parliament from 1921 to 1924. Italy, however, was taken over by Mussolini's fascist regime in 1922. His party was dissolved in 1926; shortly thereafter, De Gasperi was arrested in 1927 and sentenced to four years in prison. After one-and-a-half years, however, the Vatican helped to free him and granted him asylum. He spent the next 14 years there as a librarian until the liberation of Italy.

The first 37 years of his life made him a convinced democrat and a strong believer in European integration. A deeply religious man, in 1943 he founded the Christian Democratic Party, won the first free elections in Italy after the war, and became Prime Minister and Minister of Foreign Affairs of Italy during the difficult but formative postwar years, from 1945 to 1953.

In this position, De Gasperi became a key personality in forming the future of Europe. He became a firm believer of integration, advocated for the creation of joint European defense mechanisms, and enthusiastically supported the Schuman Plan. Under his leadership, Italy became one of the founding members of the European Community, and he became the first president of the Parliamentary Assembly of the European Coal and Steel Community in 1954.

When De Gasperi died in August 1954, the European integration process that he helped to create was already on its way.

Wartime and immediate-postwar dreamers – or, as Henri Brugmans called them, the "prophets and founders" of the integration – reinvigorated the idea of European integration and brought it to the center of politics.[24] They popularized the idea of unity as a possible solution, and crafted political party programs that offered it as a response to the lessons of the war that would help solve the main problems of the Continent. Alan Milward – probably a bit unjustly – maintained that even the "saints and prophets," as he sarcastically called the main advocates of unification, in reality only wanted to serve the interests of their own nation-states.[25] Yes, some of them did, but not all of them.

The idea of creating a united federal Europe that would act virtually akin to a single republic divided into provinces had accompanied almost the entire history of Europe. However, despite this long lineage it was unclear how viable this idea was, as no concerted attempt towards its realization had ever happened, and success was bound to be difficult. The spirit of Westphalia – the idea that individual states are the only legitimate embodiment of sovereignty in Europe – had only become stronger since the mid-seventeenth century, increasing in strength throughout the early modern period until and especially gaining predominance during the turn of the nineteenth-century, which saw the genesis of the modern nation state. Aside from a few important voices to the contrary, the superiority of the state seemed unquestionable for three hundred years; this view still exists and in most parts dominate in the present. The passionate advocacy of hundreds of people, politicians, and organizations for federalist integration came up against the thick concrete wall of the nation-states' resistance.

Nevertheless, after World War II many pragmatic politicians – who unquestionably did not ascribe to idealistic dreams and plans, but who wanted to serve their nation's practical interests – entered the ring *en masse*, from France and Germany to the Benelux countries and Italy. These politicians offered solutions to many of the unsolved and frightening questions facing Europe. They cooperated with the dreamers and started to play important practical roles in advancing European integration. The international situation – the Cold War confrontation between West and East and the task of rebuilding a working international economic system – offered a special opportunity for them. The absolute hegemon of the Western world, the United States, also wanted to create a united Western world. Some of the postwar Western politicians became influential because they supported and followed the American policy initiative, working together with the government of the United States of America to achieve greater European unity.

American plans and efforts to Unite Europe

The American aid policy to Europe definitely contributed to the fast economic reconstruction and recuperation of Western Europe, enabling the region to cure its politically dangerous vulnerabilities. Crucially, America wanted to force recipients of Marshall Plan aid towards integration. While official speeches and writing used highly diplomatic language to obscure this objective, behind the scenes American policy insiders bluntly expressed this goal. Charles Bohlen, the special assistant to George Marshall who actually drafted the Secretary of State's famous Harvard speech, consciously followed the ideas of Kennan and Clayton. He spoke honestly about the goal of the aid as "an overall plan for economic cooperation by the Europeans themselves, perhaps an economic federation to be worked out over three or four years."[26] This outcome was achieved by attaching strict requirements to the aid. For example, the plan stipulated that within the first three months of receiving aid, 60 percent of trade in aid-recipient countries must be liberalized; by June 1959, liberalized trade had to make up 89 percent of total trade. After half a century of protectionism and tariff wars, the American requirements opened up a new period in European trade relations.

The Marshall Plan also mandated a return to a multilateral payment system within the established Payment Union. This shift became the first important step in postwar integration. Barry Eichengreen and Andrea Boltho underline that "eliminating exchange control and making currencies convertible on current account (that is, allowing them to be freely bought and sold for trade-related purposes) was a precondition for reconstructing intra-European trade and creating a common market."[27] The Payment Union created an automatic mechanism for the settlement of net surpluses and deficits. This feature decisively contributed to the amelioration of the decades-long trade stagnation, which had brought European trade in 1947–1948 to more or less the same level as it had been in

1913. As a consequence, trade among Marshall-aid recipient countries grew from $10 billion in 1950 to $23 billion by 1959. Fifty years later, it has multiplied by 50 times.

Allen Dulles clearly articulated the American hope that the Marshall Plan would bring the European countries one "step nearer to the establishment of a United States of Europe."[28] Likewise, the influential Senator J. William Fulbright explicitly stated that the European Recovery Program "should be used as an instrument of European political unification." In February 1949, he even had a sharp debate with Secretary of State Acheson about the necessity of European political unification. Acheson, opposing Fulbright's view, "emphasized that there had to be more progress on an economic level before true political integration could be achieved."[29] The idea of economic integration as road to political integration was genuinely present during the preparation of the Marshall program. When Undersecretary William L. Clayton returned from Europe in May 1947, he was probably the very first to suggest the initiation of a three-year aid program to promote widespread concurrent European growth that would lead to federation. He based his ideas on the Benelux customs union. George Kennan also recommended the formation of customs union and a multilateral clearing system to pave the road for federation.[30]

President Truman appointed Paul Hoffman, an experienced automobile manufacturing executive, to head the administration of the Marshall Plan. He served between 1948 and 1950. On 31 October 1949, at the OEEC Council in Paris, he openly stated that aiding the economic recovery

> means nothing less than an integration of the West European economy . . . the building of an expanding economy . . . through economic integration . . . a single large market within which quantitative restrictions on the movement of goods, monetary barriers to the flow of payments, and eventually, all tariffs are permanently swept away.[31]

This statement represents an open and clear expression of the real American aims. After the Hoffman speech, Ernst van der Beugel, the secretary of the Dutch delegation at that Paris meeting (and later the minister of foreign affairs) concluded:

> There were parts of the speech which could lead to the belief that integration in the political and institutional sense was the ultimate aim. . . . In short America has the power, if it will be patient to impel Europe along the road of real integration.[32]

During an Oral History Interview in 1964, Paul Hoffman underlined:

> there was no hope for progress of a compartmentalized Europe and that in a postwar world Europe's future would be dim unless there was close cooperation among the Marshall Plan countries. Speaking personally, I thought

that union would first come along economic lines and that some degree of political union was certain to follow.[33]

A group of American diplomats in Paris–Ambassador Caffery at the US Embassy; Under-Secretary Clayton, who had arrived in Paris in July 1947; and later George Kennan, who travelled to Paris to aid with the project of European integration – consulted with the delegations of participating European countries to push them to create a common market. In August 1947, they expressed dissatisfaction about the progress embodied in the agreement. Consequently, from April 1948 to September 1950, the US strengthened its push. "It is this period that the impact of the US on every phase of European cooperation was the strongest than in any other period," noted Beugel. As part of it, the Americans gave the authorization for four members of the Commission to make the final decision. Thus, a "denationalized group" had to analyze all the national plans for using the American aid, evaluate them, and make the final decision upon the aid's allocation. The recipient countries' economic sovereignty, concluded Beugel, was "essentially broken."[34] All in all, the American Marshall Plan's aid policy successfully forced some cooperation among the West European countries, but did not reach its final goal of establishing a West European common market, which was supposed to be the start of the federative reorganization of Europe.

New American integration plans: looking for a European leader

The United States was not satisfied with the results of the Marshall Plan regarding its impact on integration. Thus, it engaged in continued efforts to push the west European countries into a united community. The Americans found new ways to push the countries in this direction. The State Department worked out two plans: one for economic and one for military integration. As discussed in Chapter 1, these plans were sent over to the main American representative in Europe, John J. McCloy, who presented them to his close European friend, Jean Monnet, with the task of translating them as a European initiative.

Monnet was a man for all seasons. He was a merchant, banker, financial advisor and civil servant; he worked in Europe, America, and China, but always as an *eminence grise*. During World War I, he had the idea to create an international supranational authority propelled by Franco-British cooperation to run an efficient war economy. After the war, he was appointed Undersecretary General in the newly established League of Nations, but resigned in 1922. During World War II, Monnet suggested the formation of an inter-Allied Coordinating Committee based on a joint French-British recommendation, which he would run. In 1940, Churchill sent him over to the United States to convince the Roosevelt administration to abandon its isolationist policy. Monnet established close connections and friendships with high-level Roosevelt aids, including the influential Harry Hopkins. Moreover, he became a major contributor to Roosevelt's Victory Program, an economic mobilization plan, and the Land-Lease program that financially assisted the Allies. When the Organization of European Economic Cooperation was established to run the Marshall Aid program in Europe after the war, the Belgian politician Paul-Henri Spaak nominated him to be the president of the Organization, but he rejected it. Monnet, a convinced integrationist, became the main 'translator' of American integration plans into European initiatives because of his American connections and equally close relationships with leading French, British and German statesmen. He stood behind the Schuman Plan and the Joint European Army plan as well.[35]

The failure to convince Britain

The Truman administration wanted to present its European integration plans as a genuine European initiative. Therefore, they wanted to find a European initiator and leader. It seemed natural to turn to Britain, America's closest wartime ally. "In the early postwar years," the Truman administration "pressed for UK leadership in Europe." The American effort to encourage British leadership started during the preparation of the Marshall Plan. Averell Harriman and Paul Hoffman urged the Truman administration to pressure the Atlee government."[36] Secretary of State Acheson

> made it a personal mission to convince Britain to join the European Coal and Steel Community. . . . Together with President Truman, he was convinced long-term US national interests required that Britain be a founding member of an integrated Europe.[37]

After Truman, President Eisenhower lectured the British political elites about the advantages of a European federation.[38] In fact, American presidents from Truman to Kennedy until the 1960s all tried convincing Britain first to lead, and then at least to join the already-established European Economic Community. Arthur Schlesinger, who had intimate knowledge about the Kennedy administration, recalled John Kennedy's belief that if Britain joined, "the Market could become the basis for a true political federation."[39] Even in 1962, Senator William Fulbright emphasized that "only Britain . . . has the long experience, the ancient institutions, and the over-all political maturity for leading Europe into a new era."[40] The United States was not alone in believing in the importance of British leadership for the integration process. The most influential Belgian politician of the time, Paul-Henri Spaak, who served as minister of foreign affairs and as prime minister, also tried convincing the Brits to join and lead. He had several discussions about it with Churchill. As he recalled, "the idea of an organization of Western Europe did not appeal to [Churchill]. My plans for economic integrations seemed to him, I believe, a pipe-dream."[41] Ernest Bevin, the foreign secretary of the postwar Labor government, also rejected Spaak's initiative at the end of 1945. As the *Economist* noted in December 1951, "In French and Benelux eyes Britain is still regarded as the missing component, without which the Schuman community is in danger of German domination."[42] Even Germany wanted

Britain to join. In 1960, the German president of the European Commission, Walter Hallstein, stated to the European Parliament that it would be "an act of historical importance if other European States, and in particular Great Britain" were to join.[43] Six years later, Chancellor Kurt Kiesinger of Germany repeated: "the community of Six is open for all European states that accept its goals. We should especially welcome the joining of Great Britain."[44]

Nevertheless, the British political elite – both conservative and Labor – constantly resisted. At the time when the American push for European integration was culminating in the postwar years, Britain was governed by the Labor government of Clement Atlee, with Ernst Bevin as its Foreign Secretary. Britain had been victorious in the war and was still ruling a huge empire. In this context, Secretary Bevin presented his "Grand Design" to government officials. He held three meetings between 10–15 August 1945, in which he spoke about a British-led "Western Union." Bevin described his desire for a British-led alliance from the Aegean Sea to the Baltic, and from Greece and the Mediterranean to the Low Countries and Scandinavia. He believed in three great spheres of interests, which he called the "Three Monroes," presided over by the Americans, the Soviets and the British. In September 1947, he visited French Premier Paul Ramadier in Paris and presented a grandiose plan: France and Britain, with their

> vast colonial possessions . . . could, if they acted together, be as powerful as either the Soviet Union or the United States. . . [and] occupy in the world a place equivalent to that of Russia and of the United States.[45]

It is not necessary to repeat what was discussed earlier (in Chapter 1): both the French and British colonial empires were already in the process of collapsing. This disintegration started during and immediately after the war, and was fully realized by 1960. However, this new political reality did not eliminate or indeed even influence the imperial consciousness of the British elite.

Bevin's traditional feeling of British superiority is evident in his remarks during a meeting with American representative William Clayton about the recently launched Marshall Plan. Bevin protested, as Alan Milward put it, "that the new policy of providing aid to Western Europe as an integrated bloc rather than individual countries would mean that Britain would now be 'just another European country.'"[46] Like Churchill, from time to time Bevin made different, even opposing statements about the topic. Sometimes he voiced definitive support for integration; other times he expressed reluctance. However, records from closed-door cabinet meetings show that he called Robert Schuman's integration plan a "schumania" and urged Britain to act against it. He said: "if we do nothing Schumania will spread. Better that we shd [*sic.*] take initiative."[47]

The Labor Cabinet and the British Board of Trade also opposed any kind of unification with the Continent. Instead of a customs union composed of similarly industrialized European countries, they maintained that "a Customs Union with a number of primary producing countries with a wide diversity of unexploited resources would be likely to be the advantage of the United Kingdom."

As Secretary Bevin and Prime Minister Atlee expressed in September 1947, their goal was "to reestablish Britain's position in the world. . . . One way to do this was . . . drawing the raw-material resources of the Commonwealth and Empire." Indeed, the British Cabinet set up a committee "to consider the feasibility of a customs union with the colonies or even with the Commonwealth."[48]

This stance clearly reflected that even the British business world and the government lived in the past. They simply did not recognize the change that had begun during the war and had accelerated thereafter. Instead of the traditional nineteenth-century division of labor between industrial and agricultural-raw material producing countries that had remained in place during the first half of the twentieth century, by mid-century industrialized countries had started to build a new type of labor division among themselves. With the exception of a few developed countries such as Canada, Australia, and New Zealand, most of the fifty-four British Commonwealth countries were from African, Caribbean and other non-industrial regions. Trade with those countries gradually and, then sharply, started decreasing after the war. Within just fifty years, British exports to the entire Commonwealth were roughly equivalent to British exports to Germany. Imports from Commonwealth countries were equal to British imports from the Netherlands. Both amount to less than 10 percent of British trade. Nevertheless, a government committee concluded in the summer of 1947 that "it is not our interest to encourage the idea of a European Customs Union of which the United Kingdom would be a member. . . . A general West European customs union is out of the question."[49] After the Schuman Plan for West European integration became public, the National Executive Committee of the British Labor Party published a fifteen-page statement opposing such unification:

> Britain herself is unwilling to join such a union for fear of losing her independence outside Europe. . . . [Britain is] the nerve center of a world-wide Commonwealth . . . [and] we in Britain are closer to our kinsmen in Australia and New Zealand . . . than we are in Europe. . . . The economies of the Commonwealth countries are complementary to that of Britain to a degree which those of Western Europe could never equal.[50]

The Secretary of State and the Chancellor of Exchequer prepared a Cabinet paper in October 1949 that finalized the British position on this question: "We must remain, as we have always been in the past, different in character from other European nations and fundamentally incapable of wholehearted integration with them."[51]

Beside the old reflex to be connected to the Empire and the Commonwealth, the other prevailing foreign policy idea was that Britain held a special relationship with the United States. Churchill especially had strengthened this belief during the war, and Roosevelt shared this view. However, the Truman administration did not feel similarly, although the British government still wanted to believe in it. As the preparation for the first steps of Western European integration went on, senior representatives of the British Foreign Office, the Dominions Office, and the Treasury developed a joint resolution that was accepted by the Cabinet: "We hope to secure a special relationship with USA and Canada . . . for in the last resort we cannot rely upon the European countries."[52]

In January 1950, the government even warned Oliver Harvey, the British ambassador to France, not to mention the customs union. "In fact," they underlined, "the present view of Ministers is that we must remain completely uncommitted."[53] This view was not only the standpoint of the political elite; it was shared by a huge portion of the country. As Sir Oliver Franks, the British ambassador to the United States, correctly appraised in his 1956 Reith Lecture at the BBC, the British people have increasingly "thought less and cared less" about Europe.[54] More than two generations and sixty years later, during a time when the majority of the British people voted for Brexit and gave a landslide victory for Boris Johnson based on his insistence on leaving the European Union, this assessment seems truer than ever. Edmund Dell, who chronicled Britain's rejection of the offer to join the European Coal and Steel Community, rightly stated: "Britain was bankrupt of ideas. Creativity was left to others."[55]

At last, in September 1949 (if not earlier), American Secretary of State Dean Acheson clearly realized that the British government would continue to refuse participation in the planned West European integration after he consulted with his counterpart in the British government, Bevin, and Stafford Cripps, the Chancellor of Exchequer. Acheson was forced to realize that the United States must give up the idea of positioning Britain as leader of West European integration. The head of his State Department's Planning Office, George Kennan, suggested turning instead to France as an alternative leader.[56]

Successfully blackmailing France

Indeed, the Truman administration had no other option but to turn to France. But, unsurprisingly, the Americans met with a rather similar attitude in Paris as in London. In spite of the shamefully fast French collapse after the German Blitzkrieg during the war, and even after a series of endless and hopeless colonial wars, the French political elite still saw France as the second biggest colonial power. As such, they held somewhat similar views about France's global identity as did the British. Henry Bonnet, the French ambassador in Washington, clearly expressed this self-identification as a global power:

> Our American friends appear to have an extremely simplistic conception of the unity of Europe . . . ignoring the seriousness of the problem faced by the European states, particularly France, a power having worldwide responsibilities. . . . The French Union and the construction of a Federal European state were mutually exclusive.[57]

Similarly to his English colleague Bevin, French Minister of Foreign Affairs Georges Bidault complained at the American embassy in early 1945 that "the Big Three put France in the same class with China . . . I don't like often the way your government treats us. I don't like the secondary position."[58] When Bidault visited President Truman in May 1945, he expressed his hopes for American support "in enabling France to return to her former position."[59] In the spring of 1945, the American embassy in Paris sent a memorandum to Washington with the title "What Worries the French." In this document, they summed up various famous and influential French people's fears of America's growing power. One mentioned the idea "that American imperialism will swallow up some of our colonies." Another accused the US of seeking "to block the road for France to control the Rheinland." French sensibilities, commented the Embassy, "have taken an almost pathological turn."[60] Like the Brits, the French government and a great part of the population similarly opposed the American plan of West European unification, for two basic reasons. The first, expressed in Bidault's earlier-quoted statements, was the sense that France was still a colonial great power.

However, for France there a second major concern: the "German Question." Indeed, the French had a pathological fear of German recovery and rearmament, which they believed could lead to a fourth German attack in the future. France's main aim was the destruction and mutilation of the powerful German state. Including Germany as equal partner in a federal Europe was out of the question. Between 1945 and 1950, French and American diplomats played an endless political chess game regarding the German question. The French government tried blackmailing Americans by emphasizing the growing communist danger and, insinuating that they would turn to Russia if America failed to encourage the revival of France as a world power. On 12 May 1945, the American ambassador to France, Jefferson Caffery, reported to the State Department:

> Ever since liberation . . . French foreign policy has followed a very uncertain course and has been marked by recurring efforts to draw closer to the Soviet Union, Great Britain or the United States, depending on external developments at the time. In the early part of the period the emphasis was toward the Soviet Union.[61]

On 5 May 1945, Ambassador Caffery reported his conversation with General De Gaulle, who said to him: "I would rather work with the United States than any other country. . . . [But] if I cannot work with you I must work with the Soviets."[62] A few months later, on 17 August 1945, De Gaulle told to the American ambassador:

> The decision about Germany's western frontiers would have far-reaching repercussion on French international policy. . . . [If] Germany was permitted to retain those areas [the Ruhr, the Rheinland, and Saarland] as part of a strong central Germany . . . France might be obliged to orient her policy toward Russia.[63]

Those remarks constitute explicit blackmailing by the French.

Meanwhile, the American government also blackmailed France by threatening to stop economic and military aid. After the war, France was unable to operate without major American assistance. Around the end of the war, Jean Monnet – at that time a close associate of De Gaulle – calculated that by January 1946, half of France's food supply, a quarter of its coal and raw material supply, 80 percent of its semi-finished goods, and 90 percent of its finished goods would have to come from the US. The postwar reconstruction plan of France, prepared by Monnet, necessitated American financial contributions. France even established a French Supply Council in New York with 1,200 employees.[64] France's dependence on the US was clear for the Americans as well. Ambassador Caffery suggested giving France a "generous credit on political rather than economic grounds." If the US lost interest, he argued, the French would feel abandoned and turn to communism.[65] At the National Advisory Council in Washington, William Clayton reiterated this position: a decision against a substantial loan would be a "catastrophe." Whereas the French asked for $2 billion, Clayton suggested giving them $650 million. After Leon Blum, the former French prime minister, visited Secretary Byrnes, the government provided this amount as a loan; and even more importantly, it cancelled France's Land-Lease obligations, which totaled $2.8 billion. In total, through various forms – loans, Marshall Plan aid (21 percent of the total amount spent by the US), and military assistance – the United States sent over $1 billion in assistance to France between 1945 and 1954. Additionally, America supported the French colonial war in Vietnam, later taking it over entirely.

In other words, the blackmailing race was not a match of equal partners. America had the upper hand and held the ultimate weapon. As such, the United States was able to successfully blackmail France with the withdrawal of Marshall Plan aid if they did not comply. De Gaulle was outraged, but he had to bow.[66] In early 1947, Ambassador Caffery informed Prime Minister Ramadier and foreign minister Bidault of Truman's decision to aid Greece and Turkey (a proxy for direct Soviet confrontation), and added: "From now on the situation is clear. One must choose."[67] In his 18 July 1947 memorandum, George Kennan made the stakes of France's choice clear: "We could place squarely before the French the choice between a rise in German production or no European recovery financed by the US."[68] France, indeed, had no choice. The Truman administration categorically told the French government that their desire to keep the German Ruhr area under international and not German authority would only happen if "the coal and steel industries of France and the Benelux countries were brought under its purview as well."[69] This American concept was first aired by John J. McCloy, the American high commissioner in Germany, during a conversation with his old friend, Jean Monnet. This idea became soon the central concept of the European Coal and Steel Community, formed a few years later. It is undeniable that France was not strong enough to resist such pressure; sooner or later, they had to cease their resistance and accept all of the American requirements.

Jean Monnet, with his first-hand information from America, was among the very first to recognize that the policy best suited to serve French interests was the acceptance of the American plans. He wrote in a letter to Prime Minister Couve de Murville: we are

> forced to make a short cut. Now the federation of Europe would have to become an immediate objective. The army, its weapons, and basic production would all have to be placed simultaneously under joint sovereignty. We could no longer wait, as we have once planned for.[70]

As Monnet discussed in his *Memoires*, he recognized that the Marshall Plan included Germany. "I saw no solution," he recalled,

> except to propose linking the growth of German steel production to an increase in Ruhr coke exports. . . . Only in this way could we maintain France's steel production targets, which were the key to the whole French plan.[71]

He summarized:

> A financial crisis in Paris brought the French to their knees. On September 10, the Ministry of Foreign Affairs notified Washington that all imports of needed raw materials . . . must be ceased by the end of October 1947, because French currency reserves would then be totally exhausted. . . . The French needed at least $100 million per month to live through July 1, 1948. . . . In exchange . . . the French government also declared that it recognized the necessity of the economic integration of Europe and was ready for negotiations with the European nations to achieve it. . . . On September 23 Bidault appropriately concluded that the German question had become a "lost case" for France. . . . On August 8, Bidault told American officials that publicly he still supported the harsh terms of the Morgenthau Plan, but privately we know that we have to join in the control of Germany and reorganization of Western Europe, but please don't force us to do so at the point of a gun.[72]

2.4   Jean Monnet

Born in a peasant-merchant family in the small French township of Cognac and withdrawn from school – where he was such a bad student that his teachers considered him mentally disabled – at the age of 16, Monnet spent his early years working in the family business, selling cognac in London and Canada.

World War I became a turning point in his life. Monnet developed the idea that international control and supranational authority were needed to run an efficient Allied war economy. He convinced the French prime minister to cooperate with Britain, and Monnet became a member of the Inter-Allied Maritime Transport Council. Due to his outstanding service, after the war he was appointed undersecretary general of the newly established

League of Nations, but he soon realized that the League was a powerless institution and resigned in 1922 to go back to business. He joined the American Blair Investment Bank's Paris office. During the 1930s, he spent five years in China establishing a Development Bank to finance railroad construction.

World War II, however, galvanized him to try organizing coordinated European action again, and he returned to public service. In 1939, he sent a memorandum to the French prime minister suggesting the organization of an inter-Allied coordination organization. The British government agreed, and the Coordinating Committee, headed by Monnet, was established. He even tried to convince Churchill to create a French-British Union. After the collapse of France, Churchill sent him to the United States to press for American economic mobilization to support the European war effort. He gained the friendship of intimate Roosevelt aides such as Harry Hopkins, and closely collaborated with them. Monnet also became a major supporter of Roosevelt's Victory Program, the mobilization of the American economy, and the Lend-Lease project that assisted the European allies.

After the war, Monnet turned to planning French economic reforms. He convinced de Gaulle to introduce modernizations and then a reconstruction plan for the provisional French government. De Gaulle signed a decree in December 1945 that established the Commissariat du Plan headed by Monnet, who started building up a new economic framework that combined elements of market and planned economies. He played a central role in postwar French reconstruction. When the Organization for European Economic Co-operation (OEEC) was established in 1948 to administer the Marshall plan, Paul-Henri Spaak recommended him to run the institution, but he rejected it because he believed that the OEEC was not powerful enough to realize the federalization of Europe, which had become his overarching goal.

Monnet was extremely well informed by his influential American friends about the radical changes in American policy towards Europe and Germany in light of the emerging Cold War. He understood that postwar French plans to paralyze and virtually destroy Germany, which he had supported in the beginning, were no longer realistic, and as such he helped to transform French policy accordingly.

Monnet was a special character, working via making friendly connections with influential people and then influencing them, but he was never in the foreground. True, he was not a good orator and did not like to perform in front of crowds. In a way, he was a born *éminence grise*, but an unusual sort who did not serve others, but rather used them to realize his ideas. Monnet was an interesting mix of a visionary and a man of action who was able to realize his ideas. He was very successful at convincing the French government to accept American policies, about which he had the very intimate, direct information straight from the horse's mouth. He was able to convince the French officials that in accepting the American integration plans, they could realize French interests in a different form. Following American initiatives, in 1950 he convinced French foreign minister Robert Schuman to initiate the unification of the West European coal and steel industries under a supranational authority, combining the most important strategic industries of the former enemy countries. He drafted the Schuman Declaration and then the Schuman Plan, and he was the one who realized it, as the first president of the supranational High Authority established by the six founding countries.

Somewhat later, after having received the plan of the US State Department from his influential American friend regarding the establishment of a West European joint army, he again prepared a plan to initiate the creation of a European Defense Community with a supranational army, and presented it to René Pleven, the French prime minister. This plan failed, but Monnet continued his work for integration.

In terms of the path towards further integration, Monnet advocated for the gradual sectoral integration plan, which would have started with coal and steel, followed by other sectors such as nuclear industry and transportation. He, however, was an extremely modest man without personal ambitions, and was thus open to accepting different approaches. As such, he welcomed the Dutch and Belgian foreign ministers' idea of furthering integration by creating a common market. The year the European Economic Community was established in 1958; the 68-year-old Monnet withdrew from direct administrative roles and worked towards further integration by serving as the chair of his Action Committee for the United States of Europe, a role he held for two decades. He always worked behind the scenes, using his reputation and close connections with de Gaulle, Adenauer, Brandt and Kennedy. Jean Monnet, who was often called one of the Fathers of Europe, died in 1979 at the age of 90.

2.5 Robert Schuman

Schuman is considered to be one of the founding fathers of the European Community, and not without reason. As early as May 1949, in one of his famous speeches in Strasbourg, he was already speaking about "supranational association of the European nations":

> Our century, that has witnessed the catastrophes resulting in the unending clash of nationalities and nationalisms, must attempt and succeed in reconciling nations in a supranational association. This

> would safeguard the diversities and aspirations of each nation while coordinating them . . . within the unity of the nation.[73]

Schuman had the predestination to be a "European." He was born in a mixed family in Luxembourg, from a Luxembourgian mother and French father who was a native of Alsace-Lorraine and born as a French citizen, but who became a German citizen when Lorraine was annexed by Germany in 1871. Schuman himself was born in 1886 as German citizen. He studied law, economics, political philosophy, theology and statistics at German universities in Bonn, Munich, Berlin and Strasbourg, finally receiving a law degree and setting up his own law practice in 1912. When Alsace-Lorraine was returned to France after the war, he became a French citizen in 1919.

Schuman was a deeply religious man; moreover, he was a Bible scholar and an expert in the medieval philosophy of St. Thomas Aquinas. He entered French politics as a Christian Democrat and became a member of the French parliament in 1919. He elevated along the political ladder, and in 1939 became a member of the French wartime government. After the Nazi occupation of France, he voted to give full power to Marshal Pétain, but refused to join his government and instead joined the resistance movement. He was arrested and interrogated by the Gestapo in 1940, but was released two years later.

With his background, after the war, he became an advocate for reconciliation with Germany and for European integration. During that time, he became one of the most important French politicians: he served as Minister of Finance, then as Prime Minister, and then as Foreign Minister from 1948–1952, and finally again as Minister of Justice from 1955–1956.

The American State Department initiated the integration of Europe and this plan was sent over to the American envoy, who presented it to his influential French friend, Jean Monnet. Based on these American ideas, Monnet drafted a memorandum and sent it to foreign minister Schuman. In this way, the American integration plan of Western Europe became the basis of the famous Schuman Plan, which he proposed on 9 May 1950. He suggested joint control of coal and steel production, the bases for war industries. This goal was genuinely in France's interest, but it also furthered reconciliation with Germany and also helped to reunite Germany into the European family (and as such, the plan was fully supported by the German government under Adenauer).

In his Declaration, Schuman stated:

> Europe will not be made all at once, or according to a single plan. It will be built through concrete achievements which first create a de facto solidarity. The coming together of the nations of Europe requires the elimination of the age-old opposition of France and Germany.[74]

Schuman invited all nations who agreed to join and, indeed, the governments of Italy, Belgium, Luxembourg, and the Netherlands reacted positively. The six states signed the agreement to establish the European Coal and Steel Community in Paris in April 1951.

When Schuman died in September 1963, the process of integrating Europe had already made great progress, as the Treaty of Rome, the foundation of the European Economic Community, had been agreed upon. European integration was on its way.

Robert Schuman, who had meanwhile replaced Bidault as the minister of foreign affairs, told Secretary Acheson that France would take the initiative on starting the process of European integration, but he pleaded – using a more abject metaphor than his predecessor had – "that France could not be dragged on the end of a chain."[75]

American successes, pragmatic European politicians: the coal and steel community

At last, the United States government succeeded in realizing its new European policy, including the rebuilding of Germany and its incorporation into the West European community as an equal partner. The Western European countries had to comply, and thus emerged the road of integration towards a federal Europe. In the spring of 1948, the Deputy Director of European Affairs triumphantly reported: "According to Paris, the French are as desirous as we are of bringing about the integration of Germany with Western Europe."[76]

In April 1949 in Washington, Acheson, Schuman and Bevin jointly stated their commitment to addressing the German Question according to the American plan. Bevin spoke for the group when he stated: "We want assurance on security. We want the economy of Germany to be put on a proper footing to play her part in an integrated European economy."[77]

At last, European integration was on track. Naturally, it could not happen without the influence of the leading European politicians, who each presented the integration plan as their own. First among them were Jean Monnet and Robert Schuman. Monnet, who received information about the American integration plans directly from key American officials and repackaged it as a French plan, sent his draft to Robert Schuman, the foreign minister of France. Schuman was the ideal person to present the American plans as his own. He was born in Alsace-Lorraine as a German citizen and studied in Berlin; but later became a French citizen, a parliamentarian, and then a member of government between the wars. He had rejected to join the Vichy government. Thus, Schuman had learned the lessons of the war and accepted the new realities of the postwar global power structure. Unlike other French politicians, he embraced the Marshall Plan and clearly recognized that France had to follow the American initiative. In a 16 May 1949 speech delivered in Strasbourg, he stated:

> We are carrying out a great experiment, the fulfillment of the same recurrent dream that for ten centuries has revisited the peoples of Europe: creating between them an organization putting an end to war and guaranteeing an eternal peace. . . . Our century, that has witnessed the catastrophes resulting in the unending clash of nationalities and nationalisms, must attempt and succeed in reconciling nations in a supranational association.[78]

Henry Byroad at the German desk of the US State Department in Washington, DC, drafted a letter on 28 October 1949 for Acheson to send to Schuman that voice support for France's assumption of a leadership role: it

> is time for French initiative and leadership . . . to integrate the German Federal Republic promptly and decisively into Western Europe. . . . The Germans are psychologically and politically ripe to take measures for genuine integration with Western Europe. . . . French leadership is essential and will ensure success.[79]

Schuman carried out the American plan. Based on Jean Monnet's draft (which he based on Byroad's draft), Schuman delivered a speech at the Salon de l'Horloge of the Quai d'Orsay in 9 May 1950 which became the "Schuman Declaration." He asserted:

> In taking upon herself for more than 20 years the role of champion of a united Europe, France has always had as her essential aim the service of peace. A united Europe was not achieved and we had war. . . . Europe will not be made all at once, or according to a single plan. It will be built through concrete achievements which first create a de facto solidarity. The coming together of the nations of Europe requires the elimination of the age-old opposition of France and Germany. Any action taken must in the first place concern these two countries. With this aim in view, the French Government proposes that action be taken immediately on one limited but decisive point.
>
> It proposes that Franco-German production of coal and steel as a whole be placed under a common High Authority, within the framework of an organization open to the participation of the other countries of Europe. . . . The solidarity in production thus established will make it plain that any war between France and Germany becomes not merely unthinkable, but materially impossible. The setting up of this powerful productive unit, open to all countries . . . will lay a true foundation for their economic unification . . . this proposal will lead to the realization of the first concrete foundation of a European federation indispensable to the preservation of peace.[80]

This highly idealistic speech represented a deeply *realpolitik* French acceptance of the American policy. Nevertheless, it served French interests – although in a different way than previous French governments had originally planned. While the original French plan to occupy the Saarland and keep occupation troops indefinitely in order to control the German coal and steel industry in the Ruhr area failed because of strong American resistance, Schuman accepted the American suggestion of controlling Germany by the way of integration. As André Gauron, adviser to two French prime ministers, honestly stated in his 1998 reflections on the situation,

> Under the cover of Europe, France hope[d] to use Germany's power to benefit its own economy. . . . Germany was not fooled by the French machinations. But it found them to be in its own interests, temporarily. Chancellor Adenauer's priority was to attain sovereignty with equal rights.[81]

2.6   Konrad Adenauer

Konrad Hermann Joseph Adenauer played a central role in postwar European integration although – unlike Spinelli and De Gasperi – he was not a "federalist dreamer." Rather, he was a calculating, pragmatist German politician. Born in 1867, he studied law in Freiburg, Munich and Bonn, graduating in 1900. He then started working as a lawyer in Köln, until he was elected mayor of the city in 1917; he served until 1933. Although he was a Catholic politician and mayor of a big city during the 1920s, he was removed from office by Hitler in 1933; moreover, he was actually arrested twice during the Nazi era (though only for days or weeks). Adenauer emerged at the top of German politics after the war, when he was already in his early 70s.

He always served German interests, but, in contrast to the majority of German politician of his time, in a rather flexible way, by adjusting to the requirements of international situations. A good early example of his mentality took place in February 1919, when Adenauer called for the dissolution of Prussia and the formation of an autonomous Prussian Rhineland, because that seemed to be the best way to avoid the planned French annexation of the Rhineland.

After World War II, he immediately recognized that the best way of serving German interests was to establish the best relationships with the occupying American, British, and French powers – even if it meant subordinating Germany. His past and strong anti-communism helped him to gain the confidence of Western powers, and he was able to convince them to include Germany in the Western alliance system during the sharp Cold War years. He developed a relationship with the occupying powers and worked for them. His main opponents in German politics, also anti-fascist and anti-communist social democratic politicians, targeted his centrist German position. He established the Christian Democratic Party, which became the strongest political force in German politics in the latter half of the twentieth century. When American Cold War policy established the Federal Republic of Germany in 1949, his party's electoral victory elevated him to the chair of Chancellor at the age of 73. His main opponent, the social democrat Kurt Schumacher, called him the "Chancellor of the Allies."

Although he was traditionally anti-Nazi, he denounced the Allied occupation forces' policy of denazification, arguing that it would only exacerbate growing nationalism. He also advocated for rehabilitating the millions who supported the Nazi regime back into German life. Indeed, former Nazis flooded German public life, dominated the jurisdiction, and gained positions in the government under his Chancellorship. (Even after it came to light that his government's State Secretary, Hans Globke, was one of the drafters of the anti-Semitic Nuremberg Race Laws in Nazi Germany, Adenauer kept him in the post.) In August 1950, Adenauer demanded the Western Allies free all the imprisoned war criminals, especially former Wehrmacht officers, because without them, he argued, German rearmament would be impossible. In January 1951, the amnesty legislation indeed realized his plans. Adenauer also never stopped arguing against the dismantlement of German industry, which was part of the original postwar Allied policy. He achieved the Petersberg Agreement in November 1949, which decreased the planned dismantlement; eventually it was totally halted.

Understanding the American interests to build a West European alliance against the Soviets, Adenauer became an integrationist. He offered his support for creating a union with France, the most anti-German power of the postwar years, and welcomed every idea of integration. When Robert Schuman sent him his proposal for uniting the coal and steel industries, a key French interest because it would block the road for new future German war preparations, Adenauer enthusiastically welcomed the idea, even though it was very unpopular in Germany. Indeed, he became one of the key founders of integrated Europe. As a result of his Chancellorship and *realpolitik* for fourteen years until 1963, Germany became a solid pillar of the renewed European Community. He died in 1967 with a series of very positive political achievements behind him. Although his main goal was always serving German interests and regain the face of the country after Hitler and the country's tremendous war crimes, he also served all-European interests as one of the founders of the European Union.

West German Chancellor Konrad Adenauer's postwar policies focused on regaining his country's reputation, erasing the heavy burden of the war crimes committed by Hitler-led Nazi Germany and reestablishing Germany as an equal part of the European family of nations. He was an ideal German politician for this task. Although he was a conservative, he had been removed by Hitler from his post as Mayor of Köln; moreover, he had even been arrested twice (though for very short periods of time). He established a new party, the Christian Democratic Union; was able to build strong connections with the American authorities; and successfully represented Germany at international meetings. Adenauer recognized immediately after the war that Germany had no other option but to subordinate herself to France's security interests. In a letter from October 1945, he wrote: "The only way to fully satisfy the French desire for security must in the long run lie in the economic interlocking of West Germany, France, Belgium, Luxembourg and Holland."[82] Adenauer clearly recognized that German rehabilitation was only possible through European integration. In 1946, he participated at a secret meeting of the European Christian Democratic leaders in Switzerland – among the participants was the French politicians Robert Schuman and Georges Bidault – in which they discussed the possibility of an integrated European economic system. Adenauer also participated in The Hague Congress of the Union of European Federalists headed by Coudenhove-Kalergi, which included figures like Churchill, De Gasperi, Spaak and Schuman. There Adenauer was elected honorary president of the European movement. He never stopped working on his plan. Even before he became Chancellor, he had already "declared that he was against remilitarization of Western Germany. In his view the Allies . . . defend WD [West Germany] against invasion."[83] He also expressed strong anti-Soviet feelings, and offered Germany's participation in a Western front against Stalin. In a speech at Heidelberg University, he promised that Germany would join the rest of Europe to "construct a Wall against Asia."[84] He published an article in the *Reinische Merkur* in spring 1948 welcoming the American plan to unite Western Europe: Expressing a view shared by America as well, he remarked that "A renaissance of the conception of the West can rise only as a result of fruitful understanding between Germany and France."[85] The American military governor of Germany reported: "Adenauer informed me, he had secret meeting with Bidault and also with Schuman to reach a Franco-German understanding. . . . Schuman and Adenauer are old friends from before 1933."[86]

The Americans recognized the value of Adenauer's support for the success of their plan. Although he was already 72 years old and, as American General Consul Altaffer recognized, shows the symptoms of age, "becoming more and more capricious, impatient . . . more and more isolating himself from the rank and file of the party."[87] Nevertheless, as the American consul Martin Hildebrand reported: "Adenauer [is] one of the few Germans who at the present enjoy a European reputation."[88] John McCloy expressed, "I am impressed by him. I think he is a man who firmly believes in the necessity of a French-German rapprochement."[89] That was definitely the case. Adenauer wrote in his *Memoires:*

> Schuman wrote that the aim of his proposal was not economic but highly political. There was still fear in France that when Germany had recovered she would attack France. . . . I immediately informed Robert Schuman that I agreed to his proposal with all my heart.[90]

After founding the German Christian Democratic Union, Adenauer emerged as the leader of Germany after the first elections of the newly established state in August 1949. In September, he officially became the first Chancellor of the Federal Republic. A few weeks later, he echoed the American view on European integration: "I should agree to an authority that supervised the mining and industrial areas of Germany, France, Belgium and Luxembourg." In an interview in the spring of 1950 he went as far as suggesting a union between France and Germany by merging their economies, parliaments and even citizenship.[91]

Both pragmatic politicians, Schuman and Adenauer recognized that they served their national interests by integrating their countries. This cognizance led to the gradual formation of a French-German axis, which became the engine of integration. The first major step was taken on 18 April 1951, after West Germany embraced the Schuman Declaration and signed, along with France, the Treaty of Paris. The three Benelux countries – Belgium, the Netherlands and Luxembourg – as well as Italy, also accepted the Schuman Declaration and immediately joined. They had a variety of motivations. In the case of Italy, their main goal was rather similar to that of the Germans: to rid themselves of the burden of Mussolini and their fascist past. At a cabinet meeting on 15 July 1947, foreign minister Count Carlo Sforza stated: "no national sacrifice was too great for a united Europe . . . a supreme necessity."[92] Prime Minister De Gasperi and his deputy and minister of finance, Luigi Einaudi, were also enthusiastic Europeans. The Benelux countries' postwar governments were all led by federalist dreamers – in Belgium, by Paul-Henri Spaak; in the Netherlands, by Henri Brugman. They put into practice the lessons of their wartime experiences by forming the Benelux alliance and then by pushing for integration. Quite early on, on 30 October 1945, the Dutch parliament declared the need for a "regional union in Europe."[93] In 1946, when De Gaulle suggested establishing a French-Benelux customs union – an "economic area" – the Dutch asserted their readiness to join if Britain and Germany were also invited. Both the Dutch and the Belgians worried that without the other two great powers, France would gain dominance; thus, they ultimately decided not to join. Unlike France, the Benelux countries wanted to include Germany. In the fall of 1947, the three countries sent a joint memorandum to the occupying powers that "pointed out the dependence of the recovery program in the three Benelux countries upon the economic revival of Germany."[94] These small countries actually became federalist by recognizing – as the war had taught them – that the best way to serve their own interests was to unite with the great powers.

On this basis, the six countries agreed to establish the European Coal and Steel Community (ECSC). The organization was based on supranational principles. Thus basic industries were taken from national authorities' control and put under supranational control and management. The ECSC was overseen by four institutions: (1) a High Authority headed by Jean Monnet and composed of independent appointees, (2) a common assembly with delegate members from the member countries' national parliaments, (3) a special governing council composed of national ministers and (4) a European Court of Justice to adjudicate among debating members if needed. The High Authority distributed the production quotas, and created a common market for coal (which opened on 10

Map 2.1 The six founding member countries

Source: EC06-1957-58 European Community map.svg, created by user Kolja21, CC Attribution-ShareAlike 3.0 Unported, commons.wikimedia.org/wiki/File:EC06-1957-58_European_Community_map.svg

February 1953) and for steel (which began on 1 May 1953). The headline of the organization's first bulletin signaled its overarching goal: "Towards a Federal Government of Europe."

In reality, the ECSC was very far away from realizing the idea of a United States of Europe. It basically offered a solution for the "German Question," assuaged French fears about a future German rearmament and attack, and consolidated Germany's status as an equal member of the European community, but did not offer much more. It was not a solution that would create a booming new prosperity; and it did not provide a strong social fabric to anchor the creation of a modern and prosperous Western Europe. Especially in the context of Cold War competition, it did not offer enough structural support to build a strong Western world.

Deciding how to go further

The builders of integration definitely did not want to stop at that first stage. In those years there was much discussion about a common West European market, and even about a federal reorganization of the countries. But how could Europe go further? Jean Monnet argued for a gradual sector-by-sector integration. After the coal and steel sectors, he thought about integrating the nuclear energy sector, and likely followed by agriculture and transportation. His views were based on French economic interests, namely the creation of an independent energy base for the country and a common market for French agricultural products.

One cannot forget Monnet's role in France's postwar reconstruction. In 1943, he went to Algiers to work with the Free French administration and became member of the National Liberation Committee, the French government in exile, led by General Charles de Gaulle. After the liberation of France, De Gaulle appointed him to run a government committee tasked with preparing a complex plan for reconstruction and economic modernization. As commissioner-general of the National Planning Board he prepared the Monnet Plan, as it came to be called, in 1945; the plan was accepted in early 1946.[95] His central goal was to encourage the modern transformation of France; however, unlike De Gaulle's nineteenth-century nationalistic formulation, his ideas were based on economic cooperation with Germany. Monnet clearly recognized the need of integration as a French interest *par excellence*. All of these motivations were behind his sectoral integration concept.

Most leaders from other member countries nurtured a different plan for continuation. Because the Benelux countries were small, they naturally had rather open economies. Indeed, some decades later, two-thirds of their combined GDP was represented by foreign trade – twice as big a share as the OECD countries' average. Recognizing their national interests, they became more integrationist. They wanted deeper and more complex integration. Already in 1944, their governments in exile in London discussed postwar policies and held a joint customs convention. At that time, they established the Benelux Customs Union that was institutionalized in 1948, and eventually became the Benelux Economic Union. All in all, the Benelux countries wanted broader and deeper economic integration starting with a united customs union, instead of the gradual sectoral integration proposed by Monnet. The Benelux ideas were immediately accepted by Germany and Italy, the two defeated and humiliated countries, which needed intimate integration with other west European countries in order to regain equal status in Europe.

Sectoral integration was not the ideal road for further integration for the western countries. In his analysis, the Hungarian-born American economist Bela Balassa pointed out that sector-by-sector integration requires a quasi-permanent readjustment of price equilibrium, costs and resource allocations, and a constant balancing of payment changes. These objections, he summed up, "suggest the inadvisability of integration sector by sector."[96] Balassa was right. Later economic history analysis proved that the Coal and Steel Community was unable to reach even its limited goals because national price controls and subsidies remained in place. Steel tariffs were only harmonized, not eliminated, and the sectors could not establish a real common market. This Community was also unable to made technological or organizational changes.

Nonetheless, the primary integration of the Benelux countries became a real practical engine for further integration. In May 1952, the representatives of the six member countries of the ECSC met in Paris and signed a treaty creating a European Defense Community with forty mixed divisions. The Benelux representatives suggested uniting the defense community with the Coal and Steel Community under a European Political Authority. In the fall and winter of 1952–53, representatives of the member countries formed an ad hoc assembly, headed by the Belgian Paul-Henri Spaak, and met in Strasbourg. This group adopted a draft treaty in March 1953. The details were worked out by the Assembly's Constitutional Committee, which was headed by the German politician Heinrich von Brentano. The finalized draft treaty was presented at the Intergovernmental Conference in September 1953. It called for the establishment of a supranational European Community with a common market for goods, capital and persons, governed by a bicameral parliament and a powerful executive council. This plan for a genuine federation, however, did not survive the planning phase. The French Parliament vetoed the formation of the defense community, and the entire plan collapsed.

In spite of their early failures, the Benelux politicians did not stop fighting for closer integration. In 1952, Johan Willem Beyen, the Dutch minister of foreign affairs, published another supranational integration plan. Instead of further sectoral integration in the fashion that Monnet had recommended, his plan on a customs union and common market formation between the six countries was based on the construction the Benelux countries already had. This plan also remained un-adopted. But two years later, he renewed his economic integration plan in a 1955 memorandum, suggesting that instead of sectoral integration, the countries should "create a supranational community with the task of bringing about the economic integration of Europe in the general sense, reaching economic union by going through a customs union as a first stage."[97]

2.7 Paul-Henri Spaak

Spaak was born in a political family in Belgium in 1899. His grandfather was deeply involved in politics, and his mother was a socialist member of the Senate. When World War I broke out, he felt impelled to serve his country; so although he was underage, he lies about his age and volunteered to join the army. He spent two years in a prisoner-of-war camp in Germany. After the war, in 1920, Spaak joined the Belgian Labor (later Socialist) Party.

Spaak studied law and began to practice, but then shifted to pursue a career in national politics. As a result of his family background and war experiences, he elevated quickly. He was elected to Parliament in 1932, appointed minister of foreign affairs in 1936, and became prime minister in 1938. After the German occupation of Belgium, he went into exile together with the rest of the government, and served as minister of foreign affairs in the Belgian-exiled government in London.

During that period, Spaak became the number-one advocate of European integration. He did not merely make suggestions, but acted efficiently to make his ideas realities as well. The first logical step on this road was his initiative to unite the three small neighboring West European countries – Belgium, the Netherlands and Luxembourg – all of which had suffered the same fate of Nazi German occupation during the war. He became one of the main architects of the Benelux Agreement in 1944, wherein the three neighboring countries established a borderless common market with the free movement of people, goods and capital. This agreement was the very first step towards, and example of, European integration after the war.

Paul-Henri Spaak also played a prominent role in postwar Belgian politics. He was foreign minister from 1945–1947 and then prime minister from 1947–1950, a crucial period in which European integration became a central political issue. Spaak, a genuine integrationist, helped prepare the Brussels Treaty, which established a regional defense alliance among Britain, France and the Benelux countries in 1948. His Belgium immediately joined the integration of the European Coal and Steel Community, which first included six European nations and was formalized in the Treaty of Paris in 1951. Spaak naturally became the organization's first president serving from 1952 to 1954.

In that role, he became a central force in the advancement of European integration. Shifting away from the then-dominant goal of promoting gradual sector-by-sector integration (after the coal and steel, probably nuclear energy, then transportation, followed by others), he became the main advocate for following the Benelux example. At the Messina Conference of 1955 between the six countries, Spaak was understandably chosen as chairman of a committee to work out plans for further integration. The Spaak Committee presented the Spaak Report in 1956, which suggested the formation of the European Common market. His report became the basis of the Intergovernmental Conference, which led to the Treaty of Rome in March 1957 that establishing the European Economic Community.

During the "Empty Chair Crisis" of the Community in the mid-1960s – which was caused by France's president Charles de Gaul, who opposed everything beyond the creation of a loose alliance between independent nation states–Spaak consistently rejected this view and stressed that "[t]he Europe of tomorrow must be a supranational Europe." When Spaak retired from politics in 1966, the European Community was in the midst of deep crisis (as it was when he died in 1972, unfortunately), but the framework that he significantly contributed to was strong, and this solid foundation helped to restart integration efforts in the mid-1980s.

Beyen's Belgian and Luxembourgian colleagues, Paul-Henri Spaak and Joseph Beck, supported the plan. Even Jean Monnet joined. In April 1955, Spaak sent Beyen's plan to the foreign affairs ministers of the six Coal and Steel Community member countries. An *ad hoc* committee presided over by Spaak was formed, and the Benelux initiative became the basis of new negotiations in 1955–1956. On 9 May 1955, just ten years after the end of the totalizing European war, the European Coal and Steer Community's assembly welcomed the plan. They adopted the resolution and formed an intergovernmental committee between the six member countries to continue working on further steps for integration. Their ministers of foreign affairs met in Messina on 1–3 June 1955 and established an intergovernmental committee headed by Spaak to work out the draft agreement. In May 1956, the committee's report was presented to the foreign ministers of the six countries in Venice.

Everything was prepared, and the representatives of the six countries gathered in the Palazzo dei Conservatori in Rome on 25 March 1957. They signed two treaties that established the European Economic Community (EEC) and the European Atomic Energy Committee (EAEC), which both came into force on 1 January 1958. The preamble of the treaty stated:

> Determined to lay the foundations of an ever-closer union among the peoples of Europe, resolved . . . to eliminate the barriers which divide Europe . . . anxious to strengthen the unity of their economies . . . desiring to contribute, by means of a common commercial policy, to the progressive abolition of restrictions on international trade . . . resolved by thus pooling their resources to preserve and strengthen peace and liberty, and calling upon the other peoples of Europe who share their ideal to join.[98]

The Treaty of Rome was a kind of constitution for the six member countries of the European Economic Community. It had 248 articles, four annexes, 13 protocols, four conventions and nine declarations that established the institutional network of governance, laid down the framework and roadmap for an economic union, and brought into focus the agenda for further unification. That was a major turning point in the history of European integration from sectoral integration towards a complete union.

The explicit goal of the European Economic Community was the gradual abolishment of tariffs and other trade restrictions among member countries within twelve years. As it happened, the free-trade system of the Community was actually realized somewhat earlier, within ten years. In the first decade, however, each member country still had its own external tariffs against outside countries. In 1968, the EEC unified its external tariffs as well at the exterior border of the Community. The Treaty of Rome also declared the elimination of restrictions on the free movement of labor and capital. The establishment of the free movement of goods, however, was not realized at this stage.

2.8   Walter Hallstein

Hallstein – who served as the first President of the European Commission and was reappointed three times, and who guided the European Economic Community during the first decade of its existence between 1958 and 1967 – is often called the "forgotten founding father." Without doubt, he became a committed Europeanist and a believer of the historical importance of federalization of the Continent. Through his ideas and precise organizational work, he played an important role in the history of European integration.

As a man who was born in the first year of the twentieth century, virtually started an academic career as a legal scholar in Hitler's Germany, and then elevated up the university ladder by becoming a professor and then a dean, he would naturally have had to make serious concessions to the Third Reich. Nevertheless, the war changed his life. He was drafted to the army in 1942 and sent to the Western Front as adjutant of a general, but became a prisoner of war in the summer of 1944, and was kept in an American camp in the United States until nearly the end of 1945. In the prisoner's camp he established a "camp university" to reeducate fellow German soldiers. This wartime experience shifted his goals.

After the war, he became Chancellor of the University of Frankfurt. He was also among the very first of those who were invited as guest lecturers to Georgetown University after the war, and he had a stint there in 1948. His studies on democracy and its institutions, as well as his new American credentials, gave him a special clout in early postwar Germany.

Chancellor Adenauer recognized that and in 1950–1951 appointed him State Secretary in the Federal Foreign Office, and also as head of the German delegations at the Schuman Conference on the formation of the European Coal and Steel Community and at the conferences that led to the preparation of the Paris Treaty in 1951. Hallstein started to ascend in this new career pathway. Chancellor Adenauer also sent him to head the German delegation that prepared the Treaty of Rome, which established the European Economic Community in the later 1950s. Although he shared Jean Monnet's idea about gradual sectoral further integration, he was flexible enough to accept Spaak's suggestion that they form a common market all at once.

In 1958, after the new European Community was established, the founder countries agreed to appoint Hallstein as the first head of the executive arm of the EEC, the Commission. In that role, he fundamentally shaped the EEC's institutions and policies. He developed a federalist perspective, believing that only federal reorganization could give durability to the integration project. To reach this goal, Hallstein proposed supranational projects such as the foundation of a currency union to serve the common market. He also considered creating a foreign and security union to speak with one voice, and wanted to strengthen the European Parliament by creating direct elections and budgetary power. Under his presidency, the agricultural market was completed, as well as the customs union for industrial products. The Community gradually established its own revenue from custom duties.

Nevertheless, when he presented his set of proposals, including the introduction of majority voting, in March 1965, they were met with the strongest possible opposition from President de Gaulle, who defended national sovereignty. De Gaulle responded to this challenge by provoking the "Empty Chair Crisis," which sabotaged the Community's work and forced the so-called Luxembourg Compromise that virtually paralyzed further progress of integration.

Hallstein's accomplishments provided a solid base for the European Community, and several of his failed attempts towards supranationalization were realized in later decades.

The impact of integration on economic recuperation

The establishment of the new Community became one of the important factors of postwar economic development. After the first steps of the common market were completed, tariffs gradually decreased and disappeared. The trade of goods among the member countries dramatically increased by six and a half times during the 1950s and 1960s. Trade expansion was much bigger than at any time before in history. By 1973, some of the member countries increased their exports by 10–15 times compared to the prewar years. For example, Italy's volume of exports, which was only 127 percent of its 1913 value in 1950, increased to 1,619 percent by 1973. In the case of the Netherlands, the equivalent figures were 171 percent and 1,632 percent. In 1938, 53 percent of the West European countries' imports and 64 percent of their exports were connected to other West European countries. Because of the elimination of economic nationalism, tariffs and other restrictions, trade significantly increased: both exports and imports among the member countries reached nearly 75 percent.

Together with this dramatic increase of trade, the structure of trade also started to radically transform. During the interwar decades, the traditional division of labor between industrial and agricultural countries was still dominant. As a result of integration, this labor structure started changing: imports of food and raw materials from the industrialized countries in Western Europe declined from 33 percent to 18 percent of their total trade by 1970. Industrial exports to non-industrialized, partly non-European countries dropped from 30 percent to 17 percent. The new emerging trade structure was characterized by trade between industrial countries wherein they traded industrial products and parts of products among each other. Several industrial products were produced in cooperation with the western countries: different countries produced different parts of the same industrial products that were assembled at the last stage. Cooperation between France and Britain produced the Concord airplane in 1969, which went into commercial use in 1976. The Airbus program, created through a French-German partnership in 1969, was another paradigmatic instance of this kind of cooperation. Soon after its genesis, four more countries joined, and different plane parts were produced by 55,000 workers and employees across in 16 sites. The new Airbus planes conquered half of the world market in their category by the 1980s. This new division of labor created the opportunity for production on a scale that helped to increase productivity and economic growth.

Most of the countries in Europe had re-reached their prewar (1938) economic levels between 1948 and 1950. Traditionally, scholars have conceived of the postwar reconstruction period as marking the years until countries' outputs and GDPs reached the levels of the last prewar year (1938). This concept, however, has been convincingly challenged by the Hungarian economist Ferenc Jánossy, who has redefined the concept of the postwar European reconstruction period. Jánossy argues that this period should be measured not by the time it took countries to reach the economic level of the last year before the war started, but instead by the time it took countries to reach the GDP the level they likely would have attained if the wartime devastation had not happened, and if economic growth had continued within the average long-term growth trend (determined by the average growth rate of the previous 50–70 years).[99] Measuring reconstruction time in this way means that the reconstruction period actually ended in Europe – meaning that the production output reached the levels it should have if there had been no war – only in the late 1960s (mostly in 1968, specifically). That is three decades later than the last prewar year, 1938. If we adopt this convincing interpretation of the unique postwar growth-rate, it becomes all the more startling that the member countries of the EEC increased their growth by three to four times of the interwar decades growth rate – hence the German *wirtschaftswunder*, the French *Trente Glorieuses*, and the Italian *miracolo economico*.[100]

Contrary to many dark economic forecasts, the postwar period experienced incredible economic prosperity. There were several reasons for this occurrence. One was the fast rate of reconstruction growth, and another was the extensive economic development model based on technology imports from the United States. New technology was created by the scientific and technological revolution that began during the war, led by wartime and postwar America. These spectacular advancements enabled the Atomic Age, the start of the computer revolution, the invention of chips and transistors, and the electronics revolution. The United States, which led this transformation, was in the midst of a Cold War confrontation, and as such it preferred to share technological novelties with its European allies. Consequently, West European countries experienced a major structural renewal with a permanent shift of labor and investment from lower to higher productivity sectors. Very soon, a service revolution started to transform the advanced economies. Together, all these became one factor in causing postwar prosperity.

Cooperation among the western countries also strongly contributed to the economic boom. The Geneva Declaration of 1950 initiated the building of a connected West European freeway network. The so-called "E-roads" of the interconnected European international road system covered 46,000 kilometers in 1965, and expanded to 64,000 by 1975. By that time, more than one-third of these roads were highways. Agricultural employment declined in Western Europe from 20–25 percent in 1950 down to 10 percent by the 1970s. In three decades after the war, the French agricultural population declined from 36 to 10 percent; in Germany, it declined from 5.9 million to 1.5 million people between 1949 and 1975. Mechanization and the use of artificial fertilizer caused this break-through. Agricultural productivity increased by 2.5 percent per year. The West European energy systems were revolutionized: in France, while energy consumption increased by 250 percent between 1950 and 1970, the share of coal dropped from 74 to 17 percent. Germany became the real engine of economic development and modernization. The share of modern industrial sectors – such as chemical, electrical, precision engineering, car and business machinery – increased their contribution to industrial-value added from 26 to 42 percent.

Citizens' living standards reached new heights. In 1950, a German or French citizen spent 43–45 percent of their income on food and basic supplies; by 1971, this share had dropped to 27 percent. In 1950, only 20 percent of French households owned a car; by 1972, already 60 percent had purchased one. In the early 1970s, 60–80 percent of households became mechanized. People spent 44 percent of their income on health, entertainment, culture and home goods – nearly twice as much as in 1950.

After decades of dire situations, depressions, and war, a never-before existent version of consumerism flooded Western Europe. Private consumption increased by 4–5 percent per year in the 1970s. A new modern consumption infrastructure emerged. "By the early 1970s," as one scholar put it recently, "Germany, France, as well as several smaller states, including Belgium, Holland . . . were at home with mass marketing, the supermarkets, chain retailing . . . of modern commerce."[101]

The West European countries provided an extremely successful response to the postwar challenges. Their ability to do so was significantly aided by economic integration and the development of a common market for goods. Optimism filled the air. Federalist dreamers and pragmatic integrationists alike believed – as Walter Hallstein, President of the EEC Commission, stated in 1959 – "There will be a United States of Europe, but it certainly premature to say when."[102] In 1964 he repeated this position: national sovereignty had become an obsolete doctrine belonging to yesteryear.

The first crisis and curbing further integration

The Treaty of Rome, which established the European Common Market, targeted much more than the free trade of goods: the countries wanted "an ever closer union"; continuous development towards a complex common market for goods, but also for services, capitals and labor. That did not happen. The main reason for this incomplete market integration was that some countries did not share the goal of fully developing a federal Europe.

The main opponent of further integration in the 1960s was France, under the leadership of President Charles de Gaulle. He was a nineteenth-century-style nationalist whose first requirement was national sovereignty. He only tolerated intergovernmental cooperation. He spoke about *Europe des Patries*, a merely cooperative political alliance.

De Gaulle wanted to reform and transform the European Community. To achieve his goal, he suggested a Franco-German partnership, a kind of confederation, to Chancellor Adenauer. The two countries would hold regular meetings either between the heads of state, or between the government ministers and senior officials, to discuss and coordinate policies. An assembly delegated by the national parliaments would act as an advisory body. After this Franco-German agreement was solidified, De Gaulle wanted to include the other four members of the European Community to join his confederative plan. With this goal in mind, a summit meeting was held in Paris on 10–11 February 1961 to discuss De Gaulle's suggestions. They established a group comprised of members of the six governments, headed by the Gaullist French diplomat Christian Fouchet to make recommendations.

In October 1961, Fouchet presented his plan of common foreign policy and defense to the delegates of the member states, who, worried about French domination in this policy cooperation, rejected the French draft treaty. The Benelux countries made a more federalist counterproposal, which was rejected by De Gaulle. The foreign ministers declared the impossibility of forming an agreement in Luxembourg in April 1962. At a May press conference, General de Gaulle condemned European federalist policies and criticized the partner countries and their backer, the United States of America.[103]

The hope and plan that a gradual but permanent economic integration process would pave the way for political integration and federalization had suddenly run upon the rocks. The Benelux countries still tried to counterbalance the French anti-federalist plan. Instead of the existing requirement of unanimous decisions that gave a veto right to each country, they suggested lowering the standard to a qualified majority for decision-making. A Dutch initiative proposed that the Community should create its own income sources instead of relying upon government contributions. Therefore, they suggested the introduction of an automatic Community taxation for the member countries.

In July 1965, De Gaulle vetoed these integration plans and decided to leave the Council of Ministers, the decision-making body of the Community. His boycott, as he called the "empty chair" crisis, paralyzed the entire activity of the EEC. Furthermore, he also made a strong statement, a kind of ultimatum, that if veto right was put into jeopardy, France would leave the Community.[104]

The other member countries still wanted further integration and ultimately decided to change the voting system and introduce the qualified-majority principle. In January 1966, the members met in Luxembourg and accepted the new voting system. However, they were forced to add a limiting condition: "if [at] any stage, a member state felt that its national interest might be threatened, the voting would simply switch back to unanimity." This agreement, called the Luxembourg Compromise, was a victory for De Gaulle.[105] The endangerment of European integration caused a Europe-wide reaction by farmers and industrialists, including the French National Federation of Farmers. The Union of Industries also issued communiques defending integration. Several trade unions supported the common market as well. The French daily newspaper *Le Monde* called upon the electors not to vote for De Gaulle in the coming elections on 23 October 1965.[106]

Thus the Community remained an intergovernmental organization. As Michael Baun commented, De Gaulle's triumphs appeared to be the death-knell for the realization of a supranational, federalizing Europe.[107] The "empty chair" crisis virtually paralyzed the European community for about two decades, until the mid-1980s.

The crisis, however, had deeper and broader roots than De Gaulle's policy. Four years after the empty chair crisis erupted, President De Gaulle – who lost the vote by more than 52 percent over a domestic issue, the redrawing of regional voting boundaries and the renewal of the Senate, after more than a decade in office – resigned on 28 April 1969.[108] The first Community summit in The Hague after De Gaulle's defeat, in 1969, witnessed some changes. The summit communiqué declared that Europe had reached "a turning point in its history," and spoke about "a rediscovered political will [of] the Six."

In reality, the European Economic Community remained mostly paralyzed. The huge literature about European integration does not give a real convincing answer to this question. In his convincing study *Europe Recast: A History of European Union*, Desmond Dinan discusses several events that caused the severe problems that emerged during those years. He noted that "the Luxembourg Compromise remained firmly in place." He also did not forget to mention that Leo Tindemans, Belgium's federalist prime minister, was officially asked to create a report about the future development of the Community, but this report – which contained all of his important ideas – was shelved. He discussed the possibility of Britain joining the Community (with Denmark and Ireland), and rightly commented that "British accession was especially disruptive because it brought into the EC a large country with a strong strain of Euroscepticism." He also discusses important new personalities that began to enter upon the stage such as Willi Brandt, Georges Pompidou, and Giscard D'Estaing; new institutional changes that partially strengthened intergovernmental features; new proposals for "deepening" integration that did not work; and the EC's African opening. He concluded: "Nevertheless, developments in the EC were not unremittingly gloomy. There was notable progress on regional policy, social policy, and environmental policy."[109]

In his carefully detailed, nearly 500-page-long book, *Building Europe: A History of European Unification* (2015), Wilfred Loth rightly stressed that De Gaulle remained alone and that the other five member countries remained consistent in their integrationist stance. Unfortunately, however, this uniformity did not mean that De Gaulle gave up and lost, or that the EU could return to normalcy.

> With his seven-month absence from the Council of Ministers and the meetings of the Permanent Representatives, de Gaulle had achieved nothing more than sowing uncertainty among his partners as to how France would unleash another crisis . . . That the president gave up his opposition at this juncture can only be explained in that he had come to the conclusion that he had played out his hand. . . . De Gaulle could no longer exclude the possibility that the integration of the Community would continue in a completely normal manner.[110]

In reality, integration could not continue. Aside from integrating some essentials, all further progress along the gradual but continuous road towards integration was halted for quite some time. The two decades after 1965 were gloomy, and despite a few new developments, Community integration could not continue as expected. Instead, inertia and stagnation characterized the two coming decades. Other internal factors certainly played a role in causing this near stagnation, namely a lack of strong leadership in the EEC. Walter Hallstein, the devoted integrationist president of the Commission, ended his decade-long term in 1967. After De Gaulle's resignation in 1969, there was no strong leadership in the Community. After Hallstein, four men – Jean Rey of Belgium, Franco Malfatti of Italy, Sicco Mansholt of the Netherlands and François-Xavier Ortoli of France – occupied the position over a decade until 1976. Each of them only held the office for a short period of time, and none contributed to its renewal by presenting important new ideas or actions. Even the subsequent two presidents after this group, Ray Jenkins of Britain and Gaston Thorn of Luxembourg – who both served full four-year terms – were unable to galvanize change. The only groundbreaking new idea proposed during those eight years was the introduction of the common currency, but it was not accepted by the member countries and had to wait another thirty years to be realized.

Nevertheless, the Commission's presidents were not solely responsible for stagnation. Unfortunately, the heads of governments whom they worked with were mostly not devoted Europeanists or were preoccupied with national problems.

The serious difficulties that characterized the two decades between the mid-1960s and mid-1980s in Europe also played an equally important role in retarding the integration process. The year 1968 was one of revolt, followed by paralyzing left- and right-wing terrorism, especially in Italy and Germany. Meanwhile, the impressive economic growth and postwar boom of the 1950s–1960s slowed down at the turn of the 1960s–1970s, and in 1973 a serious economic crisis shocked the Continent. The 1973 oil crisis, the 1973–1974 stock market crash, the collapse of the Bretton Woods system, and then a second oil shock in 1979–1980 undermined the international and European economies. For 16 months between 1973 and 1975, the global GDP declined by -3.2 percent and the global unemployment rate peaked by 9 percent. The decade was characterized by a new type of economic crisis, the so-called *stagflation*. Very unusually, during this period economic decline, or stagnation, and high unemployment went hand in hand with high inflation. Europe did not find a way out of this crisis for a long time. Between 1950 and 1973 the West European countries' average GDP increased by almost two and a half times, but between 1973 and 1985 it only increased by a quarter.[111]

On top of all of that, the American policy towards Europe also changed in the early to mid-1970s. The Nixon administration lost interest in America's European allies, and the ascendance of neoliberal globalization accelerated. All of these shifts required a reorientation in Europe.

Notes

1 Paul Fouracre, ed., *The New Cambridge Medieval History c. 500–700*, vol. 1 (Cambridge: Cambridge University Press, 2005). The main wave of the Great Migration, or the "Barbarian invasion," mostly took place in the centuries between 300 and 700, but later waves still arrived until the tenth century.

2 All of these are quoted in Perry Anderson, *The New Old World* (Brooklyn, NY: Verso Books, 2009), 476–477.

3 Georg Wilhelm Friedrich Hegel, *Hegel: The Letters*, trans. Clark Butler and Christine Seiler (Bloomington, IN: Indiana University Press, 1984), 114.

4 Quoted in Alexander Mikaberidze, *The Napoleonic Wars: A Global History* (Oxford: Oxford University Press, 2020), 232.

5 Claude Henri Saint-Simon and Augustin Thierry, *De La Réorganisation de La Société Européenne, De La Nécessité et Des Moyens de Rassembler Les Peuples de l'Europe En Un Seul Corps Politique* (Paris: Adrien Égron, 1814).

6 Alexander Campbell, "Peace Congress," in *The Millennial Harbinger*, ed. W. K. Pendleton, R. Richardson, and A. W. Campbell, vols 3 and 6, (Bethany, VA: A. Campbell, 1849), 705.

7 Mikhail Aleksandrovich Bakunin, "On Federalism and Socialism," in *Selected Writings of Mikhail Bakunin*, ed. Arthur Lehning, trans. Steven Cox and Olive Stevens (London: Jonathan Cape Ltd., 1973), 94.

8 Teodor Korwin Szymanowski, *L'avenir économique, social et politique en Europe* (Paris: H. Marot, 1885).

9 Richard N. Coudenhove-Kalergi, *Pan-Europe* (New York: Alfred A. Knopf, 1926).

10 Wickham Steed, "Introduction," in *The Totalitarian State against Man*, ed. Richard Nicolaus Coudenhove-Kalergi, trans. Andrew McFadyean (London: Frederick Muller Ltd., 1938), 9.

11 Coudenhove-Kalergi, *Pan-Europe*.

12 Ben Rosamond, *Theories of European Integration* (London: Palgrave Macmillan, 2000).

13 Altiero Spinelli and Ernesto Rossi, "The Ventotene Manifesto," in *The European Union*, ed. Brent F. Nelsen and Alexander C.-G. Stubb (London: Lynne Rienner, 1998), 4–6.

14 Altiero Spinelli and Ernesto Rossi, "The 1944 Ventotene Manifesto: Towards a Free and United Europe," in *Theories of Federalism: A Reader*, ed. Dimitrios Karmis and Wayne Norman (New York: Palgrave Macmillan, 2005), 199–200, https://doi.org/10.1007/978-1-137-05549-1_17, accessed October 6, 2017.

15 *"Draft Declaration of the European Resistance Movement,"* May 20, 1944, http://ucparis.fr/files/2414/4231/7458/manifesto_of_european_resistance_1944.pdf, accessed October 7, 2018.

16 Winston Churchill, *"Why Not 'The United States of Europe'?"* (Cambridge: International Churchill Society, 1938), https://winstonchurchill.org/publications/finest-hour/finest-hour-130/the-united-states-of-europe/, accessed October 7, 2018.

17 Jon Danzig, *"Winston Churchill: A Founder of the European Union,"* November 10, 2013, https://eu-rope.ideasoneurope.eu/2013/11/10/winston-churchill-a-founder-of-the-european-union/, accessed October 18, 2018.

18 Winston Churchill, "The Tragedy of Europe" (Speech, University of Zurich, September 19, 1946), www.churchillarchive.com/explore/page?id=CHUR%20 5%2F8%2F145-162#image=0, accessed October 18, 2018.

19 Roy Jenkins, *Churchill: A Biography* (New York: Farrar, Straus, and Giroux, 2002), 814–816.

20 See note 16.

21 Winston Churchill, *Kingsway Hall Speech* (London: Curtis Brown Group, November 28, 1949), www.cvce.eu/content/publication/1999/1/1/ce26cc27-30bc-4ec1-b0df-8a572f3dcc0e/publishable_en.pdf, accessed October 17, 2018.

22 Winston Churchill, "Speech in the House of Commons on 27 June 1950 (#168)," in *In the Balance*, ed. Winston S. Churchill (New York: Rosetta Books, 2014), 299.

23 Walter Lipgens, "The Formation of the European Unity Movement," In *A History of European Integration, 1945–1947*, vol. 1 (Oxford: Oxford University Press, 1982), 19, 41, 56, 115, 126, 134, 142–143, 159, 248, 259, 269.

24 Henri Brugmans, *Prophèts et Fondateurs de l' Europe* (Bruges: College of Europe, 1974).

25 Alan Milward, *The European Rescue of the Nation-State* (Berkeley, CA: University of California Press, 1992).

26 Michael J. Hogan, *The Marshall Plan: America, Britain, and the Recommendation of Western Europe, 1947–1952* (Cambridge: Cambridge University Press, 1987), 41–43.

27 Barry Eichengreen and Andrea Boltho, "The Economic Impact of European Integration" (London: Centre for Economic Policy Research, May 2008), www.researchgate.net/publication/4761629_The_Economic_Impact_of_European_Integration, accessed November 1, 2018.

28 Allen Welsh Dulles, *The Marshall Plan*, ed. Michael Wala (Oxford: Berg, 1993), 39.

29 Ernst Hans van der Beugel, *From Marshall Aid to Atlantic Partnership: European Integration as a Concern of American Foreign Policy* (Amsterdam: Elsevier Publishing Company, 1966), 73, 75.

30 Ibid., 43, 47.

31 Paul Hoffman, *Hoffman Speech*, 75th OEEC Council Meeting (Paris: Organisation for European Economic Cooperation, October 31, 1949), www.cvce.eu/content/publication/2009/4/3/840d9b55-4d17-4c33-8b09-7ea547b85b40/publishable_en.pdf, accessed October 15, 2018.

32 Beugel, *From Marshall Aid to Atlantic Partnership*, 186.

33 Paul Hoffman, "Oral History Interview," interview by Philip C. Brooks, November 25, 1964, www.trumanlibrary.gov/library/oral-histories/hoffmanp, accessed October 18, 2018.

34 Beugel, *From Marshall Aid to Atlantic Partnership*, 79, 137, 146–147.

35 Jean Monnet, *Memoirs*, trans. Richard Mayne (Garden City, NY: Doubleday, 1978).

36 Edmund Dell, *The Schuman Plan and the British Abdication of Leadership in Europe* (Oxford: Oxford University Press, 1995), 50–51.

37 Sarwar Kashmeri, "The Sun Never Sets on Britain's Eternal Question: To Be or Not to Be a European (Review of Britain's Quest for a Role: A Diplomatic Memoire from Europe to the UN by David Hannay)," *Foreign Policy Association* (blog), March 14, 2013, https://foreignpolicyblogs.com/2013/03/14/the-sun-never-sets-on-britains-eternal-question-to-be-or-not-to-be-a-european/, accessed October 16, 2018.

38 "General Eisenhower's Speech before the English Speaking Union at London, July 3, 1951," *Department of State Bulletin*, July 30, 1951, 163–165.
39 Arthur Schlesinger, *A Thousand Days* (Boston, MA: Houghton Mifflin, 1965), 720.
40 United States Congress, *Congressional Record: Proceedings and Debates of the 87th Congress*, vol. 108, Part 7 (Washington, DC: U.S. Government Printing Office, 1962), 8612.
41 Paul-Henri Spaak, *The Continuing Battle: Memoirs of a European, 1936–1966*, trans. Henry Fox (Boston, MA and Toronto, ON: Little, Brown and Company, 1971), 164.
42 "France and the Schuman Plan," *The Economist*, December 15, 1951, The Economist Historical Archive, 1843–2015.
43 Walter Hallstein, *Statement by the President of the Commission of the European Economic Community* (Strasbourg: European Parliamentary Assembly, June 24, 1960), 71, http://aei.pitt.edu/34146/1/A612.pdf.
44 Kurt Kiesinger, "December 13, 1966 Speech by Federal Chancellor Kiesinger in Front of the 5 Deutschen Bundestag," in *Documents on Germany Policy: December 1, 1966 to December 31, 1967*, ed. Gisela Oberländer, vols 1 and 5 (Frankfurt: Alfred Metzner Verlag, 1968), 59.
45 "Unsigned Minute, September 22, 1947," n.d., PRO, FO 371/67673/Z8461/G.
46 Alan S. Milward, *The Reconstruction of Western Europe, 1945–51* (Oxon: Routledge, 1984), 62.
47 *Cabinet Minutes*, C.C.(52)101st Meeting–C.C.(54)12th Meeting (London: The Cabinet of the United Kingdom, December 3, 1962), 98, www.nationalarchives.gov.uk/documents/transcript-cab195-11.pdf, accessed October 18, 2018. Minister of State Kenneth Younger, a deputy of Bevin, clearly expressed his biases and suspicions about Schuman: "I would not . . . pin too much faith to him as he is an odd personality. . . . A bachelor and a very devout Catholic who is said to be very much under the influence of the priests." In Edmund Dell, "K. Younger's Diary: 14 May 1950 Entry," in *The Schuman Plan and the British Abdication of Leadership in Europe* (Oxford: Oxford University Press, 1995), 65.
48 Carlo Sforza, "Cinqueanni a Palazzi Chigi. La Politica Estera Italian Dal 1947 al 1951," in *A History of European Integration: 1945–1947*, ed. Walter Lipgens (Oxford: Clarendon Press, 1982), 555–556.
49 Alan S. Milward, "T 236/808 London Committee, Sub-Committee for Integration of Europe, July 23, 1947," in *The Reconstruction of Western Europe 1945–51* (Oxon: Routledge, 1984), 239.
50 Walter Lipgens and Wilfried Loth, eds., *Documents on the History of European Integration: The Struggle for the European Union by Political Parties and Pressure Groups in Western European Countries, 1945–1950* (Berlin: De Gruyter, 1988), 746–753.
51 Sean Greenwood, *Britain and European Cooperation since 1945* (Oxford: Blackwell, 1992), 30.
52 Dell, *The Schuman Plan and the British Abdication of Leadership in Europe*, 68.
53 Ibid., 87.
54 Ibid., 65.
55 Ibid., 88.
56 Ibid., 11.
57 Irwin M. Wall, *The United States and the Making of Postwar France, 1945–1954* (Cambridge: Cambridge University Press, 1991), 266.
58 Jefferson Caffrey, "Memorandum to the Secretary by Ambassador Caffery," May 12, 1945 [National Archive 751.00/5–1245].
59 Joseph Grew, "Memorandum by the Acting Secretary of State [National Archive 711.51/5–1845]," in *Foreign Relations of the United States*, vol. 1 (Washington, DC: U.S. Government Printing Office, 1945), 17.

60 National Archive, *What Worries the French*, Memorandum (Paris: U.S. Department of State, March 1945), 711.51/3–2145.
61 Caffrey, "Memorandum to the Secretary by Ambassador Caffery."
62 Jefferson Caffrey, "Ambassador Caffery's Report to the Acting Secretary of State" (Paris: U.S. Department of State, May 5, 1945), NIACT 2381, National Archive.
63 Jefferson Caffrey, "Ambassador Caffery's Telegram for the Secretary of State," August 17, 1945 [National Archive 751.00/8–1745].
64 Wall, *The United States and the Making of Postwar France, 1945–1954*, 36–37.
65 Jefferson Caffrey, "Ambassador Caffery's Message to the State Department," n.d. [National Archive 851.00/4–446].
66 Albrecht Ritschl and Helge Berger, "Germany and the Political Economy of the Marshall Plan, 1947–52: A Revisionist View," in *Europe's Postwar Recovery*, ed. Barry Eichengreen (Cambridge: Cambridge University Press, 1995), 218–219; Milward, *The Reconstruction of Western Europe, 1945–51*, 147–148.
67 Wall, *The United States and the Making of Postwar France, 1945–1954*, 65.
68 George Kennan, "Memorandum Prepared by the Director of the Policy Planning Staff (Kennan)," in *Foreign Relations of the United States, 1947, the British Commonwealth; Europe*, vol. III (Washington, DC: U.S. Department of State, July 18, 1947), 202, https://history.state.gov/historicaldocuments/frus1947v03/d202, accessed October 16, 2018.
69 Wall, *The United States and the Making of Postwar France, 1945–1954*, 192.
70 Monnet, *Memoirs*, 342–343.
71 Ibid., 274.
72 Ibid., 80, 88–89.
73 Robert Schuman, *The Coming Century of Supranational Communities* (Strasbourg: Festival Hall, May 16, 1949), www.schuman.info/Strasbourg549.htm, accessed October 28, 2017.
74 Robert Schuman, *The Schuman Declaration* (Brussels: European Union, May 9, 1950), https://europa.eu/european-union/about-eu/symbols/europe-day/schuman-declaration_en, accessed October 23, 2017.
75 Monnet, *Memoirs*, 199.
76 Samuel Reber, "The Deputy Director of the Office of European Affairs (Reber) to the Director of the Office for European Affairs (Hickerson)," In *Telegram, Foreign Relations of the United States, 1948*, vol. II (Paris: U.S. Department of State, March 27, 1948), 152.
77 Ernest Bevin, *House of Commons Debate [Vol. 469 Cc2203–338]*, Parliamentary Session (London: UK Parliament, November 17, 1949), https://api.parliament.uk/historic-hansard/commons/1949/nov/17/foreign-affairs, accessed November 3, 2018.
78 Robert Schuman, *The Coming Century of Supranational Communities* (Strasbourg: Festival Hall, May 16, 1949), www.schuman.info/Strasbourg549.htm, accessed October 9, 2018.
79 H. A. Byroade, "Draft Letter to Foreign Minister Schuman Concerning German Development from H.A. Byroade to Secretary of State," October 28, 1949 [National Archive 862.00/10–2849].
80 Schuman, *The Schuman Declaration*, https://europa.eu/european-union/about-eu/symbols/europe-day/schuman-declaration_en, accessed November 1, 2018.
81 André Gauron, *European Misunderstanding*, trans. Keith Torjoc (New York: Algora Publishing, 2000), 5–6.
82 Konrad Adenauer, "Letter: 31 October 1945," in *Erinnerungen: 1945–1953*, vol. 1 (Stuttgart: DVA Verlag, 1965), 39.
83 Maurice Altaffer, "American Consul General's Report from Bremen," January 31, 1949 [National Archive 862.011/1–3149].

84 Konrad Adenauer, "Consular Report to the Secretary of State," May 22, 1949 [National Archive 862.00/5–1549].

85 Konrad Adenauer, *Erinnerungen: 1945–1953*, vol. 1 (Stuttgart: DVA Verlag, 1965), 314–315.

86 Maurice Altaffer, "American Consul General's Report from Bremen," October 22, 1948 [National Archive 862.00/10–2248].

87 Maurice Altaffer, "American Consul General's Report from Bremen," May 5, 1948 [National Archive 862.00/5–548].

88 Martin J. Hillenbrand, "American Consul's Report from Bremen," March 29, 1948 [National Archive 862.00/3–1548].

89 John McCloy, "High Commissioner McCloy's Letter to James E. Webb," October 28, 1949 [National Archive 862.00/10–2849].

90 Adenauer, *Erinnerungen: 1945–1953*, 314–315.

91 Monnet, *Memoirs*, 283, 285; Thomas Pedersen, *Germany, France, and the Integration of Europe: A Realist Interpretation* (London: Pinter, 1998), 76. As Monnet recorded, the French daily *L'Aube*, issued by the governing French Christian Democratic *Mouvement Républicain Populaire* (MRP), rushed to reject Adenauer's ideas: "Adenauer wants to build Europe around Germany and for Germany."

92 Sforza, "Cinqueanni a Palazzi Chigi. La Politica Estera Italian Dal 1947 al 1951," 501.

93 Walter Lipgens, *A History of European Integration: 1945–1947* (Oxford: Clarendon Press, 1982), 264, 267.

94 Robert A. Lowett, "Message," November 26, 1947 [National Archive 862.00/11–2647].

95 Frances M. B. Lynch, "Resolving the Paradox of the Monnet Plan: National and International Planning in French Reconstruction," *The Economic History Review* 37, no. 2 (May 1984): 229–243.

96 Bela Balassa, *The Theory of European Integration* (Westport, CT: Greenwood Press, 1961), 184–185.

97 Pierre Gerbert, *La Construction de l' Europe* (Paris: Notre Siècle, 1983), 197.

98 "Treaty of Rome," March 25, 1957, 2, https://ec.europa.eu/romania/sites/romania/files/tratatul_de_la_roma.pdf, accessed November 17, 2018.

99 Ferenc Jánossy, *The End of the Economic Miracle: Appearance and Reality in Economic Development* (London: Routledge, 1971).

100 For a more comprehensive account of this economic and consumption growth, see Ivan T. Berend, *An Economic History of Twentieth-Century Europe: Economic Regimes from Laissez-Faire to Globalization* (Cambridge: Cambridge University Press, 2016), 222–251.

101 Victoria De Grazia, "Changing Consumption Regimes in Europe, 1930–1970," in *Getting and Spending: European and American Consumer Societies in the Twentieth Century*, ed. Charles McGovern, Matthias Judt, and Susan Strasser (Cambridge: Cambridge University Press, 1998), 59, 74, 79.

102 P. Paul Finet, P. Etienne Hirsch, and P. Walter Hallstein, Interview of Three European Community Presidents, June 11, 1959, Archive of European Integration.

103 Derek Urwin, *The Community of Europe: A History of European Integration since 1945*, 2nd ed. (Oxon and New York: Routledge, 1995), 103–105; CVCE (University of Luxembourg), n.d., "The Fouchet Plans," www.cvce.eu/en/recherche/unit-content/-/unit/02bb76df-d066-4c08-a58a-d4686a3e68ff/a70e642a-8531-494e-94b2-e459383192c9, accessed November 3, 2018.

104 Andrew Moravcsik, "De Gaulle and Europe: Historical Revision and Social Science Theory," Working Paper, Working Paper Series 8.5 (Cambridge, MA: Harvard Program for the Study of Germany and Europe, 1998), Archive of

European Integration, https://ces.fas.harvard.edu/files/working_papers/PSGE_WP8_5.pdf, accessed November 18, 2018.

105 Andreas Staab, *The European Union Explained: Institutions, Actors, Global Impact*, 3rd ed. (Bloomington, IN: Indiana University Press, 2013), 12.

106 See Éva Bóka, "The Idea of Subsidiarity in the European Federalist Thought," Working Paper (Amstelveen: University of Budapest, 2005), 69–73, www.grotius.hu/doc/pub/ECICWF/boka_eva_idea_subidiarity.pdf, accessed November 2, 2018.

107 Michael J. Baun, *An Imperfect Union: The Maastricht Treaty and the New Politics of European Integration* (Boulder, CO: Westview Press, 1996), 77.

108 Dolly Haddad, "The Day France's Liberation Hero Charles de Gaulle Resigned," *RFI (Radio France Internationale)*, April 28, 2019, Digital Edition, sec. France, www.rfi.fr/en/france/20190428-general-charles-de-gaulle-resignation-liberation-war-hero, accessed November 16, 2018.

109 Desmond Dinan, *Europe Recast: A History of European Union*, 2nd ed. (Boulder, CO: Lynne Rienner, 2014), 123–156.

110 Wilfried Loth, *Building Europe: A History of European Unification* (Berlin: Walter de Gruyter, 2015).

111 Angus Maddison, *Monitoring the World Economy, 1820–1992* (Paris: Development Centre of the Organisation for Economic Co-operation and Development, 1995), 228.

3 The main institutional structure and policy agendas of the European community

The European Union is a unique, *sui generis* institution. Its combination of supranational and national characteristics places it in a class by itself. The EU's embryonic institutional structure and policy agendas were already established in the early 1950s when the European Coal and Steel Community was created. It went through important changes when it developed into the European Economic Community in 1957, and then again when it was reorganized into the European Union in 1992. Neither the institutional structure nor the policy agendas were stagnant. For example, the euro-zone was created by countries that used the common currency, and they became more integrated than those who kept their old currencies. The main policy agendas were enriched as new policy programs were introduced throughout the decades, due to changes in the number of member countries and increasing goals and tasks. Within the framework of the EU's cohesion policy, financial assistance was introduced to help less-developed regions and countries catch up.

There are several in-depth studies on this topic available for those interested in the minutia of the EU's structure (on the EU's health policy alone, for example, a book of more than 200 pages exists).[1] Rather than reiterating those details, therefore, this short chapter will sum up the main structural features of the EU.

The governing institutions of the community and their reforms

The Community is governed by six basic institutions. Some were already existent in the Coal and Steel Community; others were established later, either during the creation of the European Economic Community in 1957 or the European Union in 1992. Together they combine elements of supranational and intergovernmental governance.

The Community's quasi-governmental body is the European Commission, a supranational institution that is representative of the "European Idea." The Commission's president is nominated by party-families and elected by the majority of the European Parliament, according to the results of the European Parliament elections. The first president was Walter Hallstein of Germany; the present leader is Ursula von der Leyen, also from Germany. Under the President, the cabinet – known as the College of Commissioners – has as many members as there are member-states: in 2020, it has 27 members. The Commission has eight vice presidents, including three executive vice presidents, as well as a quasi-minister of foreign affairs called the High Representative of the Union for Foreign Affairs and Security Policy. Each commissioner, called a directorate-general, runs a department, or ministry, that is responsible for a specific policy area. The Commission has a relatively small staff – altogether, roughly 32,000 members, less than the size of several national governments. It has the exclusive right to recommend initiatives and policies, but the Commission, unlike a national government, is not a decision-making body.

Another central institution, the Council of Ministers, is composed of representatives from member countries. Thus in contrast to the Commission, it is an intergovernmental body. The Council is the major decision-maker. Originally it was the sole decider, but following the reform of the Parliament, the two became co-decision-making bodies. Decisions are prepared by the Council's preparatory body, called the Committee of the Permanent Representatives of the Governments of the Member States (Coreper). The Council's general secretariat has 3,500 staff members.

Early on, a unanimous decision was required, but later reforms allowed for three different standards. In certain cases only a simple majority is necessary; while in other cases a qualified majority is required. In the latter circumstance, 55 percent of the member states (which represent 65 percent of the EU's population) have to accept the proposal. For certain issues – such as common foreign policy decisions, EU membership, EU finances, and the harmonization of national legislation – a unanimous vote is still required.[2]

The third central institution is the Parliamentary Assembly, which originally included 142 representatives delegated by the member countries' parliaments. The Assembly that time was not a decision-making parliament, but only a consultative body. One of the Community's most important reforms occurred in 1979, when the role of the European Parliament changed. Instead of forming a delegation from the national parliaments, direct elections were introduced in every fifth year. In 2020, the number of parliamentarians is 705. The parliament general secretariat employs 3,500 people.

There are seven so-called *party-families* in the Parliament. The two major ones are the center-right European People's Party and the center-left Party of European Socialists, accompanied by several smaller groups, such as greens, regionalists, conservatives, communists, liberals and Eurosceptics. Party-families were founded to coordinate national social-democratic, conservative, populist and Green party activities on a pan-European scale. While some believe these party-families constitute embryonic all-European parties, others maintain that they are only insignificant alliances. Sometimes the allied parties within a given party-family have little in common. For example, before Brexit, British conservatives and German Christian Democrats aligned; as did several populist-nationalist parties that were in favor of national sovereignty but had little in common otherwise. In two cases, the Socialists and the Peoples' Party families suspended the memberships of some national parties. The Socialists suspended the Slovak Smer Socialna Demokracia after it formed a coalition with right-wing xenophobic-nationalist parties after the 2006 elections. The Peoples' Party family suspended the Hungarian FIDESz after it found that the latter had rejected democratic practice and the rule of law through its autocratic governance. These cases illustrate the lack of coherence within party-families. Beginning in 2014, the European party-families gained the power to nominate the President of the Commission (whom the Parliament elects), and to vet the designated commissioners at hearings before finally electing them.

The function of the European Parliament has also changed. Instead of acting as a consultative body, the Lisbon Treaty in 2010 made it a legislative parliament. EU laws are now voted on by both the parliament and the council of ministers. As a result of this change, legislation became more supranational than before, when only the intergovernmental council had voting rights.[3]

The fourth institution is the European Court of Justice, the supreme court of the EU. It is composed of three distinct entities: the Court of Justice and its subordinates, the General Court (or Court of First Instance, established in 1988) and the Civil Service Tribunal (established in 2005). The Court has judges from each member country, who are jointly appointed for a renewable 6-year term by each nation's government. There are also eleven general advocates. The court is responsible for controlling the rule of law; adjudicating disputed issues among member countries, individuals and companies; and managing appealed decisions from national courts. This institution is the EU's most federal in nature. It became so after a unanimous 1964 acceptance by member countries that national laws and constitutions should be subordinated to the European Community's laws.[4]

While the institutional governing bodies are now rather stable, they have undergone significant reforms. Some institutions gained different functions, while others were established. The first major reform occurred in 1965, when the European Coal and Steel Community's governing bodies, which were originally separate, were merged with the until that time independent governing bodies of the 1957 established European Economic Community and the European Atomic Energy Community (Euratom). A single Council and the Commission of the European Communities were created in 1967.

An important fifth institution, the European Central Bank, was established by the Treaty of the European Union in June 1998. It was created to administer the planned introduction of the common currency, the euro, and to generate the euro-zone's monetary policy. At the turn of the millennium only eleven member countries were involved, but others gradually joined. By 2020, the zone is comprised of nineteen countries.

A sixth institution, the European Council, is a body of member countries' head of states and governments that was created in 2009. While it is not a legislating institution, the Council defines political agendas, directions and priorities; in this way, it strengthens the intergovernmental character of the EU.

Twenty-three standing committees also belong to the Community's governing bodies. A few of the most important ones include the committees of Foreign

Affairs, Human Rights, Security and Defense, International Trade, Budget, Economic and Monetary Affairs, Employment and Social Affairs, Environment, Public Health, Food Safety and Regional Development.[5]

At first, the European Union's governing structure struggled to strike the ideal balance between national and all-communal interests. For decades, it was criticized for the "democratic deficit" of its governance. Reforms – such as the institution of direct elections and the assumption of a co-decision-making role for Parliament, as well as the introduction of a qualified-majority voting system to decide some issues – made the system more democratic. Following these reforms, the supranational and intergovernmental elements are better at counterbalancing and compensating for one another. While the Commission, the Parliament, the Court of Justice and the European Central Bank represent supranational, all-European Union interests very well, those of the nation-states are not neglected at all. Countries have a strong voice in the decision-making process via the Council of Ministers and the European Council, which represents head of states and governments. Together these institutions represent a relative balance.

The European Union is neither a federation nor a confederation: rather, it is a hybrid built upon the principle of consent between member states. Consensus building among more than two dozen countries, however, is always difficult – it is time-consuming, and thus slow and often delayed. Moreover, it requires a lot of compromise, which often leads to half-measures. The institutional structure of the EU, in other words, needs further reforms and improvements. These changes would be easier to implement if the institution's structure would become more supranational in character, at least for the euro-zone, which is already more supranational than the EU as a whole. The structure could be changed further by strengthening the "multi-speed" character of the Union and institutionalizing differing levels of integration between different groups of countries.

The question of democratic deficit

As stated earlier, one common critique of the European Union is that its institutions and working procedures are not democratic enough. Critics generally cite a lack of representation for ordinary citizens and a lack of accountability for institutions as central problems. EU voters, according to this view, do not feel that they have an effective way to reject a government that they do not like, and to change politics and policies that they do not support. Critics often view the low turnouts at European elections – which dropped to 43 percent in 2009 and have never surpassed 50 percent since – as one of the main expressions of this supposed disaffection.[6] Left-wing British historian and essayist, Perry Anderson, want even much further in his almost three-thousand words essay in 2007:

> Constitutionally, the EU is a caricature of a democratic federation, since its Parliament lacks powers of initiative, contains no parties with any existence at European level, and wants even a modicum of popular credibility. Modest increments in its rights have not only failed to increase public interest in this

body, but have been accompanied by a further decline in it. Participation in European elections has sunk steadily, to below 50 per cent, and the newest voters are the most indifferent of all. . . . The violation of a constitutional separation of powers in this dual authority – a bureaucracy vested with a monopoly of legislative initiative – is flagrant. . . . In fact, what the trinity of Council, Coreper and Commission figures is not just an absence of democracy – it is certainly also that – but an attenuation of politics of any kind, as ordinarily understood.[7]

In reality, since the term "democratic deficit" was first coined in 1979, the European Union has taken several important steps to improve its democratic character. Legislation passed between 1999 and 2001 made the public release of working papers and meeting reports compulsory. The institution has also promoted the direct participation of citizens. For example, the Lisbon Treaty introduced the European Citizens' Initiative, which allows EU citizens to participate directly in the creation of EU policies. Most importantly, as discussed before, the elections and role of the European Parliament was strongly democratized. Today, European citizens have a direct voice through the elected Parliament and an indirect voice through their national governments, which play a decisive role in crafting EU legislation via the Council of Europe and the council of the head of states and governments. The European Union is ruled by law: all of its policies are passed in the legal manner defined by its treaties, according to democratic values adopted by the 2001 Nice Treaty. The EU has a system of checks and balances between institutions such as the Parliament, the Commission and the European Court of Justice.[8]

Democratic deficits within the EU, however, definitely exist, but unfortunately this flaw is not at all uncommon – the democratic natures of many nation-states are equally questionable. In some countries behind the façade of multi-party elections and democratic institutions, "illiberal democracy" means authoritarian rules. In Hungary, for example, at the 2018 parliamentary elections Viktor Orbán's ruling party gained 49.2 percent of the votes, by only 2.8 million voters, while the fragmented opposition parties together gained 3.2 million votes. Nevertheless, the constitution, changed by the majority party, gave a two-thirds majority for Orbán's party in the parliament. Formally, Hungary was still a "democracy." Shortcomings, however, characterize even the most established democracies. For example, the world's oldest democratic constitution (that of America), does not call for a basic democratic majority to decide presidential elections, but instead relies upon the Electoral College system, in which delegates from the federation's member states retain the final decision-making right. In the first two decades of the twenty-first century, two candidates who received the absolute majority of the popular votes did not become president. In 2000, Al Gore received 48.4 percent, and George W. Bush 47.9 percent, half-million less votes, but Bush became the president. In 2016, Hillary Clinton gained 48.2 percent, 3 million more votes than Donald J. Trump, who had only 46.1 percent of the votes, but Trump was elected president though failed winning the majority.

In America, voter participation is also not much higher than in the EU. At the midterm elections for members of Congress, participation almost never reaches 50 percent and sometimes hardly surpass one-third of the voters; between 1978 and 2014 only once reached the level of 50 percent, and even for the presidential elections, it is generally around 53–55 percent.

But even majority voting on crucially important issues are often questionable. The essence of democracy, as often stated, is majority rule with defense of minority rights. But there is an ever existing tension between the often contradictory majority rule and minority rights. It is a commonplace that majorities can be wrong and even abusive. History produced endless examples about it. George F. Will in one of his studies quoted Henrik Ibsen's drama, "An Enemy of the People" where his central hero, Dr. Stockman declares "the majority is always wrong." George Will added: often, but not always. "It is true that the majority often is wrong, and that the majority, even when wrong, often has a right to work its will anyway."[9] What to say when the majority in a crucial question is only two-three percent larger than the minority, but democracy cannot defend minority rights. That happened when Norway had a referendum in the mid-1990s to join the European Union and 53 percent of the voters voted "no" and 47 percent "yes." That happened when Britain voted about leaving the European Union in 2016 and 51.9 percent voted for leaving but 48.1 percent wanted to remain. In this case, though 72 percent participated, altogether 27 percent of the population voted for Brexit. Democracy neglected to defend the "minority," that in both cases represented almost half of the sharply divided population. Wasn't it also a caricature of democracy?

Common policy agendas

The European Union has a budget based on the payments of member countries, which pay a membership fee of about 1 percent of their GDP to the EU budget. The Union has some additional incomes, since it also takes 75 percent of the customs duties, agricultural duties and sugar levies collected by each member state when goods enter the customs union. Nevertheless, the budget is still small if one compares it to the budget of a nation-state, which may equal one-third of the country's GDP.

Debates about increasing this fee to 2–3 percent of the GDP have been going on for quite some time. Most recently, French President Emmanuel Macron suggested it again. Increased income would widen the possibilities for supranational programs. Increased national contributions – although in a much modest way – became a EU requirement after Brexit, since Britain contributed almost 12 percent of the common budget. According to the Commission's proposal national contributions for the next (2021–2027) budget period would increase from 1 to 1.11 percent of the EU's gross national income (GNI). The European Parliament has suggested a bigger increase, to 1.3 percent. Member countries are rather polarized about the increase. Spain and Portugal are demanding a budget size in the range of 1.14–1.16 percent. On the other end of the spectrum, the five net contributors–Germany, the Netherlands, Austria, Denmark, and Sweden – do not want to accept anything larger than a 1-percent contribution, hence their nickname, the "Frugal Five."[10] If the Commission's proposal were accepted, Germany's net contribution would double from €15 billion in 2020 to €33 billion in 2027. The Netherlands' contribution would increase by 75 percent from around €7.5 to about €13 billion.

However, even EU's current, relatively small budget allows it to finance important EU-wide programs that help lower income citizens, including certain categories of farmers, and poorer countries with per capita GDP that is below three-quarters of the EU's average. These programs have a unique character because the richer countries are supporting the poorer ones. The rich countries' contribution to the EU budget is bigger and they have a negative balance between payments to and received money from the Union. In 2018, three countries – Germany, France and Italy – contributed 48.1 percent to the EU's budget. Germany, the biggest contributor, gets it back in various forms of subsidies; however, these are barely more than one-third of its payments to the EU. The situation for poorer countries is just the opposite: they receive more aid from the EU than they contribute to the common budget. Poland, the largest net beneficiary in the EU, received €8.1 billion more than it paid in 2017. The European Commission rightly called this system – in the 2020 budget proposal – "an expression of solidarity among Europeans."

The European Union introduced and currently runs many policy programs. Among the earliest was the trade and tariff policy, which eliminated tariffs among member countries and introduced common tariffs against non-member countries. The Community has duty-free or low tariffs policies for imports from developing countries. This policy also necessitated making common trade agreements with outside countries. After the introduction of the common currency at the turn of the millennium, the Community also began to regulate interest and exchange rates via its Central Bank. Later on, it introduced common security and defense policies. The EU created a joint justice organization, Eurojust, in which national law enforcement agencies, prosecutors, judges and police forces cooperate to fight organized cross-border crime. It also introduced a number of joint defense resources. The common European law enforcement agency Europol manages the cooperation of various national police authorities. The Rapid Reaction Force consists of troops from member states' armies. The European Defense Agency coordinates cooperation between nations and develops compatible weapon systems. The European Union also sends troops on various peacekeeping missions. And finally, member countries also have joint policies regarding migration and asylum. While previously every member state was responsible for its own foreign policy agendas, the Treaty of Lisbon introduced close cooperation in that area as well.[11]

The European Commission launched its first European Climate-Change Program in 2000 to decrease the dangerous global warming phenomenon. Europe was among the first region to join the Paris Agreement of 2015 to reduce greenhouse gas emissions, in an effort to limit the global temperature increase to two degrees Celsius above preindustrial levels. In 2008, member countries agreed in their famous "20–20–20 agreement" to reduce greenhouse gas emissions by 20 percent, increase the share of renewable energy by 20 percent, and make a 20 percent improvement in energy efficiency by 2020 (as compared to 1990 figures). In 2018, the EU announced that it was already ahead of those targets, and that greenhouse gas emissions had already been reduced by 23 percent. In 2014, member countries agreed to new targets for the 2021–2030 periods. The EU has committed to cutting greenhouse gas emissions by 40 percent (compared to 1990 levels) by the end of that time.

The EU has adopted a ban on single-use plastic items, among various other measures to decrease pollution. In May 2018, the EU decided upon new rules for waste management and established legally binding targets for recycling. In 2019, it announced stricter emission limits for cars and vans: from 2030 onwards, new cars must emit almost 38 percent less CO_2 on average compared to 2021 levels; new vans must emit 31 percent less on average. In December 2019, the EU adopted the ambitious objective of achieving a climate-neutral EU by 2050.[12] The European Union is at the forefront of international efforts to save the world.

In addition to these environmental efforts, several other major EU policy programs are financed from its communal budget. Although the national governments still manage education, the European Community grants financial assistance for developing education and research. During recessions it subsidizes public building projects that provide work opportunities for a large number of people. The Development Fund supports new inventions and environment-friendly projects. Some of the major programs developed through 1992 included Comett, Erasmus, PETRA, Lingua, FORCE and Tempus. Erasmus, Comett and Lingua were initially developed to promote cooperation among universities through a variety of exchanges. Lingua focused on language education in Europe; while Erasmus enabled student mobility by allowing participants to spend one to two semesters at other member countries' universities, and promoted cooperation among universities. FORCE and PETRA (integrated into the Leonardo Program) were focused on providing initial and ongoing vocational training, and on managing youth exchanges. The programs offered one to two years of post-compulsory education for vocational training, with part of the time spent in another member state. Most of these programs were intended to cultivate the idea of "European citizenship" by boosting broader language knowledge, and by enabling people to spend time in other member countries and create friendships with people living there.

However, the two central EU policies that consume the bulk (about 60 percent) of the EU's budget are the agricultural and cohesion policies, which support farmers and the less developed regions and countries of the EU.

Common Agricultural Policy (CAP)

Agriculture is a small sector of the EU-27's economy, accounting, as an average, for only 1.1 percent of the GDP and 5.1 percent of employment. These proportions are higher in Central European and the Balkan countries. In the two most extreme cases, Bulgaria and Romania, agriculture's share of GDP is 3.8 and 5.4 percent respectively, while its share of employment reaches 7.1 and 29.1 percent. At the time of this policy's introduction, France was the biggest beneficiary of the support, but nowadays CAP subsidizes the eastern and southeastern member countries the most.

Introduced in 1958, CAP was one of the EU's first major policy issues. It began subsidizing agriculture to increase the living standards of the agrarian population (who at that time only had 40 percent of the urban population's standard of living), and to bolster the nutritional self-sufficiency of the Community. This policy is also contains quality control and food safety standards. During the first decades, CAP represented nearly half of the budgetary expenses. It increased to nearly three-quarters during the 1980s (peaking at 73 percent in 1985), but later its share significantly decreased to more than one-third of the budgetary expenditure (in 2018, CAP was responsible for 38 percent of the EU budget). Most of the aid supported agricultural prices, but that was later opposed by the World Trade Organization's regulations and had to be reformed. The Uruguay Round Agreement on Agriculture imposed limits on the EU's ability to support its agricultural sector, raise barriers to imports and subsidize exports. Consequently, CAP was reformed in 1992, 1999, 2003, 2004 and 2005, in part to adhere to WTO rules. As a result, the structure of the CAP has fundamentally changed since its genesis, with a large part of former price support spending now going towards fixed, per-hectare payments to EU farmers. In 2018, CAP paid roughly €260 per hectare for land support, with provisions for increasing this aid up to €425. This funding supports 6.5 million farmers in the EU-27 countries.

According to the Organization for Economic Cooperation and Development (OECD), EU-27 subsidies accounted for 25 percent of farm revenue in 2008 (compared with 7 percent in the United States). CAP contributed significantly to the agricultural self-sufficiency of the EU, and helped it to become a major player on the world agricultural market. EU agriculture accounts for a large share of the global production: for example, it exports 26 percent of the value of cow milk, 22 percent of pork, 19 percent of potatoes, 16 percent of wheat and 14 percent of beef. In 2007, the EU was the largest worldwide importer of several raw products such as coffee, tea, and fruit (€77.4 billion); it was also the largest exporter of processed products (€75.1 billion).[13]

Nevertheless, CAP was always somewhat contradictory. One of its main problems is that big landowners (who own 24 percent of total land) and agricultural oligarchs pocket 85 percent of the support. The Central European and Balkan countries offer an extreme example of this striking systemic weakness. The *New York Times* conducted an investigation of nine countries in 2019 and concluded that in several of these countries, Mafia-style land grabs had occurred during recent decades. Former state farms were bought by powerful people connected with the governments. The multi-millionaire prime minister of the Czech Republic, Andrej Babiš, collected at least $42 million in CAP subsidies last year. In Hungary, the patronage system of Viktor Orbán's government enriches his friends and family and protects his political interests. At the end of his first government in 2002, Orbán sold 12 state-owned farming companies to politically connected clients, which became known as the "Dirty Dozen." In 2015, his government sold hundreds of thousands of acres of state farmland, much of it again to politically connected allies. As a consequence, the two richest men in the country, Lőrinc Mészáros, a schoolmate and close friend of Orbán, and Sándor Csányi, received $28 million in EU subsidies last year alone. In Bulgaria 75 percent of the subsidies ended up in the hands of about 100 landowners. Such deeply rooted corruption undermines the entire subsidy system in this region.[14] There is broad consensus that through these CAP payments, the European Union subsidizes its internal nationalist-populist enemies.

Another major issue is that CAP subsidies have the unintended consequence of incentivizing backwardness. The Netherlands owns just a little over 1 percent of the EU's agricultural area but produces almost 7 percent of the EU's agricultural output because of its advanced farming methods. In contrast, Bulgaria accounts for almost three times as much agricultural area as the Netherlands, but produces only one-seventh of the Dutch agricultural output. But because subsidy funding is determined by agricultural land mass, Bulgaria receives three times more support than the Netherlands does, despite being much less efficient.

Aiding less-developed regions

The goals of supporting cohesion and the harmonious development of member countries were already present in the Treaty of Rome in 1957. However, the effective assistance of relatively backward regions (those in which the per-capita GDP was lower than 75 percent of the Community's average) started in 1975 with creation of the European Regional Development Fund, which aimed to reduce disparities between regions. This program is the EU's most unique and selfless aid agenda. Between 1989 and 2020, a tremendous amount – €1,152,000 billion – was spent assisting less developed areas to aid cohesion. During the last budget period of 2014–2020 alone, this aid amounted to nearly €352 billion, or almost one-third of the EU budget. Some countries such as Lithuania, Bulgaria and Hungary receive 2.5–4 percent of their GDP from the EU budget. In the 2021–2027 budgetary period these aids will decrease about 22–24 percent.

The European Regional Development Fund allocated €200 billion ($225 billion) for the years 2014–2020. The funds offer financing for a broad spectrum of projects: for example, €50 million for broadband connections in rural Greece, more than €20 million for the production of airplane parts in Portugal's Alentejo region, and €65 million for a new tram line in Latvia's capital of Riga. Construction on the underground transit system in Thessaloniki, Greece began in 2006. It is one of the biggest projects to date that was funded with the help of the EU. For the 2014–2020 periods, the project has been allotted more than €400 million. In Hungary and Poland, more than 60 percent of total infrastructural investments are covered by EU assistance.

Originally, about one-quarter of the subsidies arriving from the European Union were distributed by the member countries' governments. In some countries, this system produced a hotbed for corruption, as EU revision investigations discovered. By 2023, all EU money must not only be awarded, but also actually paid out to the final recipients, without the involvements of national governments.

In a report from late 2017, the EU concluded that thanks to EU cohesion funding, Poland's GDP was projected to be 3.4 percent higher by 2023 than it would have been without such aid.[15] The European Union's assistance for less-developed regions and countries became an important factor in the catching-up process that already begun in less-developed areas (discussed in Chapter 9).

Social policy

While social policy is also an area that belongs to member states, nevertheless the European Union makes important contributions to it. Through its Single Market policy, the EU plays an important role in job creation and employment, a central issue in social-policy agendas. The free movement of capital helps create investments in less-developed areas, which significantly increase employment opportunities there. The free movement of people also creates huge employment opportunities for workers in these areas by enabling them to find work in other countries. In the 14 most developed member states, 40–80 percent of the posted workers come from less-advanced neighboring countries.

Aside from the social consequences of economic policies, as the Amsterdam Treaty phrased it, pure economic growth cannot be considered the sole goal in and of itself. The economy created and exacerbated a certain degree of social, regional and environmental imbalances that should be corrected.[16] The agricultural and cohesion policies of the EU, as discussed earlier, are rectifying actions.

The European Union also plays an important role through the creation of a common legal framework for social policy. According to the Treaty on the Functioning of the European Union (TFEU), the member states and the European Union have joint competence regarding the EU's social policy agenda. The European Social Law was defined in Article 4, paragraph 2 of TFEU as a component of the international labor law, which includes regulations governing the Council of Europe and the EU's institutions. The EU determines issues relating to workers' rights, working time, gender balance, the rights of ethnic minorities. It helps to create protections in these areas. Therefore, at a European level, the system of social law – which contains the legal norms adopted by European organizations – regulates work relations and contributes to social security.[17]

European Neighborhood Policy (ENP)

In the preparatory years leading up to the EU's major eastward enlargement, the Community launched its new Neighborhood Policy. As a 2002 Strategy Paper phrased it, "An enlarged EU will ensure and open attitude and foster common interests and activities with its neighbors in the Western Balkans, Eastern Europe and the Mediterranean."[18] In June 2003, the European Council summed up the goal of this new policy: "To work with the partners to reduce poverty and create an area of shared prosperity and values based on free trade, deeper economic integration. . . [and] cross-border cooperation." The EU stressed the need to cultivate stability in order "to avoid new dividing lines between the enlarged EU and its neighbours."[19] Beside the officially announced goals, the neighborhood policy also served as preparatory work for possible further enlargements, especially towards the east and the west Balkans.

In this framework, the EU gives financial support to neighboring countries. Its amount in the 2014–2020 budget period was €15.4 billion. The neighborhood policy included 16 partner countries: in the East, Ukraine, Moldova, Belarus, Azerbaijan, Georgia, and Armenia; and in the Middle East and Northern Africa, Israel, Jordan, Lebanon, the Palestinian Territory, Egypt, Algeria, Libya, Morocco, Syria, and Tunisia.[20]

In spite of this policy's noble goals, the results were rather limited; in some respects, it even failed. The two decades that followed, especially the 2010s, clearly showed that the main goal of the policy – creating stability around the border of the EU – miserably failed. The most important aspect of this policy was its anti-enlargement feature. Instead of accepting new member countries from the neighborhood, strengthened cooperation and support were supposed to bring neighboring countries closer to the EU. Besides helping less-developed regions and countries within the EU to catch up, the EU is also the biggest donor for the less-developed non-European countries around the European Union. It assists them through development aid, donating at least 0.7 percent of its gross national income to these regions per year.

Notes

1 See European Commission, *The European Union Explained: How the European Union Works* (Luxembourg: Publications Office of the European Union, 2012), http://eeas.europa.eu/archives/delegations/singapore/documents/more_info/ eu_publications/how_the_european_union_works_en.pdf, accessed September 8, 2018; Knud Erik Jørgensen, Mark Pollack, and Ben Rosamond, eds., *The Sage Handbook of European Union Politics* (London, Thousand Oaks, CA and New Delhi: Sage, 2007); *The European Union: A People-Centered Agenda* (Brussels: OECD Publications, 2019), www.oecd.org/eu/The-European-Union-a-people-centred-agenda.pdf, accessed January 7, 2020; Neill Nugent, *The Government and Politics of the European Union*, 7th ed. (Basingstoke: Palgrave Macmillan, 2010); Scott L. Greer et al., *Everything You Always Wanted to Know about European Union Health Policies but Were Afraid to Ask*, Observatory Study Series 34 (London: European Observatory on Health Systems and Policies, 2014).
2 "The Decision-Making Process in the Council," European Council, January 31, 2020, www.consilium.europa.eu/en/council-eu/decision-making/, accessed February 19, 2020; "Voting System," March 23, 2020, www.consilium.europa. eu/en/council-eu/voting-system/, accessed March 18, 2020.
3 Ina Sokolska, "Developments Up to the Single European Act," *European Parliament*, November 2019, www.europarl.europa.eu/factsheets/en/sheet/2/

developments-up-to-the-single-european-act, accessed December 8, 2019; Philippe de Schoutheete, "Institutional Reform in the EU," *European Policy Brief*, no. 19 (February 2014): 8.

4 "Court of Justice of the European Union (CJEU)," *European Union*, June 16, 2016, https://europa.eu/european-union/about-e0u/institutions-bodies/court-justice_en, accessed November 7, 2019.

5 The European External Action Service (EEAS) assists the High Representative of the Union for Foreign Affairs and Security Policy, the European Economic and Social Committee, the European Committee of the Regions, the European Investment Bank, and the European Ombudsman (all of which are overseen by the EU's governing bodies).

6 "Glossary of Summaries," *EUR-Lex*, January 9, 2020, https://eur-lex.europa.eu/summary/glossary/democratic_deficit.html, accessed January 20, 2020.

7 Perry Anderson, *Depicting Europe*, vol. 29, no. 18 (London: London Review of Books), September 20, 2007, www.lrb.co.uk/the-paper/v29/n18/perry-anderson/depicting-europe, accessed September 6, 2018.

8 Mathis Porchez, "The Questionable 'Democratic Deficit' of the European Union," *The New Federalist*, November 19, 2018, sec. Commentary, www.thenewfederalist.eu/the-questionable-democratic-deficit-of-the-european-union, accessed October 9, 2019.

9 George F. Will, "The Limits of Majority Rule," *National Affairs*, no. 43, Spring 2020.

10 Mehreen Khan and Guy Chazan, "Germany's Annual EU Budget Bill Set to Double to €33bn," *Financial Times*, October 27, 2019, www.ft.com/content/9c82433c-f846-11e9-a354-36acbbb0d9b6, accessed December 7, 2019.

11 "Policies of the European Parliament," *Mosaiikkiry*, https://europarlamentti.info/en/values-and-objectives/policies/, accessed May 19, 2020; "Policies–Migration and Home Affairs," *European Commission*, December 6, 2016, https://ec.europa.eu/home-affairs/what-we-do/policies_en, accessed October 8, 2019; "Cohesion Policy–Glossary," *European Commission*, https://ec.europa.eu/regional_policy/en/policy/what/glossary/c/cohesion-policy, accessed May 19, 2020; "The Common Agricultural Policy at a Glance," *European Commission*, https://ec.europa.eu/info/food-farming-fisheries/key-policies/common-agricultural-policy/cap-glance_en, accessed May 19, 2020; "EP after the Lisbon Treaty: Bigger Role in Shaping Europe," *European Parliament*, www.europarl.europa.eu/about-parliament/en/powers-and-procedures/the-lisbon-treaty, accessed May 19, 2020.

12 "Climate Change: What the EU Is Doing," *European Council*, accessed May 19, 2020, www.consilium.europa.eu/en/policies/climate-change/, accessed May 20, 2020; Jennifer Rankin, "'Our House Is on Fire': EU Parliament Declares Climate Emergency," *The Guardian*, November 28, 2019, sec. World News, www.theguardian.com/world/2019/nov/28/eu-parliament-declares-climate-emergency, accessed January 3, 2020.

13 Stefan Tangermann and Stephan von Cramon-Taubadel, "Agricultural Policy in the European Union: An Overview," no. 1302 (2013): 76; "1.6 Million Farmers Receive almost 85 Percent of the EU's Agricultural Subsidies," *European Data Journalism Network*, www. europeandatajournalism.eu/News/Data-news/1.6-million-farmers-receive-almost-85-percent-of-the-EU-s-agricultural-subsidies, accessed May 24, 2019.

14 Selam Gebrekidan, Matt Apuzzo, and Benjamin Novak, "The Money Farmers: How Oligarchs and Populists Milk the E.U. for Millions," *The New York Times*, November 3, 2019, sec. World, www.nytimes.com/2019/11/03/world/europe/eu-farm-subsidy-hungary.html, accessed January 8, 2020.

15 Kira Schacht, "How the EU Funds Its Economically Disadvantaged Regions," *DW*, May 8, 2019, www.dw.com/en/how-the-eu-funds-its-economically-disad vantaged-regions/a-48354538, accessed December 5, 2019.
16 Professor Persida Cechin-Crista et al., "The Social Policy of the European Union," *International Journal of Business and Social Science*, Special Issue, 4, no. 10 (August 2013): 10.
17 Jon Worth, "What Is a 'Social Europe'?," *The New Federalist*, August 22, 2006, sec. Economy & Trade, www.thenewfederalist.eu/What-is-a-Social-Europe, accessed October 7, 2018. The Council of Europe issued the following documents: The Convention for the Protection of Human Rights and Fundamental Freedoms (Rome: November 4, 1950); The European Social Charter (Turin: October 18, 1916); The European Code of Social Security (April 16, 1964); and the European Convention on the Social Protection of Farmers (May 6, 1974).
18 *Towards the Englarged Union*, Strategy Paper (Brussels: Commission of the European Communities, October 9, 2002), 7.
19 *Communication from the Commission to the Council and the European Parliament* (Brussels: Commission of the European Communities, March 11, 2003), http://eeas.europa.eu/archives/docs/enp/pdf/pdf/com03_104_en.pdf, accessed September 7, 2018.
20 "European Neighbourhood Policy (ENP)," Government, European Commission, December 21, 2016, https://eeas.europa.eu/headquarters/headquar ters-homepage_en/330/European Neighbourhood Policy (ENP), accessed October 9, 2018.

4 The new challenges of globalization and global political disorder – Europe's answer

Regionalization (the 1980s–1990s)

As discussed in Chapter 1, significant American contributions enabled the changing global economic and political order to emerge on the road towards integration in the immediate postwar period. However, a third of a century later, during the 1980s and early 1990s, the world's economic and political systems reached another major turning point. Both the international capitalist world economy and the world political order radically changed once again.

European integration essentially stagnated for two decades between the mid-1960s and mid-1980s, and – in contrast to the original aim – became unable to move forward on the road towards "ever closer union."[1] What were the change in the economic and political environment, what was the impact of these changes, and what kind of adjustment were needed to cope with the European Community's new situation?

The globalized capitalist world economy and the technological revolution

One of the main new challenges was the new trend towards globalization. In reality, it was not an entirely new development. During the second half of the nineteenth century, the international economy shifted markedly towards global integration. Two of the best experts on the subject, Kevin O'Rourke and Jeffrey Williamson, introduced the term "first globalization." They realized that because of a strong backlash against that trend, "The world economy had lost all of its globalization achievements in three decades, between 1914 and 1945. In the half-century since then, it has won them all back in every market but one."[2]

To be more precise, the components of global economic system – significant international trade, migration, capital investment, the establishment of subsidiaries, production abroad and an internationalized financial system – started to develop in the second half of the nineteenth century, but a truly and fully matured globalized world system had not materialized before the onset of World War I. And indeed, all that was achieved before the conflict was eliminated during and after the war.

Nevertheless, three decades of economic nationalism and a capitalist world economic system ushered in by America after World War II produced the return of globalization. This new trend was not at all inevitable. Shale Horowitz rightly recalls that

> Following two world wars and the Depression, international trade and finance had been in retreat for decades, and protectionist forces seemed dominant in all the major economies. National governments seemed bent on heavily restricting international economic transactions to preserve economic stability and fuller employment. . . . [However,] trade liberalization began in the United States and the FRG [Federal Republic of Germany] and was unilateral in character.[3]

Building upon studies by Joanne Gowa (1994) and Albert Hirschman (1980),[4] he concludes that "military externalities of trade can lead countries to modify trade policies in an effort to strengthen allies or to strengthen themselves relative to their enemies."[5] He also quotes Charles Kindleberger's landmark 1973 work on the Depression,[6] in which Kindleberger famously stated that "the world economic system was unstable unless some country stabilized it."[7]

Actually, that did really happen. The United States wanted to stabilize the capitalist world economic system, and found a good follower in postwar Germany, which wanted to hew to the US as closely as possible to regain the credibility and international status it had lost during the Hitler regime. During the rising Cold War era and in the context of a deadly race with the Soviet Union, stabilizing and connecting the economies of the so-called "free world" was a crucial Western interest. In other words, national political, military and economic interests were responsible for the genesis of globalization beginning almost immediately after the war.

The first steps towards the return to a free-trade regime occurred gradually during the 1950s and 1960s. For two decades beginning in the mid-1960s, European integration declined into crisis and countries could not make significant progress; however, globalization eventually gained real momentum and became dominant in the last third of the twentieth century. A dramatic quantitative change in worldwide economic interactions accompanied a qualitative change in the international division of labor, and together they ushered in a new chapter in the history of the capitalist world economy.

Kenichi Ohmae rightly distinguished five stages of globalization. The first occurred when companies focused on exports, established distribution offices, and employed agents abroad. In the second stage, companies established overseas branches; then, during the third stage, they relocated production to foreign countries and continents. Ohmae called the fourth stage "insiderization" by clone markets, wherein multinational companies opened local satellites in other countries and thus became able to provide targeted responses to local market requirements. And finally, during the fifth stage, global companies achieved dominant positions in the world markets.[8] The final three decades of the twentieth century saw the full realization of Ohmae's third stage, followed by the onset of the fourth and fifth stages. It is not a coincidence that the term *globalization* only appeared in *Webster's Dictionary* beginning in the 1960s, although it had been included in the standard *Oxford English Dictionary* in 1930 but had been "forgotten."

From that time on, multinational companies – those that operated in two or more countries – became the key actors of the globalized world economy. Their sheer numbers signaled this change early on. In 1970, there were about 7,000 multinationals in the world; by 2006, there were already 80,000. During this one-third of a century, about 900,000 subsidiaries and affiliates were established abroad, and the number of their employees increased by three and a half. In the early twenty-first century, multinational companies traded three-quarters of world's manufactured products. Some of the biggest multinationals have out-ranked several nation-states. ExxonMobil's revenue surpassed Turkey's GDP; General Motors income exceeded the GDPs of Denmark, Indonesia, and Poland. Toyota out-earned the GDP of Finland.[9] As Ohmae (somewhat over-) stated:

> The nation state has become an unnatural, even dysfunctional, unit for organizing human activity and managing economic endeavor in a borderless world. It represents no genuine, shared community of economic interests; it defines no meaningful flows of economic activity.[10]

He prophesizes:

> In this brave new borderless world, there remains a role – albeit it a diminished one – for government. And that is to educate the workforce; to protect the environment; and build a safe and comfortable social infrastructure.[11]

Globalization could not have reached these heights without the technology and communication revolution that occurred around the turn of millennium. The rising high-tech industries required significantly less material and became knowledge-based. Revolutionized technology made global business possible by sharply declining transportation and communication costs. A 'simple' idea, containerized shipping, patented by Malcom McLean in the second half of the 1950s soon conquered international – including transatlantic and transpacific – transportation. Container transportation developed rapidly from the late 1960s, and exponentially during the 1970s–1980s. Whereas in 1966, only 1 percent of the countries had container ports; by 1980, already 90 percent of ports worldwide could process containers. By 2013, 90 percent of global trade had become seaborne, and companies were shipping 700 million containers every year. This system made it easy to feed the international supply chains, and to deliver parts of products produced in another country or even another continent. Global production had fundamentally changed.[12]

The cost of a three-minute telephone call from London to New York, which had cost $5.30 in 1950, had become just $0.90 by 2000. Likewise, the cost of an air-transport passenger mile was $0.30 in 1950, but fell to only $0.11 by 2000.[13] The computer revolution opened a new era in communication, especially after the appearance of personal computer in the mid-1970s, and even more so after the invention of the Internet and the World Wide Web. The Internet was already existent in the 1960s but reached a turning point in early 1990s, when commercial networks and enterprises were connected, so that interconnected documents and huge amounts of data could be transmitted with ever-increasing speed. Full documentation of production plans and minute-to-minute operational commands could be in place within seconds.[14] Communication among countries and continents became entirely free via video conference programs like Skype and Zoom.

The movement of people reflects the changing world. In 1970, people could travel to 50 countries without a visa; by 2019, 100 countries were opened in this way. The number of travelers and tourists – a symbol of globalization – in 1970 has been 200 million, but by 2019 more than 1.5 billion.[15] The skyrocketing volume and value of international trade clearly signify the breakthrough of globalization in the world economy. Global trade increased in value from $1.7 trillion in 1973 to $5.8 trillion by the end of the century. During just a quarter of a century – between 1980 and 2007 – the value of traded goods and services jumped from 42 percent of the world's aggregate GDP to 62 percent. Unlike before, trade within companies and their subsidiaries abroad accounted for a great part of this figure. Similarly, the amount of foreign direct investments – which was only $112 billion in 196 – began to grow gradually to $1,215.8 billion by 2006. That year it reached 32 percent of the world's aggregate GDP. The value of daily financial transactions amounted to $15 billion in 1970. By 2000, it was already $1.3 trillion, fifty times higher than the value of world trade just thirty years before.[16]

Neoliberal theory and policy

Globalization was accompanied by globalized "market fundamentalism" and an ideological "counter-revolution": trademark ideas of Friedrich Hayek, Milton Friedman and the Chicago School of Economics. In the mid-1970s, this ideological economics campaign launched vicious attacks against state regulations and intervention, against price and wage controls, and against welfare states. They advocated instead for a self-regulated market. According to their neoliberal theories, an undisturbed market is able to solve all not only all economic, but also all human problems, including health care and education. Friedman went so far as to state: "the philosophy of welfare state" is "sending a policeman to take the money from somebody's pocket."[17] The state should not interfere in any of these areas, he argued, but should instead let them be governed by market-like forces. The state's only function should be to create monetary policy that could guarantee the market's continued proper functioning. Milton Friedman's receipt for ideal economy and society was the flat rate (16 percent) for taxation; radically decreased state expenditure; the all-round privatization of state functions; and a return to policies that made the individual (not the state) responsible for education, health care and pensions.[18]

Two central figures of the Chicago School received the Nobel Prize for economics – Hayek in 1974 and Friedman in 1976. They advised governments, and their ideas became government policy. The first steps were taken by the American and British governments. The latter opened the first regulation-free offshore Eurodollar market in London in the 1960s. President Richard Nixon closed the fixed exchange rate era of Bretton Woods in 1971; then, three years later, he abolished capital controls. Britain followed in 1979, eliminating their 40-year-old capital-control system. The New York Stock Exchange was deregulated in 1975 and a competitive deregulation race followed. The great economic powers in the so-called Group-7 (G7) organization – the United States, Canada, Japan, Germany, France, Britain and Italy – which together produced nearly half of the world GDP, agreed and followed each other to cope with uneven competition. By 1988, virtually the entire European Community had copied those policies. The Western world turned to a self-regulated market system. The IMF and World Bank advocated for and assisted with spreading this system to developing countries. Actually, the so-called Washington consensus made this policy framework mandatory as a condition for IMF assistance.[19]

America and Asia conquer huge parts of the European markets

The deregulated global capitalist system created an existential danger for Europe. With America's assistance, devastated postwar Western Europe had applied the extensive development model for a quarter of a century, based on domestic labor input and American technology imports. It worked very well to galvanize a fast recovery, but the European countries had a follower economy, and remained behind the technology leaders: the United States and Japan. From the 1970s on, Europe had to face increasing competition partly from the United States and Japan, but also from the rising low-wage "Small Asian Tigers."

The United States dominated the new computer age. The American technology company IBM established subsidiaries in Britain, Germany and France; and installed 75 percent of the computers in the entire West. American companies controlled 64 percent of the west European memory-chip and microprocessor market. These products were the determinant parts of the data processing, telecom, industrial automation and consumer electronics sectors. In the mid-1980s, eight out of ten computers sold in Western Europe came from the United States. Europe's share of high-tech production declined from 16 percent to 10 percent.[20] The American Ford Company established Ford Europe in 1967, and its Ford Fiesta became known as the "European car." Half of Ford's global production and one-quarter of General Motors' production were produced and sold in Europe. During the 1960s, an average of 2000 European scientists and engineers per year left Europe for America. American companies gradually conquered the world market, and by 1981, almost half the assets of the world's largest companies were in American hands.

Based on its exceptional postwar development, Japan also entered the European markets. Its GDP increased by nearly eight times between 1945 and 1973, and then again three-and-a-half times during the next two decades. At that time, Japan's share in the computer industry was twice as big as that of Europe. In 1985, the European Parliament's analysis found that nine out of ten video recorders sold in Western Europe came from Japan. The Japanese company Sony established its first electronics factory in Europe in 1973, and other Japanese companies quickly opened subsidiaries in Britain, France, Germany and Portugal. In the mid-1980s, the European Community's share in the European semiconductor market was only 9 percent, compared to the 56 percent American and 33 percent Japanese shares.

While America and Japan dominated the west European markets in most modern industries, the more traditional and labor-intensive textile, clothing, and leather-product markets of Europe were controlled by the "Small Asian Tigers" and – somewhat later – by China. A European Commission Working Document revealed that whereas the average European Community worker in these sectors earned roughly $12,000 per year, in Asia and other less-developed countries, workers earned only $2,000 per year; and in China, only $600. The high-wage advanced world was unable to compete with such low-wage competition. The situation was similar in the European steel industry, which dismissed 100,000 employees in the Community during this period because of competition from Asia. The European Commission reported in 1986 that the newly industrializing countries endanger "the future of industry in the Community" because of the "[fierce] competition aroused by the growth of these newly industrialized countries, which had been specializing in branches of industry similar to the Community."[21] All in all, "the European business community," as Willem Hulsink pointed out, "found itself inadequately equipped to cope with . . . the high-technology threat from the US and Japan and . . . the low-end technology threat from the newly industrializing countries."[22]

After its miraculous postwar reconstruction and modernization, Western Europe suddenly found itself far behind. Europe lost ground to international competition in technology-intensive products. European companies held only a 9 percent share of the world market in computer and data-processing products, 10 percent in software, 13 percent in satellites and launchers, and 29 percent in data-transmission services.[23] Between 1965 and 1984, the United States and Japan increased their combined share of world trade in the products of R&D (research and development)-intensive branches of industry from more than 30 percent to more than 45 percent; while the shares of France, Germany and Britain combined decreased from 36 percent to 31 percent.[24] In the mid-1980s, the collective American and Japanese output of information technology was valued at $250 billion, while the output of the seven leading European countries together was valued at only $66 billion. Europe lost ground in the production of high-tech products, and between 1970 and 1985, the EEC dropped from 88 percent to 75 percent of the average output of the 37 member countries of the Organization for Economic Co-operation and Development (OECD, established in 1961).[25]

The European Community was shocked at the loss of its economic strength in key sectors of the modern economy and recognized the need for action. In 1973, the European Commission prepared and accepted an Action Program, which stated: "The worsening positions of the European economy vis-à-vis Japan and the United States and the Third World subsequently saw a widespread acceptance on the European government agencies of the need to promote a more effectual restructuring of European industry."[26] However, nothing happened, and the situation did not change. These dangers became the central topic of French journalist Jean-Jacques Servan-Schreiber's early influential book, *Le défi américain (The American Challenge)* published in 1967. In 1980, his new book, *Le défi mondiale*, or (*The Worldwide Challenge*), followed. He described the huge American subsidiary network in Europe as the second-largest industrial force of the world, second only to American industry in America. He spoke about European "inferiority," comparing the situation to those countries in the nineteenth century that were unable to industrialize. It was a dramatic warning about the danger facing Europe and a cry for action.[27]

The rearranged world political order

Politics paralleled the radical changes in the world economic system during the 1970s–1980s, and the world political order also transformed. The first signs of changes appeared at the early 1970s. Until that time, the relationship between America and Western Europe was very one-sided: a strong America and a weak Europe meant that within this close alliance; America was unquestionable and Western Europe dependent. The spectacular revival of Europe during the 1950s–1960s changed the nature of relations, however, because America's postwar superiority began to vanish. Between 1949 and 1960, America's share of the output of the advanced world dropped from 59 percent to 45 percent. Its share in world exports also diminished from 25 percent to 15 percent. Beginning in the mid-1960s, the American current-account balance also started to diminish, and for first time since the 1890s, the country started to run a trade deficit. As Richard Nixon rightly noted in a speech, "The deficit in our balance of payment is matched by a mounting deficit in our balance of influence."[28] From the mid-1980s, the United States – which had been a traditional creditor country since the 1920s – began to be an international debtor. While in 1950, the per capita GDP of the United States was almost twice as much as Western Europe's average, in the early 1990s, that difference had shrunken to 20 percent. The European Community gradually started emerging as an economic power. Giving a clear expression of this rising balance of power, *The New York Times* published an article on the rapidly developing interdependence in the world on the bicentennial anniversary of American Independence Day, 4 July 1976. It stated: "Americans, no longer dominant in that world despite our giant size, are ever more aware that interdependence with the other industrial nations in economics, and with the Soviet Union in nuclear stability, is more and more a two-way street." Indeed, as the journal article concluded, "Independence Day" should be renamed as "Interdependence Day."[29]

Commenting on the development towards a more balanced and equal world, President Kennedy clearly expressed in 1963 that America did not want to continue its immediate postwar policy of dominating its European allies. He declared, "It is Europeans who are building Europe. . . . [T]he choice of paths to the unity of Europe is a choice which Europe must make."[30] His Independence Day speech from 4 July 1962[31] offered a "transatlantic partnership of equals" for Europe and detailed his desire for "two pillars of democracy of equal weight with leaders of equal voice."[32] Kennedy also changed trade relations with the European Community. He gained congressional authorization to decrease the tariffs by 50 percent on a reciprocal basis and to eliminate tariffs in areas where the US and EEC conducted 80 percent of the world trade. The new trade act was passed in June 1962.

Meanwhile, Cold War tensions increased in the early 1960s. In April 1961, America's failed Bay of Pigs landing in communist Cuba sharpened conflicts. Nevertheless, in June 1961, the Kennedy-Khrushchev meeting in Vienna signaled the possibility of new relations. Unfortunately, less than three months later, the Berlin Wall was constructed and created a disturbing new symbol of the divided world. In October 1962, the worst conflict of the Cold War erupted: the Cuban Missile Crisis. The deployment of Soviet missiles 90 miles away from American soil in Florida pushed the two countries to the brink of military confrontation. President Kennedy remained calm and wise, and in the end, Khrushchev was ready to compromise and withdraw. All these events, at last, slowly moderated Cold War tensions.

After the assassination of President Kennedy, his successor Lyndon Johnson wanted to continue the de-escalation that Kennedy had started. In a speech from October 1966, Johnson underlined the goals of "peaceful engagement"[33] with the Soviet Bloc, the liberalization of trade, the elimination of travel restrictions, and the promotion of cultural and scientific exchanges. He also signaled the acceptance of the Oder-Neisse border and, in 1967, praised the German strategy of bridge building towards the East, a central component of Chancellor Willy Brandt's new *Ostpolitik*. Despite this rhetoric, however, President Johnson made a sharp turn towards domestic politics. In a 1964 speech, he announced his "Great Society" plan, which he further detailed in his January 1965 State of the Union address. He introduced a path-breaking set of domestic social reform policies and signed a revolutionary Civil Rights bill. Unfortunately, the later years of his presidency was consumed and destroyed by the Vietnam War. Ultimately, Lyndon Johnson was not a foreign-policy president and did not continue the international opening that Kenned had begun.

Nevertheless, opening continued within Europe. In 1969, for the first time since the war, a social democrat, Willy Brandt, was elevated to the post of Chancellor of the Federal Republic of Germany. He opened a new chapter in foreign policy. After Adenauer's "policy of strength," his denial of the Oder-Neisse border, and his repeated conviction of German unification, Brandt gave a new direction to West German foreign policy. On 21 December 1972 in East Berlin, the two Germanys signed the Basic Treaty, in which the two states recognized each other and established normal political and trade relations. Germany also recognized the Oder-Nisse border and signed treaties with the Soviet Union and with Poland.[34] This new era was symbolized by Bradt's *Kniefall von Warschau* in 1970, when he visited Poland and kneeled down at the monument of the Warsaw Ghetto Uprising after laying a wreath.

The road towards peaceful coexistence and competition was paved. The changes were enacted in the early 1970s by the Nixon administration. Richard Nixon, the former vice president under President Eisenhower, was inaugurated as the 37th president of the United States in January 1969. He appointed the talented Harvard Professor and foreign policy expert Henry Kissinger as his main foreign policy advisor and later as his secretary of state. Nixon and Kissinger radically changed the course of American foreign policy for over a quarter of a century. They skillfully exploited the rising political conflicts between the world's two foremost communist nations, the Soviet Union and China. A few months after Nixon occupied the White House, a military skirmish erupted at the border outpost on the Ussuri River north of Vladivostok after Russian and Chinese soldiers opened fire on each other. The monolithic communist bloc became divided. China turned against the Soviet Union, and even some members of the Soviet Bloc in Eastern Europe, Albania and Romania distanced themselves from the Soviets. The strongest west European communist parties, especially in Italy, rejected the Soviet one-party system and advocated for pluralist democracy. They also rejected the traditional communist hostility against European integration and became pro-integrationist.

Kissinger recognized the great potential of playing the "Chinese card," and in July 1971 he travelled to Beijing. Nixon ended twenty-five years of a total lack of communication and connection, visiting China in February 1972. The next year he also successfully ended the tragic Vietnam War and prepared to normalize the US relationship with the Soviet Union. Three months after his visit in Beijing, Nixon went to Moscow. Kissinger masterminded the balanced geopolitical triangle of the United States, China and the Soviet Union. In the summer of 1973, Leonid Brezhnev spent a week in the United States. Over the course of these two visits, the US and the USSR signed the Strategic Arms Limitation Treaty (SALT 1) and the agreement of Nuclear War. Between then and 1975, the two countries signed 58 agreements. Trade relations were reestablished as well, and the Cold War was basically replaced by a détente.

This new situation strongly influenced American–West-European relations. The United States dropped the European Community from the center of its foreign policy: "Following a period of intense negotiations with American adversaries, it was as though American diplomats had lost the ability to negotiate with allies."[35] This change in American policy towards Europe from the 1970s on, of course, had a more complex cause. The developing balance of power between the US and the EEC played a significant part in changing relations as well. In 1964–1967, during the so-called Kennedy Round of negotiations at the General Agreement on Tariffs and Trade (GATT), the tariff conflicts between America and Europe became evident. Henry Kissinger, still a Harvard Professor at that point, was probably one of the first who realized that when he stated that "the United States is in fact creating its own rival." In his 1965 book *The Troubled Partnership*, Kissinger became the first in postwar America to express the view that an integrated and united federal Europe could be harmful for the United States. Kissinger agreed with General De Gaulle that a "confederated Europe would enable the United States to maintain influence at many centers of decision rather than be forced to stake everything on affecting the view of a single, supra-national body."[36] He also argued that

> the assumption that a united Europe and the United States would inev-itably conduct parallel policies . . . runs counter to historical experience. A separate identity has usually been established by opposition to a dominant power. . . . [Europe] will challenge American hegemony in Atlantic policy.[37]

A few years later, Kissinger's criticism of America's postwar policy towards Euro-pean integration became the guiding line of US foreign policy. He argued that the US should not further advocate for European integration. He told Nixon that the US should "make clear that we will not inject ourselves into intra-European debates on the forms, methods, and timing of steps toward unity."[38] He also suggested that America should not deal "with Brussels" (a policy he himself fol-lowed), but should instead confer directly with the head of states or governments of each of the Community member countries. French foreign minister Michel Jobert clearly recognized Kissinger's aims when he told him in June 1973: "you wish to divide Europe to strengthen your mastery."[39]

American businesses also realized the danger of stronger European competi-tion and demanded protection for American interests. The Nixon administration tried to use its new foreign policy to stabilize the Pax Americana, to ensure Amer-ica's primacy and world dominance, and to serve the country's business interests. The first victim of this policy was the previously strong Cold War alliance with integrating Western Europe. By the time of his 1971 Report to Congress, Nixon was already stating: "European unity will also pose problems for American policy, which it would be idle to ignore." Echoing Kissinger's advice, he argued against direct intervention in European affairs.[40] Both Nixon and Kissinger expressed hostility against the European Community when they spoke privately without the necessity of official diplomatic language. When the infamous Nixon tapes made public, it was revealed that Kissinger said on 16 November 1971: "Western Europe is a mess. We've given up our friends to our enemies."[41] Nixon, talking with his staff in the Oval Office, told them: "It's time for America to look after its own interests. . . . Now, in order to play the game, we can perhaps . . . split them [the European Community] up, don't let them get together."[42] Arthur Burns, the Chairman of the Federal Reserve, recalled that Henry Kissinger had flatly stated: "What we had to do adroitly is to throw a monkey wrench into the Com-mon Market machinery, for European unity in economic areas would definitely work against U.S. interests."[43] Kissinger and Nixon were both in agreement that "one of the worst mistakes we made was to push Britain into the Common Mar-ket."[44] In 1973, Nixon also brutally declared:

> The Europeans cannot have it both ways. They cannot have United States participation and cooperation on the security front and then proceed to have

confrontation and even hostility on the economic and political front . . . the day of the one-way street is gone. . . . We are not going to be faced with a situation where the nine countries of Europe gang up against the United States – the United States which is their guarantee for their security. That we cannot have.[45]

Although the Atlantic alliance and NATO survived, conflicts between the two close postwar allies emerged and America did not continue its earlier policy of building Europe back up by aiding its integration.

Civil wars, coups and regime changes

Other major geopolitical changes accompanied the significant weakening of the Western alliance during the détente years. Indeed, the entire postwar world order disappeared. The two most important historical elements of the changing world order were the collapse of the colonial systems (which had existed for centuries) and the communist system (a twentieth-century invention).

The colonial empires, as noted before, started collapsing immediately after World War II. The Asian and African colonies were liberated one after another, and the colonial regime – with very few exceptions – was basically nonexistent by 1960. Within a few years, it had totally disappeared. In spite of this highly positive historical development, the dozens of newly independent countries were faced with the tremendously difficult task of finding their way. These newly independent countries were often fractured and declined into murderous civil wars and even genocides. The Biafra war from 1967 to 1970 led to the division of Nigeria. The crisis in Pakistan led to the separation of an independent Bangladesh. Military takeovers, successful coups d'état, and coup attempts followed one another with frightening frequency. In Sub-Saharan Africa, 80 coups succeeded and while another 108 failed. Another 139 coups were discovered between 1956 and 2001. In Afghanistan, there were five coups between 1973 and 2001. In Ghana, five coups occurred between 1966 and 1981; in Sierra Leone, six coups followed one after the other between 1967 and 1998; in Uganda, five took place between 1971 and 1986; and in Thailand, four happened between 1971 and 2006. In the 1990s, the Rwandan civil war between the Tutsi and Hutu tribes led to the genocide of nearly 1 million people, 70 percent of the Tutsis, and the rape of nearly half a million women.

Instability remained unchangingly characteristic even in the early twenty-first century. In the early 2000s, coups or serious coup attempts happened in Ecuador, Peru, Guinea-Bissau, Togo, Nepal and Mauritania. Dictatorial regimes took over several countries intermittently. Ghana and Pakistan both had four, Sudan and Honduras five, Guatemala and Peru six, and Argentina had eight regimes changes from dictatorships to democratization and back. As Thomas Piketty summed up, countries were "caught in an endless alteration between revolutionary governments . . . and governments dedicated to the protection of existing property owners, thereby laying the groundwork for the next revolution or coup."[46]

During these same decades, from the 1960s–1970s on, upheavals shocked the Third World, the so-called Second World, the Soviet Union and the entire Soviet

Bloc. These regions declined into an ever-deepening crisis. During the nearly two decades-long rule of Leonid Brezhnev between 1964 and 1982, the Soviet Union lost its earlier dynamic economic growth, which was replaced by near stagnation. After Brezhnev's death, in a tragicomical way, the Soviet superpower elected two dying men one after other to lead the country: Yuri Andropov's term started in November 1982, but he died in February 1984; after his death, Konstantin Chernenko was elected in February 1984, but he died on March 1985.

At last, after those fiascoes Mikhail Gorbachev took over and started to implement long-overdue reforms. But they were too late and too little to save the country. Meanwhile, major crises hit the Soviet Bloc countries and the Bloc started melting down. Communist regimes collapsed country by country without the kind of Soviet military intervention that had rescued the Bloc during previous crises in 1953 (East Germany), 1956 (Hungary), and 1968 (Czechoslovakia). The first communist regime collapsed in Poland in 1989, followed almost synchronously by that of Hungary. The entire Soviet Bloc in Central Europe and the Balkans followed one by one, until the end of 1989. Not much later, the Soviet Union itself collapsed in 1991. Chinese communism, had nominally survived by bloodily suppressing the rising revolution at Tiananmen Square in the summer of 1989, but the country gradually turned into a modernization dictatorship and a state-interventionist capitalist economic regime behind the façades of the communist regime, the red flag, and one-party communist rule.

The communist bloc disappeared, and the Cold War finally ended. The former communist half of Europe started along its difficult road of transformation. During the first years, they declined into deep and complex crises. All of the multinational states in the region, the Soviet Union, Yugoslavia and Czechoslovakia collapsed either immediately or within a few years after the regime change. Fifteen independent countries emerged from the Soviet state. Former Yugoslavia first became four, and then by the end seven, independent countries. Czechoslovakia was separated into two independent countries. Instead of eight countries in the Central and East European area, 28 sovereign states emerged during the 1990s and started a new chapter of history.

The entire region began to follow the West in emerging on the road towards developing private market-capitalist economic systems and pluralistic democracies. The newly transforming countries all wanted to go, as the main slogan in the region expressed, "Back to Europe!" This goal had positive impact on several countries of the region for quite a while, but this transformation miserably failed in Russia and in several of the successor states of the Soviet Union. This failure to align closely with Europe led to local wars as well as civil wars in some of the successor states and in the Balkans. In the eastern half of the European continent, several countries were taken over by autocratic, dictatorial regimes which regular multi-party elections to create a façade of democracy.

Two decades later, the entire southern Mediterranean area was shocked by the so-called Arab Spring. Dramatic protests, uprisings and violent civil wars destroyed the existing regimes in Tunisia, Libya, Egypt, Yemen, Syria and Bahrain. However, hopes for a democratic revival soon died. Total regional instability, long sectarian fights and civil wars between Sunni and Shia Muslims, the violent rise of the so-called Islamic State – altogether, an "Arab Winter" – followed.

Thus at the turn of the millennium, the world declined into disorder. Thus, development was just the opposite of what Francis Fukuyama forecasted in his 1989 study on the end of history:

> What we may be witnessing is not just the end of the Cold War, or the passing of a particular period of postwar history, but the end of history as such. . . . That is, the end point of mankind's ideological evolution and the universalization of Western liberal democracy as the final form of human government.[47]

In reality, Fukuyama's former teacher Samuel P. Huntington was right when he prophesized that after the Cold War, the world would experience a new type of confrontation, not among nation-states, nor among the ideologies and regimes that embodied them, but among cultures and religions. As the title of his 1992 lecture and then 1993 study in Foreign Affairs phrased it, the ensuing scenario would be a "Clash of Civilizations."[48] The wars in Yugoslavia, Chechnya and India-Pakistan signaled the ascendancy of this kind of confrontation. Huntington rejected what he characterized as the naïve Western belief in the universality of Western values and democratization. He predicted the rise of two "challenger civilizations" – Confucian Sinic and Islam – based on a population explosion in those regions and on the rising economic power of China and connected areas of Asia. Huntington believed that this shift would lead to a fight for hegemony. Within two to three decades, this confrontation became a fact. Not even a decade of the new millennium had passed when Muslim terrorism in New York and Washington on 11 September 2001 signaled the beginning of a religious confrontation. The clash of civilizations started dominating the world.

Lack of hegemony and global governance

After less than half a century, the postwar world order was replaced by a quite chaotic new international disorder without benign hegemons. These conditions exhibited frighteningly similar features to those of the interwar decades. In the globalized world economy, however, the lack of leadership and any kind of global governance became even more dangerous. Virtually all of the existing economic institutions remained national; though their importance significantly diminished, they were not replaced by international institutions. In 1992, the Commission of Global Governance was established; in 1995, it presented a report on the crisis of global governance. The journal *Global Governance* was also established, which argued for the necessity of global governance in a period where nobody was in charge and the "boundaries between national and international arenas" were disappearing.[49] Some suggested that international institutions should do on an international scale what governments do on a national one.[50] George Soros, the famous hedge-fund magnate who profited exceedingly from globalization, called the attention to the dangers of the lack of global governance in his 1998 book *The Crisis of Global Capitalism*. He lamented, a "collective decision-making mechanism for the global economy simply does not exist." Giving the market forces "complete authority . . . produces chaos and could ultimately lead to the downfall of the global capitalist system."[51]

Certain attempts were made to fill the gap. In June 1975, the German Chancellor Helmut Schmidt and the French President Giscard d'Estaing invited the heads of the top five Western countries (G5) to assemble in Rambouillet, France to replace American hegemony with a collective-management regime that would have included North America, Japan and Western Europe. Beginning in 1976, the Group of Seven (G7) started holding annual meetings. However, the French Jacques Attali rightly characterized this body and its "meeting without any decision, whose sessions are empty, whose declarations are insignificant enough to be accepted by all."[52] Nevertheless, in 1999, the G7 group invited several other countries–Argentina, Australia, Brazil, China, Russia, India, Indonesia, Mexico, Saudi Arabia, South Africa, South Korea, and Turkey – and formed the G20. These countries represented 60 percent of the world's population, 85 percent of the world's gross products and 80 percent of the world trade. In theory, the G20 would be a competent forum to instill some order in the world system, but in practice, it does not act as an international coordinator. Through this chaotic and confrontational world disorder, the importance of the European Community as the nucleus of European government was highly magnified. In the 1970s–1980s, this realization became even more tangible as Europe itself declined into crisis.

Economic crisis and mistaken answers

Two oil crises in 1973 and 1979–1980 increased oil prices tenfold, from $3.40–3.60 per barrel in 1970–1972 to $35 in 1980. In 1973–1974, the stock-market crash shocked the economy. A deep economic crisis emerged. Based on ninety-four countries with 98 percent of the world's population, the average rate of growth of 3.4 percent from the period between 1950 and 1973 dropped to -0.1 percent between 1973 and 1987. In the same period, the "terms of trade" – the ratio of export prices to import prices – for advanced countries declined by 20 percent. Thus from the same quantity of exported goods, countries could buy one-fifth fewer imported goods;[53] industrial output declined by 13 percent. The leading economic powers were no longer the engines of European economic prosperity.

The entire decade of the 1970s was characterized by high inflation of 7–8 percent per year, but in 1974 and 1979, it reached between 10–12 percent. Between 1950–1973 and 1973–1983, consumer prices in the leading Western economies more than doubled (from an average annual of 4.2 percent to 9.4 percent), and in the Mediterranean region prices more than quadrupled (from 4.0 percent to 18.4 percent yearly increase). Unemployment, which had been extremely low – averaging 2–4 percent in Western and Mediterranean Europe between 1950 and 1973 – jumped to 5–12 percent between 1984–1993.[54] That was a new kind of economic crisis, because – in an unprecedented reversal – inflation was accompanied with near stagnation, a phenomenon immediately dubbed *stagflation*. Britain lost nearly 4 percent of its GDP, and it took three and a half years to recover to the pre-crisis level. Instead of the yearly average growth rate of 3.8 percent between 1950 and 1973, the twelve west European countries' growth rates declined to 1.8 percent per annum. Southern Europe's growth rate halved in the latter period; and Eastern Europe, instead of the 4.0 percent growth it had enjoyed before 1973, experienced a -0.8 percent annual growth rate between 1973 and 1992.[55]

Concerted European policy needed

European countries reacted with an old playbook to this new challenge. Governments increased tariffs and restrictions in an effort to defend their countries' domestic markets. The European Economic Community raised the proportion of restricted imports from 11 percent to 15 percent of total imports of manufactured goods. Restrictive tariffs for imported goods from Japan and the newly industrialized countries of Asia increased from 15 percent to as much as 30 percent of their value by the early 1980s. To keep the economy afloat, the European countries started subsidizing declining old industrial branches and increased export assistance. France paid export credits, which amounted to 5–6 percent of the value of capital goods exports between 1970 and 1978, and then increased this amount to 10 percent in 1981–1983. Some countries, such as Germany, gave tax relief to certain industries. Denmark, Sweden and Holland increased export assistance between the mid-1970s and the early 1980s from 2 percent to 28 percent, from 1 percent to 10 percent, and from 3 percent to 8 percent, respectively.[56] As an OECD analysis stated in 1987, the west European core suffered from structural rigidities that slowed the application of innovative technology. Europe's position in research and development-intensive branches worsened after 1973 because of its inability to make necessary adjustments more quickly.[57]

In the mid-1980s, governments started to realize "the failure of the national state in Europe to cope effectively with these new circumstances."[58] Revolutionary changes in technology strengthened this recognition. Europe had to become strong enough to stand on its own legs. They started to realize that "American coattails . . . are not a safe place."[59] The extensive development model based on labor input and the import of American technology was not an acceptable feasible pathway any longer. Europe needed an intensive development model that would foster independent European research and development in order to produce new inventions and independent European strategies.

A concerted European policy was needed to reach a competitive level in modern research and invention application. Europe was far behind in this arena. In the computer industry, the United States had spent five times more on research (R&D) than all the countries in Western Europe together. The US government put 8 percent of its total spending towards funding innovation. Germany and France spent 1.2 percent and 1.0 percent respectively. In 1973, Western Europe had a 21.6 percent share of the world's R&D expenditure, win comparison to the US's 33.7 percent. Japan and South Korea together spent less than 8 percent in 1973, but by 1988 they already almost at 20 percent. In that year, the spending of all the west European countries combined increased to nearly 26 percent. At the end of the 1980s, 4.1 million scientists and engineers worked in the world's R&D industry. A total of 37 percent of them were American, Japanese and South Korean; only 17 percent were West European.[60]

The requirement made clear that a single country's national policy was insufficient in sectors that required a broad sphere of research. As one Community working group report stated: "No country in Europe has the capacity to cover such a spectrum of technological options, which is the only way to achieve a satisfactory degree of technological flexibility."[61] As Wayne Sandholtz noted in his 1992 book *High-Tech Europe*, in one of the key high-tech sectors, the aerospace industry, "the states turned to collaboration only after national strategies have fallen short. . . . The period of national champion strategies (the 1970s) ended in a crisis for European telematics industries and policies; collaboration emerged in the 1980s."[62]

It was quite natural that the most modern technological sectors recognized the need for broad European cooperation first. These industries a required huge amount of investment, and the extremely rapid change in technology made a single country's national policy inefficient. As Sandholtz put it, "European collaboration in space technologies began after purely national space programs proved untenable. The sheer required scale of national investment required to join the space race and led national policy-makers to turn to cooperation." As he notes, space collaboration actually began in 1964 with the ratification of charters for the European Launcher Development Organization and the European Space Research Organization.[63]

Big corporations for European cooperation

Chief executives at twelve top European multinationals sent a letter to Étienne Davignon, the Belgian Commissioner of Industrial Affairs and Vice President of the European Commission between January 1977 and January 1981, stating that Europe's market positions were miserable and the national programs hopeless. They warned, "Unless a cooperative industrial programme of sufficient magnitude can be mounted, most, if not all, of the current IT [information technology] industry could disappear in a few years' time." Three French members of the group – GEC, Thomson and Bull – "presented a unified, clear view" and asked the French minister of industry to take up the case.[64] "Dissatisfaction with the national route of European policy making," comments one historian of this issue, "provided incentives for European big business to organise politically at the European level."[65] In January 1979, an expert group that included representatives of big business issued a report advocating that the European Community should exploit its comparative advantage "by dominating its potential internal market (which presupposes completion of the common market and monetary union) . . . [and] internationalizing capital."[66]

Charismatic commissioner Davignon was ready to address this issue, and presented his first report on telematics strategy in the same year, at the end of 1979. He invited senior officials from the ten largest computer and telecommunication manufacturers in Europe to meet. In February 1980, this group was already engaged in discussions to work out a strategy. In July 1980, the first microelectronic program was submitted to the European Council. In late 1981, Davignon invited the directors of the twelve largest information technology companies to form a European Roundtable of Industrialists. This group sent engineers and technologists to establish a technical panel. At last, 400 technologists and 150 government officials and university experts came together to work on the program.[67]

In the 1980s, the giant multinational company Philips published a booklet advocating the proper unification of the European market. It stated:

> The only option left for the Community is to achieve the goals laid down in the Treaty of Rome. Only in this way can industry compete globally, by exploiting of economies of scale, for what will then be the biggest home market in the world today: *the European Community home market*.[68]

Multinationals had

> taken up the banner of 1992, collaborating with the Commission and exerting substantial influence on their governments. . . . European business and the Commission may be said to have together bypassed national governmental processes and shaped an agenda that compelled attention and action.[69]

Another expert, Adam Harmes, similarly concluded:

> In fact, European big business played a key role in drafting the terms of the Single European Act. In 1983, two years before Jacques Delors called for a single European market . . . the European Roundtable of Industrialists . . . drew up a list of proposals that became the basis for the Single European Act. As Jacques Delors would later remark, the Roundtable was "one of the main driving forces" behind the Single Market.[70]

Big business, of course, was motivated by the goal of making larger profits, not by the possibility to creating a large European political architecture for its own sake. As Adam Smith recognized, "the consideration of his own private profit is the sole motive which determines the owner of any capital."[71] Karl Marx agreed: the capitalist's aim is the "restless, never-ending process of profit making."[72] Nevertheless, in the process of looking out for their own interests, they did a good service for Europe as well. To paraphrase the most often-quoted sentence from Adam Smith's *Wealth of Nations* about the butcher who also serves his costumers' interests in the process of increasing his own income, corporations that sought to maximize their own gain benefitted the further integration of Europe, promoting an "end which was no part of [their] intention."[73]

In February 1984, the top industrialists of the Roundtable worked out a long list of required concrete measures to "unblock the workings of the European Community." Earlier, in 1958, the main organization of the European entrepreneurs, the Union of Industrial and Employers' Confederations of Europe (UNICE), was founded and suggested the "establishment of an internal market, eliminating financial, legal and administrative obstacles." Among their recommendations, they urged "programmes of European research, development and innovation policy." In 1984, the French Chamber of Commerce and Industry – together with other institutions and the representatives from 200 leading European industrialists – organized a campaign for a new "Eurodynamism" and a break with the "Eurosclerosis" of national politicians.[74]

In the 1980s, the European Defense Industries Group, the representatives of the military industry, started also lobbying against Article 223 of the Treaty of Rome. That article left defense industrial matters outside the Community's jurisdiction and in the hands of the nation-states. The Group expressed that they "would like to see Article 223 of the Rome Treaty eliminated or narrowed in scope." An executive of the French Thomson-CSF, Europe's biggest defense electronics companies, argued:

> it was unbelievable to put together the words "Europe" and "armaments." It was a taboo. . . . Europeans as a whole felt that Europe needed more political integration. . . . And that political integration meant more cooperation in defense and armaments.[75]

Similarly, Manfred Bischoff, who soon after became the Chairman of one of the leading German military-industrial leaders, Daimler Benz Aerospace, complained about the disadvantage that European defense industrial companies faced compared to their American rivals:

> We cannot wait for full integration of the EU's single market. . . . why are there no incentives to create optional restructuring in Europe? . . . Why not a European missile company? . . . I don't care if they are German, French or Italian, as long as there's a harmonised approach.

Lord Weinstock, managing director of the British defense electronic company GEC, urged mergers between European defense companies: "We have to respond to the changes in America. They are producing giant companies through these mergers. . . . We have to form companies of sufficient size to compete effectively."[76] Serge Dassault, head of the French aircraft company, was "campaigning for an EU rule of *préférence européenne* in arms purchase to promote a pan-European defense industrial base."[77]

To gain direct impact over European Community decisions, European corporations built up huge lobbying networks in Brussels. By 1985, already 654 registered interest organizations were working in Brussels. By 2009, 15,000–20,000 similar organizations had offices and direct contacts with the EU administration.

Meanwhile, about 300 major corporations had their own independent represent-atives based there too. As a European Union archive document shows: "Some firms were establishing themselves as political insiders through engaging in a high degree of political activity." Among the 34 strongest insider companies were Royal Dutch Shell, British Petrol, Daimler Benz, Fiat, Unilever, Siemens, Bayer, British Aerospace, British Steel, Pirelli, Olivetti and Thyssen.[78]

Nothing better showcases the activity of the top business circles than the role of Wisse Dekker, the CEO of one of the biggest European multinational companies, Philips. When European Community officials were unable to produce an exact program for a unified European market, he presented his own plan, "Europe 1990," at a major Brussels gathering and sent it over to the key political lead-ers from various countries. Dekker's plan described all the required steps – the elimination of border formalities, open public-procurement markets, harmonized technical standards and fiscal harmonization – for unifying the Community's market. The European Roundtable of Industrialists, the organization of the big-gest corporations of Europe, endorsed the Dekker plan. Maria Green Cowles, the main historian of this topic, noted: Dekker's plan "was viewed by many as the precursor to the Cockfield White Paper, the [Commission's] document that outlined the Single Market or the 1992 program issued six months later."[79]

Renewed leadership: Mitterrand-Kohl-Delors and the single Europe act

The European corporate world built up its organizations and advocated for Com-munity actions, even working out plans to fulfill the unfulfilled ideas for further inte-gration and put an end to the inertia that had dominated the Community since the mid-1960s. They pushed European integration significantly farther ahead. Some of the national leaders also realized that national answers to global challenges do not work. During the 1980s, a changing of the guard in national and Community leader-ship radically altered the situation within the European Economic Community.

These major personnel changes started in 1981 when François Maurice Adrien Marie Mitterrand became the President of France. Mitterrand had a long back-ground in French political life. He started as a nationalist right-wing Catholic politician and served in Marshall Petain's Vichy Government. After a while, how-ever, he joined the Resistance movement, moved towards the political left, and served as minister in the Fourth Republic several times. He opposed many of De Gaulle's policies and became the First Secretary of the French Socialist Party. After his election to the presidency, he was reelected and served his longest term in office from 1981 to 1995.

A year after Mitterrand became president, in 1982, the Christian Democratic Union (CDU) won the German elections, and Helmut Josef Michael Kohl, the party's chairman since 1973, became the Chancellor of the German Federal Republic. Kohl also had a long career in German politics. He joined the CDU at the age of 16, received his PhD in history at Heidelberg University in 1958, and served as minister president of the state of Rhineland-Palatinate.

Both François Mitterrand and Helmut Kohl realized the crucial importance of revitalizing the European Community to answer the challenge of the newly globalized world economy and the chaotic global political situation by creating a united Europe. The two men formed an excellent team that worked together in tandem. At one of their usual meetings, a joint breakfast at the Fontainebleau Summit meeting on 25–26 June 1984, Mitterrand suggested to Kohl the appointment of Jacques Delors, his Minister of Economy and Finance, to the European Commission presidency. Kohl agreed; thus this breakfast discussion generated a turning point in the history of European integration.

Jacques Lucien Jean Delors started his political career in the French Confederation of Christian Workers, where he participated in its secularization and the foundation of the French Democratic Confederation of Labor. This socially sensitive politician became the government's social affairs adviser in 1969. As a left-wing Christian socialist, he joined the Socialist Party in 1974. Delors became member of the European Parliament in 1979, and in 1981, Mitterrand appointed him to be a member of his cabinet. Due to the French-German agreement, he became the head of the European Commission in 1985 and served in this post for ten years, until 1995.

4.1   Jacque Delors

History recognizes a few personalities as fathers of the European Union. Jacques Lucien Jean Delors, the son of a courier of the Banque de France who was born in 1925, became one of the most important. While he was not a part of the original foundation in the 1950s, he was a crucial figure in its "second coming" during the 1980s–1990s.

At the age of 20, Delors joined the same bank where his father worked as a courier, and worked there for 17 years until 1962. As a religious and socially sensitive man who was interested in social questions, he joined the French Confederation of Christian Workers and participated in the foundation of the French Democratic Confederation of Labor, but as he was ultimately a left-wing Christian socialist, he joined the French Socialist Party in 1974.

Delors studied at the Sorbonne and got a degree in economics. After his years at the bank, he joined the state's General Planning Commission and became the head of the social affairs division. From 1969 to 1972, he served as chief adviser on social affairs for the "new society" program of Prime Minister Jacques Chaban-Delmas's cabinet.

Jacques Delors had a broad view of European integration. He became a member of the European Parliament in 1979 and chaired the Economic and Monetary Affairs Committee until May 1981. His work for an integrated Europe, however, was cut short. When François Mitterrand was elected President of France, he invited Delors to serve as Economics and Finance Minister, and later as Budget Minister as well. Delors served in his cabinet from 1981 to 1984. Then, after two decades of crisis and stagnation in the integration process, two new leaders in France and Germany – Mitterrand and Helmut Kohl, who worked excellently in tandem – decided to revitalize the European Community. Mitterrand realized that the crisis-ridden economy of the 1970s and early 1980s, as well as the invasion of American and Japanese multinational companies into the European markets, required major steps and joint European action, since none of the nation-states were able to craft good solutions alone.

During a conference between the heads of states and governments of the European Economic Community, Mitterrand, at a joint breakfast discussion with Chancellor Kohl, suggested the appointment of Delors, who had proved to be an excellent and effective leader in his cabinet, to the key position of the presidency of the European Commission. Delors started his work as the Head of the Commission in 1985 and continued until 1995. This decade turned out to be the most important turning point in the history of the European Economic Community. Stagnation in the integration process ended and long-existing ideas, such as the introduction of the common currency, which had already been suggested in 1970 – were put on the agenda and realized. Delors' initiatives and leadership radically transformed the Community. As a federalist, he became an advocate and initiator of supra-European institutions. Under his leadership, as early as 1985, the building of the European Single Market started. It was already in place by 1992. Then, in three steps, the common currency was introduced at the turn of the millennium. The Community transformed into the European Union. Jacques Delors became the best and most efficient leader of the Commission, whose fingerprints are all over the European Union.

The Delors-Mitterrand-Kohl troika also benefitted from major contributions from a fourth charismatic Europeanist, Altiero Spinelli. The former prisoner from Mussolini's island prison, Ventoteno, had spent his time there dreaming about a postwar federal Europe. Later, in 1979, he became member of the European Parliament. The Parliament appointed him as General Rapporteur of the established Committee on Institutional Affairs in January 1982 to draft a proposal for a new treaty for the Community. He presented a draft treaty to the European Parliament, which accepted it in February 1984 by an overwhelming majority of 237 votes for and 31 against. Although it was never formally adopted the newly appointed president of the Commission, Jacques Delors was able to build upon it. Spinelli's "Draft Treaty Establishing the European Union" contained the following text:

> The Union shall have exclusive competence to complete, safeguard and develop the free movement of persons, services, goods and capital within

its territory. . . . This liberalization process shall take place on the basis of detailed and binding programmes and timetables laid down by the legislative authority in accordance with the procedures for adopting laws. . . . The Union must attain: within a period of two years . . . the free movement of persons and goods; this implies in particular the abolition of personal checks at internal frontiers, within a period of five years . . . the free movement of services, including banking and all forms of insurance, within a period of 10 years . . . the free movement of capital.[80]

After a few months in office, in June 1985, Jacques Delors presented a White Paper, "Completing the Internal Market," to the European Council in Milan. This document started with the following sentences:

During the recession [of the 1970s, non-tariff barriers] multiplied as each Member State endeavoured to protect what it thought was its short-term interests. . . . Member States also increasingly sought to protect national markets and industries through the use of public funds to aid and maintain non-viable companies.[81]

This document convincingly criticized obsolete defensive national policies and recommended, as an alternative, "setting the stage for a new type of association" by governance with uniform legislation, and permitting cross-border mergers to "create an environment or conditions likely to favour the development of cooperation between undertakings."[82] In accepting the ideas that the corporate businesses had already required and pushed to expand for a while, the new Commission redefined the home market as European instead of national.

Regionalization: the answer to globalization and the Maastricht Treaty

After only in one year in office, the Delors-led Commission used Spinelli's, as well as Wisse Dekker's plans (mentioned before) to create a plan for mandatory further integration. They sent the Single European Act (SEA) to the Council of Ministers in February 1986, and a few days later, to the member countries of the Community. The acceptance of the new agreement was somewhat delayed because Denmark voted 'no' the first time, but, after a positive second Danish vote, it came into effect on 1 July 1987.

The Single European Act (SEA) sought to complete the internal market of the Community by eliminating internal borders and making possible the free movement of goods, services, capital and persons by January 1993. Thanks to the creation of the Single Market, European multinational corporations largely pulled their business out of the endangered and uncertain global market. Several newly independent countries turned against foreign companies, introduced restrictions, and even nationalized certain foreign enterprises. Some governments, such as those of India and Malaysia pushed back strongly to this trend: even as early as the late 1970s, the Indian Janata Party expelled foreign companies if they refused to share their technology. The Malaysian government took over the biggest British rubber and palm oil business, the Guthrie Corporation, in 1981. As a 2004 World Bank study revealed, the governments of new developing countries forced the renegotiation of agreements with companies, which led to $371 billion in investments in their countries. The return from investment in Third World countries dropped from more than 30 percent to 2.5 percent during the 1980s.[83] The Dutch-British company Unilever, one of the world's very first multinational companies, sold more than 70 of its factories and subsidiaries outside of Europe and turned towards the European market. Germany drastically decreased its investments outside of Europe (from 40 percent to 17 percent) and redirected them to European countries. In 1986, about one-third of Norway's investment targeted Third World countries; whereas, half a decade later, this figure dropped to 4 percent. In 1991, 89 percent of Norwegian investments went to Europe.[84] During the 1960s–1970s, European multinationals reoriented their business activities, and several left the developing countries and turned to Europe.[85]

Indeed, by defending itself, Europe started to regain its competitiveness and international stature via a thoroughly integrated, centralized European market with a streamlined standard of products and a legal and regulatory system. The realization of this goal required tremendous preparatory work. A common market, for example, has to have common standards for the products to be saleable in all member countries of the community. This mandate not only created an unbelievably tremendous work for tens of thousands of products, but also required special knowledge in each of the manufacturing branches. The Community's surprisingly small bureaucracy (less than 3,500 senior administrators) was insufficient to accomplish the job. Consequently, as documents reflected, the Commission needed to involve a great number of outside experts.[86] Expert groups for assisting in this work mushroomed. In 1985, there were 700; but by 1988, there were 1,336. The Market Access Advisory Committee and the Market Access Working Group assisted in this preparatory work by "bringing together all relevant stakeholders [in a] partnership between the Commission, EU Member States and EU business."[87] The European Commission also formed a high-level strategy group made up of representatives from various industrial corporations "to oversee standardization at a strategic level and to determine the key requirements for standards in a business context."[88] The Commission worked "in close conjunction with . . . industry."[89] One European Parliament policy advisor stated, "We cannot do our work without information from interest groups . . . Sometimes it is very tempting to copy and paste their amendments."[90] One scholar has found that "about 80% of all amendments launched in the committees stem directly from interest representatives."[91]

The Single Market's laws on financial services were worked out in close cooperation with "the European Banking Federation, the European Stock Exchange Federation [and] the various insurance federations."[92] Several organizations were focused on creating "detailed drafting proposals" for the banking group."[93] The all-European auto standards were created in close collaboration with an interest group established in 1972, the Committee of Common Market Automobile Constructors. Alongside standardization, a several year-long legal and regulatory effort concluded in 1992 that created unified rules, standards, and a harmonized legal system in order to eliminate obstacles to the creation of a Single Market with the free movement of capital, goods, services, and people.

The Single-Europe project ended the restrictions on capital movement. The goal was "the establishment of a Community-wide integrated financial system"[94] with standardized rules and laws. The European Central Bank reported that the impact of regional integration in Europe increased direct investment in a range between 28 percent and 83 percent, while the incremental effect of Euro-area membership ranged between 21 percent and 44 percent. As one study found:

> The results indicate that, on average, joining the EU increased inward FDI flows from other EU countries by 43.9% .... On average, adopting the euro increased FDI from other euro area members by 73.7%. Thus, the additional effect of belonging to the common currency area can be estimated at around 20%. Indeed, the EU reduced the cost of doing business across the borders between its members, and the euro area stimulated cross-border capital flows among its members, as exchange and liquidity risk were eliminated.[95]

As part of this important change, the European Community introduced the Single Banking License, or Single Passport, in 1989. If a bank was licensed in one member country of the Community, it had the right to conduct business – including to establish branches and subsidiaries – in all other member countries. This principle became a law in the Community and led to the creation of a single system for financial legislation and regulation throughout the Community. The First and the Second Banking Directives were definitive steps towards a unified European financial market. Cross-border mergers rapidly progressed. By 2010, 166 French banks were operating under a European Passport. In 2010, 29 foreign bank branches were operating in Sweden. The merger process has advanced rapidly since the late 1980s as a result of several cross-border acquisitions. A few west European countries – France, Germany, Britain, Switzerland and the Netherlands (and the European subsidiaries of American multinational banks) – owned about half of the cross-border European banking assets. The leading European Banking groups not only operated throughout the European Union, but became all-European by ownership. A huge part of their assets were owned by other countries' investors. The foreign share of Deutsche Bank's assets, for example, accounted for 82 percent; for the Spanish company Santander, 64 percent; for the Italian bank UniCredito, 62 percent; for the French bank BNP Paribas, 41 percent; and for Société Générale, 29 percent. Each of these banks also has at least 100 majority-owned subsidiaries, and more than half have over 500 subsidiaries. A total of 16 major banks held at least 25 percent of their assets in other EU countries. The leading European banks built up huge all-European networks. In 2012, Deutsche Bank had €2 trillion assets and 3,000 branches throughout Europe with 100,000 employees, and gained 67 percent of its revenue from the European home market.[96] BNP Paribas, with its almost €2 trillion in assets and 200,000 employees (145,000 in Europe) also became a pan-European bank. Its network covers most of Western, Southern, and Eastern Europe; and of its business, 31 percent is concentrated in France, while 46 percent occurs in other European countries.[97]

Similarly to the Europeanized banking industry, manufacturing also became more and more pan-European. The member countries of the Community invested in each other. Between 1970 and 2007, their stock of foreign direct investment increased by 167 times. Before 2008, EU countries were the main recipients of global FDI. On average, between 2000 and 2007, EU countries attracted 43.1 percent of the world's FDI, while other advanced economies attracted 23.8 percent and developing countries 33 percent. (During the crises years between 2008 and 2016, the EU's share declined to 26.7 percent of the world's FDI.) As one study details, "By 2010, US $8 trillion of intra-European FDI stocks were knitting together value chains, empowering firms to serve customers across borders, and providing consumers with a vast array of goods and services. Third country inflows, with North American and Japanese firms leading the pack, have contributed a further $4 trillion to the story."[98]

Between 1998 and 2006, more than 43,000 mergers – two-thirds of the world's company mergers – happened in the European Community. "The largest European corporations" – primarily those that were registered around the end of the first decade of the twenty-first century – "have made most of their investments in the past twenty years within Europe. . . . The interlocking of the economies of Western Europe . . . has gone a great distance."[99]

Europe's industries started to become "Europeanized." As Eurostat reported in 2012, 72 percent of total inward foreign direct investments during the 1990s were intra-EU flows.[100] Joint production became widespread after all-European value chains were built up. As a study of the European Central Bank stated, in 2001, the foreign value added into corporate output "was to a major extent sourced from other euro area countries." In 1997, for example, more than a third (36 percent) of intra-EU trade imports were parts and components imported via the value chain from other member countries. The Volkswagen Group bought the Spanish car company SEAT (in 1986), the Czech Škoda (in 1991 and 1995), and the Italian Lamborghini and Bugatti (in 1998). After the collapse of communism, Volkswagen built several major factories in Slovakia – which became known as the "Volkswagen land"[101] – as well as in Hungary, Poland, Bosnia, Ukraine and Russia. In 2010, it had 61 production plants and factories in 15 European countries.[102] As of 2020, the Group employs nearly 370,000 people around the world. Daimler-Benz has a quite similar European network: 37 percent of the company's output takes place in Germany, while 64 percent of its total production is produced in other European countries.[103] By 2012, the Italian company FIAT had subsidiaries in 61 countries, and ran more than 1,000 firms with 223,000 employees. The Company became all-European with 89,000 employees employed in its European units: 50 in France, 26 in Britain, 30 in Germany, 17 in Spain, and 10 in Poland. Out of the company's 77 R&D centers, 52 were in Europe.[104]

The Airbus program began as a collaborative project between France and Germany in 1969, but soon involved Britain, Spain and other countries. As of 2020, the company has roughly 180 locations and 12,000 direct suppliers from more than 20 countries.[105] The European Central Bank's study concluded:

> [T]he internationalisation of production and, more specifically, a higher degree of vertical integration into global value chains provided in recent years critical stimulus to the European economy. First, it fostered an industrial restructuring both across the European economies and between Europe and the rest of the world, which allowed European firms to vertically specialise in those activities in which they have a comparative advantage.[106]

Regional value-chain contributions to global output became the highest – nearly 30 percent – in the European Community.[107] In the US and East Asia, this share is only 16 percent and 10 percent, respectively.

This trend of 'Europeanization' also occurred in retail trade. Giant French, German, Dutch retail companies (among others) likewise built huge networks within the EU. Between 1990 and the 2000s, the French supermarket chain Carrefour covered Greece, Italy, Poland, Portugal, Belgium, Romania, Slovakia, Spain, and the Czech Republic. As of 1997, it had 6,132 stores in 29 countries, making it the number one grocery store in Spain, Portugal and Greece; and the second largest in Italy. The German Metro Group also established a huge all-European network, employing 250,000 people in 32 countries. All in all, three-quarters of food retailing in the EU is controlled by three countries' giant retailer companies.[108] As a Bruegel Policy Brief on the markets of the 100 largest European companies stated:

> Increasingly Europe [operates] as a whole rather than [according to the dictates of] any particular country within it. The share of European sales in their total revenue is almost identical, on average, to the share of US revenue for the US Top 100, at 65% . . . . German companies are among the frontrunners of both europeanisation and globalisation. . . . French companies have europeanised rather than globalised.[109]

In the 1990s, the need for independent research and development to promote the creation of European inventions and support for innovation still existed. Using the only existing framework – the intensive development model that Europe had relied upon in the early 1980s – the European Community decided to assist. The European Strategic Programme for Research and Development (ESPRIT) launched in 1985 with 750 million ECUs (the ECU was basically equivalent with the euro, which was introduced a few years later). Further programs to inspire the development of communication and other new technologies (RACE and BRITE) followed. Eventually they were united in a single Research and Technology Development Program in 1987. From 1987 to 1991, 5.4 billion ECUs were invested in this program. Investment stood at 5.7 billion ECUs in 1990–1994 and rose to 12.3 billion in 1994–1998. The European Union's ESPRIT program established close cooperation among leading corporations such as Siemens, AEG, Bull, Thomson, Olivetti, Philips, and six other companies, which received 70 percent of the financing in the first stage of the program. Several European "showpieces," such as the Airbus program, also profited from it, and R&D activity gained momentum.[110] Within one and a half decades, employment in this sector increased by more than 400,000 people, or 34 percent. In the mid-1990s, Western Europe employed 1.6 million people in R&D.

The free movement of people became possible also in 1985, when the Schengen Agreement – originally signed by representatives from five countries on a boat near Schengen, a village in Luxembourg – took the first step in this direction. This agreement led to the gradual abolition of checks at common borders. The implementation of the Schengen Agreement started in 1995. It was initially an intergovernmental initiative that involved seven EU states, but later became incorporated into the Community's rules. Gradually all of the member countries began to join (a process that continues to this day), together with a few non-EU states such as Iceland, Norway, Switzerland, and Liechtenstein. Any person from the countries that joined can cross these internal borders without border checks. Citizens of member countries have the right to live permanently in other member countries, and have equal employment rights as well.

Furthermore, Jacques Delors gained a mandate from the European Council to examine and propose concrete measures for further integration. The Committee for the Study of Economic and Monetary Union – or, as it is usually called, the Delors Committee – was formed in June 1988 and presented its report, the Delors Report, on 12 April 1989. This report recommended the next logical steps for integration: the introduction of a single currency and monetary unification. The very first recommendation for the introduction of a common currency was made in 1970 by the Werner Committee, and it was accepted by the head of states at a summit meeting in Paris in 1972. During the decades of stagnation for the integration process, however, it was not realized.

The preamble of the Single Act – a major legislative turning point for further integration that was passed in the mid-1980s – invoked this approval of the introduction of a common currency. Nurtured by Delors and his Commission, this plan was the most ambitious step towards a federal Europe. The plan was supported by the French president and the German chancellor when they jointly appealed for political union in 1990. Luxembourg and the Netherlands soon added their support. However, a certain amount of resistance remained, and the Maastricht Treaty failed to made direct progress towards this goal, though it represented a dramatic new step in this direction.[111] It was the Delors Report of 1992 that outlined the road. It suggested three stages towards an Economic and Monetary Union that would come into effect between 1999 and 2001. The first stage, the completion of the Single Market, would be followed by the foundation of the European Central Bank (a federal monetary institute) in the second stage, and finally with the introduction of a single currency that would replace national currencies in the third stage.

When the European Central Bank (ECB) was established, the member countries' national banks became integral parts of it. The ECB is governed by a General Council, the president of the Bank, and an Executive Board comprised of six members and the governors of the national banks). Decisions are made by majority vote. The Central Bank is a note-issuing institution. It also makes open-market operations, supports operations in the foreign-exchange market, creates reserves, supervises banks and participates in policymaking. On 1 January 2002, the euro was physically introduced and replaced the national currencies in the 11 countries that had joined the monetary union. The common currency and Central Bank became the most important supranational institutions of the European Union. The introduction of the euro eliminated currency risks and provided a further push for financial integration and for mergers of the European banking sector. Cross-border financial activities have increased by 40 percent in the euro-zone. In 2008, the Single European Payment Area was also introduced, which established the same conditions for payments.[112]

The European Economic Community quickly embraced the regionalization of the Community. This was an efficient defense against globalization and the chaotic world disorder that transpired around the turn of millennium. Regionalization is the formation of a regional (in this case, European) economic bloc, a customs union of states that voluntarily organizes close cooperation to cope with global challenges. This huge economic unit of half a billion people offered an independent safe haven from global competition. According to Bjorn Hettne:

> Regionalism is thus one way of coping with global transformation, since most states lack the capacity and the means to manage such a task on the "national" level. This process is similar to state formation and nation building, and the ultimate outcome could be a "region-state," which in terms of scope can be compared to the classical empires, but in terms of political order constitutes a voluntary evolution of a group of formerly sovereign national, political units into a supranational security community, where sovereignty is pooled for the best of all.[113]

Similarly, discussing the distinction between globalization and regionalism, Grahame Thompson explains:

> Regionalisation signifies a process that draws states and groups together on the basis of their proximity, perhaps because of economic advantages . . . or perhaps because security or environmental issues can have a region-wide impact. In addition there is a possibly more pronounced *institutional* integration process that often accompanies such regionalization.[114]

Regionalization became even more important in the early twenty-first century because groups of cooperating, neighboring European countries finally became able to stand firm against strengthening international competition and confrontation. The Delors-Mitterrand-Kohl troika pulled the previously stagnant coach of the European Community far ahead. All these major reforms required the revision of the Treaty of Rome, which was accomplished in Maastricht. On 9–10 December 1991, this Dutch city hosted the European Council. There the Council drafted the new treaty, the Treaty on the European Union, which the member countries of the European Economic Community signed in the same place on 7 February 1992. That was the culmination of decades of debates on increasing economic cooperation in Europe.[115]

Notes

1 *Treaty on European Union* (Luxembourg: Office for Official Publications of the European Communities, February 7, 1992).

2 Kevin H. O'Rourke and Jeffrey G. Williamson, *Globalization and History: The Evolution of a Nineteenth-Century Atlantic Economy* (Cambridge, MA and London: MIT Press, 1999), 2.

3 Shale Horowitz, "Restarting Globalization after World War II: Structure, Coalitions, and the Cold War," *Comparative Political Studies* 37, no. 2 (March 1, 2004): 127–128, https://doi.org/10.1177/0010414003260980.

4 See Joanne Gowa, *Allies, Adversaries, and International Trade* (Princeton, NJ: Princeton University Press, 1994); Albert O. Hirschman, *National Power and the Structure of Foreign Trade*, 2nd ed. (Berkeley, CA and Los Angeles, CA: University of California Press, 1980).

5 Horowitz, "Restarting Globalization after World War II," 128.

6 Charles Kindleberger, *The World in Depression, 1929–1939* (Berkeley, CA and Los Angeles, CA: University of California Press, 1973).

7 Kindleberger quoted in Horowitz, "Restarting Globalization after World War II," 129.

8 Kenichi Ohmae, *Beyond National Borders* (Homewood: Dow Jones-Irwin, 1988), 35–39.

9 Medard Gabel and Henry Bruner, *Global Inc: An Atlas of the Multinational Corporation* (London: New Press, 2003), 2.

10 Ohmae, *Beyond National Borders*, 35–39.

11 Kenichi Ohmae, *The Borderless World: Power and Strategy in the Interlinked Economy*, 2 revised (London: HarperCollins, 1999), XVI.

12 Judah Levine, "The History of the Shipping Container," *Freightos*, April 24, 2016, www.freightos.com/the-history-of-the-shipping-container/.

13 David Kotz, "Globalization and Neoliberalism," *Rethinking Marxism* 12, no. 2 (Summer 2002): 64–79; Ivan T. Berend, *An Economic History of Twentieth-Century Europe: Economic Regimes from Laissez-Faire to Globalization* (Cambridge: Cambridge University Press, 2016), 247.

14 Art Wolinsky, *The History of the Internet and the World Wide Web* (Berkeley Heights, NJ: Enslow Publishing, 1999).

15 *The Economist*, May 30, 2020, Global Tourism.

16 Berend, *An Economic History of Twentieth-Century Europe*, 248.

17 Milton Friedman, *Tax Limitation, Inflation and the Role of Government* (Dallas: Fisher Institute, 1978), 7.

18 Ibid., 75, 79, 91.

19 See Eric Helleiner, *States and the Reemergence of Global Finance: From Bretton Woods to the 1990s* (Ithaca, NY and London: Cornell University Press, 1994), 168–170; Joseph Stiglitz, *Globalization and Its Discontents* (New York: W. W. Norton & Company, 2002), 16–17, 34, 53, 65.

20 Wayne Sandholtz, *High-Tech Europe: The Politics of International Cooperation* (Berkeley, CA and Los Angeles, CA: University of California Press, 2018), 115.

21 "Improving Competitiveness and Industrial Structures in the Community. Commission Communication to the Council," EU Commission–COM Document (European Community, February 25, 1986), 7, Archive of European Integration, http://aei.pitt.edu/6354/1/6354.pdf.

22 Willem Hulsink, *Privatisation and Liberalisation in European Telecommunications: Comparing Britain, the Netherlands and France* (London: Routledge, 1999), 101.

23 *Structural Adjustment and Economic Performance* (Paris: Organisation for Economic Co-operation and Development, 1987), 213.

24 François Duchêne and Geoffrey Shepherd, eds., *Managing Industrial Change in Western Europe* (London: F. Pinter, 1987), 36.

25 *Structural Adjustment and Economic Performance*, 214, 254.

26 Lynn Krieger Mytelka and Michel Delapierre, "The Alliance Strategies of European Firms in the Information Technology Industry and the Role of ESPRIT," in *Multinationals and European Community*, ed. John H. Dunning and Peter Robson (Oxford: Basil Blackwell, 1987), 7, 113, https://onlinelibrary.wiley.com/doi/abs/10.1111/j.1468-5965.1987.tb00314.x, accessed November 9, 2017.

27 Jean-Jacques Servan-Schreiber, *Le défi américain* (Paris: Denoël, 1967). Also see Volker Schneider, "Organized Interests in the European Telecommunications Sector," in *Organized Interests and the European Community*, ed. Justin Greenwood, Jürgen R. Grote, and Karsten Ronit (London: Sage Publications, 1992), 50.

28 Quoted in Daniel J. Sargent, *A Superpower Transformed: The Remaking of American Foreign Relations in the 1970s* (New York: Oxford University Press, 2017), 37.

29 "Interdependence Day," *The New York Times*, July 4, 1976, www.nytimes.com/1976/07/04/archives/interdependence-day.html.

30 Quoted in Ernst Hans van der Beugel, *From Marshall Aid to Atlantic Partnership: European Integration as a Concern of American Foreign Policy* (Amsterdam: Elsevier Publishing Company, 1966), 382–383.

31 John F. Kenney, "Independence-Day Address at Independence Hall" (Presidential Address, Philadelphia, July 4, 1962), www.jfklibrary.org/archives/other-resources/john-f-kennedy-speeches/philadelphia-pa-19620704.

32 Douglas Brinkley and Richard T. Griffiths, "Preface," in *John F. Kennedy and Europe*, ed. Douglas Brinkley and Richard T. Griffiths (Baton Rouge, LA: Louisiana State University Press, 1999), XVI.

33 Lyndon B. Johnson, "Remarks" (National Conference of Editorial Writers, New York City, October 7, 1966). In *Public Papers of the Presidents of the United States, 1966*, vol. II (Washington, DC: U.S. Government Printing Office, 1967), 1125–1130.

34 Gordon A. Craig, "Did Ostpolitik Work? The Path to German Reunification," ed. Timothy Garton Ash, *Foreign Affairs* 73, no. 1 (1994): 162–167, https://doi.org/10.2307/20045899.

35 Luke A. Nichter, *Richard Nixon and Europe: The Reshaping of the Postwar Atlantic World* (Cambridge: Cambridge University Press, 2015), 136.

36 Henry Kissinger, *The Troubled Partnership: A Re-Appraisal of the Atlantic Alliance*, Council on Foreign Relations (New York, London, and Toronto, ON: McGraw-Hill, 1965), 244.

37 Ibid., 39–40.

38 Henry Kissinger, *White House Years* (Boston, MA and Toronto, ON: Little, Brown, and Company, 1979), 89.

39 Quoted in Nichter, *Richard Nixon and Europe*, 132.

40 Richard Nixon, "Second Annual Report to the Congress on United States Foreign Policy – 25 February 1971," in *Public Papers of the Presidents of the United*

States: Richard M. Nixon, 1971 (Washington, DC: U.S. Government Printing Office, 1972), 232.

41 Richard Nixon, Nixon Tapes, Oval Office 617–007, November 16, 1971, 9:53 a.m.–10:13 a.m. Quoted in Nichter, *Richard Nixon and Europe*, 91.

42 Richard Nixon, Nixon Tapes, Oval Office 570–004, September 11, 1971, 12:07 p.m.–12:53 p.m. Quoted in Nichter, *Richard Nixon and Europe*, 73–74.

43 GRF, Papers of Arthur Burns, Handwritten Journals, 1969–1974, Box 1, April 3, 1973. Quoted in Nichter, *Richard Nixon and Europe*, 123.

44 Richard Nixon, HAK Telecons, Box 12, December 2, 1971, no time indicated. Quoted in Nichter, *Richard Nixon and Europe*, 123.

45 Richard Nixon, "Question-and-Answer Session at the Executive's Club of Chicago–March 13, 1974," in *Public Papers of the Presidents of the United States: Richard M. Nixon, 1974* (Washington, DC: U.S. Government Printing Office, 1975), 276.

46 Thomas Piketty, *Capital in the Twenty-First Century*, trans. Arthur Goldhammer (Cambridge, MA: The Belknap Press of Harvard University Press, 2014), 90.

47 Francis Fukuyama, "The End of History?," *The National Interest*, no. 16 (1989): 4. Also see the extended discussion in his 1992 book: Francis Fukuyama, *The End of History and the Last Man* (New York: Simon & Schuster, 1992).

48 Samuel P. Huntington, "The Clash of Civilizations?," *Foreign Affairs* 72, no. 3 (1993): 22–49, https://doi.org/10.2307/20045621; Samuel P. Huntington, *The Clash of Civilizations and the Remaking of World Order* (New York: Simon & Schuster, 1996).

49 Lawrence S. Finkelstein, "What Is Global Governance?," *Global Governance* 1, no. 3 (1995): 370.

50 See Harlan Cleveland, *Nobody in Charge: Essays on the Future of Leadership* (San Francisco, CA: John Wiley & Sons, 2002); Ingvar Carlsson, *Our Global Neighborhood: The Report of the Commission on Global Governance* (Oxford: Oxford University Press, 1995); Finkelstein, "What Is Global Governance?," 368–370.

51 George Soros, *The Crisis of Global Capitalism: Open Society Endangered* (Boston, MA: Little, Brown, and Company, 1998), XXIII, XVI.

52 Quoted in Nöel Bonhomme, "Between Political Messages and Public Expectations: G7 Summits in French and US Public Opinion (1975–1985)," in *International Summitry and Global Governance: The Rise of the G7 and the European Council, 1974–1991*, ed. Emmanuel Mourlon-Druol and Federico Romero (New York: Routledge, 2014), 92.

53 Angus Maddison, *Two Crises: Latin America and Asia, 1929–1938 and 1973–1983* (Paris: Development Centre of the Organisation for Economic Co-operation and Development, 1985), 13.

54 Angus Maddison, *Explaining the Economic Performance of Nations: Essays in Time and Space* (Aldershot: Edward Elgar, 1995), 84.

55 Angus Maddison, *Monitoring the World Economy, 1820–1992* (Paris: Development Centre of the Organisation for Economic Co-operation and Development, 1995), 62.

56 *Structural Adjustment and Economic Performance*, 229–231.

57 Ibid.

58 Michael Burgess, *Federalism and the European Union: The Building of Europe, 1950–2000* (London and New York: Routledge, 2000), 149.

59 Wayne Sandholtz and John Zysman, "1992: Recasting the European Bargain," *World Politics* 42, no. 1 (1989): 96, https://doi.org/10.2307/2010572.

60 Archive of European Integration, aei.pitt.edu/view/eusubjects/socasp.default.html, 9–10, accessed January 7, 2019.

61 Forecasting and Assessment in the Field of Science and Technology (FAST), *Eurofutures: The Challenges of Innovation–The FAST Report* (London: Butterworths, 1984), XI. Quoted in Wayne Sandholtz, *High-Tech Europe: The Politics of International Cooperation* (Berkeley, CA and Los Angeles, CA: University of California Press, 1992), 160.

62 Sandholtz, *High-Tech Europe*, 1992, 112.
63 Ibid., 104–105.
64 Ibid., 174.
65 Maria Green Cowles, "The Changing Architecture of Big Business," in *Collective Action in the European Union: Interests and the New Politics of Associability*, ed. Mark Aspinwall and Justin Greenwood (Oxon: Routledge, 1998), 112.
66 "The European Economic Community and Changes in the International Division of Labour (Report of an Expert Group on the Reciprocal Implications of the Internal and External Policies of the Community). III/1367–78-EN, January 1979," EU Commission–Working Document (Brussels: Commission of the European Communities, January 1979), 10, http://aei.pitt.edu/33770/1/A328.pdf.
67 Green Cowles, "The Changing Architecture of Big Business," 163–164, 166.
68 Wisse Dekker, *Europe 1990: An Agenda for Change* (Brussels: Chez Philips S.A., 1985), 5. Quoted in Sandholtz and Zysman, "1992," 117.
69 Sandholtz and Zysman, "1992," 116.
70 Adam Harmes, *The Return of the State: Protestors, Power-Brokers and the New Global Compromise* (Vancouver, BC: Douglas & McIntyre, 2004), 126.
71 Adam Smith, *An Inquiry into the Nature and Causes of the Wealth of Nations*, 1st ed., vol. I (London: W. Strahan and T. Cadell, 1776), 456.
72 Karl Marx, *Capital*, ed. Frederick Engels, trans. Samuel Moore and Edward Aveling, vol. I (Chicago, IL: Charles H. Kerr & Company, 1909), 170.
73 Adam Smith, *An Inquiry into the Nature and Causes of the Wealth of Nations*, 1st ed., vol. II (London: W. Strahan and T. Cadell, 1776), 35, http://hdl.handle.net/2027/osu.32435073204638.
74 Schneider, "Organized Interests in the European Telecommunications Sector," 43.
75 Quoted in Terrence Guay, *At Arm's Length: The European Union and Europe's Defence Industry* (Houndmills: Macmillan, 1998), 149–150.
76 Quoted in Guay, *At Arm's Length*, 144.
77 Quoted in Brooks Tigner, "Transatlantic Harmony Faces Many Obstacles," *Defense News* 10, no. 21 (May 29, 1995): 16.
78 David Coen, "The Role of Large Firms in the European Public Policy System: A Case Study of European Multinational Political Activity" (Seattle, WA: ECSA, 1997), http://aei.pitt.edu/2555/1/002846_1.PDF.
79 Maria Green Cowles, "The 'Business' of Agenda-Setting in the European Union" (Fourth Biennial International Conference of the European Community Studies Association, Charleston, 1995), 8, http://aei.pitt.edu/6916/1/cowles_maria_green2.pdf.
80 "Draft Treaty Establishing the European Union," February 14, 1984, 47.1–47.3, www.cvce.eu/obj/draft_treaty_establishing_the_european_union_14_february_1984-en-0c1f92e8-db44-4408-b569-c464cc1e73c9.html.
81 "Completing the Internal Market," White Paper from the Commission to the European Council (Milan: EU Communities, June 14, 1985), 5, COM (85) 310 final, Archive of European Integration, http://aei.pitt.edu/1113/1/internal_market_wp_COM_85_310.pdf.
82 Ibid., 34–35.
83 Darryl C. Thomas, *The Theory and Practice of Third World Solidarity* (Westport, CT: Praeger, 2001), 147.
84 Geoffrey Jones and Harm G. Schröter, eds., "Norwegian Direct Investments Abroad, by Country and Area, 1986–91," in *The Rise of Multinationals in Continental Europe* (Aldershot: Elgar, 1993), 135.
85 Geoffrey Jones, "Multinational Strategies and Developing Countries in Historical Perspective," Working Paper (Cambridge, MA: Harvard University, 2010), 17, www.hbs.edu/faculty/Publication%20Files/10-076_0f98ff7b-1d22-4090-b621-f1a45036a6db.pdf.

86 Heike Klüver, *Interest Group Influence on EU Policy-Making: A Quantitative Analysis across Issues*, Conference Paper (Los Angeles, CA: 11th Biennial Conference of the European Union Studies Association, April 23, 2009), 6, Archive of European Integration, http://aei.pitt.edu/33094/1/kluever._heike.pdf.

87 *Commission Staff Working Document–Accompanying Document to the Trade and Investment Barriers Report 2011*, Working Document (Brussels: European Commission, March 10, 2011), 6, 2, http://aei-dev.library.pitt.edu/46101/1/SEC_(2011)_298.pdf.

88 *Communication* (Brussels: European Commission, 1996), 3, Archive of European Integration.

89 *The Single Market* (Brussels: European Commission, 1996), 10, Archive of European Integration.

90 Quoted in Maja Kluger Rasmussen, "Lobbying the European Parliament: A Necessary Evil," *CEPS Policy Brief*, no. 242 (May 2011): 2.

91 Ibid.

92 Robert Hull, "Lobbying Brussels: A View from Within," in *Lobbying in the European Community*, ed. Sonia Mazey and Jeremy John Richardson (Oxford: Oxford University Press, 1993), 91.

93 Ibid., 88.

94 Communication from the Commission to the Council, *Programme for the Liberalization of Capital Movements in the Community* (Brussels: EU Communities, May 23, 1986), 11, COM(86) 292 final, Archive of European Integration, http://aei.pitt.edu/4029/1/4029.pdf.

95 Frederico Carril-Caccia and Elena Pavlova, "Foreign Direct Investment and Its Drivers: A Global and EU Perspective," *European Central Bank Economic Bulletin*, no. 4 (2018), www.ecb.europa.eu/pub/economic-bulletin/articles/2018/html/ecb.ebart201804_01.en.html.

96 Alan M. Rugman and Simon Collinson, "Multinational Enterprises in the New Europe: Are They Really Global?," *Organizational Dynamics* 34, no. 3 (2005): 258–272, https://doi.org/10.1016/j.orgdyn.2005.06.005.

97 "About the Group," *BNP Paribas*, March 2020, https://group.bnpparibas/en/.

98 Thilo Hanemann and Daniel H. Rosen, "China Invests in Europe" (Rhodium Group, June 2012), 9, https://rhg.com/wp-content/uploads/2012/06/RHG_ChinaInvestsInEurope_June2012.pdf.

99 Neil Fligstein, *Euroclash: The EU, European Identity, and the Future of Europe* (Oxford: Oxford University Press, 2009), 62.

100 European Union, "LUCAS Micro Data 2012," *Eurostat*, 2012, https://ec.europa.eu/eurostat/web/lucas/data/primary-data/2012.

101 "Company Plants," *Volkswagen Slovakia*, https://sk.volkswagen.sk/en/company/plants.html, accessed May 26, 2020.

102 "VW Group Reorganises Its Manufacturing Footprint," *Automotive Manufacturing Solutions*, 2014, 11.

103 Elfriede Grunow-Osswald, *Die Internationalisierung eines Konzerns: Daimler-Benz 1890–1997* (Vaihingen: DaimlerChrysler, 2006), 178, 284, 286, 346, 358–359, 365–367, 373, 376.

104 *Automotive News Europe*, March 7, 2005, 24.

105 David Slotnick, "Airbus Is One of the Most Powerful Companies in Aviation. Here's a Closer Look at Its Rise from Upstart to Industry Titan," *Business Insider Singapore*, March 27, 2020, www.businessinsider.sg/airbus-history-airliner-photos-details-2019-5, accessed January 6, 2020. Also see "Company History," *Airbus*, 2020, www.airbus.com/company/history.html, accessed January 23, 2020.

106 Filippo di Mauro, Hedwig Plamper, and Robert Stehrer, *Global Value Chains: A Case for Europe to Cheer Up*, CompNet Policy Brief (Frankfurt: European Central Bank, August 2013), 6.

107 "World Input-Output Database–July 1996," *University of Groningen Growth and Development Centre*, November 15, 2016, 2, 5, 7, 16, 93, www.rug.nl/ggdc/valuechain/wiod/, accessed November 5, 2018.

108 Rugman and Collinson, "Multinational Enterprises," 6; "Archive," *Metro Group*, accessed May 26, 2020, https://archiv.metrogroup.de/en/; EU Commission, *Green Paper on Vertical Restraints in EC Competition Policy*, COM Document (Brussels: European Union, January 22, 1997), COM (96) 721 final, Archive of European Integration, http://aei.pitt.edu/1147/1/verticle_restraints_gp_COM_96_721.pdf, accessed October 8, 2018.

109 Nicolas Véron, "Farewell National Champions," *Bruegel Policy Brief*, no. 4 (2006): 1.

110 Roger Béteille, William M. Leary, and William F. Trimble, "Airbus, or the Reconstruction of European Civil Aeronautics," in *From Airships to Airbus: Pioneers and Operations*, vol. 1 (Washington, DC: Smithsonian Institution Press, 1995); Matthias Kipping, "European Industrial Policy in a Competitive Global Economy," in *New Challenges to the European Union: Policies and Policy-Making*, ed. Elias Mossialos et al. (Aldershot: Dartmouth Publishing Co., 1997).

111 Dennis Swann, *European Economic Integration: The Common Market, European Union and Beyond* (Cheltenham: Elgar, 1996).

112 Neil B. Murphy, "European Union Financial Developments: The Single Market, the Single Currency, and Banking," *FDIC Banking Review*, n.d., 18; Emiliano Grossman, "Europeanization as an Interactive Process: German Public Banks Meet EU State Aid Policy," *Journal of Common Market Studies* 44, no. 2 (2006): 325–348.

113 Björn Hettne, *Globalization, the New Regionalism and East Asia*, ed. Toshiro Tanaka and Takashi Inoguchi (Hayama: United Nations University Global Seminar '96 Shonan Session, 1996), http://archive.unu.edu/unupress/globalism.html#Globalization, accessed October 8, 2018.

114 Grahame Thompson, "Globalisation versus Regionalism?," *The Journal of North African Studies* 3, no. 2 (June 1998): 62–63, https://doi.org/10.1080/13629389808718320, accessed June 4, 2018.

115 "Treaty on European Union" (Eur-Lex), Official Journal C 191, 29/07/1992 P. 0001–0110, https://eur-lex.europa.eu/eli/treaty/teu/sign, accessed May 26, 2020. European Central Bank, "Five Things You Need to Know about the Maastricht Treaty," *European Central Bank*, February 15, 2017, www.ecb.europa.eu/explainers/tell-me-more/html/25_years_maastricht.en.html, accessed November 7, 2018.

5 Four decades of permanent enlargement of the union and its dangers

As Cold War confrontations after World War II mobilized the United States to build a Western alliance system, American policy naturally aimed to enlarge these alliances as much as possible. The logical first step in building the "alliance of the free world" was the incorporation of Western Europe – which had been liberated and, for a while, militarily controlled by American forces – into the alliance. During the 1950s and 1960s, this goal motivated the United States government to push West European integration with the larger goal of working towards a kind of federal unity. That was, however, only the first step in alliance building. Consecutive American administrations urged the European community to accept new members and incorporate the entire group of countries that had joined the North Atlantic Treaty Organization (NATO), the anti-Soviet and American-led military alliance. When NATO was established in 1949, it had twelve members. Beside the United States and Canada, ten mostly West European countries –Britain, Belgium, Denmark, France, Iceland, Italy, Luxembourg, the Netherlands, Norway, and Portugal – joined. Between 1952 and 1955, Greece, Turkey and the Federal Republic of Germany also joined; Spain followed in 1982. American governments strongly believed that the broadest possible anti-communist alliance was needed, and that all NATO countries could also join the integration process by becoming members of the European Community. They believed that such unification would strengthen and stabilize NATO, and would create strong political cohesion among the member countries. In a speech in Frankfurt, President John Kennedy clearly expressed this traditional American concept: "It is only a fully cohesive Europe that can protect us all against fragmentation of the alliance."[1]

Creating a fully cohesive Europe was not only a noble goal, but also represented an urgent practical need. The inclusion of more and more new members was required for the creation of a more completely, truly integrated Continent. Nevertheless, while there were huge advantages to enlarging the Union, there were severe dangers as well. Including unprepared countries – countries where 'European values' and democratic systems were not valued and practiced – threatened to undermine integration, or at the very least seriously limit its depth. In other words, enlargement and calculated limitation were equally important.

To further qualify the concept of limitation, it is helpful to consider the possibility of various categories of membership. This idea is often expressed by the multispeed model of integration, where two or more groups may be integrated but also separated by different levels of integration, theoretically ranging from a group of mere free-trade-zone members to a group of federally integrated countries. It may also mean different legal statuses and rights in common decisions. Members of the free-trade zone may not have a voice in the decisions of the federalized group. Although this model is a fairly old one in theory, thus far it has not yet been realized. There are EU members in the euro-zone and EU members outside of it. But all EU member countries have the same legal status of full membership. Giving equal membership rights to different categories of participating countries with evidently different interests and goals could halt or even doom the historic process of integration. In this case, unanimous agreements are possible only at the lowest level of interest in integration. Having said that, let's go through in the various waves of enlargement, from the first wave of 1973 to the planned integration steps of the 2020s.

The first enlargement in 1973

According to America's postwar plans, the main pillar of building an allied and integrated west Europe was Britain, the United States' closest wartime and Cold War ally. The Truman administration believed that British leaders would eventually accept the American plan for the integration process. Various pro-integration speeches by Churchill and Atlee, the Tory and Labor leaders during and even after the war, had promised British leadership. Nevertheless, Britain strongly and consistently resisted American pressure and remained outside the integration process during the 1950s. In the center of Britain's interests were the Empire and the Commonwealth. Most of all, the British political elite and even a great part of the generations that came during and after the war, shared the global outlook as their ancestors had hundreds of years before. They had a strong 'island mentality' and still clung on to Britain's old imperial identity, which was only slowly starting to evaporate. They still felt a kind of superiority over the Continental countries and could not imagine being just another one of the European countries. This collective mindset was expressed in the strongest possible terms by Britain's response when the European Economic Community was established. They did not only remain outside, but, as an answer, established a counter-organization, the European Free Trade Association (EFTA), in the spring of 1960. In contrast to the six EEC member countries, Britain and her old trading partners – together with Austria, Denmark, Norway, Portugal, Sweden, and Switzerland – organized the 'outer seven' countries. This response clearly represented both the British hostility against integration and the country's enthusiasm for free trade. EFTA, however, was never as successful as the EEC, and its members did not enjoy the advantages that the members of the European Community did.

Nevertheless, despite these efforts, Britain's great-power identity was soon strongly undermined. For centuries, Britain had able to force its will upon weaker countries through its famous and successful "gunboat diplomacy" tactics. As British diplomat James Cable phrased it in 1971, it was Britain's policy to enact "the use or threat of limited naval force, otherwise than as an act of war, in order to secure advantage or to avert loss, either in the furtherance of an international dispute or else against foreign nationals within the territory or the jurisdiction of their own state."[2]

But in the fall of 1956, for the first time in British history, gunboat diplomacy failed. It actually happened after Gamal Abdel Nasser of Egypt nationalized the Suez Canal, a major waterway for British imperial rule and world trade between the Mediterranean Sea and the Indian Ocean, in July 1956. In response, British, French and Israeli troops jointly attacked Egypt. The Soviet Union sided with Egypt and even threatened atomic war. President Eisenhower warned the British government that for them the imperial project was at an end, and required its ally to withdraw. America even talked about the possibility of economic sanctions if Britain continued the war. In the end, Britain (with her allies) withdrew and Egypt was victorious. This event happened when British colonial power had already melted down considerably since the war. By 1960, it had totally collapsed. Meanwhile, the British pound also lost its status as the world's supreme currency to the American dollar. Great Britain was not really great any longer. Geographically it was now one of many the relatively small European countries; it was not even the strongest of its peers. As a *BBC* opinion article warned in 2013: "Perhaps once we finally smash the mirror we will be able . . . face ourselves shorn of that post-imperial body dysmorphia that continues to make successive British governments punch above their weight on the international stage."[3]

All these were humiliating defeats that weakened, at least temporarily, the longstanding British feeling of superiority. In this depressed atmosphere, the British government changed its traditional attitude and applied for membership in the European Community in 1961. French President de Gaulle, however, maintained that the European "Common Market is incompatible with the economy, as it now stands, of Britain," and if accepted, Britain would continue to collaborate with America and "Atlanticize" Europe.[4] Thus he vetoed British membership. Humiliated, Britain tried again in 1967, only to be rejected again by de Gaulle. After de Gaulle's resignation in 1969, Britain applied third time, and was accepted. It joined the European Community in 1973, accompanied by two of her close trading and business partners, Ireland and Denmark.

However, even after joining the EEC, Britain always remained half-heartedly and hesitantly European. The old British attitude never disappeared. As novelist Robert Harris put it in a 2017 interview with *The Irish Times*, Britain has a tendency to remember to shameful events nostalgically and to feel somewhat superior:

We have, perhaps, a sense of moral superiority which most other countries don't feel. I think that's part of the reason why we find it hard to understand Europe and why Europeans find us mildly irritating; with our constant insistence that somehow we're superior and must be given better deals and opt-outs and special treatments.[5]

Map 5.1 The first enlargement

Source: EC09-1973 European Community map.svg, created by user Kolja 21, CC Attribution-ShareAlike 3.0 Unported, commons.wikimedia.org/wiki/File:EC09-1973_European_Community_map.svg

Indeed, soon after joining, the government held a referendum on whether to stay or leave in 1975. The majority voted to remain. Early on there was only even half-hearted support for, and strong opposition against, plans for connecting Britain to the Continent by the Channel Tunnel. This idea, which had been discussed for several hundred years, finally neared realization in the 1980s when the agreement was reached. The first agreement was made with France to build the Tunnel in 1964, at a time when Britain's self-identification as a great power was in decline after its failure in Egypt and the collapse of the colonial system. As a result, Britain desperately wanted to join the European Community: 69 percent of the population supported the building of the Tunnel, and only 17 percent were against it. But this moment was only one of temporary enthusiasm. By 1985, three years before construction really started, only half of the British population supported the very reasonable and advantageous fast-rail and drive-through connection plan, while 37 percent were against it.[6] This lukewarm support symbolically expressed the British attitude towards being a part of Europe. The governments always refused to fully support the founding idea of the EU, that of an "ever closer union."[7] Britain always wanted only a "family of nations";

an alliance among independent nation states. For the UK, the only attraction was the huge free-market zone, and it always played the role of the brake, obstructing the introduction of supranational institutions and opposing deeper integration. Several times, Britain blocked attempts to develop closer military cooperation. It also opposed the introduction of the common currency and remained outside the euro-zone. The UK also opted out of the Schengen Agreement, which aimed to create a borderless Europe. To avoid further integration, Britain always advocated for further enlargement. The UK encouraged the European Union to accept more, even less prepared, new countries in order to make the Union less homogenous, and thus less able to advance towards further integration. Britain, in other words, always remained more Atlantic than European.

Nothing expresses the British attitude and policies better than Prime Minister Margaret Thatcher's speech in Bruges in 1988. In this famous speech, made when Britain had already been a member of the European Community for one and a half decades, Thatcher declared that "the Community is not an end in itself" and must not act according to "some abstract intellectual concept" and "Utopian goals." The Community must only be an "active cooperation between independent sovereign states." In her view

> To try to suppress nationhood and concentrate power at the centre of a European conglomerate would be highly damaging . . . working more closely together does not require power to be centralised in Brussels or decisions to be taken by an appointed bureaucracy. [Europe had to preserve the] Atlantic community – that Europe on both sides of the Atlantic – which is our noblest inheritance and our greatest strength. . . . Let Europe be a family of nations.[8]

To return, in 1973, the European Community already had nine member countries. At that time, the United States had already become quite successful in pushing the European Community to further enlargement. Nevertheless, that pressure was not enough, as not all the NATO members were accepted by the Community.

The 1980s: the American alliance with Mediterranean dictatorships and the second wave of enlargement

Since the end of the war, American governments had demonstrated its willingness to forge alliances with anti-communist, anti-Soviet governments even if they were anti-democratic, right-wing dictatorships. Following World War II, strategically important Mediterranean countries like Spain, Portugal, Greece and Turkey were all governed by authoritarian, part-military dictatorships. Some of these regimes had existed since the 1930s; some, such as Franco's Spain, had even been in alliance with Hitler and Mussolini. After World War II, these countries did not participate in the democratic transformation of the Continent and became politically isolated pariahs in Europe.

This state of affairs did not influence American attitude, which was well expressed by President Eisenhower when in 1960, speaking on the Salazar regime in Portugal, he took the view that "dictatorships of this type are sometimes necessary in countries whose political institutions are not so far advanced as ours."[9] Communist dictatorships were cursed daily, but anti-communist dictatorships were understandable and acceptable. Winston Churchill, who condemned communist regimes from the high moral standpoint of freedom and human rights, also expressed understanding about the bloody Franco dictatorship in Spain. In his speech about the North Atlantic Treaty in May 1949, Churchill praised Franco's Spain for services and a "most fertile and serviceable trade" during the war. Moreover, he maintained that "the conditions under which people live in Spain give far greater freedom to the individual than those under which they live in Russia." Churchill clearly expressed his reason of understanding when he said: "The absence of Spain from the Atlantic Pact involves, of course, a serious gap in the strategic arrangements for Western Europe."[10] The cynical President Nixon accepted as fact that democracy was inappropriate in Latin America, Africa, Asia and the Third World. Nixon and Kissinger did not even attempt to find explanations for collaboration with anti-democratic, dictatorial regimes. Kissinger maintained that human rights in other countries were not America's business. Nixon explicitly expressed his disinterest: "We cannot gear our foreign policy to transformation of other societies."[11] He said, "We will aid dictators if it is in our interest. . . . Take [Philippines dictator Ferdinand] Marcos – I won't lecture him on his internal structure. . . . Our concern is foreign policy."[12] All in all, human-rights rhetoric against dictatorial communism was not used against dictatorial anti-communist countries. As Helen Graham and Alejandro Quiroga have rightly argued, Spain, Portugal and Greece

> replicated the structural violence and coercion of the Cold War enemy, which meant that they actively undermined the idea of western political superiority and civility. . . . Cold War fears caused the western allies to support repressive regimes on the southern boundaries of "free" Europe. In both Spain and Greece, these international priorities determined the eventual outcomes of civil wars, guaranteeing the survival [of those regimes] . . . . Spain was excluded from Marshall Aid, and a diplomatic embargo enacted. However, by 1953, Spain had got its own US aid package, which underwrote the dictatorship and led Franco himself to declare: "at last I have won the Spanish civil war."[13]

The only aspect that mattered for the Americans and the British was a strong commitment to anti-communism. In their civil wars, Spain and Greece defeated its communist challengers. The latter did so in 1944 with powerful British contributions. When the British government informed President Truman that they were unable to keep control of Greece in 1947, Truman announced American involvement both in terms of massive financial and military assistance. An American military expert explained: "the US interest in Greece was preventing the

Soviet Union from controlling Greece, which would deny the United States access to the strategically important Aegean and eastern Mediterranean Seas and grant it to the Soviet Union."[14] The renewed civil war in Greece between 1947 and 1949 also ended with the defeat of the communists, this time as a result of strong American participation. During and after the civil wars, Greece was controlled by dictatorial right-wing or military governments. The American administration, nevertheless, signed a defense cooperation agreement with Greece in 1953, and American military installations were established.

The US government pushed the newly established European Community to accept Greece as a member. Greece applied for associate membership in 1959. Negotiations, indeed, started with Greece two years after the foundation of the EEC in the fall of 1959, and concluded in March 1961, when the association partnership agreements were signed, "based on a customs union to be established . . . over a transition period and intended to enable Greece to become at a later date, when its economic progress allows, a full member of the Community."[15]

Franco's Spain – isolated by the United States, excluded from the Marshall Aid program, and under a diplomatic boycott after the war – soon became an ally as well. Already in 1947, the US Joint Chiefs of Staff had expressed military interests in Spain. Military planners argued in mid-1947 that the US "should furnish economic aid to Spain as soon as feasible in order to strengthen her capacity for military resistance."[16] In December 1947, the National Security Council's "Report on US Policy toward Spain" announced the reorientation of American policy. In August 1950, a few weeks after the Korean War started, $62.5 million in American aid was sent over to Franco. The regime's isolation ended, and with US assistance, Spain joined the Organisation for European Economic Co-operation (OEEC) in late 1950.[17] On 26 September 1953, the preamble of an agreement between the United States and Spain on establishing American military facilities in Spain stated:

> Faced with the danger that threatens the western world, the Governments of the United States and Spain, desiring to contribute to the maintenance of international peace and security through foresighted measures which will increase their capability, and that of the other nations which dedicate their efforts to the same high purposes, to participate effectively in agreements for self-defense.

In exchange for American military bases in Spain, the US agreed to support

> Spanish defense efforts for agreed purposes by providing military end item assistance to Spain . . . to contribute to the effective air defense of Spain and to improve the equipment of its military and naval forces . . . and with the cooperation of the resources of Spanish industry to the extent possible.[18]

Between 1953 and 1961, Franco's Spain was incorporated into the "Western world," receiving $1.4 billion in aid and becoming the third largest recipient of

American assistance in Europe. The American government pushed the European Economic Community to include Franco's Spain as well. One year after the US-Spanish agreement, Helmut Burckhardt, the vice-president of the Consultative Committee of the European Coal and Steel Community, described in a Pittsburgh speech his vision for an enlarged Community with "the eventual inclusion of Scandinavia, Spain, Portugal," and others.[19]

The American Cold War policy was having its influence. When dictatorial Franco's Spain made its first applications for membership in the EEC in 1959 and 1962, the Community (although it did shelve these politically inconvenient applications for a while) eventually

> signed a Preferential Commercial Agreement with Spain . . . with highly favorable terms. European tariffs were immediately and substantially reduced by 60 percent. . . . The goal was to establish completely free trade, and all quantitative restrictions against Spanish exports were removed . . . Spain. . . [became] an "external" member of the European Community.[20]

The situation was similar regarding Turkey, whose location on the Dardanelles Straits – which controls access from the Black Sea to the Mediterranean and between the Soviet Union and the Middle East – made it a key country in Cold War politics. Turkey was a traditionally anti-Russian country, as it had fought several wars against Russia over the course of many centuries. Although Turkey was not a democracy and its political system was based on one-party rule, free elections were held in 1950, 1954 and 1957. Five governments run by Adnan Menderes followed, one upon the other. However, in delicate political situations, the army did not hesitate to launch military coup – as happened in 1960, 1971 and 1980 – which was often accompanied by massacres, such as those that took place in Bahçelievla, Taksim, and Kahramanmaraş. From the 1960s on, after Cyprus became independent, Turkish confrontations with Greece about Cyprus became a permanent source of political crisis and aggression. Regardless of these problems, the United States included Turkey in its military defense strategy and pushed Europe to build a close alliance with the country. As George McGhee, the American ambassador to Turkey, stated in a 1954 article in *Foreign Affairs*:

> The successful visit to the United States in February of this year of President Bayar of Turkey, at President Eisenhower's invitation, has highlighted one of the most significant political events of our times –Turkey's emergence as a full and responsible member of the Western alliance.[21]

This process actually started with the Truman Doctrine, the US-Turkish Ankara Agreement and then the Marshall Plan. Turkey's NATO membership failed in 1950 because Norway and Denmark voted against it, but it was realized after the Korean War. In 1951, the country was invited to join the Middle East Command to preserve the Western position at the Suez Canal. In 1954, the Balkan Pact, signed by Turkey along with Greece and Yugoslavia, set up protections against a potential Soviet aggression, and in July 1958, the IMF rushed to put together a 359 million-dollar economic-stabilization program to assist the country.

On 5 January 1957, President Eisenhower sent a message to the American Congress about the policy of protecting the countries of the Near East from Soviet danger. In March, Congress accepted the Eisenhower Doctrine, as well as the formation of the so-called Central Eastern Treaty Organization (CENTO) with the participation of Turkey, Iran and Pakistan. Turkey served as a bridge between the NATO and CENTO, and became a main player in Western Cold War policy in the area. Eisenhower invited the Turkish President to visit the US in 1959, and he visited Turkey at the end of the same year, the year of the American-Turkish Bilateral Treaty.[22] This close connection did not suffer any setbacks after the Turkish military coup of May 1960, launched by US-trained Turkish officers. The coup eliminated the democratically elected government and executed Prime Minister Menderes, along with some other members of his government.

As Eisenhower reiterated, America's prime concern remained its alliance with Turkey. He stated that it was "the best possible way to buttress US security interest in the Near East."[23] The two countries signed an agreement on the deployment of American Jupiter missiles in Turkey[24] and offered more economic and military aid to the dictatorial military regime.[25] American governments never ceased to urge the European Economic Community to admit Turkey. As an expert of the Congressional Research Service argued in a 2012 report:

> Successive U.S. Administrations and many Members of Congress have long backed EU enlargement, believing that it serves U.S. interests by advancing democracy and economic prosperity throughout the European continent. Over the years, the only significant U.S. criticism of the EU's enlargement process has been that the Union was moving too slowly, especially with respect to Turkey, which Washington believes should be anchored firmly to Europe.[26]

Successive American governments had always argued that NATO membership should be an entrance ticket for European-Community membership. This view is clearly expressed in a Congressional Research Service document regarding Turkish membership in the European Community:

> The United States believes that Turkey's membership in NATO has demonstrated that Turkey can interact constructively with an organization dominated by most of the same European countries that belong to the EU. . . . The US has been disappointed that it has not been able to use its influence to help shape a more constructive EU – Turkey relationship.[27]

At last, the American insistence worked, and in 1963, Turkey and the EEC signed the Ankara Association Agreement, which marked the beginning of the process of building close ties. This agreement was supplemented by an Additional Protocol, signed in 1970, which prepared the way for a customs union.

The acceptance of the Mediterranean countries as full members, however, only happened during in the 1980s, after all the three dictatorships collapsed in the miraculous year of 1974. In Greece, as a consequence of political turmoil caused by the Turkish invasion of Cyprus, the military junta lost power in July 1974. In January of the next year, its leading embers were sentenced to death, and the country turned to parliamentary democracy. From 1 January 1981, the country became a member of the EU.

In Spain – in what could only be described as an extraordinary and accidental historical coincidence – the bloody-handed dictator Francisco Franco, who had ruled the country for a third of a century, also died in July 1974. After rapid and successful regime change and adjustment to the formal requirements of the European Community, Spain became a full member on 1 January 1986.

Portugal was ruled by the ironhanded corporatist-authoritarian Estado Novo regime and its head, António de Oliveira Salazar, from 1932 to 1968. Even after his stroke and death in 1970, Estado Novo's regime remained in power; it was headed by regent Marcello José Caetano. In April during the miraculous year of 1974, however, the *Revolução dos Cravos*, or Carnation Revolution of the Portuguese army, ended the dictatorship. After half a century, the first free election

Map 5.2 The enlargement of the 1980s

Source: EC12-1986 European Community map.svg, created by user Kolja 21, CC Attribution-ShareAlike 3.0 Unported, commons.wikimedia.org/wiki/File:EC12-1986_European_Community_map.svg

directed the country towards a democratic transformation. Portugal applied for membership in 1977, signed a pre-adhesion treaty in 1980, and became a member of the European Community in 1986.

In spite of their rapid acceptance into the European Community within a decade of transformation, the new Mediterranean democracies were not really well prepared for full membership. After enduring four to five decades of dictatorships, their democratic transformation was not complete at the time of joining. This "New Southern Europe," as the authors of the book *Rethinking Democratization in Spain, Greece and Portugal* rightly put it, "lacked any consideration of grassroots movements and civil society as decisive ingredients of democratisation."[28] Major social and economic illnesses, such as the traditional plight of corruption, generated some doubts about these new admitters among the older member states. The average economic level (GDP per capita) of the three countries was also much lower – it was hardly more than $9,000, or only about 60 percent of the West European average. Because of these facts, "their accession was not embraced wholeheartedly. Especially French president François Mitterrand, who had opposed it initially, was afraid that the countries were not ready for membership."[29] But in the end, despite such qualms, the European Community was enlarged by three new members.

Turkey's acceptance remained more problematic and uncertain because the country was unable to accomplish the required reforms regarding the rule of law, human rights, gender equality and a new democratic constitution. Thus, an endless delay followed. Despite the country's application for membership in 1959, Turkey had to wait four decades until 1999 to be recognized as an official candidate.[30] Nevertheless, even that was too early. The country's membership did not follow, and Turkey, as often before, became an authoritarian dictatorship again after the attempted and defeated military coup in the summer of 2016. That event definitively foreclosed the possibility of Turkey joining the EU.

The 1990s: third wave of enlargement

The collapse of the Soviet Union and the end of the Cold War opened a new chapter in the enlargement of the European Union. First, some of the neutral countries that traditionally were not allowed to join any bloc formation that would endanger their neutrality decided to join in the early 1990s. That included a group of very economically advanced and rich countries: Sweden, Finland, Switzerland, Austria and Norway. They joined the British-initiated free-trade zone, EFTA, in 1960, but now wanted to be part of the rising EU. All of the applicant countries held referendums about the issue. Their populations were quite divided. In Austria, two-thirds voted to join; but in Sweden, only less than 53 percent did so. In two countries, however–Switzerland and Norway – the majority voted against joining (in the latter case, less than 53 percent of the voting population was against membership). Somewhat later, Iceland – after its application for membership during the 2008 crisis – also decided not to join.

In Western Europe, the group of countries that voted down full membership all integrated into the EU, although to different extents. Iceland, Norway and

Liechtenstein participate directly in the Single Market via the European Economic Area; Switzerland does so via bilateral treaties; and the other European neighboring microstates (Andorra, Monaco, San Marino and Vatican City) have specific agreements with the EU, which include elements of integration such as their use of the euro as their currency. Most of these countries are also part of the Schengen Area. While this integration is designed as a substitute for full membership, there are ongoing debates in a number of these countries as to whether they should join as full members. In spite of rejecting full membership, they have all developed elements of intensive integration with the EU.

In the end, three new countries–Sweden, Finland and Austria – became members of the European Union in 1995. The EU grew by 22 million people and nearly 900,000 square kilometers area. Together with Denmark, which joined earlier with Britain, this strong northwestern block strengthened the Continent's integration.[31]

The Nordic countries also started advocating for the acceptance of the newly liberated former Soviet republics, which became independent Baltic countries. These Nordic and Baltic areas have long historical connections with one another. Some of the Baltic areas belonged to Scandinavian countries in earlier centuries. The Nordic Council had already contacted the Baltic countries in 1989, when the

Map 5.3 The enlargement of the 1990s

Source: EU15-1995 European Union map.svg, derivative work created by user Kolja 21 based on Europe_countries.svg created by Júlio Reis, CC Attribution-ShareAlike 2.5, commons. wikimedia.org/wiki/File:EU15-1995_European_Union_map.svg

independence movement erupted there. Official cooperation started immediately in 1991, and in 1992, an official cooperation agreement was signed between the Nordic Council and the Baltic Assembly to form the so-called Nordic-Baltic Eight: Denmark, Finland, Sweden, Norway, Iceland, Estonia, Latvia and Lithuania. The Nordic countries were the first to open their borders and introduce visa-free regimes with the Baltics, and they supported the newly independent countries' recuperation and acceptances into the EU.

The end of the Cold War: a new opening towards the East

The possibility of the Baltic countries joining the European Union arose after the collapse of communism and the Soviet Union. That was also the case with the former Soviet Bloc countries in Central Europe, in the Balkans, and even in the western part of the former Soviet Union, where independent countries were established and looked to Europe as a new home. After the nearly half a century of Cold War confrontation, optimism filled the air. This new zeitgeist of hope was expressed clearly (though extremely naively) by American President George H. W. Bush in a speech at the United Nations General Assembly on 1 October 1990. He welcomed the end of a divided world and described its supposed transformation into a "whole world whole and free." As the head of the remaining only superpower, he spoke about a new world order of "partnership based on consultation, cooperation and collective action."[32] He talked about "shared commitment among nations, large and small."[33] A member of his government, Lawrence Eagleburger, the Deputy Secretary of State, also emphasized the importance of enlarging the group of Western democracies: "What we need to do now is to widen this circle to include many new members of the Democratic family.[34]

In the same spirit, for the first time in the history of European integration, the opening towards the previously hostile Soviet Bloc – now considered the eastern half of an integrating Continent – was initiated by the European Community itself. Jacques Delors went to Bruges in October 1989. The communist regime had already collapsed in Poland, and Hungary was set to hold free elections for the first time as well. European Commission's President Delors argued:

> The Twelve [EEC member countries] cannot control history but they are now in a position to influence it once again. They did not want Europe to be cut in two at Yalta and made a hostage in the Cold War. They did not, nor do they, close the door to other European countries. . . . The present upheavals in Eastern Europe are changing the nature of our problems . . . all the countries of Europe will benefit from the stimulus and the advantages of a single market. . . . [The Community has to help] the countries of Eastern Europe to modernize their economies.[35]

As this speech expressed, European leaders felt some degree of moral obligation. The West had left Central and Eastern Europe alone and had remained silent when some of those countries revolted. The "Yalta guilt complex" became a factor in the European reaction to the fall of communism. Europe, added German Chancellor Helmut Kohl, must not "disappoint the trust that these countries have put in us."[36] However, Europe's readiness to consider the future membership of the Central and Eastern European countries was not primarily a moral question. A new incentive, or even imperative, emerged: the regionalization of Europe as a defense against globalization. In the new world economy, as Delors stressed in the same speech, nations cannot act alone. The reality of that new world system, he argued, was that the "growing interdependence of our economies, the internationalization of the financial world. . . [made] full national sovereignty" a fiction. Europe had to consider "worldwide geopolitical and economic trends."[37]

Globalization around the turn of the millennium sharpened international competition. Beside the United States, Japan and the "Small Asian Tigers," as well as two "Large Asian Elephants" (China and India), had also entered the ring. This situation required a stronger, better integrated and more regionalized European Union. Further enlargement offered a huge advantage. Absorbing 100–200 million new, hungry consumers; a rapidly growing market; and the large, cheap, well-trained labor force next door increased the possibility for competitive exports and strengthened the economy of scale. The possibility of opening the formerly closed eastern half of the Continent and enlarging the European Union by adding the countries of Central Europe, the Balkans and the western territories of the former Soviet Union (now independent republics) offered the opportunity to neutralize one of the major disadvantages for Western Europe in relation to worldwide competition. The EU's main rivals in the global economy, the United States and Japan, already had important backyards in Latin America and Asia; Western Europe, before 1989, had nothing of the sort. By enlarging towards Eastern Europe, this disadvantage would disappear, and the Union could build a backyard with millions of well-trained and cheap workers.

Berkeley University economist, Barry Eichengreen compares the situation with the postwar American experience: after World War II, when the economic center of the United States shifted to the South, America benefited from the South's lower level of unionization, more competitive wage levels, more flexible labor market and liberal land-use policy, which helped "greenfield" investments. He states, "It is fair to ask whether the EU's expansion to the East could have a similarly invigorating effect."[38]

Britain's opposition against further integration and federalization also aided this courageous enlargement towards the east. Britain, along with Demark, advocated for further and further enlargements and the acceptances of countries that were significantly different than their Western counterparts in order to build roadblocks for further supranationalization and federalization. The complex, diverse interests of the members of the European Union opened the door for former Soviet Bloc countries. Most of those countries had never had real parliamentary democracies; they also did not have market economies, and had to set out upon on the long road towards marketization, democratization and civil-society building. Even though their economies were backwards and in ruin, they offered the possibility of a grand new opening for the Union.

Perry Anderson went even further than attributing Western Europe's interest purely to economics: quoting the Polish theorist Jan Zielonka's book *Europe as Empire*, he maintains that enlargement's

> "design was truly imperialist: power politics at its best, even though the term 'power' was never mentioned in the official enlargement discourse" – this was a "benign empire in action". . . . The emergence of the Union may be regarded as the last great world-historical achievement of the bourgeoisie . . . and what has happened to it as a strange declension from what was hoped from it.[39]

In reality, this enlargement equally served the interests of the old member countries and as well as those of the newly accepted eastern European ones because it significantly accelerated the catching-up process of the less developed members.

The 2000s: the fourth enlargement wave, three groups of potential members

At the same time as the collapse of communism (as early as April 1990 at a Dublin meeting), the European Council approved outlines for association agreements with the former communist countries. When the European Council met in Maastricht in December 1991, the Union signed the Europe Agreement – a new version of the association agreements that had been previously signed with the Mediterranean countries – with Poland, Hungary and Czechoslovakia. The next month, the Strasbourg summit decided to work out proposals, and offered immediate economic assistance for the associated countries. In May 1992, negotiations on a similar deal, the Europe Agreement, began with Bulgaria and Romania, and somewhat later with Slovenia and the Baltic states. This set of agreements took effect between 1994 and 1996.[40] At that time, the Central European countries' economic strength only reached roughly 30 percent that of the Western Europe. In some of these countries, the situation was even direr: Bulgaria's economy was only about one-tenth of Western Europe's; Ukraine and Moldova both declined into chaos and Third World poverty.[41] The Union had never considered accepting countries that were so relatively economically backward before.

The Maastricht Treaty on European Union states that any European country may apply for membership if it respects the democratic values of the EU and is committed to promoting them. In the summer of 1994, the Union's Commission clearly reaffirmed this idea as the goal of the Europe Agreements as well:

> The goal for the period before accession should be the progressive integration of the political and economic systems, as well as the foreign and security policies of the associated countries and the Union . . . to create an increasingly unified area.[42]

Indeed, the European Union assisted a gradual progressive integration. As László Andor, a former EU Commissioner, explained:

> the candidate countries already receive pre-accession funds, and benefit from visa liberalisation. Investment is also facilitated to them by the European Bank for Reconstruction and Development, which turned out to be keen to diminish its involvement in countries that have already joined the EU. On the other hand, free movement of labour and full agricultural subsidies did not come at once for the Eastern "new member states," they did not immediately join the eurozone, and many of them did not immediately enter the Schengen zone either. Altogether, *the enlargement process is by definition a transition process* [emphasis in original].[43]

As Martin Dangerfield concluded in his 2007 study, the European Union "has, by virtue of various modes of engagement, regionalized post-communist Europe into three distinct groups of states, each of which reflects different orders of priority and varied levels of privilege in EU relations."[44] The first group included Central Europe and some of the Balkan countries, the second was the West Balkans, and the third was composed of the western former Soviet republics. In a very direct and rare gesture, in June 1993 the Copenhagen Council mentioned the countries of Central and Eastern Europe as potential candidates, and laid down the exact criterion for their membership:

> The associated countries in central and eastern Europe that so desire shall become members of the European Union . . . as soon as an associate country is able to assume the obligations of membership by satisfying the economic and political conditions required.[45] [Furthermore,] membership requires that the candidate country has achieved stability of institutions guaranteeing democracy, the rule of law, human rights and respect for and protection of minorities, the existence of a functioning market economy as well as the capacity to cope with competitive pressure and market forces within the Union.[46]

At a December 1994 meeting in Essen, the European Council exactingly summed up the requirements for membership in the so-called *acquis communautaire*, a huge body of laws and rules, and presented these guidelines to the Central and Eastern European applicants. At that time, it was comprised of thirty-one chapters that took up some 80,000 pages. A huge set of Union laws and regulations had to be implemented and integrated into each country's laws, including market legislation, intellectual property protections, veterinary and plant health inspections, and industrial product testing. The supremacy of Union norms over existing national ones required the creation of new institutional and administrative structures, and often the enactment of new constitutional amendments.

The first phase of the negotiations constituted a screening process about the potential for adjustment by the candidates. Throughout this period of negotiations, the Commission monitored and controlled the candidates' progress in applying EU legislation and meeting its other commitments.[47] In the second phase, the terms of each country's entry were determined, and negotiations concluded in a draft Accession Agreement. If approved by the European Council, this document was ratified and the candidate became a member of the Union. The time between the application and ratification varied from between three to nine years.

Central Europe and the Baltics: thirteen countries join

The first group of countries from the Central European and Baltic regions presented their applications beginning in March 1994. Hungary was the first, followed a month later by Poland, Latvia, Estonia, and Lithuania. Bulgaria applied in the fall and winter of 1995, and the Czech Republic and Slovenia did so in 1996. All the applicants were thoroughly screened: the Commission sent a 200-page questionnaire about legislative achievements and general progress during the adjustment process in April 1996, with a demanding deadline of July that same year. Detailed answers were required about the entire process. Poland's response report came to 2,600 pages, for example; Bulgaria's, completed somewhat later, comprised 5,000 pages.

The Commission issued an "Opinion" document on the applications in July 1997, in which it pronounced Poland, Hungary, the Czech Republic, Estonia, Slovenia and Cyprus ready for negotiations. Slovakia, Bulgaria, Romania, Latvia and Lithuania required more preparation. At a European Council meeting in Luxembourg, the organization decided to begin the accession process in December of that year. Five more countries joined the group of candidates in February 2000, when negotiations opened with Slovakia, Latvia, Lithuania, Bulgaria and Romania.[48] Eventually, the Central European former communist countries joined the European Union in three steps. In 2004, Poland, Hungary, the Czech Republic, Slovakia, Slovenia, Estonia, Latvia, Lithuania, Cyprus and Malta became members. In 2007, Romania and Bulgaria followed; in 2013, Croatia joined.

In 2014, ten years after the first wave of those entries, a European Commission analysis entitled "25 years after the fall of the Iron Curtain: The state of integration of East and West in the European Union," retrospectively analyzed the outcome. Besides registering positive developments, the progress of new member countries and the increased cooperation between East and West, the report honestly detailed the serious shortcomings or even failures of that first chapter of Eastern enlargement. I quote this important document at length:

> Even after 25 years of democracy and 10 years of EU membership, some problematic issues persist or, indeed loom even larger in several of these new Member States: intolerance and populism, attempts at discrediting democratic policy making, corruption, as well as regular political eruptions regarding the status of minorities and their rights. These backlashes may be. . . [caused by] democratising too fast, too soon, without rooting far-reaching reforms in local mentalities. . . . The societies and political elites of the countries manifest a

Map 5.4 The enlargement of the 2000s

Source: EUCROA.png, created by user JLogan, commons.wikimedia.org/wiki/File:EUCROA.png

sceptical attitude and even resistance towards integration into larger, multi-state structures, as such integration is traditionally perceived as foreign domi-nance. . . . Democracy is not only a set of institutions and rights it also a set of practices and a state of mind. . . . [There is] a general disillusionment with the often scandal-ridden ruling political elite and in general the new style of poli-tics. . . . As a vibrant civil society is crucial to democracy, these developments make democracies in the CEE more vulnerable and less stable.

Furthermore, as the report lays out,

Populism in Central and Eastern Europe often seems to combine national-ist and social elements of demagogy . . . which repeatedly challenge, if not

destabilise, the existing democratic institutions. . . . Corruption has significant political costs and can even lead to autocratic political leadership and
economic stagnation at the same time. . . . The danger of state capture (when
external private interests take over public policy formation) seems to be a
recurrent phenomenon in some Eastern European countries as shown by
countries like Bulgaria, Croatia, Hungary, Romania and Slovakia. . . . [It] is
often linked with organised crime. However, fighting corruption is difficult
because of the involvement of high-ranking officials, attempts by governments to legalise the use of public funds for private purposes. . . [and as such]
political and economic entrepreneurs may occupy the state from inside and
regulate corruption.

Therefore, this study concludes,

> One of the major lessons of East Central European politics is that democratic
> institutions and regular elections may not always be enough. . . . Moreover,
> in recent times, the role of elites in some of these countries has appeared
> questionable or even controversial in relation to democratic standards and
> institutions. . . . EU institutions are not sufficiently prepared and authorised
> to monitor and sanction non-compliance with the rules, norms and funda-
> mental values of the EU in an efficient way, once a Member State does not
> keep its voluntary obligations.[49]

In 2020, the picture is even darker. Some members of the so-called Visegrád Four
group – composed of Hungary, Poland, the Czech Republic, and Slovakia – that
pocketed billions in EU aid, are trying to undermine further integration. They
want to limit the Community to a simple common market of independent nation
states, and regularly launch anti-EU attacks.

Does the EU accept unprepared countries? My answer to this question is definitely "yes." The Central European countries were not well prepared, and they
definitely needed much more time for establishing themselves as relatively stable
democracies. Consequently, was it a mistake for the enlargement of the 2000s to
happen that early? In certain respects my answer to this question is "no." Membership in the Union helped both post-communist transformation and catalyzed
the catching-up process, as well as jump-starting the creation of a broad regionalized community in Europe. This enlargement was advantageous for all old and
new members, from the East and West alike.

Nevertheless, the EU made two *major mistakes* when it accepted the Central
European countries as *full* members. First of all, after seriously monitoring the
completion of potential members' acceptance requirements (the *acquis communautaire*), they stopped monitoring the realization of further policies and actions
in the newly accepted countries. They also did not sanction punishing new members for the negation of European values, such as turning away from democratic
practices and the rule of law by returning back to their more traditional authoritarian practices. After their acceptance into the European Union, there was no

control at all. Several of the new members immediately stopped pursuing several much-needed adjustments that they had been required to do before acceptance, such as fighting against corruption. Some of them even eliminated the institutions that were responsible for enacting such changes, some openly allied with anti-EU Russia, and turned relatively quickly back to authoritarian practices.

This negative turn could have been avoided if the newly accepted but underprepared countries could have acquired a somewhat *different status* at first, instead of full membership. This intermediary status would ideally provide all the advantages of integration – the countries of the region could remain in a special group and acquire special legal status – while they were continuing to work towards full membership, without the fear that such countries would regress, creating harm and negatively influencing common decisions. This special status would give more time to stabilize new members, while enabling them to enjoy all the advantage of membership. The EU, however, did not create this special kind of status, and gave full membership to several countries too early.

The postponed acceptance of the West Balkans

As noted earlier, the European Union was more cautious with some areas of Central and Eastern Europe. It pursued three different approaches with respect to countries that wanted to join the EU. Countries in the eastern half of the Continent, the west Balkans, and western former Soviet countries that had become independent republics, were all considered different groups.

While thirteen Central European, Baltic, and Balkan countries were accepted, the countries of the west Balkans – Serbia, Bosnia, Macedonia, Montenegro, Albania, and later independent Kosovo – remained behind. Yugoslavia was buried by the civil war until 1995, and most of the successor countries (except Slovenia and Croatia) were in terribly bad shape. They applied for membership later. Albania and Serbia both applied in December 2009, and, at that time the European Commission signaled the possibility of their acceptance in 2015. The Serbia-Kosovo agreement in the spring of 2013 opened a road for both countries to join as well. Montenegro, having applied at the end of 2008, became a candidate in 2010; and the goal was for it to become a member before 2020.[50] The future acceptances of all these countries definitely influence considerations of security and peace. It also promises yet another extension of the EU backyard with all the economic advantages it provides, both for accepted countries and for the more advanced, older members of the EU. Yet such acceptances remained problematic for a long time.

Although these countries were not immediately accepted, their membership was not rejected either. It was postponed because the EU correctly recognized that the need for a longer period of preparation. These countries' average per capita income level reached only one-tenth of the West European average, even in 2018. With this kind of economic disparity, a true economic integration of equals is hardly imaginable. In those transitional years, the EU enacted its Stabilization and Association Process (SAP) in the western Balkan countries. It turned out that the transformation of those countries was even more difficult than anticipated, and membership was postponed much longer than originally planned. To provide a typical example, I quote from the EU regular annual progress report of 2013 about one of the candidate countries:

> There is 48% increase of corruption reports filed with the prosecutors' offices throughout Bosnia and Herzegovina. . . . [Based on the progress from 2012 to 2013, the country] is at an early stage in the fight against corruption. . . . [The country] has made limited progress in the fight against organised crime and terrorism. . . . Bosnia and Herzegovina remains a source of arms and ammunitions for criminal groups operating in the EU and Western Balkans region. Organised crime activities are mainly linked to illicit drugs trafficking, arms trafficking, economic crime, trafficking in human beings and money laundering.[51]

The Commission's 130-page report on Montenegro reflected a similar picture.[52] In 2014, the Commission's newly elected President, Jean-Claude Juncker, reacted to widespread criticism and opposition against further enlargement, stating that "negotiations would continue, but no further enlargement will take place over the next five years."[53]

The case of the western former Soviet republics

The third approach, that taken with respect to the group of western successor states to the former Soviet Union – Ukraine, Moldova, and Belarus – was even more cautious, although the EU definitely wanted to include them into the European integration system. In 1996, the European Commission expressed the desire to add Ukraine to "the European architecture drawn up by the Copenhagen European Council, to develop partnership relations with Ukraine."[54] From the Union's perspective, the integration of Ukraine would create political conditions that would prevent "any possible return to the former ways," or that would "loosen the grip of dependence upon their powerful neighbour [Russia]."[55] A few days later, the Council of Ministers envisioned incorporating Ukraine into the EU orbit. It stated its wish "to see the Partnership and Cooperation Agreement. . . [to] establish the fundamental basis for a privileged partnership with Ukraine."[56]

Thus, Cold War competition continued in a different way after the end of that confrontation. The West wanted to attract former parts of the Soviet Union, now independent countries, and bring them into the Western world. This goal was clearly demonstrated in 2002, when President George W. Bush offered a Membership Action Plan, a quasi-invitation to enter the NATO alliance, to Ukraine in order to incorporate it into the Western military organization. This invitation was a major strategic mistake and a clear provocation to Russia. Nevertheless, Ukraine president Viktor Yushchenko and Prime Minister Yulia Tymoshenko signed a statement of intention to join NATO in 2008. In the summer of 2010, however, the Ukrainian parliament voted down this plan.

In April 2007, the European Commission acknowledged its economic interests in incorporating even more former Soviet territories into the EU's sphere of interests. It presented its "Black Sea Initiative" to the European Council and the Parliament. The Commission noted that "the Black Sea region is a distinct geographical area rich in natural resources and strategically located at the junction of Europe, Central Asia and the Middle East," and it argued that the EU's presence in the Black Sea region "opens a window on fresh perspectives and opportunities."[57]

Several former Soviet republics were, indeed, waiting before the door, having already signed so-called Partnership Agreements offered by the EU. The very first agreement to sign was with Ukraine, in June 1996, followed shortly thereafter by Russia. These agreements envisioned the creation of a free-trade zone, to have come into being in 1998. The EU and its member countries assisted the transformation of the partner countries by sending financial support. Ukraine and Russia together received €4 billion between 1991 and 1997, either directly from the EU (€1.5 billion), or from member states acting individually. The Union wanted a peaceful transformation and friendly contacts with the region.[58]

Russia, however, soon turned onto a different and independent road, one that was hostile and anti-EU. On the other hand, Ukraine, Moldova, Georgia and some other successor states of the Soviet Union wanted more than just a loose association with the European Union: they looked to it as a new home. As Nicolae Timofti, the president of Moldova, phrased it, signing a political and free-trade agreement with the European Union "is the only chance that Moldova has in order to develop itself as a European country and in the European spirit."[59]

In 2003, an inter-parliamentary forum was established to build contacts among the EU Parliament and the national parliaments of Ukraine, Moldova, Belarus, Armenia, Azerbaijan and Georgia. These States also participated in the EU's Eastern Partnership program, the Organization of the Black Sea Economic Cooperation, and the Community of Democratic Choice. All were established to promote European integration. In January 2002, the European Parliament stated that Armenia and Georgia could enter the EU in the future. In 2014, the EU signed Association Agreements with Georgia, Moldova and Ukraine, and the European Parliament passed a resolution recognizing the "European perspective" of all three countries.

These former Soviet republics, of course, were extremely far from being prepared for EU participation. They had never had a democratic parliamentary system in their entire history. Economically, they were in ruins. Together, the Ukrainian and Moldovan average per-capita income level was only about 5 percent of the West European average in 2018. At that level of backwardness, real economic integration is out of question. Moreover, Russia did not hesitate to take action to reestablish its own sphere of interest by placing open and often brutal political pressure on these countries, and by blackmailing them whenever they seem to be moving too close to the EU. In August 2013, for example, as a kind of warning, Putin stopped imports from Ukraine, stating that the situation might become permanent were Ukraine to sign further agreements with the European Union. The Russians did not hesitate to say that signing such an agreement would be 'suicidal' for Ukraine. Russia also banned wine imports from Moldova and threatened to stop exporting oil if that country signed an agreement.

Moreover, the Russian government even initiated a competitive bloc organization, the Eurasian Customs Union, and tried to persuade the former Soviet-satellite countries that joining with Russia, Kazakhstan and Belarus would be more productive for them. Armenia, strongly dependent on its huge neighbor, soon gave up its efforts to gain EU partnership and in August 2013, joined the Russia-led customs union instead.[60]

The leader of Ukraine, President Viktor Yanukovych, presided over a divided country: the Ukrainian-speaking, Catholic population of the western half wanted to belong Europe; while the Russian-speaking, Russian Orthodox half in the eastern parts wanted to align with Russia. As such, Yanukovych declined to sign the association agreement offered by the EU and turned to Russia instead in November 2013. Endless demonstrations began, leading to the outbreak of a revolution in February 2014 that ousted Yanukovych from the presidency.[61] The pro-Europe demonstrators in Kiev proclaimed: "We want to live in Europe." But the dream of EU membership harbored by the majority of the population of western Ukraine was not shared by the majority of population of eastern and southern Ukraine, nor by those in the ethnically Russian-dominated Crimean Peninsula. The Putin government immediately began frightening military exercises on the Ukrainian-Russian border. Then Russian troops entered Crimea, which had a 60-percent Russian population majority and contained an important Russian naval base. Ukraine lies in Russia's historic sphere of interest, although the West did not want to accept that fact.

By offering associate membership to Ukraine in 2013, the European Union repeated the earlier mistake made by the United States and NATO. The Ukrainian civil war and the Russian intervention in 2014 created an international political crisis. If over-enlargement of the European Union is more than controversial in general, then attempting to include a stridently divided and extremely unstable Ukraine just might be suicidal. Speaking on the question of eastward enlargement, Giscard d'Estaing, the former president of France, was already arguing in 2004 "that this enlargement will water down the community is not a risk but a certainty."[62]

The attempt to enlarge the Union by incorporating former Soviet territories was a severe mistake, but at least the EU did not initiate the procedure for providing membership status. Towards the western newly independent states – Ukraine, Moldova and Belarus – the EU initiated the European Neighborhood Policy (ENP). This collective did not offer EU membership, but did entail advanced integration. All states in this group signed a Partnership and Co-operation Agreement (PCA) with the EU. The Partnership, based on the respect of democratic principles and human rights, set out the political, economic, and trade relationships between the EU and its partner countries in a ten-year bilateral treaty that was signed and ratified by the EU and the individual states. Six partnership states – Armenia, Azerbaijan, Belarus, Georgia, Moldova and Ukraine – are also participants in the Neighborhood Policy agreement.

As one scholar states:

> According to the official European Commission view, ENP is, for now at least, a "concrete alternative to enlargement" that provides for a major step forward in the EU's engagement and a device for inclusion based on genuine partnership with clear integration prospects for designated neighbours who are prepared to programme their future political, economic and institutional development according to EU norms and standards. Furthermore it does not prejudge how relations with the EU could develop further down the line.[63]

Enlargement towards the former Soviet republics, the sphere of Russian interest, seems to be out of question. Given these constraints, the European Neighborhood Policy looks to be the best way to assist and economically cooperate with that area.

Further enlargement became more than questionable after the 2004–2013 enlargements. Indeed, the European Union suffered from an "enlargement fatigue" after this eastward enlargement. A special Eurobarometer report published in July 2006 and based on data gathered in March–May 2006, which focused on attitudes towards EU enlargement, found that the EU population was divided on the issue. While in the ten new member countries, half the population supported further enlargement, the older member countries' citizens – the Germans, French, Austrians and Finns – were decisively against further enlargement. One of the reasons has to do with popular culture: in the West, dozens of films and television shows depicted Eastern criminal activities. Nearly two-thirds of Western European citizens worried about a rise in social problems, the risk of criminal activities, and the refusal of immigrants to assimilate or integrate. Thus, they opposed further enlargement.[64] This negative view remained quite longstanding and stable. The citizens of the EU member countries remained rather doubtful about further enlargement during the 2010s. In 2016, only 39 percent all EU citizens were in favor, while 49 percent declared that they were against "further enlargement of the EU to include other countries in future years."[65] Even more importantly, a majority (more than 50 percent of all survey respondents) in Belgium, Denmark, Germany, Greece, France, Italy, Luxembourg, the Netherlands, Austria, Finland and the Czech Republic – as well as in Cyprus and Portugal – were against further enlargement. Further enlargement was only supported by majorities in Bulgaria, Spain, Croatia, Latvia, Lithuania, Hungary, Malta, Poland, Romania and Slovenia and – with only a plurality – in Estonia, Ireland, Slovakia and Sweden.[66] The Union consequently expanded the postponement period again, and the acceptance of the west Balkans is the only enlargement on agenda for the new European Commission elected in 2020.

Some experts have started advocating for new types of quasi-membership. David Lane's study from 2007 excellently summed up these views about further enlargements:

> Further enlargement is politically unwelcome, and even the USA is reluctant to be able to persuade unwilling members of the European Union to take on further commitments, however strategically advantageous they are seen to be to Western interests. The realistic alternative to the enlargement of the EU is a form of integration without membership. The ENP [European Neighborhood Policy] is one such alternative. . . . Other possibilities include "privileged membership" and "gradual membership". . . . These new forms of association, however, will have . . . disadvantages for the "neighbours" . . . they will exclude them from decision making in the EU.[67]

Others – such as Martin Dangerfield, in his study "The Visegrád Group in the Expanded European Union" – have proposed various forms of possible cooperation; among others, the "involuntary alternative/substitute," which would include "mutual integration up to limits that are both politically and practically defined." This kind of cooperation would be offered to "European states whose fate is to become condemned to a 'limbo' or at best semi-permanent association with the EU" such as the East European countries.[68] Unfortunately, these proposals or similar ideas have still not been realized. No other connected membership categories were introduced and the European Union, if it wishes to accept an applicant, has to grant full membership.

Watch out Europe, reconsider further enlargement

In 2019–2020, the long-postponed west Balkans enlargement was put onto the EU's agenda again. The most important motivator for this development is the general one regarding European integration: to ensure peace on the Continent. The Balkans has traditionally been considered to be a powder keg – a place that foments frequent military conflicts that may spread throughout the Continent. While some kind of integration with the EU and the Balkans is a realistic and laudable goal, it is not evident that the situation necessitates the granting of full EU membership.

An additional argument for integrating the Balkans cites the 2015 migration crisis, when millions of people crossed the Balkans from the Middle East. According to this argument, the Balkan countries play a major role in blocking routes towards Europe. Regarding the migration danger, it is not the policies of the west Balkan countries that can make a difference, but foremost the policies of the European Union itself, in addition to those of Greece and Italy. Some European leaders also argue that a growing Russian and Chinese influence in the Balkans and Central Europe region should to be counterbalanced by EU acceptance.

None of these later arguments are valid. EU membership is not a guarantee against Russian orientation and alliance. It did not stop the Hungarian government from orienting towards Russia, China and even Turkey. Prime Minister Viktor Orbán crafted a famous metaphor in one of his speeches in 2010: "We are sailing under a Western flag, though an Eastern wind is blowing in the world economy."[69] In 2018, he participated at the Sixth Meeting of the Cooperation Council of Turkic Speaking States in Cholpon-Ata, Kyrgyzstan. In his speech, he denied the century-long scholarly recognition that the Hungarian language is part of the Finno-Ugric language family, and instead declared:

> Hungary has always focused on the cooperation of Turkic speaking states which nurture their language, culture and traditions even in the modern world. Hungarians consider themselves late descendants of Attila, of Hun-Turkic origin, and Hungarian is a relative of Turkic languages.[70]

It is indeed more than surprising that several EU leaders have recognized the decision not to enlarge the Union towards the Western Balkans as a "tragic mistake." Negotiations had already started with some countries of that region. However, at the European Council meeting on 17–18 October 2019, President Emmanuel Macron vetoed an enlargement that would have included Macedonia and Albania. In the case of Albania, Denmark and the Netherland joined. Macron rightly argued that enlargement – including that of under-prepared countries – had never strengthened, but had always weakened the EU. He also criticized the enlargement procedure. France suggested a new process with a seven stages of preliminary membership, each of which would be reversible if the candidates did not continue to make essential progress. The French plan would require the demonstration of "profound political, economic, and social transformations required for a future accession."[71] Fundamental reforms, very successful progress in the fight against corruption, the creation of a properly functioning market system, and democratic institutions would all be required. Meanwhile, the EU would increase financial assistance to help galvanize this transformation. The French standpoint reflects the lessons learned from previous enlargements, mostly in the Balkans and Central Europe. In an article in *The Globalist*, Stephan Richter rightly argues that

> Macron's stance on further EU expansion injects a much-needed dose of realism into EU affairs. . . . If a given country's civil society and governance structures are not strong enough, EU membership cannot be extended. . . . The path of Bulgaria and Romania inside the EU is a most vivid reminder that the EU's usual strategy of "hope and pray for self-reform" simply does not work. . . . Furthermore, Hungary under Orban and Poland under . . . Kaczynski are clear evidence of the fact that even countries which had relatively solid post-Communist governance structures can fall prey to irresponsible domestic elites who engage in kleptocracy.[72]

Supporters of further enlargement do not agree. László Andor – the former Commissioner of the EU, who fully understands the complexity and difficulties of the problem and rejects "blaming the reluctant group of wealthy member states" – still argues:

> The region . . . has a lot to offer to the EU facing population ageing and climate change. Progressives have to ensure that when EU nations launch a Conference on the Future of Europe, further enlargement, and specifically the integration of the Western Balkans appear among the top issues of the debate, if not at the very top. . . . The failure to move Albania and North-Macedonia into EU accession candidate status last October made the governments and the citizens of these two countries pretty upset. Friends of enlargement were appalled by the perceived arrogance and ignorance of France and the other non-supporters of the case. This was, however, not a unique hiccup, but another sign of European indecision.[73]

I argue that this possible enlargement does offer some, but not really much of an advantage for the EU; however, it could definitely seriously increase several risk factors. First of all, most of the West Balkan countries are not prepared for full membership and certainly need several decades to achieve stability and preparedness, in the real sense of the term. Some of those countries are ruled by autocratic strongmen and have a traditional Russian orientation, which could potentially strengthen the Eurosceptic anti-EU faction within the EU. It is not accidental that Viktor Orbán, Hungary's anti-integrationist prime minister, became the main advocate for West Balkans enlargement.[74] He declared: "The integration of the Western Balkans into the European Union is one of the top priorities of the Hungarian government. . . . We believe that enlargement can bring about a true reunification of Europe."[75] He also made several statements about "speeding up" Serbia's acceptance by the EU.[76] As the authors of the "Balkan Insight" rightly stated in the summer of 2019, "Relations between Serbia and Hungary could hardly be better, flourishing on the basis of what critics say are the shared authoritarian tendencies of Serbian President Aleksandar Vučić and Hungarian Prime Minister Viktor Orbán."[77] Vučić rightly called Orbán a "great friend of Serbia" and they have visited each other often during the 2020 coronavirus pandemic. President Vučić followed in Orbán's footsteps in introduce an open-ended state of emergency on 15 March 2020 and sidelining the parliament. It is a small wonder that Vučić started his political career at the age of 23 in 1993 as a member of the extremist Serb nationalist Radical Party led by Vojislav Seselj, who was later convicted of war crimes. Seselj was the leader of the region's criminal paramilitary activities and an advocate of creating an ethnically homogenous 'greater Serbia' that would cover the entire territory of Bosnia and Herzegovina, Macedonia, Kosovo, Montenegro, and a significant portion of Croatia. Vučić later became a member of the government of another war criminal, Slobodan Milošević. In Belgrade, weekly protests against him were staged in 2019 for four months with a "mile-long march across the city. They planned to vent their frustrations over escalating political violence and democratic backsliding in the country."[78]

The Serbian president Aleksandar Vučić, before even Serbia was accepted by the EU, joined Orbán in criticizing the European Union. In a televised address on 15 March 2020 – during the first tumultuous outbreak of the pandemic – he stated that "European solidarity" is just "a fairy tale," and praised China as the only nation that "can help us in this difficult situation."[79] He did not mention the more-than 100 million dollars in EU assistance that Serbia had received for health care and social recovery, but instead went to the airport to welcome the Chinese delegation, which arrived with a planeload of a few thousand dollars-worth of medical equipment. Serbia will require a long time – several decades – being an acceptable candidate for EU membership. It would be much more realistic to offer the country a special outside member status that provided assistance, and to give enough time for proper preparedness.

Viktor Orbán has expressed so much enthusiasm for EU enlargement that he even went so far as to tell Turkish and Azerbaijani leaders that Hungary would be "happy to be at your disposal to help you with your aspirations"[80] if Hungary were get the enlargement portfolio in the European Commission (which did, at last, happen). Of course, it is extremely clear to everyone, as two critics stated in 2016 and 2019, that "One of the EU's loudest critics advocates expansion – because the bigger it gets, the less integrated it becomes."[81] One of the analysts of the Budapest-based Political Capital Institute also reiterated that EU expansion furthers Orbán's aims because "the bigger the EU gets, the less integrated the union becomes."[82]

Despite these warning signs, one of the first actions of the new European Commission was to put the enlargement towards the West Balkans on its agenda. The new Hungarian Commissioner for Neighborhood and Enlargement, Olivér Várhelyi, commented:

> The European Union enlargement to the Western Balkans is a top priority for the Commission. We are working on three tracks: Firstly, today we propose concrete steps on how to enhance the accession process . . . the goal remains accession and full EU membership. Secondly, and in parallel, the Commission stands firmly by its recommendations to open accession negotiations with North Macedonia and Albania and . . . the Commission will come forward with an economic and investment development plan for the region.[83]

In May 2020, the Commission repeated "its commitment to enlargement, which remains a key policy of the European Union,"[84] but also underlined that

> the Western Balkans leaders must deliver more credibly on their commitment to implement the fundamental reforms . . . to meet all the requirements of membership. This includes supporting fundamental democratic, rule of law and economic reforms and alignment with core European values.[85]

On a 6 May 2020 videoconference between the EU and the western Balkans, EU leaders announced a huge amount of financial assistance to the six countries, including a generous €3.3-billion package for tackling the COVID-19 pandemic and assisting with post-pandemic recovery. In the final Declaration, they repeatedly emphasized the need for the Balkan countries to embark upon a serious and honest fight against corruption and organized crime; to demonstrate respect for human rights, gender equality, and minority rights; to take resolute action against human trafficking, drug cultivation, and money laundering; to stop criminal organizations from smuggling human beings, drugs, and weapons; and to cooperate with the EU in tackling ongoing migration challenges.[86] One can only hope that the European Union will take its own demands seriously by ensuring the fulfillment of all these requirements, and will withdrew its pledge if any of the countries are unable to deliver. At the moment, not one of the six west Balkans countries has fulfilled any of those requirements.

The European Union is rather ambivalent about further enlargement towards the western Balkans. As a think tank of the EU Parliament summed up in May 2020, the entire history of enlargement reflects this position. The Thessaloniki Summit (2003) opened the door to a European future for the western Balkans. However, the countries of the region have struggled to implement economic and political reforms, and because the rule of law remains particularly problematic, the EU became hesitant. However, the 2018 Enlargement Strategy for the Western Balkans gave new impetus to the enlargement policy, offering the six countries of the region a credible strategy for membership based upon enhanced EU engagement, and indicated that 2025 was a possible accession date. In June 2019, and again in October 2019, the Council postponed the decision to open negotiations with Albania and North Macedonia, despite a positive recommendation from the European Commission and the European Parliament's agreement. By delaying this decision, the European Union sent an ambiguous message to the region, reducing regional credulity of EU acceptance and potentially fueling desperate nationalistic rhetoric in the region. There is some fear that this decision could open the door to the influence of third-country powers, in particular China and Russia. These problems sparked a debate that has led to a fundamental rethinking of the EU's enlargement policy.[87]

Epidemic corruption in the Balkans

Acceptance without strict fulfilment of the prerequisites would cause serious weakening of the Union. All of the potential candidate countries of the Balkans have historically suffered from serious socio-cultural weaknesses, among them epidemic corruption. *The Economist* published an article in 2011 with the title "From Bolshevism to backhanders, corruption has replaced communism as the scourge of eastern Europe."[88] Corruption and strong anti-democratic authoritarian political arrangements continues to partially paralyze normal life in Central Europe, even in countries that have already been accepted into the EU, such as the Visegrád Four countries and Romania, Bulgaria, and Croatia. These continued issues offer serious warnings for the EU, because all these phenomena are even more devastating among other Balkan countries.

In this respect, there are huge gaps – or even abysses – between the countries of northwest Europe, Western European, central and eastern Europe, and the Mediterranean and the Balkans. In a 2013 study using the Corruption Perception

Index – which ranks countries on a scale of 1 to 100, where 100 signals a total lack of corruption (so the lower the number, the higher the corruption – the Northwest European countries were ranked around 90; the West Europeans at 70; the Mediterranean and central European nations around 50; and Italy, Greece, and the Balkan countries at around 40 (the Soviet successor states were ranked around a tragic figure of 20).[89]

The peripheral European countries are also at the bottom of the list regarding their *educational level*. In 2015, the OECD ranked 76 countries worldwide by educational level. Four northwest European countries made the top ten, in addition to several Asian countries. In contrast, the Balkan countries occupy places 40–44; while Albania and Macedonia, together with some Soviet successor states, all rank between 50th and 65th. Most of the lowest-ranked countries occur in countries that do not have European-style educational situations.[90]

***

All in all, further enlargement should be seriously reconsidered. In the 2010s, the COVID-pandemic crisis – which, in addition to the large human toll, produced severe economic consequences, is the third major crisis, together with the Great Recession of 2008–2010s and the migration crises of 2015–2016 that has hit the European Union hard. These situations have sharpened internal conflicts among the northern and southern member countries, and ameliorating these problems will require the EU to take an inward, more introspective turn and actualize the measures that the crises proved to be necessary. Further enlargement – which would increase the bloc of less-developed, authoritarian and Russian-oriented countries within the Union – would hinder the ability of the EU to perform badly needed introspection and might even forestall further steps of integration, thus weakening the European Union. Further enlargement has probably been permanently replaced by a series of better policies that include the European Neighborhood Policy, financial aid, economic integration, and associate (but not full) memberships for newly associated countries.

Notes

1 John F. Kennedy, *President's Address at the Pauluskirche, Frankfurt, June 25*, Department of State Bulletin, vol. 49, no. 1253 (Washington, DC: Office of Public Communication, Bureau of Public Affairs, 1963), 122.
2 James Cable, *Gunboat Diplomacy: Political Applications of Limited Naval Force* (London: Chatto and Windus, 1971), 21.
3 "A Point of View: The British and Their Bizarre View of Americans," *BBC News Magazine*, January 4, 2013, sec. Opinion, www.bbc.com/news/magazine-20857972, accessed May 7, 2018.
4 Charles de Gaulle, "Document IV-27: French Unwillingness to Engage in Negotiations on the United Kingdom's Entry into the European Communities," in *American Foreign Policy: Current Documents* (Washington, DC: U.S. Government Printing Office, 1969), 333.
5 Seamas O'Reilly, "Britain Has a Sense of Moral Superiority Most Other Countries Don't Feel," *The Irish Times*, October 5, 2017, sec. Culture, www.irishtimes.com/

culture/books/britain-has-a-sense-of-moral-superiority-most-other-countries-don-t-feel-1.3237161, accessed October 7, 2018.

6 Graham Anderson and Ben Roskrow, *The Channel Tunnel Story* (London: E & FN Spon, 1994), 20.

7 *Treaty on European Union* (Luxembourg: Office for Official Publications of the European Communities, February 7, 1992).

8 Margaret Thatcher, *Speech to the College of Europe ('The Bruges Speech')* (Bruges: Margaret Thatcher, September 20, 1988), www.margaretthatcher.org/document/107332, accessed September 4, 2017.

9 Quoted in Kenneth Maxwell, *The Making of Portuguese Democracy* (Cambridge: Cambridge University Press, 1995), 7.

10 Winston Churchill, *The North Atlantic Treaty* (London: Speech to the House of Commons, May 12, 1949). In Randolph Churchill, ed., *In the Balance: Speeches of 1949 and 1950 by Winston Churchill* (London: Cassell & Company Ltd., 1951), 61–62.

11 Richard Nixon, *Address at Graduation and Commissioning Ceremonies at Annapolis, Maryland* (Annapolis: Naval Academy Graduation, June 5, 1974). In "United States Naval Academy," in *Weekly Compilation of Presidential Documents*, vol. 10, no. 13 (Washington, DC: U.S. Government Printing Office, 1974), 579.

12 John Scali, "Memorandum of Conversation," February 13, 1973, 4, Gerald R. Ford Presidential Library & Museum, www.fordlibrarymuseum.gov/library/document/0314/1552556.pdf, accessed October 8, 2017.

13 Helen Graham and Alejandro Quiroga, "After the Fear Was Over? What Came after Dictatorships in Spain, Greece, and Portugal," in *The Oxford Handbook of Postwar European History*, ed. Dan Stone (Oxford: Oxford University Press, 2012), 502, 505, 507, https://doi.org/10.1093/oxfordhb/9780199560981.013.0025, accessed October 5, 2017. According to Graham and Quiroga, the position of Greece, "as the frontline against the nascent eastern bloc, brought a level of US support . . . that was sufficient to win them the civil war." Graham and Quiroga, "After the Fear Was Over?," 507.

14 William Harris, Jr., *Art of War Papers* (Fort Leavenworth, KS: Combat Studies Institute Press, 2013), 34, www.armyupress.army.mil/Portals/7/combat-studies-institute/csi-books/ArtOfWar_InstillingAggressiveness.pdf, accessed October 9, 2017.

15 Leonard Tennyson, "Athens Ceremony for EEC-Greek Association," *Bulletin from the European Community*, July 1961, 1, http://aei.pitt.edu/43690/1/A7433.pdf, accessed October 7, 2017.

16 Quoted in Oscar Calvo-Gonzalez, "Neither a Carrot Nor a Stick: American Foreign Aid and Economic Policymaking in Spain during the 1950s," *Diplomatic History* 30, no. 3 (2006): 411.

17 Ibid., 410–411, 412, 416.

18 United States Congress House Committee on Foreign Affairs, "The Mutual Security Act of 1954," in *Mutual Security Program Part 2*, vol. X (Washington, DC: U.S. Government Printing Office, 1980), 533.

19 Leonard Tennyson, "Speech by Mr. Helmuth Burckhardt, Vice President of the Consultative Committee of the European Community for Coal and Steel," *News from the European Community for Coal and Steel*, 2, Archive of European Integration, http://aei.pitt.edu/14369/1/S31.pdf, accessed June 12, 2020.

20 Ivan T. Berend, *An Economic History of Nineteenth-Century Europe* (Cambridge: Cambridge University Press, 2006), 259.

21 George C. McGhee, "Turkey Joins the West," July 1954, www.foreignaffairs.com/articles/turkey/1954-07-01/turkey-joins-west, accessed October 8, 2017.

22 Hikmet Özdemir, "The Turkish–American Relations toward 1960 Turkish 'Revolution,'" *The Turkish Yearbook of International Relations* XXXI, no. 2 (2000): 159–181.

23 Bruce Kuniholm, "Turkey's Jupiter Missiles and the U.S.-Turkish Relationship," in *John F. Kennedy and Europe*, ed. Douglas Brinkley and Richard T. Griffiths (Baton Rouge, LA: Louisiana State University Press, 1999), 117.

24 Ibid., 117–118.

25 Nasuh Uslu, *The Turkish-American Relationship between 1947 and 2003: The History of a Distinctive Alliance* (New York: Nova Science Publishers, 2003), 23.

26 Kristin Archick, *European Union Enlargement*, CRS Report for Congress (Washington, DC: United States Congress, April 4, 2012), 2.

27 Vincent Morelli, *European Union Enlargement: A Status Report on Turkey's Accession Negotiations*, CRS Report for Congress (Washington, DC: United States Congress, November 26, 2010), 13.

28 Maria Elena Cavallaro and Kostis Kornetis, "Introduction: Lost in Translation?," in *Rethinking Democratisation in Spain, Greece and Portugal*, ed. Maria Elena Cavallaro and Kostis Kornetis (Cham: Palgrave Macmillan, 2019), 3.

29 "Forty Years after the Fall of the Dictatorships–Why Greece and Portugal Matter to the European Union," *Heinrich Böll Stiftung*, April 2014, sec. Event Report, 1, https://eu.boell.org/ sites/default/files/event_report_portugal_greece.pdf, accessed October 9, 2017.

30 France and some other countries were strongly against its acceptance, arguing that historical, cultural, and religious differences separate Turkey from Europe. Turkey's relationship with the West was also changing. The followers of Kemal Ataturk looked to EU membership as the final step towards becoming a fully accepted part of contemporary civilization. The ruling Adalet ve Kalkinma Partisi (Justice and Development Party) strongly reoriented towards Turkey and embraced conservative, Muslim, nationalist values. See Heinz Kramer, "The Future of Turkish-Western Relations," *Südosteuropa Mitteilungen*, no. 1 (2013): 57, 59. And Yavuz Baydar, "Turkish-European Relations and the Importance of Visa Liberalisation," *Südosteuropa Mitteilungen*, no. 1 (2013): 90–91.

31 Edward Whitfield, *The 1995 Enlargement of the European Union: The Accession of Finland and Sweden*, Study, European Union History Series (Luxembourg: Publications Office, November 2015), European Parliament Historical Archives Unit, www.europarl.europa.eu/RegData/etudes/STUD/2015/563509/EPRS_STU%282015%29563509_EN.pdf, accessed November 17, 2017.

32 George H. W. Bush, *Address before the 45th Session of the United Nations General Assembly in New York City* (New York City: United Nations General Assembly Meeting, October 1, 1990). In *Weekly Compilation of Presidential Documents*, vol. 26, no. 39 (Washington, DC: U.S. Government Printing Office, 1990), 1498.

33 George H. W. Bush, *Remarks at Maxwell Air Force Base War College* (Montgomery, AL, April 13, 1991). In United States President, *Public Papers of the Presidents of the United States, 1991*, vol. 1 (Washington, DC: U.S. Government Printing Office, 1992), 366.

34 Lawrence Eagleburger, *US Must Adjust to Different, Challenging World* (Washington, DC: George Washington University, November 21, 1991). Quoted in Ian Clark, *The Post-Cold War Order: The Spoils of Peace* (Oxford: Oxford University Press, 2001), 182.

35 Jacques Delors, *Speech at the Opening Session of the 40th Academic Year of the College of Europe* (Bruges: European Commission, October 17, 1989), 4, 14, https://ec.europa.eu/commission/presscorner/detail/en/SPEECH_89_73, accessed November 17, 2017.

36 Quoted in Michael J. Baun, *A Wider Europe: The Process and Politics of European Union Enlargement* (Lanham, MD: Rowman & Littlefield, 2000), 10.

37 Delors, *Speech at the Opening Session of the 40th Academic Year of the College of Europe*, 7–8, 3.

38 Barry Eichengreen, *The European Economy since 1945: Coordinated Capitalism and Beyond* (Princeton, NJ: Princeton University Press, 2007), 406.

39 Perry Anderson, "Depicting Europe," *London Review of Books*, September 20, 2007, www.lrb.co.uk/the-paper/v29/n18/perry-anderson/depicting-europe, accessed November 18, 2017.

40 "Accession Criteria (Copenhagen Criteria)," in *Eur-Lex Glossary of Summaries* (Brussels: European Union), accessed June 12, 2020, https://eur-lex.europa.eu/summary/%20glossary/accession_criteria_copenhague.html, accessed June 14, 2020.

41 Angus Maddison, *Monitoring the World Economy, 1820–1992* (Paris: Development Centre of the Organisation for Economic Co-operation and Development, 1995), 201, 228.

42 *The Europe Agreements and Beyond: A Strategy to Prepare the Countries of Central and Eastern Europe for Accession*, Communication from the Commission to the Council (Brussels: Commission of the European Communities, July 13, 1994), 1, COM(94) 302 final, Archive of European Integration, http://aei.pitt.edu/2948/1/2948.pdf.

43 László Andor, "From Enragement to Enlargement," *The Progressive Post*, March 13, 2020, https://progressivepost.eu/no-category/from-enragement-to-enlargement, accessed March 30, 2020.

44 Martin Dangerfield, "The European Union and Post-Communist Europe: One Approach or Several?," *Journal of Communist Studies and Transition Politics* 23, no. 4 (December 2007): 481, https://doi.org/10.1080/13523270701674566, accessed October 17, 2017.

45 *Copenhagen European Council Presidency Conclusions* (Brussels: European Parliament, June 21, 1993), www.europarl.europa.eu/enlargement/ec/cop_en.htm, accessed October 23, 2017.

46 Ibid.

47 *Conditions for Membership* (Brussels: European Commission, European Neighbourhood Policy and Enlargement Negotiations, December 6, 2016), https://ec.europa.eu/neighbourhood-enlargement/policy/conditions-membership_en

48 See Ivan T. Berend, *From the Soviet Bloc to the European Union: The Economic and Social Transformation of Central and Eastern Europe since 1973* (Cambridge: Cambridge University Press, 2009), 88–95.

49 Péter Balázs et al., *25 Years after the Fall of the Iron Curtain: The State of Integration of East and West in the European Union*, European Commission–Directorate-General for Research and Innovation (Luxembourg: Publications Office, 2015), 10, 11, 27, 30, 35, 37, 38, 86.

50 "EU Enlargement: The Next Seven," *BBC News*, September 2, 2014, sec. Europe, www.bbc.com/news/world-europe-11283616, accessed October 8, 2017.

51 *Bosnia and Herzegovina 2013 Progress Report*, Commission Staff Working Document (Brussels: European Commission, October 16, 2013), 14–15, 53, SWD(2013) 415 final–COM(2013) 700 final, https://doi.org/10.1163/2210-7975_HRD-4679-0058.

52 *Commission Opinion on Montenegro's Application for Membership of the European Union*, Communication from the Commission to the European Parliament and the Council (Brussels: European Commission, November 11, 2010), SEC(2010) 1334 final, https://doi.org/10.1163/ 2210–7975_HRD-4679–0058, accessed November 19, 2019.

53 "The Western Balkans and the EU. In the Queue," *The Economist*, September 27, 2014.

54 *Action Plan for Ukraine*, Communication from the Commission to the Council (Brussels: Commission of the European Communities, November 20, 1996), 7,

COM(96) 593 final, Archive of European Integration, http://aei.pitt.edu/6288/1/6288.pdf.

55 Ibid.

56 *1977th Council Meeting–General Affairs–President: Dick Spring, Minister for Foreign Affairs of Ireland*, (Brussels: European Commission, December 6, 1996), PRES/96/366, Archive of European Integration, https://ec.europa.eu/commission/presscorner/detail/en/PRES_96_366, accessed October, 8, 2017. This statement dates back to the time when preparations were being made for the admittance of the original ten former communist countries.

57 *Black Sea Synergy–A New Regional Cooperation Initiative*, Communication from the Commission to the Council and the European Parliament (Brussels: Commission of the European Communities, April 11, 2007), 2, 10, COM(2007) 160 final, Archive of European Integration, http://eeas.europa.eu/archives/docs/enp/pdf/pdf/com07_160_en.pdf, accessed December 8, 1017.

58 Hermann Clement, "The Case of Russia and Ukraine," in *Economic Convergence and Divergence in Europe: Growth and Regional Development in an Enlarged European Union*, ed. Gertrude Tumpel-Gugerell and Peter Mooslechner (Cheltenham: Edward Elgar Publishing, 2003), 415.

59 David M. Herszenhorn, "Russia Putting a Strong Arm on Neighbors," *The New York Times*, October 22, 2013, sec. World, www.nytimes.com/2013/10/23/world/europe/russia-putting-a-strong-arm-on-neighbors.html, accessed October 19, 2017.

60 Ibid.

61 "Day of the Gangster Pygmy," *The Economist*, November 30, 2013, sec. Leaders, www.economist.com/leaders/2013/11/30/day-of-the-gangster-pygmy, accessed December 6, 2017.

62 Quoted in Michael Gehler, "From Paneurope to the Single Currency: Recent Studies on the History of European Integration," *Contemporary European History* 15, no. 2 (2006): 282.

63 Dangerfield, "The European Union and Post-Communist Europe," 488.

64 *Attitudes towards European Union Enlargement* (Brussels: European Commission, May 2006), https://ec.europa.eu/commfrontoffice/publicopinion/archives/ebs/ebs_255_en.pdf, accessed January 3, 1018.

65 Ibid.

66 *What Do Citizens' Opinions and Perceptions Mean for EU Enlargement?* Policy Brief, MAXCAP Policy Task Force (Berlin: Freie Universität, May 2016), http://userpage.fu-berlin.de/kfgeu/maxcap/sites/default/files/sites/default/files/policy-briefs/maxcap_policy_brief_03_0.pdf, accessed December 6, 2017.

67 David Lane, "Post-Communist States and the European Union," *Journal of Communist Studies and Transition Politics* 23, no. 4 (December 2007): 476, https://doi.org/10.1080/13523270701674558, accessed November 5, 2017.

68 Martin Dangerfield, "The Visegrád Group in the Expanded European Union: From Preaccession to Postaccession Cooperation," *East European Politics and Societies* 22, no. 3 (August 1, 2008): 630–667, https://doi.org/10.1177/0888325408315840, accessed November 9, 2017.

69 "Orbán and the Wind from the East," *The Economist*, November 14, 2011, sec. Eastern Approaches, www.economist.com/eastern-approaches/2011/11/14/orban-and-the-wind-from-the-east, accessed October 19, 2017.

70 Gábor Sarnyai, "Hungary and Turkey on Finding Common Ground in the Past, Present and Future," *Hungary Today*, October 9, 2018, sec. Emphasized, https://hungarytoday.hu/hungary-and-turkey-on-finding-common-ground-in-the-past-present-and-future/, accessed November 16, 2018.

71 "Non-Paper Reforming the European Union Accession Process," November 2019, www.politico.eu/wp-content/uploads/2019/11/Enlargement-non paper.pdf, accessed January 6, 2020.

72 Stephan Richter, "Thank God for France's Sense of European Realism," *The Globalist*, February 18, 2020, www.theglobalist.com/france-emmanuel-macron-germany-eu-expansion-western-balkans/, accessed March 21, 2020. Also see Andrew Rettman, "What Does Macron Really Want on Western Balkans?," *EUobserver*, November 12, 2019, https:// euobserver.com/enlargement/146583, accessed November 29, 2019.

73 László Andor, "From Enragement to Enlargement," *The Progressive Post*, March 13, 2020, https://progressivepost.eu/no-category/from-enragement-to-enlargement/, accessed May 12, 2020.

74 Alexandra Brzozowski, "Hungary Wants Montenegro and Serbia to Join EU before 2025," *Euractiv*, October 3, 2019, sec. Future EU, www.euractiv.com/section/future-eu/news/hungary-wants-montenegro-and-serbia-to-join-eu-before-2025/, accessed January 3, 2020.

75 Edit Inotai, "Hungary's Celebrations over Enlargement Post May Prove Premature," *Balkan Insight*, September 11, 2019, https://balkaninsight.com/2019/09/11/hungarys-celebrations-over-enlargement-post-may-prove-premature/, accessed January 3, 2020.

76 "PM Orbán: Hungary Is Keen to Speed up Serbia's Accession to the European Union," *About Hungary*, February 12, 2018, http://abouthungary.hu/news-in-brief/pm-orban-hungary-is-keen-to-speed-up-serbias-accession-to-the-european-union/, accessed January 5, 2020.

77 Ana Curic and Blanka Zöldi, "Illumination of Serbia, Hungarian Style," *Balkan Insight*, June 26, 2019, https://balkaninsight.com/2019/06/26/illumination-of-serbia-hungarian-style/, November 5, 2019.

78 Aleks Eror, "Two Decades after the Fall of Milosevic, Dictatorship Is Returning to Serbia," *World Politics Review*, May 14, 2019, https://111f3ba6dc4 14209b980802ea03ea4fd.pages.ubembed.com/eb9bf9ca-621c-466a-9667-2137acd1b7bc/c.html?closedAt=0, accessed January 4, 2020.

79 Zachary Evans, "Serbian President Labels European Solidarity 'Fairy Tale', Says Only China Can Assist in Coronavirus Response," *National Review*, March 16, 2020, www.nationalreview.com/news/coronavirus-outbreak-serbian-president-aleksandar-vucic-labels-european-solidarity-fairy-tale-says-only-china-can-assist-in-coronavirus-response/, accessed May 2, 2020.

80 "Hungary EU Nominee Insists He Will Not Be Orban's Man," *France 24*, November 14, 2019, www.france24.com/en/20191114-hungary-eu-nominee-insists-he-will-not-be-orban-s-man, accessed January 8, 2020.

81 Lili Bayer, "Viktor Orbán's Vision of a Bigger, Looser Europe," *Politico*, September 6, 2016, www.politico.eu/article/viktor-orbans-vision-of-a-bigger-looser-europe-hungary-european-union-brexit/, accessed October 7, 2018.

82 Ibid.

83 *A More Credible, Dynamic, Predictable and Political EU Accession Process–Commission Lays Out Its Proposals* (Brussels: European Commission, February 5, 2020), https://ec.europa.eu/commission/presscorner/detail/en/IP_20_181, accessed May 3, 2020.

84 *Council Conclusions on Enlargement and Stabilisation and Association Process* (Brussels: European Council, June 18, 2019), www.consilium.europa.eu/en/press/press-releases/2019/06/18/council-conclusions-on-enlargement-and-stabilisation-and-association-process/, accessed December 7, 2019.

85 *Enhancing the Accession Process–A Credible EU Perspective for the Western Balkans*, Communication from the Commission to the European Parliament, the Council, the European Economic and Social Committee and the Committee of the Regions (Brussels: European Commission, February 5, 2020), 2, COM(2020) 57 final, Archive of European Integration, https://eur-lex.europa.cu/legal content/EN/TXT/PDF/?uri=CELEX:52020DC0057&from=EN, accessed May 3, 2020.

86 "Zagreb Declaration, 6 May 2020," *European Western Balkans*, May 6, 2020, https://europeanwesternbalkans.com/2020/05/06/zagreb-declaration-6-may-2020/, accessed May 29, 2020.

87 "A New Approach to EU Enlargement," *European Parliament Think Tank*, March 11, 2020, www.europarl.europa.eu/thinktank/en/document.html?reference=EPRS_BRI(2020)649332, accessed May 11, 2020.

88 "From Bolshevism to Backhanders," *The Economist*, April 14, 2011, www.economist.com/europe/2011/04/14/from-bolshevism-to-backhanders, accessed May 2, 2020.

89 "Corruption Perceptions Index 2013," *Transparency International*, www.transparency.org/en/cpi/2013, accessed June 14, 2020.

90 *PISA 2015* (Brussels: OECD Publications, 2018), www.oecd.org/pisa/pisa-2015-results-in-focus.pdf, accessed November 8, 2019.

6 The triple crises and escaping ahead

2008–2020

After the historic renewal of the European Community and the foundation of the Single Market, the common currency and the European Union, and an unparalleled boom period around the turn of the millennium, very soon everything changed, and not for the better. Roughly one and a half decades after the Single Market began – less than a decade since eleven countries had started to use a common currency, and only half a decade since the major enlargement that included the first large group of Central European countries (when the Union started to become pan-European); in other words, right after the most successful boom of European integration – the deepest crisis since World War II hit the Continent. Actually, it was a series of different kinds of crises, including a serious economic recession followed by a shocking migration 'invasion' of the Continent before a full recovery had occurred. And then, just when Europe recovered from this latter crisis, an unparalleled health crisis – the coronavirus pandemic, along with the even deeper recession that it produced – followed. These triple crises hit Europe very hard over a dozen years, between 2008 and 2020.

The economic recession of 2008

Around the turn of the millennium, the EU-15 countries experienced a great boom. Between 1992 and 2005, their aggregate GDP increased by 58 percent and the average per-capita income by 60 percent, but then all of the sudden, economic growth stopped. The first sign of change appeared in 2007. On 17 and 18 September of that year, thousands of agitated people cued in front of various branches of the British Northern Rock Bank for two days to withdraw funds. The bank did not have the money. The Bank of England rescued it by providing $4.4 billion and guaranteed 100 percent coverage for these withdrawals.[1]

During the same period, Ireland became one of the most prosperous and richest countries in Europe. From the 1990s, the economy grew by an unprecedented annual 6–12 percent, and the country's national income trebled in the last third of the twentieth century. The population had twice as much disposable income as the European Union's average in 2006. Many newly wealthy Irish people bought new homes, and residential mortgage lending grew annually by 25 percent. Between 2003 and 2007, their share elevated from 40 percent to 65 percent of the country's GDP. Such an unprecedented real estate boom pushed the home prices sky-high. In just a few years between 2000 and 2006, house prices increased by three times. In 2006 in Dublin, an acre of land sold for €95 million. The income level of the population could not match this rise and in 2006, all of the sudden, there were no longer enough home buyers. House prices stopped rising, and then dropped by 18 percent: the housing bubble suddenly burst, and Ireland declined into economic crisis.

Relatedly, Greece accumulated a huge amount of debt by spending irresponsibly. Instead of the original budget of €2.5 billion for the 2004 Summer Olympic Games, the government spent nearly €10 billion.[2] Greece had also built up its welfare state partly by accruing debt, and enacted unwise policies like decreasing the retirement age to 58 years, and in some areas even to 48 years – irresponsibly low. The country accumulated huge deficits, but hide them, doctoring statistics and lying about their level of indebtedness. All of these problems came to the surface after the elections of 2009, when the new government of George Papandreu made the falsifications public. It turned out that the budgetary deficit and public debt had reached 110 percent of the GDP.[3] Meanwhile, tax collection collapsed because of corruption, leading even the prime minister to announce that the Greek economy was "a sinking ship."[4]

The world economy was over-expanded and over-financialized, but also deregulated and thus overspeculative and risky. During this period, it expanded wildly: daily financial transactions jumped from $15 million in the mid-1970s to $1.3 trillion by 2004, and direct foreign investments totaled $2.5 trillion. All of the sudden, however, giant American banks started collapsing one after another. In March 2008, the major American investment bank Bear Stearns collapsed. The New York Fed provided a $29 billion bailout and Bear Stearns avoided default. In September 2008, two more giants followed. One was the American Investment Group (AIG), which was saved by the Federal Reserve's two-year, $85 billion loan. In mid-September 2008, on the same day, two other giants hit rock bottom. Merrill Lynch – which had $1.4 trillion in assets and nearly 2 million accounts, with quarterly revenue of $4 billion – went bankrupt, and, as an emergency measure, it was sold to Bank of America for $50 billion. On the same day, the single-most significant event of the financial crisis occurred. Lehman Brothers, a traditionally solid bank – established in 1850, with 25,000 employee and $639 billion assets – filed for bankruptcy on 15 September 2008. The Bank was unable to repay its $619 billion in debts. This collapse was the largest in history, as its assets far surpassed those of previous bankrupt giants. This event ignited a

> subprime mortgage-induced financial crisis that swept through global financial markets in 2008. Lehman's collapse was a seminal event that greatly intensified the 2008 crisis and contributed to the erosion of close to $10 trillion in market capitalization from global equity markets in [October] 2008.[5]

These events became some of the most dramatic days in Wall Street's history. The *New York Times* concluded: "once-proud financial institutions have been brought to their knees as a result of hundreds of billions of dollars in losses because of bad mortgage finance and real estate investments."[6]

Financial-economic crisis in Europe

This series of collapses of American banking giants caused a dramatic panic in the international financial markets. The American Nobel Laureate economist Joseph Stiglitz stated the financial crisis that flooded the globe had a clear "Made in the USA" label on it.[7] In actuality, it was not only "American made"; it was equally created in Europe as well. However, it is true that the collapse of the American giant financial institutions frightened banking institutions all over the world from giving loans, and that an international liquidity crisis thus emerged. It generated a chain reaction. In modern financing, most of the old credits are payed back from fresh, new credits. In the liquidity crisis, crediting stopped, and therefore a great number of debtors became unable to get new loans to repay old credits. Several countries of Europe were highly indebted. Turn of the millennium prosperity in deregulated neoliberal financial markets had led to high risk-taking. Huge new investments were based on credits. High prosperity, in other words, went hand-in-hand with high indebtedness.

The small island country Iceland became a textbook example. Whereas the fishing industry had formerly dominated, in the early twenty-first century, Iceland became a banking giant. The three leading banks of the country had assets of 1,450 billion Icelandic krona in 2003, and had increased their assets by roughly ten times by 2008. They bought Norwegian banks and British industrial companies, they gave loans all over Europe, and the amount of their loans in 2007 was 430 percent of the entire country's GDP. The three banks' total assets elevated to an amount that was ten times Iceland's GDP. As usual in the financial world, Icelandic banks based their extraordinary expansion on borrowing money. By 2007, their short-term debts were fifteen times larger than the entire foreign reserve of the country's national bank. In a single year, 2005, these Icelandic banks doubled their debts. Thus, they grew their businesses with others' money. Frightening signs had already started to appear in 2006–2007, when the country's central bank reported the danger to the government. After the collapse of the Lehman Brothers in America and the severe international liquidity crisis that emerged, the Icelandic banks (like all the others) were unable to get new loans. One of the three leading banks, the Glitnir Bank, had debt that matured in October 2008. At that time, the bank had to repay €1.4 billion in debt. Similar trouble hit the other big bank, the Landsbanki, which became unable to pay 300,000 British depositors, who wanted to withdraw their money from their accounts. The British government retaliated and frozen the bank's assets in Britain. In October 2008, all three giant Icelandic banks collapsed. By the next month, the Icelandic krona had lost almost 60 percent of its value. In February 2009, even the government collapsed. The country's GDP dropped by 6.7 percent that year.

Reckless, borrowing financed banking; a housing boom with skyrocketing prices that was sustained by unsteady mortgage loans; and a borrowing-based consumption boom increased the indebtedness of banks, governments, and population alike. The crisis became like an epidemic. Beside Iceland, Greece, and Ireland, in addition to a whole series of Central, Eastern and Southern European countries–Hungary, Latvia, Estonia, Lithuania, Bulgaria, Romania, Italy, Spain, and Portugal (all European Union countries), as well as Ukraine, Russia, and Serbia – declined as a result of this severe economic crisis. Around the turn of the millennium, the transforming Central and Eastern European countries were mostly credit-boom countries with weak economies, and as such, they were strongly exposed to the crisis. In 2009, five countries of that region suffered from double-digit economic decline: Lithuania's GDP declined by 17.4 percent, Ukraine's by 14.8 percent, Estonia's by 14.3 percent, and Slovenia's by 8.1 percent. Already by the fourth quarter of 2008, exports in these transition countries had dropped by 5–15 percent; in the first quarter of 2009, they fell by another 10–25 percent. By 2011, Hungary, Latvia and Romania had all but collapsed, and the IMF and the EU had to bail them out.

The European Union intervened: in March 2009, the EU, the IMF, the World Bank and the European Bank of Reconstruction and Development – together with about 40 private banks that had business with the region – made an agreement in Vienna to keep lending to the region. This so-called Vienna Initiative saved the region from banking and crediting collapse. Nevertheless, in the worst period of the crisis (late 2011), lending to these countries still declined between $35–75 billion, and EU-based banks started selling their assets in the region. The European Union immediately helped again: a second Vienna Initiative in January 2012 reached an agreement to keep the region's financial institutions working. Surprisingly, the fact that about 87 percent of baking capital in Central Europe was in foreign hands – it was mostly held by Austrian, German, French, and Scandinavian entities – kept crediting stable. In addition, the EU had already sent over huge amount of money to the newly accepted countries: between 2000 and 2006, it had contributed €80 billion in assistance for less-developed regions. Indeed, between 2007 and 2013, the Union sent over one third of its entire budget to that region as aid for less-developed areas. The EU's agricultural policy doubled the income of the peasants in the area as well.

The economic crisis of the newly accepted former communist countries was not a great challenge for the European Union. The combined GDP of the three hardest-hit countries of the region represented only 2 percent of the EU's total GDP. Their loss was roughly equal to the decline of Greece. The countries of the Mediterranean region and Ireland – which have gained the pejorative nickname "PIIGS" (Portugal, Italy, Ireland, Greece and Spain) – represented a much bigger problem. Italy's public-debt level was the third biggest in the world. Already by the mid-1990s, it had reached 120 percent of the country's GDP – a twice as high as allowed under EU regulations. In 2011, Italy's debt totaled $2,578 trillion – sums that even the entire EU could not swallow. By the end of 2011, Italy and Spain had accumulated $3.3 trillion in debt. In 2012, the Spanish banks were bailed out by the IMF for a second time. Three of the PIIGS – Ireland, Greece and Portugal – went bankrupt and had to be bailed out by the IMF and the EU, to the tune of €80 billion.

Very soon, the economic crisis became all European. Part of the reason is because reckless lending and borrowing characterized the most advanced North-western European countries as well. Between 2000 and 2007, a housing boom and skyrocketing house prices occurred across Europe: prices rose by 100 percent in Ireland and 135 percent in Spain, but 108 percent in France and 128 percent in Britain. Even in Sweden, Norway, and Denmark this increase reached between 80–82 percent; only Germany and the Netherlands were immune. They experienced housing-price increases of only 18 percent and 38 percent, respectively. British banks wrote down $300 million; across the entire euro-zone, they were unable to get back between $500–800 billion in credit that had been loaned.

In 2008–2009, Europe declined into a serious recession. The equity market lost half of its value, and the car industry suffered tremendous losses. Jaguar-Land Rover in Britain and Volvo in Sweden were bailed out. About $14–15 trillion of the value of companies globally was erased. In 2009, the aggregate GDP of the euro-zone dropped by 4.2 percent; and then by another 0.7 percent in 2010. The unemployment rate neared 10 percent as 20 million people lost their jobs. Among young people (those under 25 years of age), the average unemployment rate was 22 percent; in Greece and Spain, it reached 47 percent and 49 percent, respectively.

The European Union rushed to work out a rescue plan. On 12 October 2008 at a Paris meeting, the countries agreed to prepare a coordinated plan to save the banks. On 26 November, the Commission announced a €200-billion recovery package. In December 2008, the European Economic Recovery Plan pumped a huge amount – equal to 5 percent of the EU's aggregate GDP – into the Community. Britain, France and Germany also created national stimulus packages. Denmark announced a 100 percent guarantee on savings and Germany rescued the Hypo Real Estate Bank. The British Treasury paid out £500 billion in bank rescues and recapitalized the Royal Bank of Scotland and Lloyds. Nine countries supported their banks, spending almost $5 billion. Bank rescues reached 82 percent of the GDP in Britain, 70 percent in Sweden and 40 percent in the Netherlands. Countries also created automatic stabilizers that worked without direct government action.

The first uncertain signs of recovery appeared as early as 2010, when the EU-27 countries together returned to economic growth: growth reached 1.8 percent in 2010 and 1.5 percent in 2011. Nevertheless, in 2010, six countries still suffered further decline: Iceland's rate was -4.0 percent, Greece's was -3.5 percent, Romania's was -1.9 percent, and Ireland's was the smallest at -0.4 percent. In 2011, only Greece was still experiencing further decline.

Collapse of the euro currency?

In 2012, decline returned to a few countries again. At that time, the most frightening factor was the debt crisis, which significantly deepened in 2011. The possibility of default in two or three euro-zone countries, the extended crisis in Greece, the delayed stabilization of Italy and Spain, and panic in the financial markets started to endanger the common currency. When it debuted at the turn of the millennium, the euro was an immense success. It was a triumph for those who had advocated for federalization, since the common currency – together with the European Central Bank – became the most supranational institutions that the EU had ever had, and further weakened the intergovernmental character of the Union. It had significant financial advantages, including the elimination of conversion costs and exchange rate fluctuations; it also helped to create price equalization and to unify the financial market. When the EU's euro was introduced, its value was on par with the American dollar: one euro was equal to one dollar. In a few years, however, it became much stronger and surpassed the value of dollar by 50 percent (€1=$1.50). It immediately became a second reserve world currency and in a few years, one-quarter of the world's financial transactions used the euro.

In January 1999, eleven EU member countries–Austria, Belgium, Finland, France, Germany, Ireland, Italy, Luxembourg, the Netherlands, Portugal and Spain – enthusiastically introduced it. Britain, Denmark and Sweden opted out, and remained with their national currencies. Before and even during the crisis, between 2001 and 2011, six other countries–Greece, Slovenia, Cyprus, Malta, Slovakia and Estonia – joined. When the currency crisis erupted, 17 EU countries used the euro; moreover, six non-member countries, mostly European mini-states, had also introduced it. Ten member countries, on the other hand, had not qualified to introduce it yet. The Maastricht Treaty introduced the "convergence criteria:" only countries that had less than 1.5 percent inflation or 2 percent long-term inflation, budgetary deficits lower than 6 percent, and public debt lower than 60 percent of the GDP could join the common currency. Several peripheral member countries could not meet these standards; later, in the next decade, it turned out that they did not even want to join.

In spite of the great initial success of the euro, the common currency had, indeed, some dangerous weaknesses. Two major mistakes at its introduction endangered the currency in an economic crisis situation. First of all, monetary unification was introduced without fiscal unification. Fiscal policy – decisions made regarding taxation and spending – remained in the hands of national governments. This structure had never occurred in history before. Consequently, some irresponsible, reckless national fiscal actions endangered the common currency. Additionally, the European Central Bank was not a fully authorized national bank, since it was not authorized to be the lender of last resort, an essential part of any national bank's function. This structure meant that it could not lend to governments or buy government bonds in order to back government spending. These functions are crucial in a crisis situation.

A second major weakness was caused by the huge differences in the economic levels between the countries that used the euro. When the European Community was established, the six founding members' levels of economic advancement were very similar. Their per-capita GDP was around $6,000–7,000. Most of those countries had also quite similar socio-cultural backgrounds. The EU's radical enlargements gradually eliminated these similarities. The first country with a rather different economic level, Ireland, was accepted in 1973; at that time, its per-capita GDP only reached 58 percent of the members' average. When Greece, Spain and Portugal joined, they likewise reached between 58–63 percent of the average EU level. The enlargements of the 2000s made an exceptional difference among member countries, since the Central European, Baltic and Balkan countries represented only 56 percent, 21 percent and 10 percent of the average West-European level, respectively. In this diverse context, the one-size-fits-all monetary policy had rather different consequences on the heterogeneous group of countries. Before the crisis, the euro led to low interest rates and thus cheap credit, which generated a decrease in savings and an increase in reckless spending. Peripheral countries also lost the ability to increase interest rates when the economy overheated. On the other hand, in crisis years, the weaker peripheral countries did not have the opportunity to devaluate their currency – the most important weapon for less-developed countries looking to improve their competitiveness. They also lost the possibility of help from their national banks to buy government bonds in order to pay back debts. In other words, crisis-ridden, less-developed countries lost the ability to maneuver and cope with the crisis. These weaknesses in the fiscal structure behind the euro became disastrous for the common currency during the crisis. While the financial crisis generated by the recession was only a temporary, short-lived problem in the United States and across most of the world, it became a severe crisis in the European Union that exposed momentous structural problems with the new common currency.

During this time, experts and the media, good economists and bad journalists, all equally criticized the introduction of the euro, and did not exclude the possibility of its collapse in a few weeks' time. On 28 November 2011, The *New York Times* declared: "Eighteen months into a sovereign debt crisis . . . the endgame appears to be fast approaching for Europe."[8] During the same month, *The Economist* asked in an article on the euro: "is this the end?"[9] In December, this excellent and well-balanced weekly magazine published an article with the title "A comedy of euros," stating, "sooner or later, the euro will be beyond saving."[10] The stable and rich countries, especially Germany, were harshly criticized because they did not want sharing the burden of the poorer nations. France suggested issuing euro-bonds instead of national bonds, which – when backed by the strong countries – would have helped the weaker countries acquire more money on the bond markets and pay back their new debts, but Germany rejected it. The *New York Times* harshly attacked Angela Merkel:

> At the center of it all sits Germany, leading the bloc of Northern European countries. . . . Any proposals to share the burden with the heavily indebted countries by collectivizing European debt . . . are rejected out of hand, largely for fear of a political backlash.[11]

The media complained about lack of leadership and action: "The European Union has a particularly acute version of leaders-who-will-not-lead."[12]

The collapse of the common currency became an everyday topic and a real possibility. All of the sudden, the entire enterprise of the common currency was deemed "artificial." The EU "built an economic and legal superstructure without a linguistic, cultural, historic and civic base. . . . But now the inherent flaws are undermining the project."[13] American pro-integrationist economist and Nobel laureate Paul Krugman – punningly recognized as one of the "funding fathers" of the euro suddenly became one of those "deeply impractical romantics" who were led by "the dream of European unification, which the Continent's elite found so alluring that its members waved away practical objections."[14]

The deep debt crisis of the peripheral countries naturally generated a banking crisis in the advanced West European countries as well. These countries – Britain, France and Germany – were the main buyers of bonds from weaker peripheral countries within the Union, and became the lenders of credit to them. In December 2010, the French, German, British, Dutch and Belgian banks together owned nearly €1.8 trillion in poisonous bonds from the PIIGS countries. By the end of 2011 and into the summer of 2012, America and other countries became hesitant to buy European bonds at all, and even a portion of Germany's bonds remained unsold. Meanwhile, the value of the euro significantly dropped from $1.5 to $1.1 compared to the US dollar.

"The Euro is Already Saved!"

On 25 April 2013, Jörg Asmussen, member of the Executive Board of the European Central Bank, proudly proclaimed: "The euro is already 'saved.' It will survive this crisis, it will emerge from it stronger and more countries will join the euro in the future."[15]

What happened? To sum up in two words: Mario Draghi. As the congenial Italian president of the European Central Bank famously bluntly announced during the deepest moment of crisis in the summer of 2012: the Bank "will do whatever it takes" to save the euro.[16] He launched a series of heroic actions, indeed. In early August 2012, the Bank started a massive purchasing run to buy government bonds. Since according to its rules, the Bank could do so directly from the governments, Draghi found another way: the Bank bought the bonds on the secondary market from private persons and institutions. As a result of this action, the bond rates dropped dramatically from their previous levels, which had been very high, and eased the burden of member countries' governments. The Central Bank also used the method of quantitative easing, pumping €1 trillion in freshly printed new money into the euro-zone's economy. This policy continued until the fall of 2016. From this new money, the Bank funneled almost half-a-billion euros into cheap long-term credit in order to recapitalize banks. It also increased its reserve capital to 9 percent of the Bank's assets so that it would be able to cover sudden losses.

The European Union, although it acted slowly and with many delays, nonetheless acted efficiently when bailing out collapsing banks and forcing austerity measures in crisis-ridden countries in order to cut expenditures, decrease debts, and reestablish the balance of trade and payments. The European Commission, the European Central Bank, and the International Monetary Fund (the so-called "troika") bailed out all of the bankrupt euro-zone countries–Ireland, Spain, Portugal, Cyprus, Greece – as well as some of the non-euro-zone countries, such as Latvia, Hungary, Bulgaria, and Romania. As a consequence, all of these countries were once again able to repay their debts. Most of these countries needed only one bailout, but Greece needed three, totaling €289 billion ($330 billion). Ireland's banks were bailed out by €64 billion in assistance from the EU and IMF, plus an additional €17.5 billion from Irish reserves – €85 billion altogether. Spain's financial-support package amounted to €100 billion. Altogether, for an entire decade, between November 2008 and August 2018, the troubled countries received €544.05 billion in total bail-out payments.

However, it is important to recognize that this bailout money was conditional: the countries that received it had to introduce harsh austerity measures. These measures were very painful, since they required countries to cut state expenditures, but also wages and pensions, in crisis-ridden countries such as Greece, Ireland, Portugal and Spain. Understandably, the austerity measures were extremely unpopular and generated strong anti-EU sentiment. In Greece, Angela Merkel was represented in newspapers in a Nazi uniform and a Hitler mustache.[17] Several critics maintained that the measures were counterproductive and could even undercut the Union. True, the austerity measures definitely caused political troubles and strengthened anti-EU populist parties; nonetheless, within a few years, the plan had essentially worked. By the fall of 2015, the average budgetary deficit in the euro-zone had decreased to -2.1 percent of the GDP, and even in the most critical cases – in countries like Greece, Italy and Spain – this figure was not higher than -4.0 percent. Current accounts became balanced; Greece, Italy and Spain experienced 2.5 percent, 2.0 percent, and 0.5 percent surpluses, and the euro-zone as a whole enjoyed a 2.8 percent surplus. Economic growth returned even in the two most severe cases, Greece and Italy. In 2015, Spain reached 3.1 percent annual growth compared to the previous year. The euro-zone's average growth rate was 1.5 percent and its industrial output increased by 5.1 percent. No one spoke about the collapse of the euro any longer. As *The Economist* had already concluded in the spring of 2013: "The pessimists did not overestimate the euro problems, so much as underestimate the political will to do enough to stop a euro break-up."[18] A European Union policy paper stated in February 2018: "After a decade of struggle the Eurozone today is an island of relative stability in a turbulent era."[19]

Escaping by running ahead: the euro-zone

The economic-monetary crisis of 2008 undermined and endangered the entire project of European integration. How could the EU climb out of that big hole? The crisis of the euro definitely required more than "first aid" from the European Central Bank. It demanded the correction of the currency's "birth defects" and further integration. In this context, two major steps deserve the most attention: the EU's advancement towards the development of a banking union and a quasi-fiscal union.

The first steps towards the establishment of a banking union were taken in the middle of the deep euro currency crisis in May of 2010. That month the EU established the European Financial Stability Facility for three years with €440 billion in funding by the member states. In a year's time, this amount was increased to €780 billion. The goal of this institution was to create a temporary safety net by giving "first aid" to troubled banks. Two days later, on 11 May 2010, the European Council decided to establish a permanent institution for the same task and the European Financial Stability Mechanism started working in July 2012. Funding came from issuing bonds, initially €500 billion in value. The Stability Mechanism acted within the EU as the IMF does internationally did, as such was soon nicknamed the European IMF. In this way, the EU guaranteed loans for troubled banks. Moreover, the EU signed an agreement with the IMF to double the amount of these loans. This task, which had previously belonged to the national governments, now became Europeanized. It represented a major step forward in the process of European integration, even if only for the euro-zone countries.

The other important step for further integration was the correction of the central weakness of monetary union, the lack of fiscal union. On 30 January 2012, the attendees of the European summit meeting agreed to prepare a Treaty on Stability, Coordination and Governance in the Economic and Monetary Union. It was signed on March 2 of that year by all the heads of states or governments, except for those of Britain and the Czech Republic. Furthermore, in the fall of 2013, the euro-zone countries founded the European Single Supervisory Mechanism. The European Central Bank took over the supervision of banks from the nation-states across the entire euro-zone. When three major banks – the Spanish Banco Popular, the Italian Veneto Banca and Banca Populare di Vicenza – went bankrupt in 2014, they were saved by this new European institution, instead of by the Spanish and Italian governments.

In November 2017, Mario Draghi stated: "We are now three years into the life of European banking supervision, and the track record so far is encouraging. . . . In short, European supervision and European monetary policy have proven to complement each other well."[20] The *Financial Times* reported in the summer of 2017: "The European banking union . . . is shaping up to be the most significant transformation brought about by the financial crisis. . . . [It] will revolutionise European economic and political relations beyond imagination."[21]

The EU's new rule ended the system of bailing out banks nationally by using taxpayer money. That system was understandably unpopular. If banks' profits went into private pockets in "normal" times, critics questioned, then why did banks' losses become public losses during times of crisis? Why the banks were compensated by public – in other words, taxpayer – money? The new EU "bail-in" (instead of bail-out) system forced the banks' huge creditors to take a big part of the losses by writing off a portion of their debt. At the same time, this new policy also introduced risk sharing among creditor and debtor countries, meaning that it mandated transfers from surplus (creditor) countries to deficit (debtor) countries. In other words, it was a major step towards Europeanizing the banking industry.

Nevertheless, the banking union remained only half built. In 2014, the European Commission suggested finishing the construction by foundation the last missing pillar of the system, the European Deposit Insurance Scheme, which would Europeanize the protection of smaller deposits by taking it over from national governments. Germany opposed the introduction of the Scheme, arguing that it would be a transfer union; thus Spanish, Irish, or Romanian depositors would back their lost deposits using German and French financial sources via transfer. After years of inaction and silence, this idea was revitalized in November 2019 when Olf Scholz, Germany's minister of finance, returned to the issue and supported a solution: the creation of a joint European fund to be used if national funding failed. If agreements follow, the ensuing further integration of the euro-zone will represent a major step forward.[22]

In the years when the European Union coped with the devastating financial and economic crisis, it avoided the collapse of the common currency; however, well before a full recovery from the complex crisis could take place, a totally different new major disaster shocked the Continent: an unparalleled migration crisis.

Migration crisis, 2015–2016

Historically, immigration in Europe is a rather new phenomenon. In the nineteenth century, Europe was a classic emigration continent, from which 50–60 million people emigrated. This trend continued (though in a much more moderate way) into the first half of the twentieth century. After World War II, Europe stopped sending huge numbers of emigrants abroad.

During the mid-1940s to the 1960s, migration continued fundamentally within Europe. Expelled Germans from Central and Eastern Europe went back to Germany; destitute, jobless people from Mediterranean countries went to various West European countries to work. Most of them later returned home. Immigration from outside Europe was well organized in Germany. The country badly needed workers, and signed agreements with Italy and Spain in 1955 and 1960, respectively, then with Turkey in October 1961 to send "Gastarbeiters" to Germany for two years. The country also made similar agreements with Portugal, Morocco, Tunisia and Yugoslavia. In 1964, Germany signed a new treaty with Turkey that allowed for a longer stay for guest workers, and even enabled workers to bring family members. In the end, half of the Turkish guest workers remained in Germany, establishing families and gradually increasing the number of Turkish immigrants in the country to 2.7 million. In 1960, only 0.7 million of Germany's population was foreigners; by 1980, there were already 5 million. Switzerland and Luxembourg also invited guest workers: at their peaks, about one-quarter and one-third of the labor force, respectively, were non-European guest workers. During the 1960s – 1970s, about 220,000 guest workers arrived to Europe every year, and their numbers increased to 500,000 in the late 1980s. By that time, France, Britain and Italy each had about 4 million immigrants.

Across the whole of recorded European history, 1985 was the very first year in which the number of immigrants surpassed the number of emigrants. At that time, Europe's permanent immigrant population was about 8–10 million people. During the next quarter of a century, thus until 2010, about 300,000–400,000 people applied for asylum annually in the EU-15 countries and about one-quarter, thus about 100,000, were accepted.[23] Beginning in the 1960s, after the collapse of the colonial system, non-European immigration to several West European countries became significant. Millions moved from Africa and Asia; many of them were French, British, Dutch people who had previously lived permanently in the colonies. Together with them, quite a lot of colonized people arrived as well, including those who had closely collaborated and served the colonizers. By the turn of the 1950s–1960s, about 10 million people had returned from the colonies, among them 1 million French people from Algeria in 1962 alone. Another major wave occurred later, when 4 million "retornado" from Africa settled in Portugal after the collapse of Portuguese colonial regime there in 1974.

At the beginning of the twenty-first century, the situation radically changed and accelerated. Tragic climate change uprooted millions in sub-Saharan Africa, and wars (especially major civil wars and tribal conflicts) pushed out millions of people from the Middle East, Asia and Africa. The globalized world economy, opportunities for cheaper travel and greater job opportunities attracted huge masses from poverty-ridden areas of the world. A Gallup Poll that surveyed 150 countries – which accounted for 93 percent of the world population between 2009 and 2011 – presented a shocking and tragic picture. A total of 40 percent of the Nigerians, 33 percent of sub-Saharan Africans, and millions of Asians – altogether 630 million adults – wanted to move to other places, 48 million of them planned to do it within a year, and 19 million had already made preparations. The polls also revealed that 145 million potential migrants would prefer to go to the United States and 142 million to the European Union, two obvious places where they hoped to find a better life. The same Gallup Poll also reflected that an additional 36 million people from the European peripheries, mostly from the Eastern half of the Continent, were considering moving to Western Europe.[24]

Around the turn of the millennium, immigration to Europe became a permanent mass phenomenon. By 2014, non-European immigrants living in Europe numbered 33.5 million, while there were 18 million migrants from the peripheral European countries living in the EU-28 countries. More than three-quarters of non-European immigrants settled in five countries: 7 million in Germany, 5 million in Britain, 5 million in Italy, 4.7 million in Spain, and 4.2 million in France.[25] Besides the legal immigrants, various estimations also calculate that about 3–10 million illegal immigrants were living in Europe in 2008. That year, roughly 12 percent of Europe's population was immigrants, but their share in some of the advanced EU-15 countries was higher: in Ireland and Austria, they represented 16 percent of the population; in Germany and Sweden, 15 percent; in Spain, 13 percent; in Belgium, 12 percent; and in France, the Netherlands, and Britain, 11 percent.[26] Only a few East-European EU member countries such as Bulgaria, Estonia, Lithuania, Latvia, Poland, and Slovakia preserved their traditional negative migration balance and had at least 1,000 more emigrants than immigrants each year; the most extreme case, Romania, had 160,000 more emigrants than immigrants annually.[27]

Except in very few countries such as Switzerland, the immigrant population gradually became legal residents and citizens. In the first decade of the twenty-first century, more than 7 million immigrants acquired citizenship in the EU-27 countries; in 2013 alone, 1 million did so. A 1990 European Commission Report declared that integration is "inescapable, the immigrants have to be one of us socially, economically and, at least in a rudimentary sense, politically." In 2000, the Commission's Family Reunification Directive stressed the importance of family unification for the integration process.[28] France speaks about assimilation, while Germany and the Netherlands prefer multiculturalism. Sweden and the Netherlands offer language and history courses free of charge (some are even compulsory), assistance with housing, and employment help. All these opportunities were components of an immigration process that was organized and well regulated – until the mid-2010s.

In 2015, immigration to Europe surpassed every previous migration figure. Bedsides the huge numbers of people, immigration became chaotic and fell totally out of control of the normative legal frameworks. In the summer and fall of that year, 5,000–10,000 illegal migrants turned up daily in Greece, Italy, Spain, France, Germany, the Netherlands and Britain. Whereas 23,000 migrants arrived to Europe in October 2014, the number of migrants that came to the Continent in October 2015 increased to 220,000. They arrived from Pakistan, Afghanistan, sub-Saharan and North Africa, Turkey, and the Middle East; they escaped from wars, massacres and hunger in Syria, where half of the population (12 million people) was displaced; and from wars and civil wars in Iraq, Eritrea, Tunisia, Sudan and Nigeria. They sometimes arrived on boats, sometimes wandering throughout the Balkans and Central Europe on foot. Many of them met the legal definition of "refugee," but an equal number of people arriving were economic migrants. The human-trafficking business boomed, as traffickers charged $1,000–4,000 per person to smuggle migrants into Europe. In the first half of 2015, 1,600 migrants died on the Mediterranean Sea; altogether, since 2000 some 23,000 Africans and Middle Eastern people have perished. In August 2015, 70 decomposing corpses were found in a sealed Hungarian truck on the Austrian side of the Hungarian-Austrian border. It was quite symbolic that the shocking incident was discovered a couple of kilometers away from the place where European leaders discussed plans "to devise new ways to cope with the migration crisis."[29]

Unorganized, uncontrolled, frighteningly chaotic masses of people went through the entire continent without any legal checks and or even administration. The greatest migration "invasion" in history shocked Europe, but Angela Merkel of Germany declared her readiness to welcome them in with open arms.[30] Germany became the central target country for migrants; indeed, the country received more than one and a half million of them in 2015, and more than 1 million in 2016. The European Union worked out a plan of compulsory distribution of immigrants according to a quota among member countries, but some of them – among others, Hungary and Poland – flatly rejected this policy. The Hungarian Orbán government built fences at its southern borders and handled the migrants inhumanly, although only a very small fraction of migrants – in 2015, for example, only 58,000 – settled in Hungary.

In the end, the migration crisis also caused a political crisis within the Union and in several member countries including Germany, where at least a part of the population rejected the immigrants because they were frightened by the increased crime that was a consequence. For a portion of Europe's population, one of most the frightening elements of the "migrant offensive" was the high percentage of Muslims among them. Their "otherness," the lack of assimilation by certain earlier Muslim immigrants, and racism definitely played a role in the backlash against immigration.

In the context of several recent Muslim terrorist attacks across Europe, Muslim immigrants represented a special concern. The European Union produced an interesting analysis of Muslims in Europe in 2009. Muslim immigration had already begun during the postwar reconstruction period. Turks settled in Germany, Bangladeshis and Pakistanis in Britain, Algerians and Moroccan in France, but also former colonial Muslims in the Netherlands and Spain. In some of those countries, they represented between 2 percent and 9 percent of the population, but mostly remained separated from the native inhabitants and had a "Muslim first" identity. In 2008, half of Germans and Spaniards had unfavorable views about Muslims. In Britain at that time, 26,500 anti-Muslim incidents were reported. Muslims have mostly marginal positions in European societies: in Germany, Germans earns twice as much as Muslims in the highest bracket; in Spain, Spanish people earn four times more. However, the educational differences are even larger. One-third of Muslims under age 34 have educational qualifications that are three times lower than those among native Europeans. Only half of Muslim males between the ages of 16 and 24 are active economically; across all of society, this figure only reaches 68 percent. A study by the Center for Strategic and International Studies concluded: "the immigrant Muslims of Western Europe have remained poorer, less educated, and more socially marginalized."[31]

Racism definitely plays some role, but it would be mistaken to label the entirety of anti-Muslim and anti-immigration sentiments as racist. Very unfortunately, mass Muslim immigration was accompanied by various terrorist actions undertaken by a small group of fundamentalist Muslims. The whole world remembers the deadly 2001 attacks against New York and Washington by fundamentalist Saudi Muslim terrorists. Relatedly, in the mid-2010s, Islamist terror attacks shocked Paris, Nice, London, Köln, Berlin, Madrid and several other European cities in a row. The list of the attacks, as *Deutsche Welle* reported in 2017, is terrifying: Madrid in March 2004, Brussels in May 2014, London in July 2005, Paris in January and again in November 2015, Copenhagen in February 2015, Istanbul in January 2016, Brussels in March 2016 and Nice in July 2016. The most frightening series occurred in 2017: Paris in February, March and April, in

London in March and June, Manchester in March, Stockholm in April, Barcelona in August and Berlin in December.[32] All of these fueled the rise of opposition against immigration and against the traditional parties and governments that supported it.

Against a new pressure of migration

The 2015–2016 migration crisis and the significant mistakes of the Union in handling it generated changes in EU policy. The European Council adopted resolutions aimed at controlling and administering migration on 18 February and on 7 and 18 March 2016. Accordingly, the EU has provided financial and administrative support to countries that have accepted the main bulk of the migration flow, in particular Greece, to assist with border control and processing asylum requests, in accordance with EU rules.

The second element of the new policy was an agreement with Turkey. According to this agreement, Europe would only accept migrants on the condition that their asylum requests were submitted and approved in Turkish territory. Migrants who illegally arrived in Greece from Turkey would be sent back. In exchange, Europe paid €3 billion in compensation to Turkey in 2016–2017, and then another €3 billion later on.

Thirdly, the EU established border controls – the European Border and Coast Guard Agency (Frontex) and the European Asylum Support Service – for asylum seekers. After this policy was enacted, the number of migrants to Europe more than halved. In 2017, the EU tightened its migration policy. At a Brussels summit on 19 October 2017, the member states decided to ensure full control over the borders. Moreover, the conclusions of the European Council indicate its readiness to respond and suppress any attempts to illegally cross the borders of EU member states. All these arrangements, however, could not eliminate the possibility of further danger, and the situation has definitely not been resolved. The United Nations World Migration Report 2020 clearly reflected the strong pressure of mass migration:

> The number of international migrants is estimated to be almost 272 million globally, with nearly two-thirds being labour migrants. This figure remains. . . [at 3.5%] of the world's population. . . . However, the estimated number and proportion of international migrants already surpasses some projections made for the year 2050, which were in the order of 2.6 per cent or 230 million.[33]

The bulk of migrants continue to target the two most advanced regions of the world, the United States and Europe. As spring approached in 2020, the danger of a new crisis appeared. A report in early March 2020 clearly reflected the first signs of the return of mass migration. A new wave of fighting in northern Syria renewed the potential for a mass Syrian flight to Turkey, and since that report was published nearly a million Syrian migrants are now in movement. Pushing aside the 2016 agreement with the EU,

> Turkey has thrown open its borders with Greece to thousands of refugees and other migrants trying to enter Europe, and has threatened to send 'millions' more. Turkey hosts 4 million refugees, some 3.6 million of them from Syria. Previously, their movement inside Turkey was strictly regulated and under a 2016 deal with the European Union, Turkey tightened border controls. Since Ankara announced last week that it would not impede those seeking to enter Europe, thousands of Afghans, Iranians, Syrians, Pakistanis and others from Africa and Asia have rushed to try their luck.[34]

As another report stated,

> The Turkish government announced that it was no longer able to support a deal made with the European Union in 2016 to prevent migrants from crossing into Europe. Shortly afterward, thousands of men, women, and children set off for the border with Greece, attempting to leave Turkey by land or by sea, only to meet barbed-wire fences and security forces.[35]

The report presented a picture frighteningly similar to the situation in 2015. The last sentence of the report, nevertheless, signals that the European response has changed compared to 2015. Greece, indeed, has responded by closing its borders, sending huge military and police forces, and trying to stop migrant boats. Greek authorities have arrested people who have illegally crossed the border. Some 24,000 attempts to pass have been thwarted. According to the UN's International Organization of Migration, 13,000 have gathered at the border, which stretches 212 kilometers.[36]

The EU has still failed to present a generally accepted agreement on migration that will be followed by all member countries. Recently, four EU countries made a new attempt to break the deadlock over migration policy. At a meeting in Birgu, Malta, interior ministers from Germany, France, Italy and Malta signed an agreement to relocate accepted refugees. They proposed the establishment of "a temporary emergency mechanism," which means that rescued migrants would be relocated to other EU member states that volunteer shelter after arriving at Mediterranean ports.[37] The voluntary plan will be presented to the EU's 24 other interior ministers at a meeting in Luxembourg in October 2020. It is unclear how many member states will sign up.[38] The only visible sign of a new European policy is the strong and successful effort to stop the chaotic, uncontrolled mass immigration crisis from resurfacing and to avoid a compulsory quota for sharing refugees. The EU is trying to find a common policy solution, but progress is very, very slow.

By the end of the 2010s, the financial-economic crisis, the common-currency crisis, and the first wave of the European migration crises had all ended (or, with respect to the latter, had at least temporarily waned). As such, the European Central Bank decided to return to normalcy, and ended its recession-era stimulus measures and special bank interventions. The Bank forecasted an impressive 2.3 percent economic growth.[39] But at this point, in the first quarter of 2020, the coronavirus pandemic hit Europe very hard and caused an even bigger and deeper economic crisis than the one created after 2008. The consequences of these three shocks during a dozen of years frightened the EU with collapse.

The COVID-19 crisis

Is the coronavirus pandemic a watershed that may open up a new chapter in international relations and European affairs? The answer to this question seems evident since the pandemic is a serious alarm bell. All of the sudden, international socio-economic connections were severed; on top of that, Europe was still reeling from the effects of the tariff wars that Trump's America initiated in the late 2010s. International value chains stopped working and countries closed their borders. This accidental event exhibited the fragility of global economic connections. "Leviathan [is] unleashed . . . the state must be unbound," *The Economist* maintained on late March 2020. The EU is "getting . . . out of the way of national governments. Fiscal rules are being quietly abandoned, allowing national governments to spend heroic amounts to allay the crisis." Health care, the number one priority during the pandemic, does not belong to the common policy sphere of the EU, but to national governments, according to EU treaties. In this environment, as *The Economist* stated, "Keeping national governments from actively working against one another would be triumph enough for Brussels."[40]

In March 2020, serious scholars, leading journals and media outlets all came out with severe warnings about the future of the existing world order, and several of them heralded the end of globalization and cooperation among countries. On 16 March 2020, *Foreign Affairs* asked, "Will the Coronavirus end globalization as we know it?"[41] *Foreign Policy* stated on 12 March 2020 that "The coronavirus is killing globalization"[42]; on the same day, the *New York Times* published an article on the topic entitled "A Global Outbreak Is Fueling the Backlash to Globalization"[43]; even the not-so-definite *Bloomberg News* maintained on March 21 that "The Coronavirus Might Kill Globalization."[44] On 2 April, *BBC News* also asked the same question: "Will coronavirus reverse globalisation?"[45] On 16 May 2020, the always-balanced magazine *The Economist* published its leading article with the title "Goodbye globalization."[46]

Globalization and cooperation among countries were already under attack from both the radical Left and nationalist Right before SARS-CoV-2 flooded the world. The pandemic immediately raised serious questions about globalization's future after countries closed their borders and the flow of millions of tourists, as well as the delivery of product parts from international value chains, stopped and the entire international system suffered deadly blows. The number of passengers at one the world's busiest airports, London Heathrow, dropped by 97 percent, Mexican car exports fell by 90 percent, South Korea's exports almost halved in May 2020, and India's nationalist government declared a new era of economic self-reliance. Moreover, the pandemic arrived at a time when trade wars had eroded decades-long interconnections among countries. *The Economist* described these challenges to globalization as "three body-blows": the financial crisis after 2008, the American-Sino trade war, and the pandemic crisis in 2020. The events of hardly more than one decade severely "wounded the open system of trade. . . . Wave goodbye to the greatest era of globalization – and worry about what is going to take its place."[47]

Should we forecast the end of cooperation and globalization? These events, one must not forget, represent not only the recent policies of some great powers, but also fall within a century-long historic trend. Globalization emerged because technological and economic development established its basis and requirements. World wars and major crises could stop it only temporarily, as evidenced by the last one and a half centuries. True, global connections and the mass movement of people massively helped the spread of the virus from China throughout the world, and countries naturally responded by reestablishing roadblocks to global connections and closing borders that were once intended to remain permanently open. These policies may have some permanent consequences. Raphael S. Cohen called the attention to the fact that the worldwide shock of the unprecedented terrorist attack against the United States on September 11, 2001 permanently changed airport security and border control but did not halt international travel; it merely "added a layer of screening." The coronavirus pandemic might have some similar permanent consequences:

> States may more actively manage the health care industry to ensure a national ability to produce critical items like masks, ventilators and prescription drugs in the event of crises. . . . Many countries . . . already take a similar hands-on approach to overseeing their defense industrial bases, so such a shift in the health care sector . . . would hardly be . . . a fatal blow to globalization at large. Above all, the primary reason why globalization will persist – perhaps in a modified form – is that the underlying drivers of the trend remain intact.[48]

The 2020 pandemic clearly showed the vulnerability of global economic connections and national economies when faced with unexpected shocks. There are definitely lessons to learn and changes to put into effect. The role of the main players of the global economy and the entire geopolitics of globalization may change, as several forecasts signal with further declining role of the United States and the increasing role of China.[49]

Recent debates and discourses, however, have questioned not only the future of globalization, but also virtually the entire future roadmap of the world. It has often been repeated that "crises shape history." In the winter and spring of 2020, several scholars and journalists prophesized radical changes to come. "Nothing remains the same"; "the world will be totally different" and not recognizable any more. Will power shift back permanently to national governments, as happened during the crisis? The Nobel-laureate economist Joseph Stiglitz is right to warn:

> In the world's advanced economies, compassion should be sufficient motivation to support a multilateral response. But global action is also a matter of

self-interest. As long as the pandemic is still raging anywhere, it will pose a threat – both epidemiological and economic – everywhere. . . "No man is an island . . ." Nor is any country – as the Covid-19 crisis has made abundantly clear. If only the international community would get its head out of the sand.[50]

Unfortunately, this kind of cooperation remains elusive, and the world may continue to act against it basic interests. One school of thought, as the British *Guardian* calls our attention to, looks at crises as glimmers of possibility: "Ideas that used to be seen as leftwing seem more reasonable to more people. There's room for change that there wasn't beforehand. It's an opening." Alternatively, pessimists warn that "emergency measures will become permanent, so enmeshed in daily life that we forget their original purpose." They warn that history also teaches that

> disasters – and especially pandemics – [have the] tendency to inflame xenophobia and racial scapegoating. When the Black Death came to Europe in the 14th century, cities and towns shut themselves to outsiders – and assaulted, banished and killed "undesirable" community members, most often Jews. In 1858, a mob in New York City broke into a quarantine hospital for immigrants on Staten Island, demanded that everyone leave and then burned the hospital down.[51]

Xenophobia, pointing to an enemy, is one of the most important weapons for populists. This is expressed by the author of a *Foreign Policy* article, who worries about the fate of democracy when advising "How to prevent the Coronavirus from Eroding Democracies."[52] On the other hand, "plenty of observers have rushed to predict that the COVID-19 pandemic will seriously harm the political fortunes of populists, or even make populism the outbreak's first ideological casualty."[53] As a study by Walter Russell Mead for the Hudson Institute and published in the *Wall Street Journal* stated on 23 March 2020: "Will Coronavirus Kill Populism?"[54] Similarly, according to the *Brookings Institution*, "The coronavirus is exposing the limits of populism."[55] On 7 April 2020, the *World Politics Review* provided a detailed analysis of "How Populists Will Leverage the Coronavirus Pandemic."[56]

I do not want to go down the road of promoting contradictory and sometimes naïve forecasting about the supposed radical change of the post-pandemic world. Richard Haass' view seems to be more realistic:

> [T]he world following the pandemic is unlikely to be radically different from the one that preceded it. COVID-19 will not so much change the basic direction of world history as accelerate it. . . . Waning American leadership, faltering global cooperation, great-power discord: all of these characterized the international environment before the appearance of COVID-19, and the pandemic has brought them into sharper-than-ever relief. They are likely to be even more prominent features of the world that follows.

Haass' forecast for Europe is rather gloomy. The pandemic throughout

> Europe has also highlighted the loss of momentum of the European project. Countries have mostly responded individually to the pandemic and its economic effects. But the process of European integration had run out of steam long before this crisis. . . . The principal question in the post-pandemic world is how much the pendulum will continue to swing from Brussels to national capitals, as countries question whether control over their own borders could have slowed the virus's spread.[57]

When the coronavirus pandemic hit the world in 2020, Europe was hit very hard: at least 4–5 million people were infected and COVID-19 killed a quarter of a million people that spring. It led to unavoidable country closures in order to introduce social distancing measures, which virtually closed the European economy as well. Economic decline caused by the pandemic ended a promising period between 2013 and 2019, the most recent post-crisis years in Europe, where economic growth had returned to the normal EU average of about 2 percent per year. The stable northwestern core countries of the Union had 1.5–2 percent annual growth, and some of them–Luxembourg, Sweden and Denmark – experienced rates of 2.1–3.4 percent. Nine countries had slower growth – between 1 percent and 2 percent per annum – but the less developed, mostly new member countries in the eastern part of the EU had an impressive 2.6–4 percent annual growth rate. (Ireland again demonstrated an outstanding and unique 8.7 percent, and in 2019 invested more than 43 percent of the value of its GDP into the economy.) In 2019, average investments in the EU countries reached 22 percent of the GDP.

This promising trend was stopped by the coronavirus pandemic and the economic crisis it caused. One must not forget that this was the third crisis in a dozen years that hit the European Union hard during the 2010s. About one-third of the economic activity of the European Union, as the European Commission's economy chief Paolo Gentiloni calculated, stopped "practically overnight." The Union, he continued, "will experience a recession of historic proportions this year,"[58] and warned that "Europe is experiencing an economic shock without precedent since the Great Depression."[59] This report predicted a 7.5 percent decline of the EU's economy in 2020 (in contrast to the worst crisis year of the Great Recession in 2009, when the decline was at 4.5 percent). The IMF also provided its first systematic assessment of the economic consequences of the coronavirus pandemic. The forecasts of the best expert bodies are already available.

The analyses also clearly clarified that the COVID-19 recession hit the member countries very unevenly. Some countries such as France – and especially the Southern members, such as Italy, Spain, Portugal and Greece – were hit harder, and their GDP may drop by 8–10 percent this year. Germany, which handled the coronavirus crisis in an exemplary way, is nonetheless predicted to experience a decline of 6.5 percent in 2020. According to EU predictions, some countries such as Poland and Austria will lose somewhat less, but will likely still decline between 4.5 and 5.5 percent.

While a rebound is expected in 2021, recovery will be gradual: current forecasts predict about 6 percent in the EU and 6.3 percent in the euro-zone, on average. Recovery may take 2–3 years in the best case. The worst part of the economic recession is its consequences for the debt burden of the member countries. It is already foreseeable that it might be as high as 20 percent of GDP on average, but the already heavily indebted member countries might be pushed to the brink. According to the already visible facts, the ratio of debt to GDP will likely exceed 200 percent in Greece; 150 percent in Italy; and 100 percent in Spain and Portugal, but also in Belgium and France. As happened during the financial crisis of 2008, the deep financial and debt crises of some euro-zone member countries may once again endanger the common currency. Nevertheless, in the spring of 2020, it is too early to evaluate the entire situation. As the British journal *The Guardian* rightly stated, around the end of April 2020, "the European economy is in a slow-motion car crash with the coronavirus. Initial impact has been made. The full scale of the damage will not be clear for months to come."[60]

Escaping by running ahead: coronabond?

Waiting until the culmination of the crisis to act would be a fatal mistake. Current decisive action is badly needed. The European Central Bank recommended that the euro-zone finance ministers put forth a stimulus package of about €1.5 trillion ($1.6 trillion) and – similarly to what it did during the financial crisis of 2008 – itself launched a $750 billion emergency debt-buying program to keep borrowing costs low. Christine Lagarde, the new president of the Bank, followed in the footsteps of her predecessor by announcing on 30 April 2020: "These purchases will continue to be conducted in a flexible manner over time."[61]

In the spring of 2020, the euro-zone ministers discussed the possibility of easing the burden of the most endangered countries (mostly those in the South) and decided upon a €540 billion ($590 billion) rescue deal to help the bloc's coronavirus-stricken economies. This amount, as impressive as it is, is only about one-third of the package that the Central Bank considers necessary. Furthermore, this amount of bailout funding is partly not additional money. It includes €240 billion ($261 billion) from the European Stability Mechanism (ESM), a bailout fund that was created during the euro-zone crisis. Countries will be able to access up to 2 percent of their respective GDP until the COVID-19 crisis is over. Another €200 billion is to be made available as loans to companies from the European Investment Bank. The only additional public funding was €125 billion (1 percent of the euro-zone GDP) in loans through the newly created Support to Mitigate Unemployment Risks in an Emergency (SURE). SURE provides for financial assistance from the EU to affected member states, but although it will help, it will also increase the already high level of indebtedness for troubled countries.

The optimal solution would be to transfer the additional debt to an all-European body. This possibly was on finance ministers' agenda in the form of issuing a joint EU 'coronabond' to cover the extra debt burden caused by the COVID-19 crisis. This solution would, indeed, mobilize about €1.4–2.1 trillion, or 10–15 percent of the EU's GDP, in the form of joint bonds. The finance ministers, however, would not agree to it. That outcome had already happened several times before. It occurred during the Great Recession after 2008, when Germany, the Netherlands and some of the Nordic countries opposed jointly sharing the burden by issuing Eurobonds. It happened again in February 2020, when, in a debate about the next EU budget, the so-called "frugal four" – as the Netherlands, Austria, Finland and Sweden were called – strictly opposed increasing the budget above 1 percent of the GDP. They also opposed the idea of creating a "transfer union," or sharing the burden by mutualizing it. From their position, it is logical to weigh the irresponsibleness of individual nations' fiscal decisions when deciding whether or not the EU should provide support. One of the German parliamentarian stated: "Every country should ask itself whether it bears some responsibility for the situation it is in."[62] In the spring of 2020, Dutch Finance Minister Wopke Hoekstra repeated his country's opposition to so-called Eurobonds or coronabonds – both instances of jointly issued debt. He argued that those policies "would turn the EU into some kind of a transfer union, where the countries in the North would have to permanently fund those in the South, which some believe are not fiscally responsible."[63] He added that would be unreasonable to expect his nation to "guarantee the debts that others make."[64] Transfers from rich to poorer countries in this way would undoubtedly be a form of debt cancellation. Nevertheless, Italy's deep crisis may easily undermine the common currency. A decade ago, the Greek crisis almost destroyed the euro currency. But Italy has the world's eighth-largest economy in the world – ten times bigger than that of Greece, and more than one-tenth of the EU's total.

Some governments, including some of the richest member countries, gave an immediate answer. On 25 March 2020, nine European heads of states and governments – Belgium, France, Italy, Luxembourg, Spain, Portugal, Greece, Slovenia and Ireland – wrote to the president of the European Council calling for a common response backed by common borrowing that would mutualize the extra burden. "What the Euro Area need in reality is not more loans to Member States," they argued, but "a strong political agreement to mutualise the cost of this crisis."[65] Italian Prime Minister Giuseppe Conte strongly criticized the cheapness of the EU's loan program from the bailout fund as a "totally inadequate tool," and also said that Italy had no intention of applying for such a loan.[66] In other words, the new crisis revitalized fundamental questions about integrating, and demonstrated the need to progress further down the road towards fiscal federalism by placing taxing, borrowing and spending under the control of the European Parliament.[67]

The solution, however, is not a technical question, but a principal one. Germany's foreign minister, Heiko Maas, and finance minister, Olaf Scholz, both advocated for fast and united action to combat the crisis: they proclaimed, "We need a clear expression of European solidarity in the corona pandemic."[68] Jürgen Hardt, a German CDU politician, emphasized that this crisis threatened the very idea of modern Europe. He said that Germany, the Netherlands and others with economic and financial power must duplicate the response of the United States after World War II:

> Germany benefited very much from the European recovery program (also known as the Marshall Plan), which was financed mainly by the US and helped us back on our feet after the Second World War. I think we need something like that now from the economically stronger European countries. It would be a strong signal to those countries who doubt the EU right now.[69]

European solidarity among EU member countries is strikingly missing, and the crisis may reopen longstanding North-South fault lines and feed nationalism and far-right populism. Italian and Spanish leaders have warned that the EU itself is at risk of falling apart.[70] Matteo Salvini and other populist politicians speak about leaving the European Union. He recently asked, "Why do we want to stay in the EU? It is useless"; and more than two-thirds (67 percent) of Italians agreed (in contrast to in November 2018, when 47 percent felt the same way). Even if it does not happen, the COVID-19 crisis may severely weaken the appetite for integration. As one analysis stated:

> Neither Italy nor Spain will be anxious to follow the UK's messy exit. But sharply Euro-skeptic governments could take over in both Madrid and Rome. Populist parties are likely to be strengthened elsewhere. The evident lack of solidarity, from the suffering many to the embattled few will likely kill efforts to expand Brussels' authority.[71]

The European Union has to learn a few lessons: "Bigger transfers and significant debt mutualisation would be hard, but as a down payment to avert catastrophe and to set the EU on the path to stability, they would be worth it."[72] Responsible European leaders understand this requirement. *Euronews* reported on 19 May 2020 that Emmanuel Macron and Angela Merkel held a joint video press conference to announce an agreement to issue coronabonds to help troubled countries with an additional €545 billion. Chancellor Merkel shifted radically away from the traditional German attitude – which she had once held as well – by deciding to support the mutualization of additional burdens. She declared, "The EU must act together; the nation state has no chance if it acts on its own. This is the biggest challenge in the history of the EU."[73] This offer has to be accepted by all the member countries, but Merkel has provided a rationale for countries that have traditionally opposed such measures by stating that this extraordinary time necessitates unusual, extraordinary measures; and that such efforts will not become the new norm, but will instead act as once-in-a-lifetime emergency steps.[74]

There are also alternatives to the coronabond. One would be to issue per-petual or consol bonds. The great advantage of this alternative is that although the issuers would have to pay interest forever, because there is no maturity time, they would not have to repay the principal. In other words, it is not a debt, but an equity. This idea of issuing common bonds with the European Central Bank as the buyer was presented in an article entitled "Helicopter Money" by Donato Masciandaro, a Bocconi University economist, in April 2020. This suggestion was repeated in May by George Soros in an interview with a Dutch journal.[75]

The "frugal" countries' counter-proposal offered another alternative: jointly raising money and loaning it to countries with low interest.[76] In May 2020, the EU was already offering low-interest loans for member countries, which could get hundreds of millions of euros in this form. European-Commission President Ursula von der Leyen unveiled an official EU plan on 27 May 2020 that even went somewhat further than the Macron-Merkel proposal. In a speech at the European Parliament, she said:

> Our unique model built over 70 years is being challenged like never before in our lifetime or in our Union's history. The common European goods we have built together are being damaged. . . . There is the Single Market that needs to recover. . . . And there are four freedoms that need to be fully restored. The crisis has huge externalities and spillovers across countries. None of that can be fixed by any single country alone. . . . A struggling economy in one part of Europe, weakens a strong economy in another part. This is about all of us. And it is way bigger than any of us. This is Europe's moment."[77]

She announced a plan to jointly borrow €750 billion to help EU states recover from the COVID-19 economic crisis. The proposal, as the *Reuters* news agency reported, maintained that it

> breaks new ground in several ways. First, it envisages the EU issuing a large quantity of debt, boosting the commission's next budget to an unprece-dented 1.85 trillion euros. The bonds – dubbed "Next Generation EU" – will be collectively backed by member states through the EU budget, increasing their appeal to investors. And they will be repaid over a long period of time, potentially stretching to 2058. . . . [The amount] will be handed to member states in the form of grants and will not count towards national debt. This is a big shift from previous aid packages, where the EU offered aid in the form of cheap loans. It will come as a relief to indebted governments.[78]

The proposal was unprecedented in the history of the European Union, and definitely different from the EU's answer to the 2008 crisis. This is, indeed, the time for the European Union to grow above itself, turn inward and begin repara-tion work, and institute further integration steps, which are badly needed. This is, indeed, Europe's moment. The opposing "frugal" countries represent only

42 million people, or less than one-tenth of the EU's population. Some compromise is hopefully possible. The fact that in one of the "frugal" countries, Finland, the social democratic-led five-party coalition government joined with those who support the mutualization of extra burden, offers great promise. This compromise is a radical demonstration of solidarity and will hopefully become a symbol of a European Union that comes out of the pandemic crisis stronger and more unified. If such crucial steps towards solidarity are not made, the newly closed borders of the member countries during the pandemic might become a symbol for the future of Europe. The old Continent demonstrated after World War II that it can learn from history, and hopefully will do so again.

Escaping by running ahead: steps towards military integration

Escaping from complex and frightening crises always requires eliminating weaknesses, adding missing elements (in this case, of integration), and thus – as Mother Courage does in Berthold Brecht's eponymous drama – escaping by running ahead through the front lines. The migration crisis naturally revitalized the necessity for border defense and for gaining control of the Mediterranean Sea in order to stop illegal entry into the Union's territory. The EU had already established the European Agency for the Management of Operational Cooperation at the External Borders (Frontex) in 2004. Frontex, however, was not well financed or equipped. In 2014, the External Sea Border Surveillance Regulation was introduced, and a common EU migration and asylum policy was enacted. In June 2015, in the middle of the migration crisis, the EU launched a common military campaign to "identify, capture and dispose of vessels as well as enabling assets used or suspected of being used by migrant smugglers or traffickers."[79]

During the difficult years of the decade-long set of crises, some further steps towards a closer integration were also taken in the military field. The idea of military integration, the creation of a joint European army, is as old as the integration process itself. It was placed onto the European Community's agenda in 1950, but it did not happen because the French parliament voted it down in 1954. In November 2014, the European Union elected a new president, Jean-Claude Juncker, the former prime minister of Luxembourg. Juncker, an old-guard federalist, advocated for military unification during his election campaign. In July 2014, at his speech at the European Parliament, he pointed out: "even the strongest soft powers cannot make do in the long run without at least some integrated defence capacities."[80] He always stressed that "defence integration is our best – and only – option."[81] *Deutsche Welle* reported on 11 November 2016 that the President of the European Commission repeated this suggestion to reporters in Berlin:

> The European Union needs to overhaul its defense strategy and work towards creating a European army. . . . We have a lot to thank the Americans for . . . but they won't look after Europe's security for ever. . . . We have to do

this ourselves, which is why we need a new approach to building a European security union with the end goal of establishing a European army.[82]

Juncker put this program on the EU's agenda during this period of dangerous crisis. Against the frightening signs of disintegration, did he suggest a new area of integration in order to counterbalance the dividing pressures of the crisis? That was probably one of his reasons. After he made his declaration, Ursula von der Leyen, then the German defense minister, immediately agreed: "Our future as Europeans will one day be a European army."[83] Germany's assent was not surprising. The *Deutsche Welle* had already reported in June 2016 that a *Weißbuch*, a German defense White Paper, had been prepared that argued strongly for the creation of a European army, although Angela Merkel had ordered her government to keep it secret. That was a radical change in German opinion. As an expert at the US Army War College's Strategic Studies Institute explains, the German White Paper

> represents a paradigm shift in two important respects. . . . What is perhaps most significant is the declaration that Germany will be willing to not simply anticipate in but also *initiate* such coalitions. This is a major departure from the past, in which Germany consistently sought to exercise hard power solely through established multilateral institutions [i.e. NATO].[84]

Resurfacing the idea of a joint European army in 2014–2016 was not, of course, accidental. Juncker himself mentioned Russian aggression in Ukraine as a reason to show strength. He, however, wanted to negate rumors that his call was connected with the American election that had occurred a few days earlier, when Donald Trump was elected president of the United States. In her earlier statement, von der Leyen also added that a European army would "strengthen a European pillar in the transatlantic alliance."[85]

In reality, both of them had certainly considered the possible consequences of the election of Trump, who, during the election campaign, stated several times that "NATO is obsolete."[86] The existence of the American security shield, which had unquestionably existed since the war, became uncertain when the US president declared his commitment to America First principles. Indeed, at a NATO meeting in early 2017, Trump made headlines for refusing to reaffirm the US's commitment to the famous Article 5 principle, which states that an attack against one NATO member is considered an attack against all members.

In 2016, another new factor contributed to EU leaders' recommendations for military integration: that summer, Britain voted in a referendum to leave the European Union. Britain, of course, was always against further integration. The country had previously opposed military integration many times when the issue resurfaced again and again. The British daily newspaper *The Guardian* stated in 2015: "In the past David Cameron, the British prime minister, has blocked moves to create EU-controlled military forces."[87] In 2016, the journal added: "Former defence secretary Liam Fox warned darkly that 'Europe's defence intentions are a dangerous fantasy' that risked cutting the UK off from the US."[88] The *Financial Times* quoted a British government spokeswoman as stating: "Our position is crystal clear that defence is a national, not an EU responsibility and that there no prospect of that position changing and no prospect of a European army."[89]

After Brexit relieved the EU of Britain's strong internal opposition, the endangered European Union started to act. The newly elected French President Emmanuel Macron was among the first heads of states who also urged military unification. He said that Europe cannot be protected without a "true, European army." At the centenary celebration of the end of World War I, the *BBC* reported that Macron "warned of the 'leprosy' of nationalism spreading worldwide and declared that he had been struck by the similarities of current times and the period between World War One and World War Two." Regarding cyber security, he also said: "We have to protect ourselves with respect to China, Russia and even the United States of America." Europe, Macron emphasized, had to be able "to defend itself better alone."[90] In an interview published in the *Economist* in November 2019, Macron called NATO "braindead": "The instability of our American partner and rising tensions have meant that the idea of European defence is gradually taking hold."[91]

Foreign Policy reported on 22 May 2017 that Germany had started to build a quasi-European army: "Germany and two of its European allies, the Czech Republic and Romania, quietly took a radical step down a path toward something that looks like an EU army" by announcing "the integration of their armed forces."[92] Similarly, Germany and France made initiatives together regarding military cooperation between their nations and the remaining EU-27 countries. *Reuters* reported in November 2017: "European defense planning, operations and weapons development now stands its best chance in years as London steps aside."[93] The defense ministries of the two countries jointly declared that they wanted to galvanize the creation of a common EU defense policy. In September they made a detailed list of proposals, including the future creation of a joint permanent EU command headquarters.[94]

In November 2017 at the EU summit in Bratislava, 23 countries of the EU-27 accepted the French-German recommendation. The Permanent Structured Cooperation on Security and Defense (PESCO) was established. In a joint statement, the French and German ministers of defense stressed that it is "high time to strengthen our solidarity and European capacities in defence."[95] Although they repeated that they wanted to remain transatlantic, they also expressed their commitment to also providing for a force that was "more European."[96] They asserted that the creation of an EU military force would help "reinforce the EU strategic autonomy to act alone when necessary, and with partners whenever possible."[97]

Officials of the United States, ignoring President Trump's announced anti-European protectionist policy, arrogantly "raised new questions and doubts about these European plans, expressing concerns that they could . . . cut out United States military manufacturers from bidding on certain European projects." The American ambassador to NATO clearly declared that "Washington did not want Pesco or a new European Defense Fund 'to be a protectionist vehicle for E.U.' "[98]

The EU's High Representative for Foreign Policy and Security, Federica Mogherini, characterized the founding of PESCO (with some degree of overstatement) as a historical breakthrough: "This is a historic achievement. . . . It is also the start of a journey on which we will embark together. This is the beginning of a new story, and not the closing of a page."[99] The EU, as she announced, was "currently working on over 50 projects to follow up the decision by 23 EU members to create a common defence fund."[100] In the summer of 2017, a European Commission's reflection paper offered a highly interesting picture on the present defense capacity of Europe in comparison with America's defense forces. While America has 330 million citizens and spends €545 billion on defense, the EU member countries together hold nearly 500 million citizens yet spend only €227 billion, or slightly less than half that amount. The paper also documented the fragmentation of weaponry in Europe. The American army has one type of battle tanks; the EU countries together have 17 types. The US has four kinds of destroyer frigates; the EU countries have 29 kinds. Instead of the US's eight types of fighter plans, Europe has 20 types. Altogether, compared with the 30 types of weaponry used by the American armed forces, the various forces of Europe use 178 different types. The Commission recommended standardizing and unifying the weaponry; aside from other great advantages, this streamlining could save the EU countries about €26 billion per year, altogether.[101]

In December 2017, PESCO submitted a list of 17 projects that will be jointly implemented. They are focused on crisis response in the southern neighborhood of Europe. Italy, Spain, Portugal and Greece became involved in between 9–16 projects, but the Central European member countries are the focus of only 1–4 projects. The Baltic countries, Poland and some of the Nordic countries that feel threatened by Russia have expressed skepticism about Europe-only military projects and have expressed their preference for NATO involvement. As such, the movement towards joint military action has illuminated some serious fissures.[102]

Nevertheless, in June 2018, nine countries accepted Emmanuel Macron's initiative and agreed upon a new European Intervention Initiative. This entity will operate independently from PESCO and "will be tasked with quickly deploying troops in crisis scenarios near European borders."[103] The French minister of defense stated: "we will create a European strategic culture. We will be ready to anticipate crises and respond quickly and effectively."[104] In May 2017, the EU initiated the Preparatory Action on Defense Research, which supported defense-related research and technology developments directly from common EU funds for the first time. A few months later, in December 2017, the launch of the European Defense Industrial Development Program provided €500 million in co-financing for the joint industrial development of defense equipment and technologies in 2019–2020. For the period between 2021 and 2027, the amount is expected to reach €13 billion, out of which €4.1 billion will go towards collaborative research projects and €8.9 billion towards capability development, making the EU one of the top four defense R&D players in Europe. All these sums will directly come from the common EU budget, and will coexist with the various national and multinational sums dedicated to military technology. As experts at the *Carnegie Endowment for International Peace* summed up around the end of 2019:

> European defense cooperation has made unprecedented strides since 2014 and further progress is expected under the new European Commission. Driving these developments are a combination of internal and external factors. Among them is a more challenging security environment in Europe, the disruptive impact of the Brexit negotiations and the election of U.S. President Donald Trump, demands for deeper European Union (EU) integration.[105]

Although these steps towards military integration only represent the very first ones along a long road, nonetheless European military integration has started to inch forward. According to the 2018 Eurobarometer survey, defense is popular among EU citizens as well, with some 68 percent of respondents demanding that the EU do more on the subject.

Nevertheless, there are still stable and strong roadblocks on the way towards the full realization of a joint European army. Germany believes that a common European army is still several decades away. Nowadays, 80 percent of the development for defense capabilities and two-thirds of the acquisition for defense capabilities in Europe takes place on the national level, and cooperation is rather limited. Furthermore, as the Carnegie analysis noted, "European militaries remain heavily dependent on the United States for critical capabilities and strategic enablers during operations. These include strategic airlift, air mobility, medevac, [and] air-to-air refueling," in addition to several other areas.[106] Brexit also significantly weakened the EU military capacity: the Union lost 40 percent of its defense R&D and about a third of its airlift capability. Military experts are skeptical that the EU could manage to take on ambitious missions without Britain. Berlin still continues to regard NATO as the cornerstone of European security and hopes that US support for the alliance will revert back to normal after the Trump presidency.

Most importantly, the biggest obstacle is that the member countries of the EU are strongly divided regarding European self-defense. The northernmost countries – Sweden, Denmark and the Netherlands – together with several Central European countries who are close neighbors of Russia – such as Poland and the Baltic states – oppose the EU's plans for strategic autonomy and view NATO and the American alliance as more effective defenses against Russia. Some of them have even sought to boost bilateral defense ties with the Trump administration, and Poland even decided to host a new US military base in its territory. Some other countries, such as Hungary and Bulgaria, have a strong Russian orientation. Only a very strong joint French-German action will be able to convert the interest in close military cooperation into the tangible creation of a military union. A positive result is still far away.

***

In the years between 2008 and 2020, the European Union survived a complex triple set of crises and made some important attempts to go further with integration. The 2010s were, and the 2020s remained, difficult periods in the history of integration. The complex economic-financial and currency crises, the migration crisis, and the dual health and economic crisis produced by the coronavirus pandemic clearly demonstrated both the inner problems and strengths of the European Union. Meanwhile, the crises also significantly strengthened internal nationalist-populism opposition to the European Union, as well as the hostile enemies that surround it.

Notes

1 Jeremy Atack, "Financial Innovations and Crises: The View Backwards from Northern Rock," in *The Origins and Development of Financial Markets and Institutions: From the Seventeenth Century to the Present,* ed. Larry Neal and Jeremy Atack (Cambridge: Cambridge University Press, 2009), 1.

2 Simon Nixon, "Will Greece Be an Olympic Winner?," *MoneyWeek,* October 31, 2005, https://moneyweek.com/21363/will-greece-be-an-olympic-winner, accessed October 9, 2017.

3 "Greece Acknowledges Debt Concerns," *BBC News,* November 30, 2009, http://news.bbc.co.uk/2/hi/business/8387190.stm, accessed November 1, 2018.

4 Niki Kitsantonis and Matthew Saltmarsh, "Greece, Out of Ideas, Requests Global Aid," *The New York Times,* April 23, 2010, Web Edition, sec. Business, www.nytimes.com/2010/04/24/business/global/24drachma.html, accessed November 6, 2017.

5 Nick Lioudis, "The Collapse of Lehman Brothers: A Case Study," *Investopedia,* November 26, 2019, www.investopedia.com/articles/economics/09/lehman-brothers-collapse.asp, accessed December 19, 2019.

6 Andrew Ross Sorkin, "Lehman Files for Bankruptcy; Merrill Is Sold," *The New York Times,* September 14, 2008, Web Edition, sec. Business, www.nytimes.com/2008/09/15/business/15lehman.html, accessed October 7, 2017.

7 Joseph E. Stiglitz, "The Current Economic Crisis and Lessons for Economic Theory," *Eastern Economic Journal* 35, no. 3 (2009): 282.

8 Landon Thomas Jr., "Time Runs Short for Europe to Resolve Debt Crisis," *The New York Times,* November 27, 2011, Web Edition, sec. Business, www.nytimes.com/2011/11/28/business/global/pressure-builds-in-europe.html, accessed October 16, 2017.

9 Ryan Avent, "Is This the End?," *The Economist,* November 25, 2011, www.economist.com/free-exchange/2011/11/25/is-this-the-end, accessed October 18, 2017.

10 "A Comedy of Euros," *The Economist,* December 17, 2011, www.economist.com/leaders/2011/12/17/a-comedy-of-euros, accessed October 20, 2017.

11 Nicholas Kulish and Steven Erlanger, "Even as Governments Act, Time Runs Short for Euro," *The New York Times,* November 12, 2011, Web Edition, sec. World, www.nytimes.com/2011/11/13/world/europe/for-european-union-and-the-euro-a-moment-of-truth.html, accessed November 1, 2017.

12 Thomas L. Friedman, "Who's the Decider?," *The New York Times,* November 15, 2011, Web Edition, sec. Opinion, www.nytimes.com/2011/11/16/opinion/whos-the-decider.html, accessed October 28, 2017.

13 David Brooks, "The Technocratic Nightmare," *The New York Times,* November 17, 2011, Web Edition, sec. Opinion, www.nytimes.com/2011/11/18/opinion/brooks-the-technocratic-nightmare.html, accessed October 16, 2017.

14 Paul Krugman, "Boring Cruel Romantics," *The New York Times,* November 20, 2011, Web Edition, sec. Opinion, www.nytimes.com/2011/11/21/opinion/boring-cruel-euro-romantics.html, accessed October 16, 2017.

15 Jörg Asmussen, *Saving the Euro* (London: The Economist's Bellwether Europe Summit, April 25, 2013), www.ecb.europa.eu/press/key/date/2013/html/sp130425.en.html, accessed October 17, 2017.

16 Mario Draghi, *Speech*, Global Investment Conference (London: European Central Bank, July 26, 2012), https://www.ecb.europa.eu/press/key/date/2012/html/sp120726.en.html, accessed October 20, 2017.

17 Aya Bach, "Merkel as Hitler?," *Deutsche Welle*, April 18, 2013, Web Edition, sec. Germany, www.dw.com/en/merkel-as-hitler/a-16753456, accessed October 20, 2017.

18 Anton La Guardia, "All Hope Not Lost," *The Economist*, December 22, 2012, sec. Charlemagne (Opinion), www.economist.com/europe/2012/12/22/all-hope-not-lost, accessed October 23, 2017.

19 Daniel Gros, "The Eurozone as an Island of Stability," *Centre for European Policy Studies*, February 19, 2018, www.ceps.eu/ceps-publications/eurozone-island-stability/, accessed November 6, 2018.

20 Mario Draghi, *European Banking Supervision Three Years On*, Welcome Address (Frankfurt am Main: ECB Forum on Banking Supervision, November 7, 2017), www.ecb.europa.eu/press/key/date/2017/html/ecb.sp171107.en.html, accessed October 30, 2017.

21 Martin Sandbu, "Banking Union Will Transform Europe's Politics," *Financial Times*, July 25, 2017, sec. Opinion, www.ft.com/content/984da184-711c-11e7-aca6-c6bd07df1a3c, accessed November 7, 2017.

22 Sam Fleming et al., "German Eurozone Banking Plan Wins Cautious Backing," *Financial Times*, November 6, 2019, www.ft.com/content/6e6eb2a6-0088-11ea-b7bc-f3fa4e77dd47, accessed January 3, 2020.

23 Elspeth Guild et al., "New Approaches, Alternative Avenues and Means of Access to Asylum Procedures for Persons Seeking International Protection," *CEPS Paper in Liberty and Security in Europe*, no. 77 (January 2015), www.ceps.eu/ceps-publications/new-approaches-alternative-avenues-and-means-access-asylum-procedures-persons-seeking/, accessed October 16, 2017.

24 Neli Esipova, Julie Ray, and Anita Pugliese, *Gallup World Poll: The Many Faces of Global Migration* (Geneva: International Organization for Migration, 2011), https://publications.iom.int/system/files/pdf/mrs43.pdf, accessed November 1, 2017.

25 "2015 Migration and Migrant Population Statistics," *Eurostat*, https://ec.europa.eu/eurostat/statistics-explained/index.php?title=Migration_and_migrant_population_statistics&oldid=477804, accessed June 15, 2020.

26 Christian Dustmann and Tommaso Frattini, *Immigration: The European Experience*, Discussion Paper (Bonn: IZA, 2011), www.ssrn.com/abstract=2023575, accessed October 25, 2017.

27 *Eurostat Yearbook 2011, Europe in Figures* (Luxembourg: European Union, 2011).

28 *Policies on Immigration and the Social Integration of Migrants in the European Community* (Brussels: Commission of the European Communities, September 1990), SEC(90) 1813 final, Archive of European Integration, http://aei.pitt.edu/1261/1/immigration_policy_SEC_90_1813.pdf; *On a Community Immigration Policy*, Communication from the Commission to the Council and the European Parliament (Brussels: Commission of the European Communities, November 22, 2000), COM(2000) 757 final, Archive of European Integration, http://aei.pitt.edu/38186/1/COM_(2000)_757.pdf, accessed October 28, 2017.

29 Alison Smale and Melissa Eddy, "Grisly Discovery in Migrant Crisis Shocks Europe," *The New York Times*, August 27, 2015, Web Edition, sec. World, www.nytimes.com/2015/08/28/world/europe/bodies-austria-truck-migrant-crisis.html, accessed November 5, 2017.

30 Andrea Thomas, "Germany's Merkel Sticking to Open-Arms Migrant Policy," *Wall Street Journal*, November 13, 2015, sec. World, www.wsj.com/articles/

germanys-merkel-sticks-to-open-arms-migrant-policy-1447437314, accessed October 25, 2017.

31 Steffen Angenendt et al., *Muslim Integration: Challenging Conventional Wisdom in Europe and the United States*, CSIS Transatlantic Dialogue on Terrorism (Washington, DC: Center for Strategic and International Studies, September 2007), https://csis-website-prod.s3.amazonaws.com/s3fs-public/legacy_files/files/media/csis/pubs/070920_muslimintegration.pdf, accessed October 16, 2017.

32 "Madrid to Manchester to Barcelona: A Chronology of Terror in Europe," *Deutsche Welle*, August 17, 2017, www.dw.com/en/madrid-to-manchester-to-barcelona-a-chronology-of-terror-in-europe/a-38949481, accessed January 7, 2018.

33 *World Migration Report 2020* (Geneva: International Organization for Migration–United Nations, 2019), 2, www.un.org/sites/un2.un.org/files/wmr_2020.pdf, accessed January 17, 2020.

34 Andrew Wilks and Nicholas Paphitis, "AP EXPLAINS: The New Migration Crisis at Europe's Borders," *ABC News*, March 3, 2020, https://abcnews.go.com/International/wireStory/ap-explains-migration-crisis-europes-borders-69353175, accessed May 2, 2020.

35 Alan Taylor, "Thousands of Migrants Attempt to Cross into Europe from Turkey," *The Atlantic*, March 2, 2020, sec. In Focus, www.theatlantic.com/photo/2020/03/thousands-of-migrants-attempt-to-cross-into-europe-from-turkey/607321/, accessed May 2, 2020.

36 Wilks and Paphitis, "AP EXPLAINS."

37 "Key EU Countries Agree on Sea Migrant Redistribution Scheme," *Deutsche Welle*, September 23, 2019, www.dw.com/en/key-eu-countries-agree-on-sea-migrant-redistribution-scheme/a-50549610, accessed January 8, 2020.

38 Jennifer Rankin Lorenzo Tondo in Palermo and Lorenzo Tondo, "EU Nations Come to Italy's Aid over Relocating Migrants," *The Guardian*, September 23, 2019, sec. World News, https://www.theguardian.com/world/2019/sep/23/eu-nations-come-to-italys-aid-over-relocating-migrants, accessed December 8, 2019.

39 Jack Ewing, "Europe's Central Bank, Lagging behind Counterparts, Faces Eventful 2018," *The New York Times*, December 13, 2017, Web Edition, sec. Business, www.nytimes.com/2017/12/13/business/economy/ecb-draghi-rates.html, accessed November 8, 2018; Jack Ewing, "E.C.B. Shifts Guidance, as Europe Moves toward Normalcy," *The New York Times*, March 7, 2018, Web Edition, sec. Business, www.nytimes.com/2018/03/07/business/economy/ecb-euro-italy.html, accessed December 1, 2018.

40 "More Europe or Less?," *The Economist*, March 21, 2020, sec. Charlemagne (Opinion), www.economist.com/europe/2020/03/21/more-europe-or-less, accessed May 2, 2020.

41 Henry Farrell and Abraham Newman, "Will the Coronavirus End Globalization as We Know It?," *Foreign Affairs*, March 16, 2020, www.foreignaffairs.com/articles/2020-03-16/will-coronavirus-end-globalization-we-know-it, accessed May 2, 2020.

42 Philippe Legrain, "The Coronavirus Is Killing Globalization as We Know It," *Foreign Policy*, March 12, 2020, sec. Argument, https://foreignpolicy.com/2020/03/12/coronavirus-killing-globalization-nationalism-protectionism-trump/, accessed May 6, 2020.

43 Peter S. Goodman, "A Global Outbreak Is Fueling the Backlash to Globalization," *The New York Times*, March 5, 2020, sec. Business, www.nytimes.com/2020/03/05/business/coronavirus-globalism.html, accessed May 4, 2020.

44 Andrew Browne, "The Coronavirus Might Kill Globalization," *Bloomberg*, March 21, 2020, www.bloomberg.com/news/newsletters/2020-03-21/the-coronavirus-might-kill-globalization-bloomberg-new-economy, accessed April 25, 2020.

45 Jonty Bloom, "Will Coronavirus Reverse Globalisation?," *BBC News*, April 2, 2020, sec. Business, www.bbc.com/news/business-52104978, accessed May 7, 2020.

46 "Goodbye Globalisation," *The Economist*, May 14, 2020, Print Edition, sec. Leaders, www.economist.com/leaders/2020/05/14/has-covid-19-killed-globalisation, accessed April 28, 2020.

47 Ibid.

48 Raphael S. Cohen, "The Coronavirus Will Not Stop Globalization," *Lawfare* (blog), April 12, 2020, www.lawfareblog.com/coronavirus-will-not-stop-globali zation, accessed May 8, 2020.

49 Farrell and Newman, "Will the Coronavirus End Globalization as We Know It?."

50 Joseph Stiglitz, "World Must Combat Looming Debt Meltdown in Developing Countries," *The Guardian*, www.theguardian.com/business/2020/apr/07/world-must-combat-looming-debt-meltdown-in-developing-countries-covid-19, accessed April 19, 2020.

51 Peter C. Baker, " 'We Can't Go Back to Normal': How Will Coronavirus Change the World?," *The Guardian*, March 31, 2020, sec. World News, www.theguardian.com/world/2020/mar/31/how-will-the-world-emerge-from-the-coronavirus-crisis, accessed May 5, 2020.

52 Florian Bieber, "How to Prevent the Coronavirus from Eroding Democracies," *Foreign Policy*, March 30, 2020, Print Edition, https://foreignpolicy.com/2020/03/30/authoritarianism-coronavirus-lockdown-pandemic-populism/, accessed May 7, 2020.

53 Jan-Werner Müller, "How Populists Will Leverage the Coronavirus Pandemic," *World Politics Review*, April 7, 2020, https://111f3ba6dc414209b980802ea 03ea4fd.pages.ubembed.com/eb9bf9ca-621c-466a-9667–2137acd1b7bc/c. html?closedAt=0, accessed May 7, 2020.

54 Walter Russell Mead, "Will Coronavirus Kill Populism?," *Wall Street Journal*, March 23, 2020, sec. Opinion, www.wsj.com/articles/will-coronavirus-kill-pop ulism-11585004780, accessed May 8, 2020.

55 Thomas Wright and Kurt Campbell, "The Coronavirus Is Exposing the Limits of Populism," *Brookings Institution* (blog), March 5, 2020, www.brookings.edu/blog/order-from-chaos/2020/03/05/the-coronavirus-is-exposing-the-limits-of-populism/, accessed May 6, 2020.

56 Müller, "How Populists Will Leverage the Coronavirus Pandemic."

57 Richard Haass, "The Pandemic Will Accelerate History Rather than Reshape It: Not Every Crisis Is a Turning Point," *Foreign Affairs*, April 7, 2020, Web edition, www.foreignaffairs.com/articles/united-states/2020-04-07/pandemic-will-accelerate-history-rather-reshape-it, accessed May 9, 2020.

58 Lorne Cook, "EU Forecasts 'Recession of Historic Proportions' this Year," *Associated Press News*, May 6, 2020, sec. Global Trade, https://apnews.com/86f0b8 41f06affc7b825333163dfd50f, accessed May 19, 2020.

59 Jack Parrock and Natalie Huet, "EU Forecasts 'Recession of Historic Proportions' This Year," *Euronews*, May 6, 2020, sec. Europe, www.euronews.com/2020/05/06/eu-forecasts-recession-of-historic-proportions-this-year, accessed May 23, 2020.

60 Daniel Boffey, "Coronavirus Delivers a 'Moment of Truth' on the Meaning of the EU," *The Guardian*, April 23, 2020, sec. World News, www.theguardian.com/world/2020/apr/23/coronavirus-delivers-a-moment-of-truth-on-the-meaning-of-the-eu, accessed May 24, 2020.

61 Peter Bofinger, "The 'Frugal Four' Should Save the European Project," *Social Europe*, May 4, 2020, www.socialeurope.eu/the-frugal-four-should-save-the-european-project, accessed May 29, 2020.

62 Miles Johnson, Sam Fleming, and Guy Chazan, "Coronavirus: Is Europe Losing Italy?," *Financial Times*, April 6, 2020, www.ft.com/content/f21cf708-759e-11ea-ad98-044200cb277f, accessed May 6, 2020.

63 H. J. Mai, "The Coronavirus Could Tear the EU apart," *Vox*, April 21, 2020, www.vox.com/world/2020/4/21/21228578/coronavirus-europe-eu-eco nomic-crisis-eurozone-debt, accessed May 8, 2020.

64 Doug Bandow, "One Victim of the COVID-19 Pandemic: European Integration," *The American Conservative*, April 9, 2020, www.theamericanconserva tive.com/articles/one-victim-of-the-covid-19-pandemic-european-integration/, accessed May 17, 2020.

65 Shahin Vallee, "What Is at Stake Is . . . Well, Everything!," *The Progressive Post*, April 27, 2020, https://progressivepost.eu/spotlights/what-is-at-stake-is-well-everything/.

66 Gavin Jones and Angelo Amante, "Italy PM Extends Virus Lockdown, Says Euro Zone Rescue Plan Inadequate," *Reuters*, April 10, 2020, www.reuters.com/arti cle/us-health-coronavirus-italy-conte-idUSKCN21S1YL, accessed May 18, 2020.

67 Also see Daniel Dombey, Guy Chazan, and Jim Brunsden, "Nine Eurozone Countries Issue Call for 'Coronabonds,'" *Financial Times*, March 25, 2020, www.ft.com/content/258308f6-6e94-11ea-89df-41bea055720b, accessed May 4, 2020; Andrey Khalip and Gabriela Baczynska, "Nine EU Leaders Call for Joint Debt Issuance for Coronavirus Spending," *Reuters*, March 25, 2020, www. reuters.com/article/us-health-coronavirus-eu-letter-idUSKBN21C1SC, accessed April 18, 2020.

68 "Coronavirus: Germany Urges 'European Solidarity' to Combat Economic Fallout," *Deutsche Welle*, June 4, 2020, www.dw.com/en/coronavirus-germany-urges-european-solidarity-to-combat-economic-fallout/a-53026997, accessed June 15, 2020.

69 Mai, "The Coronavirus Could Tear the EU apart."

70 Katherine Butler, "After Coronavirus: How Will Europe Rebuild?," *The Guardian*, April 12, 2020, sec. World, www.theguardian.com/world/2020/apr/12/after-coronavirus-how-will-europe-rebuild, accessed May 7, 2020.

71 Bandow, "One Victim of the COVID-19 Pandemic."

72 "The European Union Is Having a Bad Crisis," *The Economist*, May 14, 2020, Web Edition, sec. Leaders, www.economist.com/leaders/2020/05/14/the-european-union-is-having-a-bad-crisis, accessed May 30, 2020.

73 Crispus Nyaga, "EUR/USD Soars to Two-Week as German Economic Sentiment Rises," *Invezz*, May 19, 2020, sec. EUR, https://invezz.com/news/2020/05/19/eur-usd-soars-to-two-week-as-german-economic-sentiment-rises/, accessed June 1, 2020.

74 Alice Tidey, "Macron and Merkel Back EU Bond to Raise €500bn for Europe's Recovery," *Euronews*, May 18, 2020, sec. News_News, www.euronews. com/2020/05/18/macron-and-merkel-back-eu-bond-to-raise-500-billion-for-covid-19-recovery-plan, accessed May 30, 2020.

75 Donato Masciandaro, "Covid-19 Helicopter Money: Economics and Politics," *Centre for Economic Policy Research*, no. 7 (April 20, 2020): 23–45, https:// doi.org/10.2139/ssrn.3561244, accessed May 3, 2020; George Soros, "Perpetual Bonds Could Save the European Union," Interview by Dorinde Meuzelaar, May 22, 2020, www.georgesoros.com/2020/05/22/ perpetual-bonds-could-save-the-european-union/, accessed May 30, 2020.

76 Philipp Grull, " 'Frugal Four' Working on Counter-Proposal to Franco-German Recovery Fund," *European Business Review*, May 21, 2020, sec. Europe, www. europeanbusinessreview.eu/page.asp?pid=3830, accessed May 30, 2020.

77 *Plenary Speech by President Von Der Leyen on the EU Recovery Package* (Brussels: European Parliament, May 27, 2020), https://ec.europa.eu/commission/press-corner/detail/en/speech_20_941, accessed June 2, 2020.

78 Lisa Jucca, "Breakingviews–Europe's Bond Taboo Finally Broken by Pandemic," *Reuters*, May 27, 2020, German Edition, sec. Breakingviews, https://de.reuters.

com/article/us-eu-coronavirus-breakingviews-idDEKBN2332EF, accessed June 2, 2020.

79 Giovanni Faleg and Steven Blockmans, *EU Naval Force EUNAVFOR MED Sets Sail in Troubled Waters*, CEPS Commentary (Brussels: Centre for European Policy Studies [CEPS], June 26, 2015), 1, Archive of European Integration.

80 Jean-Claude Juncker, *A New Start for Europe: My Agenda for Jobs, Growth, Fairness and Democratic Change*, Opening Statement (Strasbourg: European Parliament Plenary Session, October 22, 2014), 11, www.eesc.europa.eu/resources/docs/jean-claude-juncker-political-guidelines.pdf, accessed October 14, 2017.

81 "In Defence of Europe," *EPSC Strategic Notes*, no. 4 (June 15, 2015): 2, https://cdn.cursdeguvernare.ro/wp-content/uploads/2016/09/strategic_note_issue_4.pdf, accessed November 5, 2017.

82 "Juncker Calls for an EU Army," *Deutsche Welle*, October 11, 2016, www.dw.com/en/juncker-calls-for-an-eu-army/a-36337676, accessed November 6, 2017.

83 Andrew Sparrow, "Jean-Claude Juncker Calls for EU Army," *The Guardian*, March 8, 2015, sec. World News, www.theguardian.com/world/2015/mar/08/jean-claude-juncker-calls-for-eu-army-european-commission-miltary, accessed November 5, 2017.

84 John R. Deni, "Germany Embraces Realpolitik Once More," *War on the Rocks*, September 19, 2016, sec. Commentary, https://warontherocks.com/2016/09/germany-embraces-realpolitik-once-more/, accessed November 6, 2017.

85 Sparrow, "Jean-Claude Juncker Calls for EU Army."

86 Ashley Parker, "Donald Trump Says NATO Is 'Obsolete,' UN Is 'Political Game'," *The New York Times*, April 2, 2016, sec. Politics, www.nytimes.com/politics/first-draft/2016/04/02/donald-trump-tells-crowd-hed-be-fine-if-nato-broke-up/, accessed November 3, 2017.

87 Sparrow, "Jean-Claude Juncker Calls for EU Army."

88 Jennifer Rankin, "Is There a Secret Plan to Create an EU Army?," *The Guardian*, May 27, 2016, sec. Politics, www.theguardian.com/politics/2016/may/27/is-there-a-secret-plan-to-create-an-eu-army, accessed November 7, 2017.

89 Duncan Robinson and James Shotter, "Jean-Claude Juncker Calls for Creation of EU Army," *Financial Times*, March 8, 2015, www.ft.com/content/1141286a-c588-11e4-bd6b-00144feab7de, accessed October 8, 2017.

90 "France's Macron Pushes for 'True European Army'," *BBC News*, November 6, 2018, sec. Europe, www.bbc.com/news/world-europe-46108633, accessed November 25, 2018.

91 Emmanuel Macron, "Emmanuel Macron in His Own Words (English)," trans. *The Economist*, November 7, 2019, www.economist.com/europe/2019/11/07/emmanuel-macron-in-his-own-words-english, accessed January 4, 2020.

92 Elisabeth Braw, "Germany Is Quietly Building a European Army under Its Command," *Foreign Policy*, May 22, 2017, https://foreignpolicy.com/2017/05/22/germany-is-quietly-building-a-european-army-under-its-command/, accessed December 7, 2017.

93 Robin Emmott, "EU Signs Defense Pact in Decades-Long Quest," *Reuters*, November 12, 2017, sec. World News, www.reuters.com/article/us-eu-defence-idUSKBN1DD0PX, accessed January 6, 2018.

94 Robin Emmott and Gabriela Baczynska, "Germany, France Seek Stronger EU Defense after Brexit: Document," *Reuters*, September 12, 2016, www.reuters.com/article/us-europe-defence-idUSKCN11I1XU, accessed September 5, 2017.

95 Alex Barker, "Paris and Berlin Push for Tighter Defence Co-Operation," *Financial Times*, September 12, 2016, www.ft.com/content/fd637b0e-7913-11e697ae-647294649b28, accessed October 7, 2017.

96 Steven Erlanger, "U.S. Revives Concerns about European Defense Plans, Rattling NATO Allies," *The New York Times*, February 18, 2018, Web Edition, sec. World, www.nytimes.com/2018/02/18/world/europe/nato-europe-us-. html, accessed November 6, 2018.

97 "Part 3 – Permanent Structured Cooperation on Defence PESCO," *European Union*, August 16, 2018, https://eeas.europa.eu/headquarters/headquarters-Homepage/49449/part-3-permanent-structured-cooperation-defence-pesco_ me. Also see Michael Peel, "EU States Poised to Agree Joint Defence Pact," *Financial Times*, November 7, 2017, www.ft.com/content/29f6fe76-c2eb-11e7-a1d2-6786f39ef675, accessed January 6, 2018.

98 Erlanger, "U.S. Revives Concerns about European Defense Plans, Rattling NATO Allies."

99 "Foreign Affairs Council," *European Council*, November 13, 2017, www.consil ium.europa.eu/en/meetings/fac/2017/11/13/, accessed November 5, 2018.

100 Aurora Bosotti, "Dawn of the EU Army? 'FULL SPEED Ahead' with Defence Plans, EU Foreign Affairs Chief Warns," *Express*, November 25, 2017, sec. World, www.express.co.uk/news/world/884091/European-Union-army-military-news-EU-foreign-minister-Brussels-defence-security-video, accessed November 5, 2018.

101 *Reflection Paper on the Future of European Defence* (Brussels: European Commission, June 7, 2017), https://ec.europa.eu/commission/publications/reflection-paper-future-european-defence_en, accessed January 9, 2018.

102 Justyna Gotkowska, *The Trouble with PESCO*, trans. Jim Todd, Point of View 69 (Warsaw: Centre for Eastern Studies [OSW], 2018), 6, 16, 18, https://aei.pitt. edu/93565/1/pw_69_pesco_ang_net.pdf, accessed January 7, 2019.

103 Yasmine Salam, "Nine EU States, Including UK, Sign off on Joint Military Intervention Force," *Politico*, June 25, 2018, www.politico.eu/article/uk-to-form-part-of-joint-eu-european-defense-force-pesco/, accessed December 6, 2018.

104 Judy Dempsey, "Trump May Be Doing the European Union and NATO a Big Favor," *Washington Post*, July 6, 2018, sec. Global Opinions, www.washing tonpost.com/news/global-opinions/wp/2018/07/06/trump-may-be-doing-the-european-union-and-nato-a-big-favor/, accessed January 5, 2019.

105 Erik Brattberg and Tomáš Valášek, *EU Defense Cooperations: Progress Amid Transatlantic Concerns* (Washington, DC: Carnegie Endowment for International Peace, November 2019), https://carnegieendowment.org/files/WP_Brattberg_Valasek_EU_Def_Coop_v3.pdf, accessed January 4, 2020.

106 Ibid.

7 Disappointment and anger

The rise of anti-EU populist nationalism

The triple crises generated a host of controversial responses, but one main effect was the marked rise of nationalist populism. The dramatic consequences of the 2008 economic crisis and the introduction of the restrictive austerity measures that had strongly aided Europe's recovery already had quite dramatic consequences. Masses of people felt the decline of their incomes, were angry about the lack of responsibility shown by high risk-taking banks, and blamed governments for bailing out these financial institutions with taxpayer money. The resultant desperation was an additional response founded upon people's existing feelings of disappointment. The Great Recession followed a nearly two decade-long opening of the income scissor. For nearly half a century during the Cold War, political interests had somewhat counterbalanced the business community's inherent drive for more profit, moderating extreme income inequality in the postwar period. Besides the arms race, capitalist and communist regimes engaged in a welfare race as well, which positively impacted both systems. This competition helped drive the formation of welfare capitalism and moderated income inequality. When the Cold War ended, capitalism's genuine inner drive for profit at any cost flourished in a mostly uncontrolled environment, and inequality started to increase. People realized the growing gap among fellow citizens, and that widening disparity generated dissatisfaction and anger.

To see the impact of the welfare race between the confronting regimes, it pays to recall a famous episode from the late 1950s: the Nixon-Khrushchev Kitchen Debate that took place in Moscow in July 1959. The end of the Cold War again proved that even the most positive historical developments can also have dangerous negative consequences. The senseless division of the world and the terribly expensive and explosive arms race ended, but it also ended the social, welfare and cultural races between capitalism and socialism. Nixon and Khrushchev's notorious Kitchen Debate epitomizes the ways in which competition between the two Cold War powers positively contributed to both societies' advancement in this respect.

Nixon and Khrushchev: the kitchen debate

At an American exhibition in Moscow that took place in July 1959, the two leaders visited a model of an American kitchen, where they subsequently entered into a harsh debate about which system, communism or capitalism, was superior – in essence, which system offered more to its people. After Nixon pointed to a colored TV set that did not yet exist in Russia, Khrushchev immediately countered that the Soviet Union would have the kinds of products and appliances widely available within a few years. Nixon explained that this kitchen is "our newest model . . . built in thousands of units for direct installations in the houses. In America, we like to make life easier for women." He added: "any steel worker could buy this house . . . after twenty years, many Americans want a new house or a new kitchen. Their kitchen is obsolete by that time. . . . The American system is designed to take advantage of new inventions." Khrushchev did not hesitate to accuse Nixon of condescension: "You think the Russian people will be dumbfounded to see these things, but the fact is that newly built Russian houses have all this equipment right now." In response, Nixon praised

> this competition . . . in which you plan to outstrip us, particularly in the production of consumer goods. . . . If this competition is to do the best for both of our peoples, there must be a free exchange of ideas.[1]

Nixon was right: when the welfare race ended after 1989–1991, income inequality immediately started to increase.

Growing inequality and insecurity

Inequality is measured by the Gini coefficient on a scale between "0" and "1." These numbers represent extreme cases: the hypothetical "0" means that every citizen has the same income, while "1" means that one person gets the entire income of a country. Thus, the lower the index number, the more equals the income distribution, and vice versa; higher numbers reflex higher inequality. In his famous book *Capital in the Twenty-First Century*, Thomas Piketty used a formidable amount of statistical data to prove that the generally accepted theory offered by American Nobel prize-winning economist Simon Kuznets – that inequality has, and will continue to, decrease with the development and maturity of capitalism – is nothing but an ideological Cold War theory; it is not actually true. Capitalism has the inner tendency to increase profit and inequality, and the historical events of the postwar period have shown that only outside, non-economic, mostly political factors can generate opposite trends in a manner that is predominantly only transitorily. As Piketty documented, Gini coefficient studies that measured differences within and among countries showed that inequality had actually steadily increased from the late 1700s to the mid-twentieth century. In 1820, the average number within countries across the world was 0.43, and by 1913, it had already risen to 0.61; across countries, the average Gini coefficient was 0.16 in 1820, but it was 0.55 in 1950.

However, during the Cold War decades – between 1950 and the 1980s – the welfare race produced an "egalitarian revolution." In the mid-1980s, most European countries had relatively equal income distributions, and the Gini figures were mostly in the low range of 0.20–0.25. But after the collapse of communism and the Soviet Bloc, inequality started to increase once again. By the 2010s in Greece, Italy, France, Germany and Britain, Gini coefficient valued had reached between 0.30–0.34. Income inequality had increased significantly within the rich countries and had actually returned to the levels seen under early capitalism. The global Gini index in 2000 was already 0.66, higher than in 1820.[2] During the one and a half decades between 1985 and 2000, the West European Gini coefficient had already increased from 0.27 to 0.35. Only Sweden, Denmark, and Finland preserved the more egalitarian system, and therefore experienced index numbers of 0.25–0.28. The United States' index of 0.41 was surprisingly similar to Russia's, which went from being very egalitarian under communist rule to becoming extremely unequal (0.41). Its Gini coefficient moved relatively close to the values of extremely unequal Third World countries such Zambia (0.57), Namibia (0.59) and South Africa (0.63). Likewise, inequality also increased in some of the other formerly egalitarian communist countries: the Gini coefficients of Bulgaria, Croatia, Poland and Bosnia elevated to 0.30–0.37.[3]

Social differences started to broaden, and the income of the top one percent of the population sharply increased after the end of the Cold War. The world index of incomes shows that it increased by 6.8 percent per annum, while the average income of wage-earning adults only increased by 2.1 percent. Between the 1960s and 1992, the average income of a manager jumped to 10–17 times that of a factory worker, and that figure further increased to 13–25 times by 2000. In Britain, the average manager income jumped to 25 times higher than the average worker's income. In advanced countries that kept their postwar social-policy orientations, such as Germany and Sweden, this discrepancy was smaller – 11 and 13 times, respectively.[4] Growing inequality after a half-century of decrease became one of the main factors of dissatisfaction throughout Europe. According to a relatively recent report, 119 million – or almost one-quarter of Europe's population – are at risk of poverty and social exclusion.[5]

This situation is closely connected to the rise of neoliberal globalization, when counterbalancing state regulations were eliminated and the freedom of the market became almighty. Governments accepted the main prophecy advanced by the "saints" of neoliberalism: that the market can aptly govern not only the economy, but even society and social policy as well. Globalization changed the world, equally influencing the most advanced and the less-developed countries in the sense that it limited the rule of national governments without replacing this influence with international governance.

As is usual in times of marked change, globalization produced winners and losers. The globalized economic system served the more advanced countries and their multinational corporations, which were the monopolists of technological innovation. The latter created enormous new markets for their products. Multinational corporations proliferated, partly stripping down national governments and institutions of economic control. Several of them became more prosperous than some well-established but relatively small European states. They made use of the cheap labor forces located in the peripheral countries of Europe and the Third World.

After nearly half a century, however, the advantages and disadvantages of globalization have begun to shift. A number of developing countries, particularly the Asian Small Tigers and then China and India, rapidly industrialized, and have shot straight to the top of the list of global exporters. They successfully competed with the affluent core countries, even within the latter's domestic markets. In China and several other Asian countries, poverty markedly decreased and living standards increased; thus inequality among countries started to decrease. Within countries in Europe and the West, just the opposite happened: income inequality increased.

Parallel with these trends, in the globalized world economy, employment in certain layers became uncertain because of marked technological and structural changes in modern economies. Most wealthy countries began restructuring their economies. Agriculture, which employed about 70 percent of the active work force until the early nineteenth century and still about 30–35 percent until the mid-twentieth century, decreased to 2–4 percent in advanced countries. This long-term trend was also accompanied by deindustrialization. The manufacturing labor force declined from 40–45 percent of the gainfully occupied population in the early twentieth century to 15–25 percent by the early twenty-first century. The onset of dangerous climate change and the ensuing defense against it – decreasing pollution – also contributed. The use of coal declined, and many coal-heated power stations in the West were closed. The coal industry, together with strongly polluting industries such iron and steel, largely moved to Third World countries. Most coalmines shut down even in Belgium, where the coal industry was a leading sector and a major export industry. Sheffield, the heart of the British steel industry, became a rust-belt area. (In the wonderful 1997 English comedy film *The Full Monty*, jobless steel workers from the region retrain to become striptease performers.) Blue-collar workers in traditional sectors faced stagnating wages and growing joblessness.

Manufacturing employment, on the other hand, was increasingly replaced with employment in financial and other service-sector branches. Millions of new jobs were created, but these jobs required new knowledge, computer literacy, and much higher qualifications. This fundamental restructuring of the socioeconomic system greatly devalued unskilled labor. Education became emphatically emphasized, leaving behind those who did not have more advanced schooling. Already by the 1980s, 75 percent of the unemployed people in Italy had no more than eight years of elementary education, and 45 percent of them had even less. In Germany at that time, unemployment among unskilled workers was twice as high as that of skilled workers.[6]

These unpleasant trends were somewhat counterbalanced by the huge boom years around the turn of the millennium. Ten West European countries virtually doubled their average per-capita incomes between 1989 and 2003, from $15,880 to $31,071. The three Mediterranean countries together with Ireland increased their average per-capita income level by nearly four times – from $5,902 to $22,280 – during the same thirteen years.[7] As Europe elevated and became richer, its share of the world's foreign direct-investment stocks became almost equal to the American share (34 percent and 35 percent, respectively) at the end of the 1980s. By the early twenty-first century, the European share (39 percent) had already significantly surpassed the American share (21 percent). Europe regained the leading role in world exports as well. At the turn of the millennium, its share of global exports reached 43 percent, while the combined share of the United States, Canada, and Australia was only 19 percent and the rising countries of Asia accounted for 27 percent.[8]

Nevertheless, after the booming years of economic expansion at the turn of the millennium, the unregulated, highly speculative, and risk-taking Western economies sunk into the economic crisis of 2008, the Great Recession, the most severe one since the Great Depression of the early 1930s. The recession produced devastating social consequences, joblessness and wage cuts. The young generation was unable to successfully enter the job market. For example, during this period the youth unemployment rate in the Mediterranean countries approached 50 percent. In Europe, the long period of crisis between 2008 and 2017 generated devastating revolts and political upheavals.

The 2015–16 migration crisis significantly strengthened the nationalist-populist revolt that had been gaining traction. Immigration became a weapon for right-wing forces, who argued that the elites and those who supported immigration were undermining job security for 'white' workers. They contended that multiculturalism was endangering national European cultures and characteristics.

The political revolt against the elite

The traditional groups of workers, who lacked the requisite skills for the new economy, were simply unable to adjust to the new economic reality and faced mounting peril, insecurity and despair. Disillusioned and desperate workers became angry, believing that they had been betrayed, and grew hostile with the elites of their countries. They became easy fodder for revolting politicians and demagogues. A great part of the working class – the much-touted "proletariat," as socialists labeled them – that had long served as the base for leftist revolutionary movements, now flocked to right-wing demagogues. This shift was not an entirely new phenomenon, for it had already happened in similar situations such as the interwar period, when hordes of desperate workers joined fascist movements. One third of the members of the Nazi party in Germany were workers. In 1939, the Hungarian Nazi Arrow Cross Party won 40 percent of the vote in working-class regions.

These workers, who felt that they had been forgotten and left behind, coalesced with a part of the endangered middle class, and joined extremist parties led by demagogue politicians. The French populist demagogue Marine Le Pen and the British advocates for Brexit, Boris Johnson and Nigel Farage, successfully recruited them in the 2010s. In a way, this jump from left to right is understandable because both kinds of extremism share one basic thing in common: a revolt against the establishment. The establishment is considered to be responsible for the negative changes and often called the enemy of "pure, ordinary people."[9] Once again, left-wing and right-wing revolts produced an alternative leadership that promised radical change. Self-promoting billionaires such as Silvio Berlusconi and Donald Trump, who presented themselves as anti-establishment, self-sacrificing saviors of "the people," attracted poor and under- or unemployed workers, from the people of southern Italy to coal miners and steelworkers in the United States.

In this new environment, huge groups of workers and employees turned against the elite, lost confidence in their former representatives and social-democratic parties, and perceived immigrant workers as their enemies. Social democratic and left-leaning liberal parties lost their followers and consequently their self-confidence. Social democracy turned towards the Third Way and shifted to the center. The Italian philosopher Norberto Bobbio recognized this trend in the 1990s, and talked about "political *baisse*" between political Right and Left, when both of them became ready "to recycle itself as something totally new, something which goes beyond the traditional distinction (neither left nor right), or combining the positive values of both sides to produce a modern, innovative movement."[10] This new political development undermined traditional party organizations. The mass parties, as well as parties that had been based on class issues or cohesive ideologies, declined. In the 1990s, membership in political parties was half of what it had been in the 1960s. In Italy, Sweden, and Denmark, membership in political parties dropped to one-quarter of previous mid-century levels; and in Britain to one-fifth.

One of the main losers was the social democratic party, the oldest party-organization umbrella, which had been around since the late nineteenth century. Social democrats had run the governments of several countries largely since the war; in 2000, they were in power in ten of the fifteen member countries of the European Union. During that time, however, they dropped their old identity as working-class parties with close connections to trade unions, and modified their programs. Such shifts had occurred before. For example, the German Social Democratic Party, which was established in 1863 as a workers' party, declared in its Bad Godesberg program from 1959 that the Party represented the entire nation. That meant a shift to the middle. Similarly, more than once in the second half of the 1960s and again in the 2010s, social-democratic parties participated in grand coalitions created with right-of-center parties. The fact that former left-wing parties began to work together with right-wing parties was troublesome: "those 'ideologically weird' coalitions tend to alienate voters . . . by implying that there was little real difference between establishment right and left."[11] A part of the workers' base of the party in Germany considered party leader Gerhard Schröder a traitor when, as Chancellor of the country, he introduced new labor market laws that made it easier to dismiss workers and put a time limit on unemployment benefits that forced unemployed people to accept any low-wage job after a certain period of unemployment. This change definitely helped the German economy, but it was very bad for the workers. Similar changes characterized the administration of Tony Blair, the leader of the British Labour Party, who advocated for the Third Way. As prime minister, he instituted neoliberal policies and represented British "great power" interests. At the national elections the German Social Democratic Party in 1998, he gained 40 percent of the votes, but in 2017, he acquired hardly more than 20 percent. In February 2018, *Deutsche Welle* reported that the right-wing populist Alternative für Deutschland party had overtaken the Social Democratic Party in a national opinion poll for the first time.[12] In the 2017 French presidential election, the social-democratic candidate gained only 6 percent of the votes. In several Central European countries, social democracy virtually disappeared.

Citizens' participation in elections has also dramatically shrunk. After the war, voter participation in European elections was 88 percent on average; in contrast, between 1999 and 2002, 40 percent did not vote in Britain, 38 percent did not in Portugal, and 37 percent did not in Ireland. Analysts blamed political apathy, anti-political feelings and disillusionment with democracy.[13] Others diagnosed the crisis as one of political representation. Earlier parties were formed around central conflict lines of identity: working class versus bourgeoisie, urban versus rural, church versus state.[14] Those lines no longer exist in the same ways.

These changes were also related to the shift of traditional decision-making power from national parliaments to international corporations, Brussels, the European Central Bank. Old power structures weakened, and postwar party formations collapsed and were replaced by new types of parties and party structures. Instead of representing social groups, the new parties declared that they represented "national interests" – meaning the state.

Around the turn of the millennium, several parties disappeared. With rare exceptions, this extinction decimated almost all of the communist parties throughout the Continent, from France and Italy to Eastern Europe. The same happened to the strongest Christian Democratic Party, that of Italy, as well as to several agrarian parties. Importantly, the surviving social democratic parties shifted to the middle, adopting neoliberal economic policies; therefore, instead of attracting workers, they attracted public service employees. Several new single-issue parties appeared, such as the Green Party. In 2008, there were thirty-five such environmental parties in Europe. Feminist movements also strengthened.

The most important new development in this area was the spectacular rise of populism, or as Andrej Zaslove phrased it, "populism as a new party type."[15] These parties rejected the "corrupt political elite," offered "straight talk," and declared that they "served the people." There were characteristically left-populist and right-populist parties, with a significant majority of parties that were right-wing, nationalist, and often xenophobic and racist. Most of the populist parties, however, rejected the old left-or-right distinction, and even denied the existence of this distinction by mixing left and right agendas in their programs. Their masses basically gathered behind 'strong' autocratic leaders, who talked as people do around the kitchen table. Around the turn of the millennium, several new populist parties were established throughout Europe: the Forza Italia, the Lega Nord, and the Alleanza Nazionale in Italy; the Fremskrittspartiet in Norway; the Fremskridtspartiet in Denmark; the Sverigedemokraterna in Sweden; the Freiheitliche Partei Österreichs in Austria; the Vlaams Blok in Belgium; the Front

National in France; the Alternative für Deutschland in Germany; the Perus-
suomalaiset in Finland, the Fidesz in Hungary; and several others throughout
Central and Eastern Europe.

Around the mid-2010s, nationalist-populist parties gained ground, becoming
victors of national elections and members of coalition governments and single-
governing parties in several countries. In the 2010s, populist parties were in
power (or formed a significant part of coalition governments) in Austria, Hungary, Croatia, Estonia, Finland, Italy, Latvia, the Netherlands, Poland, Serbia,
and Slovakia. In Greece in 2015, the Syriza party gained 36 percent of the votes
and formed the government. They attacked Germany and the West in order to
subordinate and exploit other countries.[16] In 2018, the Movimento 5 Stelle, or
Five Star Movement, became the biggest party of Italy. It gained almost one-
third of the votes and formed the government in coalition of an extreme populist
party, the Lega Nord. Altogether, populist parties in Italy gained 70 percent of
the vote. In Austria, the Freedom Party gained 27.7 percent and became part of
the coalition government in 2017.

The real home of populism, however, became Central and Eastern Europe
and the Balkans. In Poland, the Prawo i Srawiedliwość, or Law and Justice Party,
took power. In recent decades, Slovakia has almost always been led by populists:
Vladimir Mečiar in the 1990s, and then Robert Fico's Smer Party in the early
twenty-first century. The Nations in Transit Organization, which has tracked the
progress and regression of democracy in Central and Eastern Europe, the Balkans, and Eurasia since 1995, reported in 2016 that in Central Europe and the
Balkans

> populism and corruption have eroded once-promising democratic institu-
> tions. In Eurasia, personalist authoritarianism has gone from a burgeoning
> trend to an entrenched norm. This year, 18 of the 29 countries in the survey
> suffered declines . . . the most since 2008, when the global financial crisis
> fueled instability. . . . For the first time in the report's history, there are now
> more Consolidated Authoritarian regimes than Consolidated Democracies.[17]

Authoritarianism flooded the Balkans: Alexandar Vučić in Serbia, Milorad Dudik
in the Bosnian Republika Srbska, and Albin Kurti and Levizja Vetevendosje in
Kosovo. Several others with similar platforms are also in power. The Balkans, and
virtually the entire Central and Eastern European area, has almost never experienced democratic political systems in the last two centuries. The region was traditionally ruled by autocratic governments during the nineteenth and twentieth
centuries. As the American economist and Nobel Laureate Paul Krugman wrote
(quoting a friend's remark when the Berlin Wall collapsed): "Now that Eastern
Europe is free from the alien ideology of Communism, it can return to its true
path: fascism. We both knew he had a point."[18]

The eastern part of Germany, the former Soviet-Bloc GDR, exhibited major similarities. West Germany invested nearly €2 trillion in the East after unification, but the
East never surpassed two-thirds of the per-capita West German GDP; thus its population has always felt that they had been "left behind." Today, 30 years after the collapse

of communism and German unification, this part of the Federal Republic is the nest of right-wing nationalism. It is dominated by the Alternative für Deutschland Party, which received twice as many votes there than in the Western part of the country. The German media often describe the former East Germany as experiencing a "collective psychological disorder spurred by the fact that the experience of two [fascist and communist] dictatorships was never properly dealt with."[19]

The political fault lines between East and West were clearly expressed by a 2014 poll, which showed that on average, 28 percent of the population of the European Union felt that immigrants would take their jobs. In Germany, where most of the immigrants settled, this percentage was only 13 percent; and in Sweden, which also accepted a lot of immigrants), this figure was only 7 percent. However, in the Central European countries, which did not experience large immigrant resettlement, the majority of people worried that their jobs would be taken by immigrants: in Hungary 52 percent had this feeling; in the Czech Republic, 51 percent felt this way.[20]

While the main concern of the governments and peoples in Central and Eastern Europe is immigration, in reality, their real problem is *emigration*. An IMF analysis about migration in Central and Eastern Europe sharply reflected this problem: emigration in this region is much higher than immigration. As the report stated, "During the past 25 years, nearly 20 million people (5½% of the CESEE population) are estimated to have left the region. . . . By [the] end [of] 2012, Southeastern Europe (SEE) had experienced the largest outflows, amounting to about 16% of the early-1990s population." Cumulative GDP growth would have been 7 percent higher in 2012 without emigration.[21]

Nationalist-populist attacks against the European Union

Some populist parties were left wing, but most of them right wing with mixed left- and right-wing programs. Populism – as one of its best experts, Cas Mudde, called our attention to – is a "thin" ideology, and in most cases appears in combination with other ideologies. In early twenty-first-century Europe that added factor was in most cases nationalism. In the early twenty-first century, populist-nationalists turned against the European Union and attacked the "dictatorial bureaucrats of Brussels" who were supposedly endangering national sovereignty. Instead of integration and cooperation they prefer as their leading slogans "Italy First" (Berlusconi), "Austria First" (Haider, similarly to Trump's later "America First"), and "über alles" (Orbán) in Hungary. These nationalistic rallying cries express the idea of the strong 'sovereign' nation-state. They successfully influenced up to at least one-quarter of the population in France and the Netherlands; were able to mobilize more than half of the population in Britain and Hungary; and won over three quarters of Italy's electorate. They have won majorities in parliaments of several Central and Eastern European countries. The so-called Visegrád Four countries (Hungary, Poland, Slovakia, and the Czech Republic) all support the nationalist-populist agenda that opposes the EU.

European nationalist-populists use the typical demagogue techniques of proclaiming in heated oratory, telling lies and half-truths, and repeating them over and over until they became a kind of "evident truth" for many. Half-truths are often over-simplified explanations for existing problems, and tend to name a single cause that is supposedly responsible for innumerable problems. In demagogic conditions, that kind of rationale is much more appealing to many people than the complicated truth that each problem has countless causes. An oversimplified answer is itself a half-truth or a lie. As part of this technique, nationalist-populists always point to an enemy, inside and/or outside the country, as the cause of the nation's problems. The enemies can be a variety of "others": the EU, a segment of society, the very rich, an ethnic or religious minority, Jews, immigrants, and Muslims have all been presented as "enemies of the nation." Appealing to hatred, popular prejudices, anxieties and fear helps to mobilize the masses. We learned this lesson from history: Hitler masterfully convinced his followers that the Jews, a single enemy, were responsible for all of Germany's miseries: the Jews, Judaism, communism and capitalism were supposedly adhered together in a secret international Jewish conspiracy. Mussolini similarly combined elements of anti-capitalism with his fascist ideology. Replacing the Marxist idea of international class struggle between the bourgeoisie and the proletariat with the idea of a struggle between bourgeois and proletarian nations, Mussolini presented Italy as one of the latter, which had to fight for its rights. Nowadays, several countries have declined into post-truth politics once again.

One of them is Britain, where the earlier-mentioned populist technique was successfully used by Boris Johnson, the main advocate for Brexit, when he declared that if Britain left the EU, "we can take back control of our borders." Did he forget that Britain had opted out of the Schengen Agreement, and thus already had control over its borders? In the same piece, Johnson also argued that "above all we could take back control of our powers to pass laws and set tax rates." Did he not know that the EU has no uniform tax rates and that each country sets its own rates? And again in the same piece, he mentioned that "we can reorient the UK economy to the whole world, rather than confining ourselves to an EU that now amounts to only 15% cent of global GDP." In reality, the EU represented 24 percent of the world's GDP at that time, more than the US's 22 percent. Britain actually oriented (not ordered!) 56 percent of its trade to the EU, while only 12 percent of it went to Britain's own Commonwealth. How characteristic that in one single speech he presented a lot of misinformation and lies.[22]

It is a common knowledge that the uniform standardization of products is a prerequisite for every national market or common market that a group of countries participates in, such as the European Single Market. Without uniform standardization, products would not be salable. Britain earned billions because it was able to exploit the EU's standardized markets. Ignoring this basic reality, Johnson – even before he entered to politics, as a journalist based in Brussels – caricatured EU standardization by highlighting a few extreme examples: "After five months' study the EEC Commission has decided snails should be categorized as fish, not meat."[23] Then he added:

> Brussels bureaucrats have shown their legendary attention to detail. . . . All 12 member states have agreed that an un-stretched condom should be 16 centimeter long. However, the EC has dismissed Italian plans for a maximum

condom width of 54 millimeters. . . . [The] spokesman of the Commission's standards division said: "This is a very serious business."[24]

One of the strongest nationalist arguments is that national sovereignty is threatened by the European Union, which – according the British populist argument – represents French interests, or – according to French and Polish nationalist arguments–German interests. To quote Boris Johnson again: "The European Community . . . is ruled by France. . . . [They] are dressing up French national interests as the European dream." He also spoke about French "networks" in the EU, using the Nazi term for it: "Delors . . . now have a dense network of *gauleiters*. . . . There is no British counter network."[25]

Marine Le Pen, the head of the French right-wing nationalist-populist Front National (renamed as Rassemblement National, or National Rally), said in one of her speeches:

> I don't want this European Soviet Union. . . . The EU is deeply harmful, it is an anti-democratic monster. [The EU's treaties only] promote German interests. . . . My warning is: Be careful Ms. Merkel. . . . [S]he wants to impose her policies on others. . . . The French want to regain control of their own country.[26]

Similarly, Jaroslav Kacziński, a member of parliament and the head of the Polish anti-EU nationalists, launched an infuriated attack against the anti-nationalist opposition in August 2004, calling them traitors: "In Poland there was and . . . still is a genuine front for the defense of German interests." This front "consists of informants of the German secret services. . . . This is a very big group of people who live from German money and act as if they were independent scholars and journalists.[27] Populist nationalists are in a permanent battle against the European Union to regain national sovereignty. In the Netherlands, Geert Wilders's Partij voor de Vrijheid (Freedom Party) announced its program as such: "Millions of Dutchmen are fed up with the Islamization of our country. Fed up with mass-immigration, asylum, terror, violence and insecurity. . . . The Netherlands will be sovereign again . . . we must leave the European Union."[28]

Boris Johnson compared the consequences of Britain's EU membership to the Battle of Hastings in October 1066, when the Norman-French army defeated the English army and initiated the Norman conquest of England. He quoted the words of historian John Gillingham, who said that it was "a catastrophe for the English. . . . As William of Malmesbury wrote in 1125, England today is the home of foreigners and the domain of aliens." The memory of the conquest, Johnson added, "is one of those many things that put us in two minds, about whether to rejoice in our links with the continent, or whether to be dismayed."[29] Marine Le Pen similarly announced: "I want to destroy the EU. . . . I believe in a Europe of nation-states."[30] Elsewhere she elaborated,

> Do we want an undemocratic authority ruling our lives, or would we rather regain control over our destiny? . . . A cage remains a cage. . . . The European

Union has become a prison of peoples. Each of the 28 countries. . . . has slowly lost its democratic prerogatives. . . . Different economies are forced to adopt the same currency. . . . [The EU Parliament is] based on a lie: the pretense that there is a homogenous European people.[31]

7.1　Marine Le Pen

Marine Le Pen was born in 1968, the third daughter of Jean-Marie Le Pen, a former French Foreign Legion soldier who fought in colonial wars in French Indochina and Algeria, and was proud of his past, including that he "tortured because it was necessary."[32] During World War II, he was an admirer of Marshal Pétain and an enthusiastic reader of fascist French collaborators who, after the war, were imprisoned, such as Charles Maurras, or even executed, like Robert Brasillach. He remained a right-wing nationalist, an open anti-Semite, and a hater of the European Union when he turned to politics. When his daughter Marine was 4 years old, he established his own party, Front National, in 1972, together with Pierre Bousquet, a former member of the Waffen SS; Jacques Bompard, a member of the colonialist OAS; and Roland Gaucher, a Nazi collaborator. To be fair, eventually he skillfully rid the party of his fascist collaborator-rivals and monopolized leadership.

Marine closely worked together with her father. After graduation from law school, she worked for six years, but at the age of 18, she joined her father's party, and lived and worked for Front National. In 2000, she became a member of the party's Executive Committee, and in 2003, she was elected as vice president. She has married and divorced twice; both of her former husbands were Front National functionaries. Her third partner is the Secretary General of the Front National as well as her vice president. The Front appears to be her entire real family.

Marine Le Pen was devoted to her father and worked closely with him until his retirement in 2011, when she took over the Front and continued where her father left off. She compared Muslims 'taking over' certain suburbs and streets to the Nazi occupation of France. She offered nothing but a repetition of her father's politics. But she was a much shrewder tactician, and skillfully distanced herself from his father's mistakes. She renounced anti-Semitism, banned skinheads from the Front's meetings, and purged some openly fascist leaders of her party. When, in April 2011, her father repeated his favorite anti-Semitic remark that the gas chambers were an unimportant detail of the war and called on France to ally with Russia in order to "save the 'white world,' "[33] the hard-nosed, steely gazed Marine Le Pen did not hesitate to state that her father was experiencing a mental downturn, and then removed him from the Party. She even changed the compromised name of the party to Rassemblement National.

Marine, who has gained the nickname of *la peste blonde* (echoing both *la peste noire*, the Black Death, and the *la peste brune*, or Nazi menace), has started repackaging the Party – or, as *The Economist* put it, she has embarked on a project of *dédiabolisation* (de-demonization) to save the Front National. The French political scientist Michel Winock observed: "whereas Jean-Marie was anti-abortion, socially conservative, and a staunch advocate of small government, Marine is pro-choice, gay-friendly, and economically interventionist, with a populist streak . . . Islam now represents the enemy, when it used to be the Jews for Daddy's radical right."[34]

While she quite rationally dropped the toxic elements in the Front's program, she retained the key elements of extreme nationalism and xenophobia, especially its anti-Muslim, anti-immigration, and anti-European Union agenda, mixed with a kind of anti-Anglo-Saxon capitalism and anti-German sentiment. She promised to reestablish morals, and to fight against senseless egoism, internationalism ("mondialism"), and "perverse liberalism." Her program is a strong nationalist-populist platform that will supposedly "protect ordinary people," "our French workers." Advocating for a strong state and attacking the "perverse effect" of over-privatization, she accuses the European Union "that accelerates all of this." The EU, she repeated thousands of times, is against the core interests of France. "I don't want this European Soviet Union. . . . The EU is deadly harmful, it is an anti-democratic monster . . . promote German interest."[35] She began to build an anti-EU block of supporters, an alliance of Eurosceptic parties and forces, in the name of liberty: "A cage remains a cage. . . . The European Union has become a prison of peoples."[36]

Exploiting Muslim terrorist actions in France, she demanded actions such as the expulsion of foreigners who supposedly preach hatred, as well as those who have dual citizenship. Marine Le Pen promised that if she gains power, she will pull France out of the euro-zone and, during her first six months in office, hold a referendum on France's continued membership in the European Union. If Marine Le Pen gains power in France, it would likely be the death knoll of the European Union.

This "freedom fight" is even more grotesque when it occurs in small countries that have never really had national sovereignty, have never been able to defend themselves alone, and have always tried to achieve foreign policy goals through alliances with neighboring great powers. At present, these countries are strongly dependent on foreign investment, foreign bank loans and multinational companies that establish their modern industrial sectors. Moreover, they also enjoy substantial aid from the European Union, which it gives to support their catching up with the West. In the EU's last budgetary period between 2014 and 2020, Poland pocketed €27 billion annually and Hungary received €40 billion altogether: thus these two countries got almost 12 percent of the entire EU budget (€156 billion annually). Hungary financed 55 percent of its entire infrastructure spending during that period with EU money; similarly, Poland covered 61 percent of it using this aid. The right-wing nationalist prime minister of Hungary, Viktor Orbán – whose country has arguably profited the most from EU aid and investments – became the leader of this "freedom fight" against the EU:

> Today, 168 years after the great Wars of Independence of the European peoples [in 1848], Europe, our common home, is not free! . . . Today in Europe it is forbidden to speak the truth. . . . It is forbidden to say that Brussels is now stealthily devouring more and more slices of our national sovereignty. . . . The peoples of Europe may have finally understood that their future is at stake. . . . We should not allow Brussels to place itself above the law. . . . We must put steel in our spines, and we must answer clearly, with a voice loud enough to be heard far and wide. . . "Shall we be slaves or men set free – That is the question, answer me!"[37]

7.2 Viktor Orbán

As Hungary's prime minister since 2010, Orbán has gradually introduced authoritarian rule, subordinating both the Parliament and its jurisdiction to his government. He has become one of the main enemies of the European Union, even as his Hungary has pocketed huge amounts of EU assistance the organization provides to less-developed regions and countries in the Union. In the seven-year budgetary period from 2013 until 2020, the EU allocated $40 billion in aid to Hungary. Orbán also reoriented his foreign policy towards autocratic countries: Russia's Putin, Turkey's Erdoğan, and China's Xi. He exerts significant influence on the rest of the so-called Visegrád Four group, neighboring former communist countries in Central Europe, and is attempting to build an anti-EU alliance.

Who is Viktor Orbán? He was born into an impoverished rural family in Hungary in 1963. His parents received many advantages from the communist Kádár regime. His father Győző joined the communist party, attended evening college courses free of charge, and earned an engineering degree. The family rose to solidly middle-class status. Viktor was sent to the Eötvös Loránd University in Budapest and graduated law school in 1987. At that time, Hungary was undergoing a unique transformation process. By the following year, the Kádár regime, which had emerged after the defeat of the 1956 revolution, ended. Kádár retired and reform communists took over and implemented radical reforms. A multiparty system was introduced, and the 1956 revolution was rehabilitated as a genuine people's uprising against Stalinism and Russian occupation. Privatization of the economy commenced, market prices were introduced, the first subsidiaries of Western multinational companies were opened and – in February 1989 – the decision was made to hold the first free multi-party elections in the spring of 1990.

The newly graduated Orbán began working at a Management Training Institute, but two years later, he left his job and became a professional politician in 1989. He considered himself a born leader and loved power. In high school, he served as the head of the school's Communist Youth Organization. As he later explained, he was a naïve and devoted supporter of communism. In March 1988, he established the FIDESz (Alliance of Young Democrats) party with 36 of his friends. By the end of the year, there were 21 political parties in existence in the country. At that time, Orbán became a devoted (certainly also a 'naïve') liberal democrat. The communist regime had virtually dissolved. A few months before the free elections, Imre Nagy, the executed communist leader from the 1956 revolution, was reburied. Orbán was one of the speakers at the catafalque before a crowd of 250,000 on 16 June 1989. He delivered a passionate anti-communist speech that earned him fame. In an aggressive and threatening tone, he demanded free elections (which had already been decided on and announced some time earlier) and the withdrawal of the Soviet troops (which was also an arranged issue). FIDESz, however, won only 5.4 percent in the first free elections in March 1990.

In 1993, he disbanded FIDESz's collective leadership and took over as the party's unquestioned leader. The prominent Austrian journalist Paul Lendvai, who met Orbán in September 1993, reported in his *Orbáns Ungarn* that Orbán "made a strong impression as a consistent liberal democrat who strongly criticized the right-wing nationalist policies of the first post-communist government of József Antall." Nevertheless, in the next elections in 1994, FIDESz again barely exceeded 5 percent of the votes. The results suggested to Orbán that FIDESz had little chance of winning power if it remained one of many liberal democratic parties. He also recognized that there was a vacuum on the other side of the political spectrum. The power-loving Orbán did not hesitate to easily change his political convictions and transform his party into a right-wing nationalist organization in April 1995. Strong nationalism provided him a huge throng of supporters. He began speaking of a nation of 15 million Hungarians (including more than 2 million Hungarians who live in neighboring countries and another 3 million, even third generation emigrants all over the world; only 10 million live in Hungary), and started mourning the anniversary of the Trianon Treaty of 1920, which cut off two-thirds of the previous Kingdom of Hungary, as a "Day of National Unity." Similar to the Horthy regime before World War II, when Hungary started reoccupying lost territories with the help of Hitler, Orbán used this exulted nationalism to powerfully envision the reconstruction of a "greater" Hungary. For example, in his speech at the centennial anniversary of the Trianon Treaty in June 2020 (which was published by the Office of the Prime Minister), he stated:

> Thousand year-old Hungary was stabbed from behind by the Budapest traitors [meaning the 1918 democratic revolution and liberal

Jews] . . . . They paralyzed and demoralized its army. . . . [The Western powers] redesigned Central Europe without any moral scruples. . . . We will never forget that. There were some who always hated the Hungarians. They united to eliminate us from the globe. . . . Even the biggest cannot avoid making historical justice. . . . What belongs together will unite. . . . Hungarians, just as the human heart sometime shrinks, sometimes enlarges. . . . We are safeguarding the Carpathian Basin as our mission. . . . We were not as strong as now in the last hundred years. . . . Our intellectual, economic and cultural attraction is strengthening day by day. . . . Compared to Western Europe our country is the island of peace and security. To keep it in this way, we are rapidly developing our new army. . . . There is no nation on earth which could survive the last hundred years behind us. . . . We not only survived but we are before victory again. . . . A new order will born. . . . Tremendous changes are before the gate. . . . We are those who change the fate of Hungary. Our generation, the fourth Trianon-generation fulfill its mission. We lead Hungary to the gate of victory.[38]

At a mass rally in March 2016, he accused all previous governments of wrongdoing: "Liberal democracy was not capable of openly declaring . . . that they should serve national interests. Moreover, it even questioned the existence of national interests."[39] Orbán declared himself the savior and unifier of the Hungarian nation. He rejects liberal democratic principles and speaks about a "declining" corrupt West. Orbán turned to Putin's Russia, Erdoğan's Turkey and Xi's Communist China as friends and examples and praised the "Eastern wind" as the most powerful force in the world. Dictatorships, he argued, secure "stability," which is the primary interest: "The new state that we are building is an illiberal state, a non-liberal state . . . it applies a specific national approach in its stead."[40] The Orbán regime, as foreign journalists have recognized, has effectively become a "Führer democracy."[41] As populist demagogues do in general, he always needed an enemy, and found it in George Soros, the Hungarian-born multi-billionaire Hungarian-born Jewish American philanthropist. Orbán uses Soros as a scapegoat to symbolize the "evil" behind everything that is bad. His coded anti-Semitic propaganda increased his popularity.

Orbán subordinated the Constitutional Court by appointing his cronies. For the first time in Hungarian history, a small group of close friends hold all the leading positions in the government. After his new election victory and absolute majority in the Parliament, he amended the constitution as many times as he needed to, and enacted laws to easily ban demonstration on the bogus premise that it could "disturb people in the neighborhood." A new 2018 law requires previous governmental approval if "two or more people" want to discuss public issues in public places. The regime had eliminated elementary democratic principles and practices. In 2012, the world media was shocked by Orbán's claim that the EU's aid to Hungary amounted to colonialism: as the BBC reported, "Hungarian PM Viktor Orban denounces EU's colonialism."[42] *Politico* also published parts of his speech on March 16.[43] As the BBC stated, "Orban has launched a scathing attack on the European Union, accusing it of treating the country as a colony." At a huge rally in Budapest, he said that the nation "will not live according to the commands of foreign powers."[44] He accused the European Union of oppression and 'likened its pressure on the country . . . to communist-era dictatorship.' "[45]

The European People's Party suspended Orbán's FIDESz's membership in the "party family," and his authoritarian system was strongly indicted by the Sargentini Report and, more than once, by the European Parliament. During the coronavirus pandemic, Orbán introduced absolute, uncontrolled power and started to govern by decree. Nevertheless, the EU continues to send huge amount of money to his regime, remains passive, and lets him try to undermine European integration.

All these lies about an oppressive, even colonizing European Union that supposedly represents foreign interests, were compounded in Central and Eastern Europe by a series of strongly anti-Western attacks that described the West as a corrupt, declining power and that idealized a defense of endangered Christian and national values. Orbán often speaks about the decline of the liberal West and the "decadent and 'money-based' west," and instead embraces a "work-based society . . . of a non-liberal nature."[46] In one speech, he scolded, "Liberal values today incorporate corruption, sex and violence." He also added the white supremacist argument that "Western Europe . . . forgot about the white working class."[47] He emphasized that the

> defining aspect of today's world can be articulated as a race to figure out a way of organizing communities, a state that is most capable of making a nation competitive. [A] trending topic in thinking is understanding systems that are not Western, not liberal, not liberal democracies, maybe not even democracies, and yet making nations successful. Today, the stars of international analyses around the world are Singapore, China, India, Turkey, Russia. And I believe our political community rightly anticipated this challenge. . . [w]e are searching for (and we are doing our best to find, ways of parting with West European dogmas, making ourselves independent from them).[48]

In June 2020, Orbán painted a stark vision of the end of Western and EU "dominance":
The world is in tectonic transition. The United States is not at the throne of the word anv longer, the European Union is in deep crisis and wants to escape with a

"salto mortale" [a deadly jump], Eurasia is developing in tremendous speed. . . . A new order will born.[49]

Orbán often repeats that he is building "a national Christian era. . . . We could also define our current situation in comparison with the Horthy era," when Hungary "started flourishing and achieved outstanding diplomatic, military and economic results."[50] It is really surprising – although fitting – that Viktor Orbán compares his regime to the interwar Hungarian Horthy regime, an openly racist, anti-Semitic government in the closest possible alliance with Mussolini and Hitler.

The unpopular migration crisis in the mid-2010s and the EU's mistakes in handling it provided an excellent opportunity for him, and he masterfully exploited it, indeed. When the EU wanted to establish a quota to distribute immigrants among member countries during the big migration crisis, and proposed sending 1,300 immigrants to Hungary – a country of 10 million–Orbán declared: "We know how it works. If we allow them to tell us who to accept, they will then force us to serve foreigners in our own country, and at the end they will push us out from our own country."[51] He also threatened in a State of the Nation speech: "We shall teach Brussels, the people smugglers and the migrants that Hungary is a sovereign country . . . gangs shall not hunt our wives and daughters."[52]

In March 2020, when the coronavirus spread extremely rapidly all over the closely interconnected world, in which millions of people were travelling and visiting other countries, Orbán immediately wanted to make political profit from it. According to the World Tourism Organization, Europe received about 750 million visitors per year in 2019–2020. Tourists from China, the early epicenter of the disease, made more than 140 million journeys abroad (mostly in Europe and the United States) during that time; likewise, China is one of the favorite tourist destinations for Europeans as well. Neglecting these facts, however, Orbán connected the spread of disease with illegal migration, since "many migrants come from Iran or through Iran, one of the centers of the disease."[53] He recently also announced: "We are fighting a two-front war: one front is called migration, and the other one belongs to the coronavirus. There is a logical connection between the two, as both spread with movement."[54]

Another major political windfall he engineered from the coronavirus was the acquisition of unlimited personal power through governing by decrees. As *The Guardian* reported in its article "Coronavirus is now contaminating Europe's democracy" on 1 April 2020: "In Hungary Viktor Orbán has been allowed to rule by decree during this state of emergency without any clear time limit and special measures include jail terms for spreading misinformation. Since 1989 no politician has been so powerful in the region."[55] Indeed, it even allows him to imprison those who spread "misinformation." What is false is, of course, decided by him. In just the first month, the authorities initiated legal actions against more than one hundred people, mostly those who had made critical remarks against the government.[56] It is a powerful weapon to frighten people and shut down free speech and free media. Orbán's establishment of absolute, uncontrolled power generated a European Union-wide outcry demanding retribution. The news and opinion website *Vox American* (established in 2014) labelled the Hungarian government's step a "coronavirus coup" that unmasks the real character of Hungary's nationalist-populist autocratic regime, which – although it has maintained the façade of democracy –

> has not been a democracy for years. . . . The new law, a so-called "coronavirus coup" enacted in the crisis atmosphere of a pandemic, strips off that veneer. It is an uncharacteristically crude measure, one that makes the more subtle reality of what's happened to Hungarian democracy quite obvious.[57]

In its resolution on 17 April 2020, the European Parliament stated that Hungary's decisions to prolong the state of emergency indefinitely, to authorize the government to rule by decree, and to weaken the Parliament's oversight, are "totally incompatible with European values."[58] In a session on 13 May 2020, the EU Parliament discussed the issue again and repeated the language of its previous declaration: "Decisions in Hungary to prolong the state of emergency indefinitely, to authorise the government to rule by decree, and to weaken the Parliament's oversight, are 'totally incompatible with European values.'" The EU "specifically asked for payments to Hungary to be stopped, in the framework of the new financial perspectives and the recovery plan, unless rule of law is respected. They also criticized the passive attitude of the Council." The Parliament "called on the Commission to make full use of all available EU tools and sanctions to address this serious and persistent breach, including budgetary ones, and urged the Council to put back on its agenda the ongoing Article 7 procedure" to suspend certain rights of member countries, such as voting right in EU decision making "against Hungary."[59]

The anti-EU campaign combined with anti-Soros attacks in Eastern Europe

Nationalist-populists all over Central and Eastern Europe combine their anti-EU campaign with vicious attacks against George Soros. This Hungarian-born American multi-billionaire is, as they say, behind the EU's policies, and several EU leaders are "in his pocket." This masterful selection of an 'enemy' who is behind everything that is bad, including the EU's policies and the crisis of mass immigration, is closely connected with the name of Viktor Orbán. He famously said: "We will fight against the Soros Empire and what it does and plans against Hungary . . . if they gain power, want to realize the big plan to crash Hungary."[60]

Orbán's demagoguery became the most notorious nationalist-populist peers, and ignited a similar blaming campaign against Soros in other countries in the region. George Soros, a multi-billionaire philanthropist who established his Open Society Fund in the late 1980s all over the Eastern world to assist opposition movements in communist countries, has been attacked by Orbán – who, ironically, was actually was one of Hungary's Open Society Fund grantees; he was sent over to Oxford through a Soros grant. According to Orbán, Soros wants to settle Muslims in Europe and Islamize Hungary and the Continent. Soros supposedly dictates poisonous policies for the European Union as well. He is behind the 'liberal conspiracy' against the nation. Orbán stated in a speech at the European Parliament: "It is important information that George Soros and his NOGs [*sic.*; Non-Governmental Organizations] want to transport one million migrants to the EU per year . . . and [he] provides a financial loan for it."[61] His parliamentary majority amended a 2011 law in April 2017 and declared: "The faked civil organizations of George Soros in Hungary and the world are spy organizations and we are determined to stop it."[62] In June 2018, Hungary enacted "Stop Soros" legislation. The capital city and the country were flooded with government posters that read, "Don't let George Soros have the last laugh!"[63]

In reality, Orbán's anti-Soros campaign was not very original; he just followed Vladimir Putin's advice. The signal was given by Putin's Russia in 2015 when they closed Soros's NGO in Russia after blaming it for anti-government activity. Russia pressured former Soviet bloc countries to do the same: as one Russian commentator stated, "This list [of NGOs] will be interesting for the East European and Balkan countries as well; banning the faked civil organizations under Western control and the groups that collaborate them is highly recommended for the East European countries."[64] The official Russian-government TV program abroad, Russia Today, broadcasted a program on 4 November 2015 that maintained that Soros was behind the Islamization of Europe and that was a "threat to the existence of European peoples because they become dissolved in a so-called diverse society of different people, different religions, different cultures, different values." "The Hungarian prime minister is the only one" – declared the TV host – "that has any sense."[65]

Putin gave the signal in 2015, and Orbán's adoption of his position in 2017 marked the spread of this campaign to the other countries of the region. Anti-Soros denunciations flooded the entire region. Romanian Prime Minister Liviu Dragnea repeated that Soros has "fed evil in Romania."[66] Krystyna Pawlowicz, a Polish parliamentarian who is close to Kacziński, declared: Soros is the "most dangerous man in the world"[67] and is "openly and brazenly financing the anti-democratic and anti-Polish element with a view to fight Polish sovereignty and indigenous Christian culture."[68] Soros finances "anti-Christian and anti-national activities."[69] Macedonia blamed Soros for the illegal wiretapping of top leaders and suggested that he was the source of political crisis in the country.[70] In Bulgaria he was called a "liberal terrorist,"[71] and in Serbia he was linked to the Rothschilds, the Jewish banking family, in an anti-Semitic manner.[72]

Populists always like to pick up a scapegoat, and selecting Soros for a target was a masterful decision. As the Slovak Jan Orlovsky explains: "You couldn't come up with a better enemy figure today. . . . George Soros brings up all of the stereotypes we have lived with all our life – about Jews, bankers and, in Slovakia, also about Hungarians."[73] Jacek Kucharczyk, who runs the Institute of Public Affairs in Warsaw, added: "Because he promotes liberal values, has a Jewish background and is a billionaire, he is the perfect figure for explaining to hard-core voters why the world is the way it is."[74] Rafal Pankowski, who leads a Polish anti-racism organization, stated, the "current tendency to see Soros as a central figure in an alleged global Jewish conspiracy" is intimately connected to the growing xenophobia in the region.[75] It was indeed highly convenient to point fingers at Soros and label him an "enemy of the nation" – a phrase intended to signal that he was dangerous because he was a rich American and Jewish, but, since everyone knew it, the demagogues did not have to say so explicitly.

Britain leaves the European Union

Nationalist-populist attacks against the European Union became vicious and strong throughout Europe during and after the economic-financial and migration crises in the 2010s. These attacks by nationalist-populist parties, however, did not actually gain power in the West; they predominantly gain footholds in several countries of Central Europe, where the attacks culminated. Nevertheless, the strongest sign of discontent came from the West, since the only country that actually left the EU during those years was a Western one, Great Britain. Was it paradoxical? Not at all. Britain was never enthusiastic for European integration, did not want to join the European Community even when America pushed the UK to lead it. The country's real interest was the British Empire and the Commonwealth, and the political elite and a great part of the population still lived in the past glory within their minds. Many people share the view that Britain is not just another European country, but also a special world power. When the British government applied for membership in the 1960s it was because the country was shocked by the failure of traditional "gunboat diplomacy" in Egypt in 1956, and then by the total collapse of the colonial Empire by 1960.

Interestingly enough, however, this shock wave had only a temporary impact on the British way of thinking. Two years after joining the European Economic Community, the government already held a referendum about remaining in or leaving the Community. At that time the vast majority, more than 67 percent, have voted to remain. As discussed before, the governments always opposed further integration and any form of supranationalization and only wanted to enjoy the advantages of the huge common market. Britain opted out of the Schengen Agreement and the common currency. In other words, Britain was always a half-hearted member of the EU. More than half a century after the collapse of the Empire, a part of the population is still living in the past and reveling in the dream of British exceptionalism. This deeply rooted feeling is probably best characterized by the British historian and professor at the University of London, Orlando Figes. His 2019 book *The Europeans* describes the emergence of "Europeanness" among Europeans in the nineteenth-century, and examines why the Brits did not develop this sentiment and remained mostly estranged from this cultural shift on the Continent:

> The British had a firm belief in their superiority to the Europeans, indeed to all foreigners. They believed that Britain was the envy of the world because of

its ancient libraries and traditions of parliamentary government and the rule of law. . . . Their confidence was rooted in their country's military victories against the continental powers, especially the French, in the conquests of the British Empire, and in Britain's status as the first industrial society. Isolated from the Continent by their geography, the British had a strong sense of their special character, based upon their history of long-unconquered island. . . . European travel confirmed Britons in their view of Europe's moral backwardness.

Figes also quotes Henry Mayhew's "German Life and Manners" from 1864: "traveling southward from England is like going backward in time – every ten degrees of latitude corresponding to about a hundred years in our own history. . . . In Germany we find the people, at the very least, a century behind us in all the refinements of civilization."[76] Nothing exemplifies the survival of this mentality better than a relatively recent poll that asked people in Britain, France, the US, and Germany which of the wartime allies contributed most to defeating Nazi Germany. The clear winner in France, Germany and the United States was the United States; less than 10 percent of respondents in those countries chose Britain. But in Britain, almost half (47 percent) of the respondent said that Britain played the most significant part. Only less than a quarter of British respondents voted for either the US or the Soviet Union. A commentator noted: "the British are so proud of their own wartime role that they misunderstand it."[77] This mentality remained extremely strong among the elite, Tory party members, older generations; and among less educated people, especially in the countryside.

An accidental event converted these deeply rooted feelings into action. David Cameron, the Tory prime minister, got the idea during a discussion that an inner-party conflict with the strong Eurosceptic wing of the party could be resolved by holding a referendum on EU membership. Although he wanted Britain to remain, he still decided to hold a referendum to quash this faction, expecting they would lose. This was a rather unfortunate tactical maneuver because holding a referendum was not a widespread popular demand. On 23 June 2016, the surprising result shocked the country. Roughly 52 percent voted to leave the Union, while 48 percent voted to remain. However, there are some important details. Only a bit more than half of the UK population participated. A total of 12.9 million registered voters did not vote, and another 18.1 million people were not even registered. Out of the 33.5 million who voted, 17.4 million wanted to leave. In other words, barely more than one quarter (27 percent) of the population decided this crucial step. True, the referendum did not have compulsory biding legal consequences for the government. In spite of this, the new government – since David Cameron, who campaigned for remaining, resigned – took it as a compulsory decision by the people. The referendum was followed by three difficult years filled with sharp confrontations. The younger and more educated urban population, who wanted to remain, opposed the older rural population, who were for leaving; thus the country was sharply divided nearly in half. Moreover, the population of some members of the "United Kingdom," such as

Scotland and Northern Ireland, voted mostly to remain. It became clear that the unity of the United Kingdom was endangered by leaving the EU. Despite voting to remain in the UK in 2014, before the Brexit referendum, Scotland is preparing to hold another referendum to vote for independence from England in order to remain part of the EU. In Northern Ireland, the possibility of a renewed civil war has appeared on the horizon. When Boris Johnson made his agreement with the EU, one central problem was the impossibility of avoiding a hard customs wall between the Irish Republic and British Northern Ireland, which was harshly rejected by the northern Irish population. Despite the volatile political history behind that issue, Johnson decided to agree to a customs wall between Northern Ireland and England, and thus Northern Ireland virtually remained in the EU. His decision alienated the Irish Protestant loyalists who had fought a brutal war for thirty years against the IRA and Sinn Féin (the northern Irish party that wanted to reunify Ireland), and they cried betrayal.

7.3 Boris Johnson

Alexander Boris de Pfeffel Johnson was born in 1964 in a family with an ethnically mixed background. His great-grandfather, Ali Kemal, was a Muslim Turkish minister in the last Ottoman government, who was lynched during the Atatürk revolution. That pushed his grandfather to ask for asylum in Britain. Boris was raised in an upper middle-class family, and studied at the famous Eton boarding school and then at Oxford University, the 'factories' that produce the British political elite. There he developed his eccentric British persona. He started working as a journalist in the Thatcher era in Brussels, the city where his father had worked as a so-called 'Brussels bureaucrat' for the European Commission starting in 1973. As a reporter, he never attempted to be fully truthful and had nothing positive to say about the EU, which he always described with biting sarcasm, even inventing stories and quotations. As he later put it: "The longer I stayed in Brussels . . . the more obvious it was that Europe would never work . . . it has been the object of 500 years of British diplomacy to ensure that continental Europe is not united against our interests." He perennially attacked Delors, the "homo foederalis" who supposedly acted only to further the "Delors' Plan to Rule Europe," as he titled one of his articles in 1992. According to his view, there was no longer any reason for integration: "There will be no war between France and Germany, and the Soviet threat is a busted flush." He described the Union as a nonsensical and self-serving bureaucratic institution.

Although he did not understand the importance of standardization of products for a common market, he caricatured it by focusing solely on a few extreme examples, such as: "After five months' study the EEC Commission has decided snails should be categorised as fish, not meat."[78] Or:

"All 12 member states have agreed that an unstretched condom should be 16 centimeter long. However . . . dismissed Italian plans for a maximum condom width of 54 millimeters."[79] For years, Johnson depicted European integration as serving French interests against Britain: "The European Community . . . dressing up French national interests as the European dream . . . they deserve admiration for one huge geo-political coup" [and for their] "semi-annual humiliation of the British Government." As his former colleague John Palmer concurs: "As a journalist he is thoroughly irresponsible, making up stories."[80] Another colleague, Jean Quatremer, adds that Johnson's motto is: "Never let the facts interfere with a good story."[81]

When Prime Minister David Cameron decided to hold a referendum on remaining in or leaving the European Union in 2016, Johnson first hesitated about what position to support, as he told Cameron, but then recognized that heading the "Leave" campaign might be the road to power. His irresponsible demagoguery was based on bombastic misinformation, lies, and the delusional promise of regaining Britain's lost world-power status. His lack of knowledge or irresponsible lies also led him to declare that if Britain left the EU, the Single Market would remain open to it, and that thus there was nothing to lose – only everything to win. He argued: "It is overwhelmingly in the economic interests of the other EU countries to do a free-trade deal, with zero tariffs and quotas, while we extricate ourselves from the EU law-making system."[82] As he repeatedly said, his idea was for Britain to have their cake and eat it too.

The conservative and elitist Boris Johnson, like other populists, did not hesitate to employ leftist rhetoric in order to present Brexit as a populist project against big corporations: "It is we who want to give power back to people. It is we who want to stand up against the corporatist and elitist system. . . . Although some very large banks and multinational companies profit from the EU system,"[83] the people are not. And although he originated from an immigrant family, he also used popular anti-migrant arguments: "migrants are disproportionately coming to Britain. . . . If we stay, we are tying ourselves to a broken Eurozone economy while simultaneously accepting unlimited migration of people. . . . The only way to restore democratic control of immigration policy is to vote to leave on 23 June."[84]

Johnson has often repeated that he is a "one-man melting pot"[85] and thus genuinely not racist, but he also said: "I have prejudged [certain ethnic groups] about the greater likelihood of being mugged by young black males than by any other group. And if that is racial prejudice, then I am guilty. And so are you baby . . . racism is natural."[86] Elsewhere he stated, "We must begin the re-Britannification of Britain."[87] As Stephen Castle wrote in the *New York Times on* 4 October 2017:

"Shaggy-headed, bombastic and full of bravado and sunny optimism as he brushed aside the clouds hanging over Britain's fraught withdrawal from the European Union. . . . Boris Johnson was exactly where he wanted to be . . . at the center of attention. . . . Mr. Johnson's jovial, bumbling persona belies a ferocious ambition."[88]

Although it may be tragic for sharply divided Britain, Brexit – which Johnson helped to realize – definitely helped his carrier and ultimately carried him to 10 Downing Street.

After three years of long political skirmishes, demands, and the rejection of the possibility of holding a second referendum, at last new elections gave the upper hand to the Tory Party. Headed by a new leader and prime minister, Boris Johnson, the UK stepped out of the European Union at the end of January 2020. The Tory elite and its extreme Johnson government are running after the illusion of a "global Britain." Theresa May – who failed as prime minister to maneuver her country on the turbulent waters of politics between 2016 and 2019 – expressed the Brexiters' illusions best when she stated: Brexit "should make us think of global Britain, a country with self-confidence and the freedom to look beyond the continent of Europe and to the economic and diplomatic opportunities of the wider world." *The Economist* that quoted May's statement added: "Talk of 'global Britain' fosters dangerous illusions."[89]

The forecasts and signs for Britain's future are pretty dark: companies and financial institutions are already escaping, and the tremendous tasks of preparing and signing new trade agreements with dozens and dozens of countries and of keeping the United Kingdom united loom. What will be the impact of Brexit upon the European Union? One fact is already proven: Britain's exit from the Union did not ignite a wave of similar exits, as several modern Cassandras forecasted when they warned about the death knell of the EU. Otherwise, the impact is rather contradictory. On the one hand, it is evidently harmful. Clearly the loss of a well-developed Western country – second biggest economically in the bloc after Germany – that had represented 12 percent of the EU's GDP represented a large shift. Not only did post-Brexit UK not contribute to the European Union's budget (with a net £8.9 billion pounds, more than $11 billion), but it also did not remain within the EU's common market; thus its removal weakened all-European value-chain networks. Europe consequently became less Europeanized.

Several calculations tried to measure the possible losses of Brexit for the EU-27. Despite dire predictions from some corners, all agreed that the potential losses are not substantial and that real output – according to an IMF analysis – would only fall by 0.2 percent, although some countries such as Ireland may lose about 2.5 percent of growth; the Netherlands, Denmark, Belgium, and the Czech Republic were also expected to experience greater than average losses. In the case of a hard landing, in which the UK fails to come to a trade agreement with the EU – an outcome that is becoming more plausible – the European output loss might be somewhat larger: 0.5 percent for the EU-27 and 4 percent for Ireland,

given the substantial increases in both tariff and non-tariff barriers.[90] The RAND
Corporation's experts calculated that in the case of a hard landing, Britain's GDP
would decline by 5 percent in the ten years after Brexit and the country would
lose $140 billion, compared with its projected figures if it had retained EU mem-
bership. The economic loss of the EU during that same decade was expected to
be only about 0.7 percent.[91]

Regardless of the overall mildness of Brexit's anticipated negative effects for
the EU-27 countries, some regions and sectors on the Continent will be hit
harder. The EU's European Committee of the Regions calculated that sectors
such as transport vehicles, machinery, electronics, textile and furniture, vegeta-
bles, foodstuff, wood, and chemicals and plastics may lose markets. Such losses
will disproportionately hurt certain regions in France (Midi-Pyrénées), Germany
(Stuttgart and Tübingen) and Italy (Emilia Romagna). Companies would lose
important markets in the electronics sector in the Czech Republic (in Střední
Morava); the transport-vehicle industry in Romania (in Vest) and Germany (in
Niederbayern); the machinery sector in Ireland, the Czech Republic, and the
Netherlands; and the furniture sector in Italy (in Tuscany and Marche), Bulgaria
(in Severozapaden), Ireland and Latvia.[92]

On the other hand, Britain was the leading anti-integrationist member country. Throughout its more than four-decades-long membership, it has always
opposed any steps towards further integration, and has always pushed the EU to
accept more new member countries that were less and less prepared, in order to
undermine the road towards federalization. Britain is now out of the EU. The
removal of this countervailing anti-integrationist weight will definitely strengthen
the influence of integrationist Germany, and may, in the long run, encourage better cohesion and catalyze further integration for the remaining EU-27.

All forecasts are, of course, hypothetical. The next decade and decades will
show the real consequences of Brexit for both Britain and the European Union.

Notes

1 Richard Nixon and Nikita Khrushchev, *The Kitchen Debate*, Debate (Moscow:
   Central Intelligence Agency, July 24, 1959), www.cia.gov/library/readingroom/
   docs/1959-07-24.pdf, accessed October 12, 2017.
2 Thomas Piketty, *Capital in the Twenty-First Century*, trans. Arthur Goldhammer
   (Cambridge, MA: The Belknap Press of Harvard University Press, 2014), 13–15.
   Piketty successfully rejected the postwar theory of Simon Kuznets, which maintained that early capitalism was characterized by high inequality that decreased
   under mature capitalism.
3 Ibid.
4 Ivan T. Berend, *An Economic History of Twentieth-Century Europe: Economic
   Regimes from Laissez-Faire to Globalization* (Cambridge: Cambridge University
   Press, 2016), 270.
5 "Europe 2020 Indicators–Poverty and Social Exclusion," Europe 2020 Strategy Report (Eurostat, August 2019), https://ec.europa.eu/eurostat/statistics-
   explained/index.php/Europe_2020_indicators_-_poverty_and_social_exclusion,
   accessed October 6, 2019.

6 Hans-Georg Betz, *Radical Right-Wing Populism in Western Europe* (Basingstoke: Macmillan, 1994), 31; Ryan Avent, "Black and Jobless in America," *The Economist*, May 2, 2011, sec. Economist, www.economist.com/free-exchange/2011/05/02/black-and-jobless-in-america, accessed October 9, 2017.

7 See *Pocket World in Figures 2006* (London: Economist Books, 2005); *Pocket World in Figures 2015* (London: Economist Books, 2014).

8 Maddison Angus, *The World Economy: A Millennial Perspective* (Paris: OECD Publishing, 2001), 147.

9 Michael Hameleers and Rens Vliegenthart, "The Rise of a Populist Zeitgeist? A Content Analysis of Populist Media Coverage in Newspapers Published between 1990 and 2017," *Journalism Studies* 21, no. 1 (January 2, 2020): 20, https://doi.org/10.1080/1461670X.2019.1620114, accessed April 19, 2020.

10 Norberto Bobbio, *Left and Right: The Significance of a Political Distinction* (Chicago, IL: University of Chicago Press, 1996), XIII.

11 Amanda Taub, "How Germany's New Coalition Explains Europe's Uncertain Future," *The New York Times*, February 11, 2018, Web Edition, sec. World, www.nytimes.com/2018/02/11/world/europe/europe-politics-far-right.html, accessed November 5, 2019.

12 "Germany's Far-Right AfD Overtakes Social Democrats in Poll," *Deutsche Welle*, February 19, 2018, www.dw.com/en/germanys-far-right-afd-overtakes-social-democrats-in-poll/a-42648964, accessed October 3, 2019.

13 Gianfranco Bettin and Ettore Recchi, eds., *Comparing European Societies: Towards a Sociology of the EU* (Bologna: Monduzzi, 2005), 244–247.

14 Michael Saward, "Making Representations: Modes and Strategies of Political Parties," *European Review* 16, no. 3 (July 2008): 271–286, https://doi.org/10.1017/S1062798708000252, accessed September 5, 2017; Zsolt Enyedi, "The Social and Attitudinal Basis of Political Parties: Cleavage Politics Revisited," *European Review* 16, no. 3 (July 2008): 289, https://doi.org/10.1017/S1062798708000264, accessed October 7, 2017.

15 Andrej Zaslove, "Here to Stay? Populism as a New Party Type," *European Review* 16, no. 3 (July 2008): 319–336, https://doi.org/10.1017/S1062798708000288, accessed September 8, 2017.

16 Alexis Tsipras, "Alexis Tsipras: 'Non à une zone euro à deux vitesses '," *Le Monde*, June 2, 2015, sec. Opinion, www.lemonde.fr/economie/article/2015/06/02/alexis-tsipras-non-a-une-zone-euro-a-deux-vitesses_4644263_3234.html, accessed October 18, 2017. Also see Helena Smith and Graeme Wearden, "Tsipras Lambasts 'Absurd Proposals' of Creditors for Greece Debt-Deal Failure," *The Guardian*, May 31, 2015, sec. Business, www.theguardian.com/business/2015/may/31/greece-alexis-tsipras-lambasts-absurd-proposals-creditors-for-debt-deal-failure, accessed December 1, 2017.

17 Nate Schenkkan, "*The False Promise of Populism*, Nations in Transit (Washington, DC: Freedom House, 2017), https://freedomhouse.org/report/nations-transit/2017/false-promise-populism, accessed February 4, 2018.

18 Paul Krugman, "What's the Matter with Europe?," *The New York Times*, May 21, 2018, sec. Opinion, www.nytimes.com/2018/05/21/opinion/europe-euro-democracy-wrong.html, accessed October 7, 2019.

19 Maik Baumgärtner et al., "Why Is the Former East Germany Tilting Populist?," *Der Spiegel*, November 17, 2017, Web Edition, www.spiegel.de/international/germany/eastern-germany-and-its-affinity-for-populists-a-1177790.html, accessed January 9, 2018. See also: Isaac Stanley-Becker and Alexandra Rojkov, "The German Election Was a Fault Line of East-West Tensions, Key to the Rise of the Far Right," *Washington Post*, September 26, 2017, sec. Europe, www.washingtonpost.com/world/europe/the-german-election-was-a-fault-line-of-

east-west-tensions-key-to-the-rise-of-the-far-right/2017/09/26/e9189efc-9e1c-11e7-b2a7-bc70b6f98089_story.html, accessed March 7, 2018.

20 Uuriintuya Batsaikhan, Zsolt Darvas, and Inês Goncalves Raposo, *People on the Move: Migration and Mobility in the European Union*, Blueprint Series 28 (Brussels: Bruegel, 2018), www.bruegel.org/2018/01/people-on-the-move-migration-and-mobility-in-the-european-union/, accessed January 28, 2018.

21 Ruben Atoyan et al., "Emigration and Its Economic Impact on Eastern Europe," *IMF Staff Discussion Note* 16, no. 7 (July 2016): 8, https://doi.org/10.5089/9781475576368.006, accessed September 28, 2017.

22 Boris Johnson, "Please Vote Leave on Thursday, because We'll Never Get This Chance again," *The Telegraph*, June 19, 2016, www.telegraph.co.uk/news/2016/06/19/please-vote-leave-on-thursday-because-well-never-get-this-chance/, accessed September 7, 2017.

23 Boris Johnson, *Lend Me Your Ears* (London: HarperCollins, 2004), 29.

24 Ibid., 37–38.

25 Ibid., 43–45.

26 Marine Le Pen, Interview with Marine Le Pen: "I Don't Want this European Soviet Union," Interview by Mathieu von Rohr, *Der Spiegel*, June 3, 2014, www.spiegel.de/international/europe/interview-with-french-front-national-leader-marine-le-pen-a-972925.html, accessed September 6, 2017.

27 Klaus Bachmann, "Reason's Cunning," *Eurozine*, August 10, 2007, www.eurozine.com/reasons-cunning/#footnote-16, accessed October 9, 2017.

28 *Concept-Verkiezingsprogramma 2017–2021* (Partij voor de Vrijheid, 2017), www.pvv.nl/visie.html, accessed June 6, 2018.

29 Johnson, *Lend Me Your Ears*, 178–181.

30 Le Pen, Interview with Marine Le Pen: "I Don't Want this European Soviet Union."

31 Marine Le Pen, "Marine Le Pen: After Brexit, the People's Spring Is Inevitable," *The New York Times*, June 28, 2016, Web Edition, sec. Opinion, www.nytimes.com/2016/06/28/opinion/marine-le-pen-after-brexit-the-peoples-spring-is-inevitable.html, accessed October 6, 2017.

32 Alan Cowell, "Le Pen Accused of Torturing Prisoners during Algerian War," *The New York Times*, June 4, 2002, sec. World, www.nytimes.com/2002/06/04/world/le-pen-accused-of-torturing-prisoners-during-algerian-war.html, accessed September 17, 2017.

33 Joel Dreyfuss, "Will Marine Le Pen's Changed Tone Be Enough to Win over France?," *Washington Post*, January 23, 2017, sec. Opinion, www.washingtonpost.com/news/global-opinions/wp/2017/01/23/will-marine-le-pens-changed-tone-be-enough-to-win-over-france/, accessed December 17, 2017.

34 Cécile Alduy, "The Devil's Daughter," *The Atlantic*, September 19, 2013, sec. Global, www.theatlantic.com/magazine/archive/2013/10/the-devils-daughter/309467/, accessed October 6, 2017.

35 Marine Le Pen, Interview with Marine Le Pen: "I Don't Want This European Soviet Union," Interview by Mathieu von Rohr, *Der Spiegel*, June 3, 2014, www.spiegel.de/international/europe/interview-with-french-front-national-leader-marine-le-pen-a-972925.html, accessed November 5, 2017.

36 Marine Le Pen, "Marine Le Pen."

37 Viktor Orbán, "The Time Has Come for Opposition and Resistance," https://gatesofvienna.net/2016/03/viktor-orban-the-time-has-come-for-opposition-and-resistance/, accessed September 19, 2017. The quotation in the last sentence is from an 1848 poem by mid-nineteenth century Hungarian poet Sándor Petőfi, which started the Hungarian revolution that occurred that year.

38 Translation from Hungarian by me.

39 Viktor Orbán, "Speech at the XXV. Bálványos Free Summer University and Youth Camp," *Budapest Beacon*, July 26, 2014, https://budapestbeacon.com/

full-text-of-viktor-orbans-speech-at-baile-tusnad-tusnadfurdo-of-26-july-2014/, accessed November 15, 2017.

40 Ibid.

41 Orlando Crowcroft, Review of *Viktor Orbán: How One Man's Will to Power Created "Führer Democracy" in Hungary (Book Review)*, by Paul Lendvai, *Newsweek*, October 20, 2017, sec. Culture, www.newsweek.com/viktor-orban-europes-new-strongman-688480, accessed October 2, 2018.

42 "Hungarian PM Viktor Orban Denounces EU's 'Colonialism,'" *BBC News*, March 16, 2012, sec. Business, www.bbc.com/news/business-17394894, accessed September 28, 2017.

43 "Orbán Accuses EU of Colonialism," *Politico*, March 16, 2012, www.politico.eu/article/orban-accuses-eu-of-colonialism/, accessed September 29, 2017.

44 "Hungarian PM Viktor Orban Denounces EU's 'Colonialism.'"

45 "Orbán Accuses EU of Colonialism."

46 Kester Eddy, "EU Urged to Monitor Hungary as Orban Hits at 'Liberal Democracy'," *Financial Times*, July 30, 2014, sec. World, www.ft.com/content/0574f7f2-17f3-11e4-b842-00144feabdc0, accessed June 7, 2017.

47 Orbán, "Speech at the XXV."

48 Ibid.

49 "Magyarország Ismét Győzelemre Áll," *Miniszterelnok*, June 6, 2020, www.miniszterelnok.hu/magyarorszag-ismet-gyozelemre-all/1, accessed June 28, 2020.

50 Viktor Orbán, *Prime Minister Viktor Orbán's State of the Nation Address* (Budapest, February 28, 2016), www.kormany.hu/en/the-prime-minister/the-prime-minister-s-speeches/prime-minister-viktor-orban-s-state-of-the-nation-address, accessed November 1, 2017.

51 Viktor Orbán, *A Szabadság És a Függetlenség Történelmünk Vezércsillaga* (Budapest, March 15, 2015), www.kormany.hu/hu/a-miniszterelnok/beszedek-publikaciok-interjuk/a-szabadsag-es-a-fuggetlenseg-tortenelmunk-vezercsillaga, accessed September 18, 2017.

52 Tamás Székely, "'State of the Nation': Prime Minister Viktor Orbán's Sunday Speech in Full–Video!," *Hungary Today*, March 2, 2016, https://hungarytoday.hu/state-nation-pm-viktor-orbans-sunday-speech-full-video-16050/, accessed October 19, 2017.

53 "Orbán Viktor: Kapcsolat van a migráció és a koronavírus-járvány között," *Magyar Nemzet*, March 10, 2020, https://magyarnemzet.hu/belfold/orban-viktor-egyertelmuen-kapcsolat-van-a-migracio-es-a-koronavirus-jarvany-kozott-7872191/, accessed May 20, 2020.

54 Peter C. Baker, "'We Can't Go Back to Normal': How Will Coronavirus Change the World?," *The Guardian*, March 31, 2020, sec. World News, www.theguardian.com/world/2020/mar/31/how-will-the-world-emerge-from-the-coronavirus-crisis, accessed May 3, 2020.

55 Karolina Wigura and Jarosław Kuisz, "Coronavirus Is Now Contaminating Europe's Democracy," *The Guardian*, April 1, 2020, sec. World News, www.theguardian.com/world/commentisfree/2020/apr/01/coronavirus-contaminating-europe-democracy-viktor-orban-seize-more-power, accessed May 19, 2020.

56 See the report of the Hungarian media: "Rákapcsolt a Rendőrség: 87 Eljárást Indított Rémhírterjesztés Miatt," *Hírklikk*, May 14, 2020, https://hirklikk.hu/kozelet/rakapcsolt-a-rendorseg-87-eljarast-inditott-remhirterjesztes-miatt/363675, accessed June 3, 2020.

57 Zack Beauchamp, "Hungary's 'Coronavirus Coup,' Explained," *Vox*, April 15, 2020, www.vox.com/policy-and-politics/2020/4/15/21193960/coronavirus-covid-19-hungary-orban-trump-populism, accessed May 20, 2020.

58 "EU Coordinated Action to Combat the COVID-19 Pandemic and Its Consequences" (Strasbourg: European Parliament, April 17, 2020), www.europarl.

europa.eu/doceo/document/TA-9-2020-0054_EN.html, accessed May 20, 2020.

59 "Hungary and COVID-19: Debate on Fundamental EU Values under Threat," *News Briefing European Parliament*, www.europarl.europa.eu/news/en/agenda/briefing/2020-05-13/3/hungary-and-covid-19-debate-on-fundamental-eu-values-under-threat, accessed June 24, 2020.

60 Viktor Orbán, *Orbán Viktor Ünnepi Beszéde Az 1848/49. Évi Forradalom És Szabadságharc 170. Évfordulóján* (Budapest, March 15, 2018), www.kormany.hu/hu/a-miniszterelnok/beszedek-publikaciok-interjuk/orban-viktor-unnepi-beszede-az-1848-49-evi-forradalom-es-szabadsagharc-170-evfordulojan, accessed September 5, 2018.

61 Viktor Orbán, *Prime Minister Viktor Orbán's Speech in the European Parliament* (Brussels: European Parliament Meeting, April 26, 2017), www.miniszterelnok.hu/prime-minister-viktor-orbans-speech-in-the-european-parliament/, accessed March 6, 2018.

62 László Valki, "Lex CEU – a felsőoktatási törvény módosítása," in *Jogtörténeti parerga: ünnepi tanulmányok Mezey Barna 60. születésnapja tiszteletére*, ed. Révész T. Mihály and Gosztonyi Gergely (Budapest: Eötvös Kiadó, 2013), 271–282.

63 Nick Thorpe, "Hungary Vilifies Financier with Posters," *BBC News*, July 10, 2017, sec. Europe, www.bbc.com/news/world-europe-40554844, accessed June 3, 2018.

64 Andre Lowoa, "Nemkívánatossá Nyilvánítják Soros György Alkalmazottait," *Armageddon Nyomában* (blog), May 24, 2015, http://nyomaban.blog.hu/2015/05/24/nemkivanatossa_nyilvanitjak_soros_gyorgy_alkalmazottait, accessed September 9, 2017; Valki, "Lex CEU – a felsőoktatási törvény módosítása."

65 Paul Craig Roberts, "Soros's 'European Values' Mean Losing Your National Identity," *Russia Today International*, November 4, 2015, sec. Opinion, www.rt.com/op-ed/320747-soros-european-values-orban/, accessed October 16, 2017.

66 Vanessa Gera, "Demonization of Soros Recalls Old Anti-Semitic Conspiracies," *The Times of Israel*, May 16, 2017, www.timesofisrael.com/demonization-of-soros-recalls-old-anti-semitic-conspiracies/, accessed September 6, 2017.

67 Ibid.

68 Przemek Skwirczyński, "Polish MP Demands 'Pest' Soros Is Stripped of Country's Highest Honour," *Breitbart*, September 21, 2016, sec. London/Europe, www.breitbart.com/europe/2016/09/21/polish-mp-demands-pest-soros-is-stripped-of-countrys-highest-honour/, accessed September 16, 2017.

69 Jon Henley, "George Soros: Financier, Philanthropist – and Hate Figure for the Far Right," *The Guardian*, February 8, 2018, sec. Business, www.theguardian.com/business/2018/feb/08/george-soros-demonised-by-populists-nationalists-and-right-wing-press, accessed March 4, 2019.

70 Jamie White, "'Stop Soros' Movement Sweeps Europe," *Infowars* (blog), January 26, 2017, www.infowars.com/stop-soros-movement-sweeps-europe/, accessed October 6, 2017.

71 Rick Lyman, "After Trump Win, Anti-Soros Forces Are Emboldened in Eastern Europe," *The New York Times*, March 1, 2017, Web Edition, sec. World, www.nytimes.com/2017/03/01/world/europe/after-trump-win-anti-soros-forces-are-emboldened-in-eastern-europe.html, accessed October 5, 2018.

72 Lianne Kolirin, "Anti-Soros Campaign across Europe Is Drenched in Antisemitism," *The Jewish Chronicle*, May 16, 2017, www.thejc.com/news/world/anti-soros-campaign-across-europe-is-drenched-in-antisemitism-1.438614, accessed June 5, 2018.

73 Lyman, "After Trump Win, Anti-Soros Forces Are Emboldened in Eastern Europe."

74 Gera, "Demonization of Soros Recalls Old Anti-Semitic Conspiracies."

75 Ibid.

76 Orlando Figes, *The Europeans: Three Lives and the Making of a Cosmopolitan Culture* (New York: Metropolitan Books, 2019), 340–341.

77 Timothy Garton Ash, "Britain's Pride in Its Past Is Not Matched by Any Vision for Its Future," *The Guardian*, May 21, 2020, sec. Opinion, www.theguardian.com/commentisfree/2020/may/21/britains-pride-past-not-matched-vision-future, accessed June 1, 2020.

78 Johnson, *Lend Me Your Ears*.

79 Ibid., 38.

80 "Boris Johnson Dossier in Full," *The Sunday Times*, September 9, 2018, www.thetimes.co.uk/article/boris-johnson-dossier-in-full-cpdrwfzj3, accessed March 20, 2019.

81 Josh Lowe, "Boris Johnson's Best Brussels Dispatches," *Newsweek*, February 22, 2016, sec. World, www.newsweek.com/boris-johnson-london-mayor-telegraph-brussels-dispatches-429010, accessed December 4, 2017.

82 Boris Johnson, "Tory Candidates Need a Plan for Brexit–Here's Mine in 5 Points," *The Telegraph*, July 3, 2016, www.telegraph.co.uk/news/2016/07/03/tory-candidates-need-a-plan-for-brexit-heres-mine-in-5-points/, accessed December 2, 2017.

83 Peter Dominiczak, Steven Swinford, and Ben Riley-Smith, "Boris Johnson: Change the Whole Course of European History by Backing Brexit," *The Telegraph*, June 19, 2016, www.telegraph.co.uk/news/2016/06/19/boris-johnson-change-the-whole-course-of-european-history-by-bac/, accessed October 7, 2017.

84 Boris Johnson and Michael Gove, "Getting the Facts Clear on the Economic Risks of Remaining in the EU – Vote Leave's Letter to David Cameron," *The Telegraph*, June 4, 2016, www.telegraph.co.uk/news/2016/06/04/getting-the-facts-clear-on-the-economic-risks-of-remaining-in-th/, accessed October 7, 2017.

85 Laura Kuenssberg, "Profile: London Mayor Boris Johnson," *BBC News*, April 12, 2012, sec. UK Politics, www.bbc.com/news/uk-politics-17534804, accessed November 1, 2017.

86 Boris Johnson, "Am I Guilty of Racial Prejudice? We All Are," *The Guardian*, February 21, 2000, sec. UK News, www.theguardian.com/uk/2000/feb/21/lawrence.ukcrime3, accessed December 2, 2017.

87 Boris Johnson, "This Is a Turning Point: We Have to Fly the Flag for Britishness again," *The Telegraph*, October 18, 2018, www.telegraph.co.uk/politics/0/turning-point-have-fly-flag-britishness/, accessed January 8, 2019.

88 Stephen Castle, "Boris Johnson Takes Center Stage in U.K. Leadership Shadow Play," *The New York Times*, October 3, 2017, Web Edition, sec. World, www.nytimes.com/2017/10/03/world/europe/uk-boris-johnson-conservatives.html, accessed November 26, 2017.

89 Adrian Wooldridge, "Global Britain or Globaloney," *The Economist*, sec. Bagehot, accessed June 24, 2020, www.economist.com/britain/2018/03/15/global-britain-or-globaloney, accessed June 30, 2020.

90 Jiaqian Chen et al., "The Long-Term Impact of Brexit on the European Union," *IMF Blog* (blog), August 10, 2018, https://blogs.imf.org/2018/08/10/the-long-term-impact-of-brexit-on-the-european-union/, accessed February 28, 2019.

91 "Examining Economic Outcomes after Brexit," *RAND Corporation*, accessed June 24, 2020, www.rand.org/randeurope/research/projects/brexit-economic-implications.html, accessed June 25, 2020.

92 François Levarlet et al., *Assessing the Impact of the UK's Withdrawal from the EU on Regions and Cities in EU27*. (Brussels: European Committee of the Regions, 2018), http://dx.publications.europa.eu/10.2863/572180, accessed January 18, 2019.

8 An increasingly hostile international environment

At the end of the Cold War, Europe's security became guaranteed more securely than ever before. There were no hostile neighbors, no real enemies. The alliance with the United States was stable, and former Soviet Bloc countries including Russia became friends and wanted to join the European Union, which was already an economic superpower with twelve integrated member countries. This surprisingly idyllic situation, however, did not last for long. Soon after the turn of the millennium, the European Union was surrounded by enemies. One of its outstanding sign is Turkey's changing position regarding the EU.

Turkey: from candidate to enemy

Turkey has a long relation with European integration and the EU. As previously discussed, the United States pushed the European Economic Community to accept all European NATO member countries, regardless of their political regimes – some had autocratic-dictatorial systems – and preparedness levels. As a consequence, the Community, dependent upon American security guarantees, signed the Ankara Treaty in 1963, which granted associated status to Turkey. At that time, full membership was still impossible because Turkey's political and human-rights situations stood in sharp contrast with EU's requirements. The country, however, applied for full membership in 1987, joined the EU's Customs Union in 1996, and – although the process was extremely slow – became an official EU candidate in 1999. In 2005, accession negotiations started and the full membership seemed to be within reach. Meanwhile, economic ties significantly strengthened. After 1996, Turkey's trade with the EU increased sevenfold and came to represent 41 percent of Turkey's global trade; thus the EU became the most important partner of the country. In addition, two-thirds of the foreign direct investment in Turkey originated from the EU-25.

Turkey's membership remained questionable for several reasons. One of them is the result of geography. The EU's fundamental documents definitively state that member countries must be European: "Any European State which respects the values referred to in Article 2 and is committed to promoting them may apply to become a member of the Union."[1] Turkey's acceptance would make the concept of Europe extremely relative and could open the door for Near Eastern and

North African countries as well, since Turkey is not a European country – only 3 percent of its territory belongs to, and only 14 percent of its population lives on, the European continent.

Nevertheless, there is some ambiguity in the EU's definition of Europe. This classification, according to the European Commission and Council, is "subject to political assessment."[2] That phrase makes Turkey's qualification rather uncertain, because politically Turkey's strategic location and military strength have been important for the EU. Nevertheless, when Morocco applied for membership in 1987, the application was rejected because it was not a European country. On the other hand, the geographical statuses of Cyprus and Malta are also not absolutely clear (are they European or African?), but they were accepted in 2004. Certain island territories that are held by European countries but are themselves definitely not European – namely the Spanish Canary Islands, Ceuta, and Melilla off the northern coast of Africa; the Portuguese Azores and Madeira; the French 'overseas departments' of Mayotte and Réunion in the Indian Ocean, French Guiana on the northern Atlantic coast of South America, and Guadeloupe and Martinique in the Caribbean – are all members of the European Union. (When the North African country of Algeria was a French colony in the 1950s, it was also part of the European Community as well, until its independence in 1962.)

Preserving the so-called "European values" – the rock-solid foundation that the Union is built upon – is even more important than considerations based on geographic location. As the Copenhagen European Council stated in 1993:

> Membership requires that the candidate country has achieved stability of institutions guaranteeing democracy, the rule of law, human rights and respect for and protection of minorities, the existence of a functioning market economy as well as the capacity to cope with competitive pressure and market forces within the Union.[3]

Even if the EU is flexible regarding geographic considerations, its basic values are crystal-clear and biding. Turkey, which applied for membership, was never able to realize the European value requirements, and increasingly wants to fulfill them less and less. As the 2008 Commission Report on Turkey's preparedness found, the country has functioning market economy for the first time, but is still missing virtually all the other basic requirements.[4] The entire accession process hit a dead end in 2005.

The first major roadblock for Turkey was Cyprus, a new member country that entered the EU in 2004. Turkey attacked and had occupied more than two-thirds of the island since 1974, and Turkish EU membership could not proceed without Turkey's withdrawal. Equally, or even more importantly, Turkey was unable to fulfill most of the requirements for applying countries summarized in the 35 chapters of the *Acquis Communautaire*. More than a decade after negotiations began, only one chapter's requirements had been fully accomplished by Turkey. The country was unable to fulfill the basic requirements of membership due to harsh violations of democratic institutions, the rule of law, women's rights and human rights in general, as well as the oppression and even military actions the government undertook against the Kurdish minority.

The Western European member countries, especially after the 2004 over-enlargement and the Muslim terrorist attacks in the 2010s, have started to oppose further EU enlargement. France explicitly turned against it, and Austria called for ending talks with Turkey.[5] The final blow came in 2016, when, after a failed military coup against Prime Minster Recep Tayyip Erdoğan in July, the government brutally eliminated the opposition and the freedom of press: tens of thousands of people were arrested, including journalists and teachers. Erdoğan, who started as an enlightened modernizer, turned towards open dictatorship and pursued the re-Islamization of Turkey, including enacting a religious reorganization of the entire school system. Turkey's foreign policy orientation also changed and the country invited close cooperation with Russia, the archenemy of the EU, including in the areas of trading policy and even military orientation. Turkey went so far as to buy Russian armaments instead of NATO ones. Erdoğan even tried to mobilize the Turkish minority in Germany against the Merkel government. In 2015 and then again in 2020, he opened refugee camps in Turkey and sent millions of migrants to Europe, significantly contributing to the European migration crisis.

Although Turkey's official candidacy has not yet been nullified by the EU, it has no real meaning any longer. Turkey became a hostile neighbor allied with Putin's Russia, dangerously weakening EU's security. After a meeting with Erdoğan in 2018, French president Macron dropped the pretense of diplomatic language and flatly said, as the BBC reported, that "it was time to end the hypocrisy of pretending that there was any prospect of an advance in Turkey's membership talks with the EU."[6]

Putin's Russia became hostile

After the collapse of communism and the Soviet Union, the fifteen successor countries that were established in the 1990s as independent states in its place all declined into deep crisis. They wanted to adjust to being part of Europe, but did not know how to work towards that goal. On top of grappling with the tremendous shock of the USSR's collapse, they faced the dual tasks of creating modern sovereign states, which had never existed there in the given form before, and of transforming into capitalist private-market economies, which they had also never experienced in a real sense. Completing these formidable tasks necessitated decades; speaking from 2020, it is evident that not even 30 years has been enough time for those changes to take place.

When the Soviet government collapsed, Russia, a giant superpower, lost its identity. All of the sudden the huge country, which had ruled over the subordinated Bloc beyond its western borders, lost all of its satellite "allies" and even the ancient birthplace of the Russian state – the region from Ukraine and Belarus to the Baltic sea, the Kievan Rus', where Vladimir the Great Christianized Russia in the ninth century. Russia, a former empire and the victor of two world wars, became a poor country where alcoholism reached extreme heights, death rates soared, and life expectancy was about ten years shorter than in Europe in the 2010s. Large numbers of ethnic Russians, about 25 million, became also minorities in the neighboring, newly independent countries.

Another major factor in the tragic developments in the former Soviet Union successor states, especially in Russia, was the mistaken Western policy towards them. Following old instincts and practices, NATO considered Russia a potential enemy, and therefore started to recruit and then include Soviet successor states. They surrounded Russia with missiles placed in former Bloc countries next to its borders. The 1987 Intermediate-Range Nuclear Forces Treaty between the US and Russia, which had banned land-based weapons with ranges 310 and 3,420 miles, was abandoned. The US installed various types of missiles – including the high-tech Aegis Ashore missile defense system – near Russia. At the time, America asserted that the measures were intended against North Korea and Iran and would not affect Russia's deterrence capability. Now, years later, Washington no longer denies that the global missile defense system is intended to oppose Russia.

NATO also included the Baltic countries, former Soviet republics, and – during the presidency of George W. Bush – planned to include Ukraine. The first official relations between the Baltic States and NATO were initiated almost immediately after their regained independence in 1991, when NATO invited Central and Eastern European countries to create a joint institution, the North Atlantic Cooperation Council. In 1994, all three Baltic countries applied for NATO membership. At the NATO Summit in 1999, the organization named twelve potential membership candidates, which included the Baltic States. That year, the first group of former Soviet Bloc countries, Poland, Hungary and the Czech Republic already joined NATO. They were followed by Bulgaria, Estonia, Latvia, Lithuania, Romania, Slovakia and Slovenia in 2004. Albania and Croatia joined in 2009, and Montenegro followed in 2017. In 2019, NATO officially recognized four more aspiring members from the region: Bosnia, Georgia, North Macedonia and Ukraine. In other words, NATO virtually surrounded Russia, which significantly increased the country's fears and feeling of isolation. Cold War-era experts like Henry Kissinger and Zbigniew Brzezinski, both veteran American foreign policy gurus, immediately criticized NATO policy towards Russia and Ukraine. Kissinger characterized the developments as steps towards a mistaken goal of "breaking Russia" instead of trying to "integrate" it.[7] Brzezinski spoke about the need for "Finlandization," or neutralization, regarding Ukraine, in order to avoid violating Russia's sphere of interests.[8]

The European Union followed a similarly mistaken policy as that of the United States, signing association agreements that established three Deep and Comprehensive Free Trade Areas in Georgia, Moldova and Ukraine. It also alienated Russia by building cooperation in the region via Mobility Partnerships with Armenia, Azerbaijan, Georgia and Moldova – evident steps to bind them to the European Union. The EU announced that its "key goal is to bring Ukraine closer to the EU."[9] The EU had already signed a partnership agreement with Ukraine in June 1996, under the framework of the Eastern Partnership project. The EU's

summit meeting in Vilnius in November 2013 ratified the association agreements, which sought the further Europeanization of Armenia, Georgia, Moldova
and Ukraine. As part of the EU's €11 billion package supporting Ukraine, in
April 2015, the European Commission also established a Neighborhood Investment Facility and adopted a €70 million Special Measure for Private Sector
Development and Approximation. The EU planned to complement the program
with a loan-guarantee facility of €40 million. EU Commissioner Johannes Hahn
visited Ukraine five times in a short period and participated in the International
Conference on Support for Ukraine in April 2015, as well as the 12th Annual
Meeting of the Yalta European Strategy in Kiev in September 2015.

It was not a secret that the EU had even more ambitious plans: In the 2010s,
Štefan Füle, the European Commissioner for Enlargement and European Neighbourhood Policy, talked in several public speeches about full EU membership for
Ukraine, Moldova and Georgia. In May 2014 in Kiev, he stated, "If we want to
be serious about transforming the countries in Eastern Europe, then we also have
to seriously use the most powerful tool we have to transform: enlargement." In
an interview for the German journal *Die Welt*, Füle also announced that "the
association agreement with Ukraine is not the ultimate goal of our mutual cooperation"; the EU's long-term aim is the creation of framework "that allows the
enlargement policy to be continued beyond current ambitions together with
deeper integration."[10]

Russia's old paranoia of being encircled by hostile enemies – certainly based
on past experiences, as Mongols, Napoleon's French army, and Germany (twice
in the twentieth century) have all invaded the country – was fueled by NATO's
presence at its borders and the EU's enlargement attempts towards post-Soviet
space territories. Russia was definitely shocked. As a special subcommittee of the
British House of Lords stated: Britain and the EU

> made a "catastrophic misreading" of Russia and President Vladimir V. Putin
> and "sleepwalked" into the Ukraine crisis . . . member nations [were] insen-
> sitive to the degree of Russian hostility toward European Union efforts to
> negotiate a closer political and economic relationship, known as an "associa-
> tion agreement," with Ukraine.[11]

After the humiliating decade of the 1990s, Vladimir Putin took power in 1999–
2000 and soon adopted the stance that he was a historical personality, a second
Vladimir the Great, who would return Russia to great power status. In April 2005,
virtually all the world's media reported on a nationally televised speech in which
Putin stated that the breakup of the Soviet Union was "the greatest geopolitical
tragedy of the [twentieth] century."[12] He wanted to turn back the clock and reestablish as much as possible of the old empire. He did not hesitate to launch coun-
terattacks. As Ukraine and Moldova became closer to the EU, Russia blackmailed
them by blocking their imports and canceling oil deliveries. Russia's growing
feelings of endangerment, well lacking real ground, generated further aggression,
including the deployment of a new ground-launched intermediate-range cruise

missile targeting Europe and the US (in violation of the 1987 Intermediate-range Nuclear Forces Treaty). In recent years, Russia has demonstrated its readiness to use its military force by employing its forces in South Ossetia, Georgia, and Moldova; by seizing Crimea; and by sustaining armed conflict in the Donbas in Ukraine.

Russia also started its first expeditionary military operation in Syria in 2015, and eventually entered the war in order to demonstrate its strength and build up its influence in the Middle East. Complementing its earlier installment of an air base in Egypt, Russia increased its engagement in the war in Libya in order to become a key player in competition for the Mediterranean area, in order to return to a position of broad influence. Russia has also built or upgraded seven military bases in the Arctic region, and has gained control of the Suez Canal. Moreover, in late 2019 Russia demonstrated its force and military capabilities by surging ten submarines into the North Atlantic, which had not happened since the Cold War. Russia keeps a sizeable military presence along the EU's eastern frontiers from the Baltic to the Black Sea, which represents an immense danger for the Union.[13]

During this period, Russia became increasingly hostile against the EU and overreacted. As an EU analysis clearly stated in 2016, the country has repeatedly tried to portray European integration as a malign force, and has tried to divide the EU. In several speeches, President Vladimir Putin declared that Russia was ready to defend – even militarily – the interests of Russian and Russian-speaking peoples in neighboring areas, including those located partly inside the EU, if they felt endangered and asked for help.[14]

Putin's main goal was to reestablish Russia as a great power, and to reunite as many former parts of the Soviet Union as possible. To achieve the goal of reuniting the now-independent republics, he launched a rival integration plan, the Eurasian Economic Union, and ushered in the formation of a Customs Union that included as many former Soviet republics as possible. At first, Russia, Belarus and Kazakhstan joined. Somewhat later, Armenia's leadership changed its policy, gave up its EU orientation and also joined, together with Kyrgyzstan. This Union is also planning to introduce a common currency. The explicit goal is progress towards political integration. They signed the Collective Security Treaty Organization with eight other former Soviet republics.

In 2018, Russia was an economically weak country: its per-capita income level was just 20 percent of the United States' per-capita income level, and only roughly 60 percent of the per-capita income levels of the former Soviet Bloc satellites. Nonetheless, it tried to increase its international status through showings of military strength. Russia, of course, remained a strong military-nuclear power even after the collapse of the Soviet Union, with more than twice as many strategic ballistic missiles (almost 1,600 versus 750), and more submarines than the United States. President Putin, however, went much further and started modernizing and developing the Russian military. The new Russian National Security Strategy stated in December 2015 that its goal is "strengthening Russia's status as a leading world power." Besides the inherited nuclear arsenal, Putin started investing nearly one-third of Russia's budget – a huge part of the revenue obtained from the country's oil income – into new armaments, modernizing and increasing the nuclear arsenal, and strengthening the country's military power. While in 2006, the country dedicated $27 billion, or 2.4 percent of its GDP, to these goals, in 2016, it spent $69 billion, or 5.3 percent of its increased GDP. As a consequence, Russia elevated to become the second-most commanding military power in the world.[15] In a televised speech to a joint session of both houses of parliament in early 2018, Putin announced the successful development of a new type of missile system, a "low-flying, difficult-to-spot cruise missile . . . with a practically unlimited range and an unpredictable flight path, which can bypass lines of interception and is invincible in the face of all existing and future systems of both missile defense and air defense."[16]

Russia is increasingly flexing its military muscles. It regularly launches military provocations in the air and seas against NATO and the EU, especially in the neighboring Baltic and Nordic countries. Between March and October 2014 alone, it committed 40 provocations. In 1999, 2009, and again in December 2017, the Royal Navy monitored Russian warships in the North Sea and escorted one of them after it skirted British waters. Several similar provocations happened in that area. In January and April of that year, provocations even happened in the English Channel. Russia also often attacks the undersea cables that carry most global communications and monetary transactions. Russia performed its usual Zapad (West) military exercises next to the EU's borders and organized joint exercises with China. The head of the British Armed Forces, Air Chief Marshal Stuart Peach, warned of a "catastrophic threat."[17]

The Guardian, arguing against Brexit, added:

> What makes everything more dangerous is that Putin's Russia has a vital interest in the EU's break-up. . . . The risk is that Brexit could trigger a Breakit through a succession of other exits forced by the angry factions and thereby add too many crises for the EU to cope with. What happens then to Europe's nations big and small, one dares not imagine?[18]

A few weeks later in July 2016, just before the two-day NATO summit in Warsaw met to discuss the Russian danger, the *Financial Times* reported from Berlin that Chancellor Angela Merkel "said Moscow had undermined European security in 'words and deeds' by infringing Ukraine's borders and 'profoundly disturbed' Nato's [*sic*.] eastern members who therefore require the unambiguous back-up of the alliance."[19] This feeling of Russian danger does not equally characterize all of the EU and European NATO member countries, but, as a 2017 Rand Corporation analysis stated:

> European countries that share a border with Russia have been living with the possibility of a Russian invasion for the better part of their history, and this experience generally has a strong impact on how they view Russia in the context of the Ukrainian crisis – this is particularly true for the Baltic States and Poland and, to a lesser extent, Finland and Norway. . . . [The Baltic

countries] were concerned about Russian propaganda in Estonia or Latvia and that Russia's attempt to influence and mobilize Russian minorities in Estonia and Latvia could exacerbate tensions in the Baltic region.[20]

The Kremlin's central foreign policy goal became the weakening, and, if possible, dismantling of both the EU and the Western – meaning American-European – alliance. In 2013, an article published in a Russian military journal explained the so-called Gerasimov Doctrine, as it has become known.[21] It discussed 'hybrid' warfare, preferring the use of nonmilitary over military measures. Exploiting the conflicts and weaknesses of the West, the Russians are working to build alliances with some of the member and candidate countries of the EU and NATO, including Italy, Hungary and Turkey, and to establish security cooperation, arms sales and joint military exercises with Western Balkan countries such as Bosnia, Serbia, Kosovo and Macedonia. President Putin supported Serbia, opposed Western interventions and the UN decision regarding Kosovo's declared independence from Serbia, and sought to build political cooperation to undermine the West. In 2015, the London School of Economics and the South East European Studies at Oxford held a conference on Russia's presence and policies in the Balkans that discussed many of these issues.[22] In addition to diplomacy, a primary component of Moscow's strategy is launching a war of disinformation in order to influence elections and referenda. As *Politico Europe* summed up in an article titled "Russia's plot against the West,"

> Moscow sees liberal democracy as a threat and therefore must defeat it, either by force of arms in Ukraine and an attempted coup in Montenegro, or through non-violent means in the West, bringing us down to the Kremlin's own, depraved level through corruption, disinformation, and support for nationalist political movements. . . . Europe's political stability, social cohesion, economic prosperity and security are more threatened today than at any point since the Cold War, Russia is destabilizing the Continent on every front.[23]

Putin views building close connections with some, and if possible many, EU member countries as an important weapon. Vladimir Chizhov, Russia's ambassador to the EU, claimed: "Bulgaria is in a good position to become our special partner, a sort of a Trojan horse in the EU."[24] Some of the Central European and Balkan countries, such as candidate country Serbia and member countries Hungary and Slovakia, may play similar roles. Putin is building important economic connections with Greece and Cyprus as well. Cyprus is used by Russian big business to create offshore firms. In addition, around the time when Cyprus became an EU member also became the biggest investor in Russia. Investments from the small island country accounted for one-fifth of total foreign investments there – in 2006, almost $10 billion. Russian trade connections with Bulgaria are also very strong. Russia is the country's second-most important trade partner and the Russian Lukoil is one of the biggest companies operating in Bulgaria. It generated around 25 percent of Bulgaria's tax revenues in early twenty-first century. Bulgaria had planned to host the future Burgas-Alexandroupolis pipeline as well.[25]

One of Russia's fighting instruments against the European Union is its 'oil weapon.' Several countries in Europe and the EU are strongly dependent upon Russian gas and oil deliveries. Russia delivers more than one-third (in 2015, 37.5 percent) of total European gas imports. Quite a few countries – Estonia, Lithuania, Finland, Slovakia and Bulgaria – import 100 percent or nearly 100 percent of their gas from Russia. Eighty-seven percent of Balkan gas imports come from Russia; in Greece, the Czech Republic, Hungary, Slovenia, and Poland, this percentage is between 50 percent and 75 percent. Thirty-five percent of the EU's overall crude oil imports come from Russia; Germany, Poland and the Netherlands are the main recipients. Additionally, 85 percent of Russian exports for various refined oil products are delivered to Europe.[26] Russia has never hesitated to use its oil supplies as a weapon and to stop delivering necessary supplies in order to blackmail dependent countries. The situations in Ukraine and Moldova provide key examples of Russia's use of oil as leverage.

In October 2014, the European Council decided to decrease oil dependence from Russia through joint actions instead of national solutions. The EU worked to reorient its supply chain buying from other oil-producing countries and creating joint-buying agreements, which gives the EU a much stronger position in the market. The EU also made progress towards its goal of achieving energy security by 2030. In the decade leading up to that deadline, the EU is working to encourage a 30-percent decrease in consumption; another 27 percent of consumed energy resources must be from renewable sources.[27] According to the integrated plans, conventionally fueled cars will be halved by 2030 and totally eliminated by 2050. In the energy sector one cannot achieve sudden change, but all of these long-term plans are already underway. The portion of renewable energy within the entirety of the EU's energy consumption is significantly increasing: in just the few short years between 2007 and 2015, this figure increased from 9.7 percent to 16.4 percent. In another four decades, according to the plan, renewable energy will account for 60 percent of the EU's overall energy consumption. To achieve that, investments in solar and wind energy production are significantly increasing.[28] Oil dependence from Russia is gradually decreasing.

So, while Russia currently holds some strategic advantages, in the long term the oil weapon is not really frightening for Europe. EU's combined economy is almost 15 times the size of Russia's. Even with all of its oil wealth, Russia's GDP is barely as big as Belgium's and the Netherlands' combined. The EU's population is three and a half times the size of Russia's; its military spending is seven times larger. In the first decade of the twenty-first century, EU bought 56 percent of Russia's exports and supplied 44 percent of its imports, while Russia bought only 6 percent of the EU's products, and supplied just 10 percent of the goods the Union bought from abroad. Russia's economic importance for the EU is not very significant.

Nonetheless, counterbalancing the Russian military danger will require faster military unification of the European Union. As discussed before, only the very first steps towards this goal have been taken. Time is pressing, since together with Turkey, Russia and another military power, China, have turned increasingly hostile as well.

A new rival: China and the Balkan silk road

As part of a broad international expansionist policy, the new rising superpower, China, is on the economic offensive all over the world, through Chinese firms' direct investment in advanced and less developed economies. As one study put it in 2012:

> The take-off was only recent: annual inflows [were] . . . less than $1 billion (€700 million) yearly in 2004–2008. . . [but then] tripled from 2006 to 2009. . . to roughly $3 billion . . . and tripled again by 2011 to $10 billion (€7.4 billion) for the year. The number of deals with a value of more than $1 million doubled from less than 50 to almost 100 in 2010 and 2011. . . the change in trend line is what matters.[29]

China's three-year plan of infrastructural investments includes Africa, Latin America and other parts of the world. Part of the $174-billion plan has gone towards building a Digital Silk Road. This project started in 2018 with a $25 billion investment and about 30 satellites. In the spring of 2020, China completed its own Global Positioning System (GPS), which quickly began to compete with the American GPS system, which until then had dominated. China's rival system debuted in 30 countries that had already signed agreements. The system was constructed in three phases. The first was completed in 2000 to provide services to China; the second, finished in 2012, provided services to the Asia-Pacific region; and the third, which wrapped up in May 2020, provided global services. Since 2000, China has launched 54 satellites. In December 2019, it launched another 24 operational satellites, and put the last ones in place in March and May 2020. They will serve 70 countries all over the world.[30] All these projects are parts of the planned $1 trillion Belt and Road Initiative in Asia, Russia, Eastern Europe and the Middle East.[31] A recent study summarized the stakes of this investment project for the West:

> [The] Hudson Institute Director of the Center on Chinese Strategy . . . believes China has a secret plan to displace the United States as the world's leading superpower, but there's nothing secret about its high-tech military buildup. . . . Nor is there anything secret about China's global ambitions. It aims to integrate Eurasia into a Chinese economic sphere under the multi-trillion-dollar Belt and Road Initiative, and to use its 5G broadband dominance to lead a Fourth Industrial Revolution. Huawei's website has advertised China's plan for global economic supremacy since 2011; China has proclaimed it with great fanfare. . . . China's military ambition is important, but subordinate to an economic and technological vision. . . . China's

current regime is cruel, but no crueler than the Qin dynasty that buried a million conscript laborers in the Great Wall. China was, and remains, utterly ruthless.[32]

With this leading superpower goal, China also started to compete with the EU. It sought to attract member countries and integrate them into a Chinese-Eurasian economic sphere of interests. The cruel dictatorial system headed by the absolutist lifelong leader President Xi Jinping tried to effect world domination by weakening rival great powers – not only the United States, but also the European Union. This goal became more realistic during the second half of 2010s, when the United States gave up its ambitions for world leadership, vacating the position it had dominated during the last three-quarters of a century, since World War II. President Trump's "America First" policy – which, practically speaking, amount to an "America alone" policy – and his administration's hostility against the Atlantic alliance opened the door for Chinese actions. Russia and the populist regimes on the Balkans and Central Europe – especially EU member countries that want to counterbalance the vilified influence of Brussels – are also potential agents for China. Ambitious China is exploiting the uncertain and chaotic world order by using its economic power as a political weapon to gain ground and influence all over the world. One study stated:

> China's interests in Europe are manifold – from access to new technologies, high-tech assets, and knowledge, to broader commercial access into the European market and entrance to third markets (such as the United States) via European corporate networks. Chinese investors are looking for brand names to improve marketability of their products – both at home and abroad – assuming a key role in integrated regional and global value chains. . . . Total Chinese investment in Europe, including mergers and acquisitions (M&A) and green-field investments, now amounts to $348 billion, and China has acquired more than 350 European companies over the past 10 years.[33]

China follows a diversified strategy in Europe, focusing on capital investments in the western EU countries and large infrastructure development projects in the less-developed peripheries. The country targets strategic assets and research-and-development networks. Seventy-five percent of total investments in the largest and wealthiest European countries and in the EU went there in 2017. State-run Chinese companies have taken their buying sprees to Europe. For example, Chem China took over Pirelli in Italy in 2017; in 2018, China's Cosco Port Holding Co. acquired the terminal in Zeebrugge, Belgium's second largest port. According to the Organization for Economic Cooperation and Development's latest figures, Chinese state-run companies now control 10 percent of European container terminal capacity, including in the three of Europe's largest ports: Euromax, Antwerp and Hamburg. Chinese foreign direct investment in Europe increased tenfold over a decade, peaking at €37.2 billion in 2016.[34]

China's control of major ports and dominant supply of important investments not only allows the country to penetrate continental Europe, but also enables her to influence EU foreign policy, especially with respect to itself.[35]

In Central, Eastern, and Southeastern Europe, Chinese investments represent a small percentage compared to the core EU countries, but the political consequences are much bigger. More than 70 percent of investments come from Chinese government-backed, state-owned companies; this dependence has significantly endangered European sovereignty and security.

China's efforts met with strong support in the Eastern half of Europe, where anti-EU populist forces gained power and tried to counterbalance EU connections with Russian and Chinese ones. The Hungarian government of Viktor Orbán, which gained power in 2010, had already declared its Global Opening Policy by 2011. This policy was followed in 2012 by a new foreign economic policy orientation, the Eastern Opening Strategy. "The main objective of this policy," an EU analysis stated, "has been to reduce the dependency of Hungary's economy on trade with Europe through increased economic relations with the East."[36] Poland followed the same policy by diversifying its exports, which were previously overly dependent on the EU (77 percent in 2014). Poland built the most developed relations with China and signed a strategic partnership in December 2011. The same report summarized China's interests in the region:

> Hungary has a specific strategy towards China . . . and was the first to work towards a closer partnership. Poland is the only country among the V4 [Visegrád Four] that is a founding member of the China-led Asian Infrastructure Investment Bank (AIIB). . . . Domestic media echoed the importance of the country's role as a gateway to China while international media reported about a new Chinese-Hungarian "special relationship," which caused mixed feelings. . . [at] the EU institutions. In 2010, Hungary alone took in 89% of the Chinese capital flow to the CCE [Central-East European] region. By 2014, the amount of Chinese investment had . . . increased . . . from $0.65 million in 2005 to. . . $556 million, according to Chinese statistics, which is by far the highest in the region. . .
>
> [China] plans several infrastructure-related investments in the coming years: China wants to transform Szombathely airport . . . and Debrecen airport, two small country airports in Hungary, into major European cargo bases.[37]

In May 2017, President Xi Jinping organized the Belt and Road Forum, in Beijing with the participation of presidents and prime ministers from Russia, Turkey, Greece, Hungary, Poland, Serbia and the Czech Republic. The Chinese government signed economic and trade agreements with 30 governments, including several former Soviet republics such as Belarus, Georgia, Armenia; and with a series of Balkan countries, among them Albania, Bosnia, Montenegro, and Serbia. The Chinese Export-Import Bank also signed a loan agreement with the Serbian government regarding the modernization of the Hungarian-Serbian Railway Line.

President Xi Jinping launched the Belt and Road Initiative in 2013 and started building a transport route and logistic corridor, the Balkan Silk Road. In 2014, China also signed the "gate towards Europe" agreement with Greece.[38] Chinese investment in that country started in 2009 when the Ocean Shipping Company, the biggest in China, leased half of the Greek state-owned Piraeus Port Authority's container port for 35 years for €678 million, and then bought a 51 percent majority of the port for another €280.5 million in 2016. In the same year, China's State Grid Corporation purchased a 24 percent stake in Greece's power-grid operator ADMIE.

These Chinese investments in Greece are a part of the 17+1 (formerly 16+1; Greece formally joined in 2019) Initiative established in Warsaw in 2012, which targeted trade and economic relations with Central and East European countries. Summits for this group were organized by the Beijing-based "Cooperation between China and Central and Eastern European Countries" and held every year in one of the member countries' capital cities. In 2013, the Chinese-CEE Investment Cooperation Fund was opened with $500 million in funding from two Chinese banks. In 2016, a second China-CEE Investment Fund was launched with $11 billion. In 2017, the Bank of China opened a subsidiary in Hungary and a branch in Belgrade. Chinese companies are building a Danube bridge in Belgrade with a $260 million Chinese loan. The Chinese Export-Import Bank will finance 85 percent of the Belgrade-Budapest high-speed railroad, a $2.89 billion project.

In connection with major Chinese investment projects in the region, trade contacts also increased. Between 2009 and 2014, the total trade between China and the region doubled to more than $60 billion. This investment was highly concentrated in five countries of the region – Poland, the Czech Republic, Hungary, Slovakia and Romania – which constitute 80 percent of trade exchange. The possible political consequences and dangers for the EU are evident.

Trade connections were significantly advanced by the realization of the EU-China rail transport system, which has increased trade a hundredfold from 2011, when the first regular connections were opened. Nearly 7,000 freight trains were launched in both directions; they transport about 4 percent of overall EU-China trade. There are also plans to build industrial parks along the railway routes to attract Chinese investors. China is also interested in developing the so-called China-Europe Land-Sea Express Line, which would connect Chinese ports with the port of Piraeus in Greece. The relatively less-developed Balkan and Central Eastern European countries need foreign investments and are still strongly dependent upon Western Europe in this respect. The motivations for China's investments are, of course, not at all solely economic; they represent a deliberate effort to weaken European Union connections and dependency.

Understandably, "China's involvement in expanding transport corridors via the Balkans has sparked major controversy within the EU."[39] The European Parliament analyzed the China-East European connection, after 2012, when the so-called "16+1 framework for cooperation" was established:

> Since 2012, China has engaged 16 central and eastern European countries (CEECs), including 11 EU Member States and five Western Balkan countries

under the 16+1 cooperation format, which it has portrayed as an innovative approach to regional cooperation. Although framed as multilateralism, in practice this format has remained largely bilateral and highly competitive in nature . . . in 2012 the CEECs had enthusiastically embraced this form of cooperation as a chance to diversify their EU-focused economic relations.[40]

Meanwhile, 16+1 became 17+1; as *The Diplomat* summarized in November 2017, "the 17+1 framework for cooperation is China's most advanced sub-regional diplomatic initiative in Europe." The European countries that are involved are all EU members or in the process of negotiating their accession to the EU. China took advantage of the struggles of the 2010s to solidify its power:

> In the aftermath of the financial crisis, Beijing initiated this format with the promise to foster investment, economic and trade cooperation, and to bring connectivity projects to the region . . . with the aim to facilitate Chinese access to the European market, to export China's excess capital and labor, and to build its global power.[41]

The European Parliament recognized the dangers that China's aggressive investments posed for European unity and, in 2015, called on "EU Member States to speak with one voice to the Chinese Government, particularly in view of Beijing's present diplomatic dynamism. [The 17+1 group] should not divide the EU or weaken its position vis-à-vis China."[42]

The Chinese Balkan Silk Road project is a long-term building plan for economic connection that has already made China a major complement to the EU's investors. As the author of a major study on this topic concluded:

> The Balkan Silk Road project cannot ignore the risks of creating investment and lending dependencies for countries in the region. . . . [I]ndividual countries interested by the Balkan Silk Road project are exposed to the risk of excessive dependence on Chinese state-led investment.[43]

This danger is accelerated by the fact the China is already the second-biggest trade partner to Europe. China initially targeted smaller and economically vulnerable states in Central and Eastern Europe. Once Chinese state-owned enterprises establish footholds in these countries, they moved on to other larger and more influential, but still economically vulnerable, countries. Following this logic, China turned to Italy. Chinese influence on Europe was significantly strengthened by making an important agreement with Italy, the EU's third-biggest economic power and the first G-7 country to form such a pact. In the spring of 2019, in the presence of Chinese president Xi, Italian Prime Minister Giuseppe Conte signed an agreement to join China's Belt and Road project. Economic Development, Labor and Social Policies Minister Luigi Di Maio happily announced the €20-billion Chinese investment project. China is especially interested in acquiring the port in Trieste. As the *South China*

Morning Post reported, "it would connect the Mediterranean to landlocked countries such as Austria, Hungary, the Czech Republic, Slovakia and Serbia, all of which are markets that China hopes to reach."[44] German Foreign Minister Heiko Maas commented the agreement: "If some countries believe that they can do clever business with the Chinese, then they will be surprised when they wake up and find themselves dependent."[45] A report in *Deutsche Welle* added: "But Italian officials are apparently happier to be dependent on faraway China than on the EU bureaucracy in Brussels."[46] This dependence may significantly strengthen populist-authoritarian forces and governments by weakening EU's economic supremacy in this region. In countries where populism is emerging and in those where it is already in power, Chinese economic connections, major investments and trade relations may significantly strengthen the governments' anti-EU policies and independence from Brussels.

China is consciously working on its project to keep Europe divided. It has furthered this goal by including countries from Southern, Central, and Eastern Europe into its sphere of interests via the "17+1" initiative. China has made a simple calculation: creating bilateral agreements with governments of EU member states that are in some way dissatisfied with the European Union will divide Europe and prevent the EU from facing it with a united front.

This Chinese policy became easier because the rising conflict and division between Europe and President Donald Trump's United States. Many partners of America, such as Australia, India, Japan, and several member states of the European Union, are critical of the US policy towards China. For quite a while, Europe was even happy to counterbalance Trump's America with China. As French President Macron phrased it: Europe has been naïve regarding China's efforts.

However, the EU's soft stance on China has started to change. The European Commission released a strongly worded White Paper on 12 March 2020 and presented it to the European Council on 21–22 March, around the time that China's President Xi Jinping began his state visit to Italy. The paper warned of the security dangers created by China's penetration of Europe. It also demanded a united stand against China, and – as French President Macron urged – "strategic autonomy" for Europe.[47] Nevertheless, hardly any real action has happened, although there are a few exceptions. The EU has created an investment screening mechanism to address foreign (including Chinese) takeovers of European companies. The Netherlands also decided to prevent China from acquiring one of its sensitive semiconductor equipment companies. Despite these outliers, real major action is still lacking but strongly needed.[48] In an article in *Foreign Affairs*, Stephen M. Walt even called the attention to a potential new role for NATO and the American-European alliance: counterbalancing China's power. This threat could "provide NATO with a strategic rationale it has lacked since 1992 and keep the trans-Atlantic partnership going for a bit longer."[49]

Although rising great-power China is physically far away from the West, its activity and presence in the European Continent and growing influence among Southern and Central Eastern European EU member and candidate countries became part of the challenges that contributed to the creation of the increasingly dangerous and hostile environment surrounding the Union.

Russian-Chinese military cooperation

The logic of the new world order pushed Russia and China from confrontation into friendly relations and military cooperation. The *Moscow Times* reported in its article "Russia and China Take Military Partnership to New Level" in October 2019:

> With the irreversible worsening of their relations with the United States, both Russia and China have seen the obstacles to broadening their coopera-tion to more sensitive areas disappear. Furthermore, the arms race in areas of breakthrough technology (such as hypersonic weapons, artificial intelli-gence, and automated systems) and the United States' attempts to activate the potential of its allies like Japan and Israel is actually pushing Moscow and Beijing to cooperate in these areas.[50]

In a speech at the Valdai Forum, President Putin of Russia emphasized "that Russia is helping China to create a missile launch detection system." According to Putin's assessment of the state of Russian-Chinese relations: "This is an allied relationship in the full sense of a multifaceted strategic partnership." Another aspect of cooperation, the Russian journal reported,

> could be the transition to joint strategic command post exercises. . . . The countries have agreed to hold annual maneuvers that are the top of a pyramid of other exercises carried out by Russia and China since 2005, both under the aegis of the Shanghai Cooperation Organization and on a bilateral basis. . . . In 2017, Chinese navy ships carried out joint exercises with their Russian counterparts in the Baltic, sparking ire among a range of NATO countries. In July 2019, the first joint patrol by Russian and Chinese long-range bomber aircraft took place over the Pacific Ocean: an explicit demonstration of the possibilities of joint action in the event of a conflict with the United States.[51]

The Russian newspaper finished the report by underlining that Russian-Chinese military cooperation may successfully counterbalance NATO.

Loosening alliances and rising hostility: the United States

Certain critics have earlier maintained that the European Union is nothing else than a part of the American "empire":

> Europe surrendered to the United States. This rendition is the most taboo of all to mention. . . . The one contemporary text to have captured the full flavour of the transatlantic relationship is, perhaps inevitably, a satire, Régis

Debray's plea for a United States of the West that would absorb Europe completely into the American imperium. . . . The paradox is that when Europe was less united, it was in many ways more independent.[52]

In a way, this view is close to the reality of the first postwar decades (as presented in earlier chapters), though never quite to the extent of the situation described here. The close connections between the United States and Europe started to loosen half a century ago and were quite broken by the 2010s. Russian, Turkish and Chinese attempts to weaken the European Union and surround it from the east and southeast by a hostile ring has created economic, political, and – especially for nearby EU countries – military danger. It may even prove to endanger the European integration process in general. This danger, however, was multiplied by the consequences of the changes in American policy towards the European Union.

Looking back from 2020, it may seem like the Trump presidency in the US represented a very sudden shift. In reality, it was not. The changing relations between Europe and America have a half-century history. The relationship between the United States and the European Union gradually changed. It started to shift in the late 1960s and reached its culmination in the late 2010s. For several decades, the EU's strong alliance with the US and its membership in the US-led military alliance NATO, formed the rock-solid base of the EU's foreign relations. This relationship was established before European integration started; moreover, as discussed before, the postwar American Marshall Plan (1948–1952) and US policy played a major initial role in European integration. During the decades of Cold War, postwar American presidents – Truman, Eisenhower and Kennedy – were strongly supportive of European integration and actively worked for it. The American Cold War foreign policy was built on the transatlantic alliance and on close military cooperation in NATO, then an American interest *par excellence.*

However, the American-West European alliance that had offered a nuclear-defense umbrella for Europe and formed the base of West European security, gradually and slowly started losing support from the United States. Initially, President Lyndon B. Johnson stopped making further efforts to strengthen the European Economic Community during the 1960s because of his preoccupation with domestic reforms and then with the Vietnam War. The real change, however, happened in the 1970s during the Nixon presidency, when the American administration revised its European policy. As the United States forged path-breaking agreements with two of its most formidable enemies, China and the Soviet Union, European alliances lost their central importance for the US. Moreover, the American government looked to integrating Europe as a rival, and preferred to forge bilateral relations with individual member countries. Nevertheless, the alliance and NATO remained intact and important during the entire twentieth century.

Further distancing continued after the end of the Cold War during the second half of the 1980s and especially after 1991, when the Soviet Union collapsed. As Robert Gilpin explains, this shift was mutual. From European perspective,

> the end of the Cold War . . . and the decreased need for close cooperation [between] the United States [and] Western Europe . . . have significantly

weakened the political bonds. . . . [Furthermore,] during the Cold War, the United States and its allies generally subordinated potential economic conflicts within the alliance to the interests of political and security cooperation.[53]

After the Cold War, "national priorities changed and the Western allies assigned a higher priority to their own national (and frequently parochial) economic interests. A shift in American policy had already become evident during the Reagan and Bush Administrations."[54] A greater emphasis on nationalism continued under the Clinton administration, as economic security displaced military security. Priorities further changed for Europe, which became less "willing to follow American leadership, much less tolerant of America's disregard of their economic and political interests, and more likely to emphasize their own national priorities."[55] According to Gilpin, protectionism slowly and gradually started to gain ground in America, as exemplified by the Multifiber Agreement of 1973, which restricted textile and apparel imports from developing countries, violating General Agreement on Tariffs and Trade (GATT) rules. Informal trade barriers emerged, and, in the US Trade Act of 1974, punitive actions were introduced against "unfair trade."[56] Nevertheless, the free trade system was not seriously endangered.

This gradual policy shift was replaced by a dramatic policy turn after the 2016 presidential elections, during the Donald J. Trump presidency. During the presidential election campaign, Trump expressed his views about the obsoleteness of NATO several times. When two journalists asked him about it on 23 March 2016, he answered in the following way:

I think NATO may be obsolete. NATO was set up a long time ago . . . when things were different. . . . We were a rich nation then . . . far more than we have today, in a true sense. And I think NATO . . . doesn't really help us, it's helping other countries.[57]

Then, in a foreign policy speech on 27 April 2016, he said:

We have spent trillions of dollars over time on planes, missiles, ships, equipment, building up our military to provide a strong defense for Europe and Asia. The countries we are defending must pay for the cost of this defense, and if not, the U.S. must be prepared to let these countries defend themselves.[58]

The new president touted his nationalist America First policy and often repeated his view that the US carried an unequal burden for others. Together with his strong admiration of dictators, especially Vladimir Putin, Trump immediately cooled down US-EU relations to their chilliest level since World War II. Trump's first visit in Europe and the NATO summit made it crystal-clear that the EU could not count on him. In one particular episode, he refused to repeat the crucial Article 5 covenant that an attack on one of the member countries is an attack against all member countries.

Several of Trump's other speeches and statements about European affairs were similarly offensive to the EU. He declared that it was a good idea for Britain to leave the Union. A day after the Brexit referendum, just before a trip to his Scotland golf club during his campaign, a *Washington Post* journalist asked him, "How would the Trump administration approach the Brexit, should you be elected president? And Scotland voted 62–38 to remain. Should Scotland leave the U.K., as many people are talking about?" Trump's answer was an enthusiastic, populist, anti-EU statement:

> People want to take their country back. They want to have independence, in a sense, and you see it with Europe, all over Europe. You're going to have more than just . . . what happened last night, you're going to have, I think many other cases where they want to take their borders back. They want to take their monetary back. . . . They want to be able to have a country again. So, I think you're going have this happen more and more. . . . I think it will turn out to be a good thing. Maybe not short term, not, but ultimately I think it will be a good thing. . . . It's not staying together. It's a really positive force taking place.[59]

In his first interview in Britain with one of the leading Brexiters, Michael Gove, for *The Times* in January 2017, Trump said he thought the UK was "so smart in getting out." Speaking just before his inauguration, he also promised a quick trade deal between the US and the UK after taking office – without knowing that trade negotiations could not even start until Britain left the EU two years later.[60]

His first visit at NATO and the EU made a shocking impact. As the British *Guardian* reported, "he denied saying things he had said, then said things that showed he did not understand. It may, mercifully, have passed off without apocalyptic mishap, but Donald Trump's first transatlantic trip as US president still left European leaders shaken."[61]

Trump also praised the anti-EU right-wing French populist Marine Le Pen as the "strongest candidate"[62] during the French presidential campaign. Trump's anti-EU attitude became even more apparent during the 2018 G-7 meeting in Canada, when he refused to sign a joint agreement. Furthermore, at his second NATO meeting, he viciously attacked Germany; during his 2018 visit to England, he undermined Theresa May by criticizing her plan to remain in the European common market and suggested that hard-liner, hard-landing advocate Boris Johnson would make a good prime minister. On top of these open conflicts, the next day Trump met with President Putin in Helsinki. Trump treated him as a new friend and ally, rejecting the conclusions of the US's own intelligence agencies and the Department of Justice, which had just indicted twelve high-ranking Russian intelligence officers for the 2016 cyberattack on the American elections. He had a two-hour secret meeting with Putin with only translators in attendance; and afterwards he confiscated the translators' notes.

Trump's America turned also sharply against the global free-trade regime. The US pulled out of the Trans-Pacific Partnership Agreement and started renegotiating the North Atlantic Treaty Organization (NAFTA) agreement with Mexico and Canada. In the framework of his new America First policy, Trump remarked that he had "a lot of problems"[63] with the EU's trade policy. Moreover, he entered into an open trade war against the EU, declaring it not only a rival but a foe. As one EU commentary phrased it,

> The utterances of President Trump about the "terrible Europeans", or Germans, "giving a bad deal" to the US for decades also emerge from an irrational belief that bilateral or even sectoral trade surpluses are somehow caused by "bad deals." . . . Much has been written about the fundamental drivers of trade surpluses or deficits in the case of the US: essentially macroeconomic determinants (e.g. spending more abroad), complemented by sectoral competitiveness in terms of price, quality, reputation or design. They are therefore first of all US-driven – US deficits begin and end at home – and the sectoral issues are largely a matter of competition on the own merits and not at all of a "deal."[64]

It became crystal clear for the European allies that the US could not be counted upon as a solid and trusted ally any longer, as the Trump administration was hostile towards the EU. Europe responded immediately to America's trade-war warnings: "The European Union stands ready to react swiftly and appropriately in case our exports are affected by any restrictive trade measures from the United States."[65] The European Commission's spokesperson warned that "restrictive trade measures from the United States" would face a robust response from Europe. "If European exporters have to pay tariffs, that will become a two-way street. Then U.S. exporters will have to pay tariffs here,"[66] announced the EU's budget commissioner Guenther Oettinger. Although this exchange was just a war of words, it was followed by a real trade war.

In the spring and summer of 2018, President Trump, indeed, announced the introduction of 25 percent and 10 percent tariffs for steel and aluminum imports to the US, respectively. The EU responded by announcing the introduction of tariffs against major US export items to Europe, with about $3.5 billion in EU duties. As the *New York Times* reported in early March 2018, "Trade partners respond in kind to tariff plans."[67] In February 2020, as *Reuters* reported, Trump sharpened his attack against the EU, complaining,

> Europe has been treating us very badly. . . . Over the last 10, 12 years, there's been a tremendous deficit with Europe. They have barriers that are incredible. . . . So we're going to be starting that. They know that.[68]

On another occasion, Trump called the EU an enemy: "We have allies. We have enemies. Sometimes the allies are enemies, but we just don't know it." He threatened to introduce 25 percent tariffs on cars and parts imports from Europe. Tariff war between "allies" has emerged. Economic alliances and cooperation were undermined.[69]

This new situation became even more pronounced as differences and conflicts also emerged in various other areas of the US-EU relationship. The two allies stopped working together on banking regulation, and American and EU regulatory policies are diverging in general. Similar diverse policies have separated the two former allies in the arena of environmental policy as well. While the EU has remained one of the most strident supporters of responsible environmental policy, in the summer of 2017, America left the Paris Agreement of April 2016, which had been globally accepted by 175 countries (189 as of February 2020; Turkey and Iran are the only significant non-signatories). Differences also surfaced in foreign policy. Whereas Europe rightly considered Putin and Russia as enemies, Trump fostered a cooperative relationship with Putin. Disagreements on foreign policy issues – from Russia to Israel and Iran – seem to be ever-multiplying.

The radically changing American policy towards Europe and the lost trust between the two in the context of an increasingly difficult international situation continues to endanger Europe and frighteningly weaken the European Union. This situation is, however, only one side of the coin. Europe has to recognize the need for stronger cooperation and unification so that it can stand alone and face hostilities and dangers without relying on America. One of the leading American media organizations rightly concluded:

> Trump's bullying could turn out to be exactly what a fractured European Union (EU) needed in order to band closer together. His attacks on the European Union's shared policies – like climate change, free trade and defense – have forced EU countries to jointly defend their goals and strengthen ties with other global allies.[70]

These prophesy might turn out to true, but it is too soon to tell: it will take time for positive impacts of Trump's America First policy to manifest in Europe.

***

The rising hostility of neighbors in the East, in southern Europe, and on the other side of the Atlantic Ocean definitely created a dangerous situation for the European Union, especially because outside and inside hostilities against the EU are closely connected. In May 2019, Jyrki Katainen, vice president of the European Commission (and former prime minister of Finland) rightly noted that outside challenges have never been so hard:

> Countries like Russia, China but also the United States have challenged us harder than before. . . . We are (for the) first time in the history in a situation where the President of the United States and (the) President of Russia seem to share the same view on Europe: the weaker, the better.[71]

Vice President Katainen also connected these outside dangers to the populist hostility that opposes the Union from the inside. Russia, he emphasized, is responsible for boosting some of those populist parties, which are shaking the EU and represent an internal challenge:

> The EU is also challenged from within. . . . [These parties] want to weaken and fragment the EU – and some of those have also very close connection to

Russia, to President Putin. So Russia has obviously financed some of those parties, they have interfered to our democratic processes, for instance referenda or national elections in order to weaken the EU.[72]

Connected outside and inside hostilities against the Union require a firm answer from the member countries, enacted through closer economic and military cooperation and integration. How much time will be needed to answer the challenges with real action is still an open question.

Notes

1 "Article 49 of the Treaty on European Union" (Official Journal of the European Union, 1992), https://eur-lex.europa.eu/legal-content/EN/TXT/PDF/?uri=CELEX:12008M/TXT&from=EN, accessed October 3, 2018.
2 *Legal Questions of Enlargement*, Briefing (Brussels: European Parliament, May 19, 1998), www.europarl.europa.eu/enlargement/briefings/23a2_en.htm, accessed October 3, 2018.
3 *Presidency Conclusions–Relations with the Countries of Central and Eastern Europe*, Official Positions of the Other Institutions and Organs (Copenhagen: European Council, June 21, 1993), 7A, III, www.europarl.europa.eu/enlargement/ec/cop_en.htm, accessed October 6, 2018.
4 *2007 Annual Report on Phare, Turkey Pre-Accession, Cards and Transition Facility*, Report from the Commission to the Council, the European Parliament and the European Economic and Social Committee (Brussels: Commission of the European Communities, December 22, 2008), COM(2008) 880 final, Archive of European Integration, http://aei.pitt.edu/45571/1/ com2008_0880.pdf.
5 Kathleen Schuster, "Turkey-EU Relations: Which Countries Are for or against Turkish Accession?," *Deutsche Welle*, September 6, 2017, https://p.dw.com/p/2jR53, accessed October 4, 2018.
6 "Macron Tells Erdogan: No Chance of Turkey Joining EU," *BBC News*, January 5, 2018, sec. Europe, www.bbc.com/news/world-europe-42586108, accessed October 4, 2018.
7 Graham Allison, "U.S.-Russia Relations: What Would Henry Kissinger Do?," *The National Interest*, September 28, 2015, https://nationalinterest.org/feature/us-russia-relations-what-would-henry-kissinger-do-13953, accessed October 5, 2018.
8 Terry Atlas, "Brzezinski Sees Finlandization of Ukraine as Deal Maker," *Bloomberg.com*, April 11, 2014, sec. Business, www.bloomberg.com/news/articles/2014-04-11/brzezinski-sees-finlandization-of-ukraine-as-deal-maker, accessed October 5, 2018.
9 Anita Tregner-Mlinaric, *Policy Brief on How to Accelerate the Process of Bringing Knowledge to the Market Including Promising Practices from EU and Ukraine and Recommendations*, Policy Brief (Luxembourg: European Union, August 17, 2017), https://ri-links2ua.eu/object/document/401/attach/D4_3_Policy_brief_RILINKS2UA_final.pdf, accessed October 6, 2018.
10 Christoph B. Schiltz, "Ukraine, Moldova and Georgia Are Expected to Join the EU," *Die Welt*, May 30, 2014, sec. Politics, www.welt.de/politik/ausland/arti cle128540032/Ukraine-Moldau-und-Georgien-sollen-in-die-EU.html, accessed October 5, 2018.
11 Steven Erlanger, "Britain and Europe 'Sleepwalked' into the Ukraine Crisis, Report Says," *The New York Times*, February 20, 2015, Web Edition, sec. World, www.nytimes.com/2015/02/21/world/europe/britain-europe-ukraine-house-of-lords-report.html, accessed October 6, 2018.

12 "Putin Calls Collapse of Soviet Union 'Catastrophe'," *The Washington Times*, April 26, 2005, www.washingtontimes.com/news/2005/apr/26/20050426-120658-5687r/, accessed October 5, 2018.

13 Steven Pifer, *The Growing Russian Military Threat in Europe* (Washington, DC: Testimony, U.S. Commission on Security and Cooperation in Europe Meeting, May 17, 2017), https://www.brookings.edu/testimonies/the-growing-russian-military-threat-in-europe/, accessed October 6, 2018; Jakub Grygiel, "Vladimir Putin's Encirclement of Europe," *National Review*, March 19, 2020, www.nationalreview.com/magazine/2020/04/06/vladimir-putins-encirclement-of-europe/, accessed May 3, 2020.

14 See Vladimir Putin, "Russia: The Ethnicity Issue," *Nezavisimaya Gazeta*, January 23, 2012, Archive of the Official Site of the 2008–2012 Prime Minister of the Russian Federation Vladimir Putin, http://archive.premier.gov.ru/eng/events/news/17831/, accessed October 7, 2018; Patrick Nopens, *Beyond Russia's 'Versailles Syndrome'*, Security Policy Brief (Brussels: Egmont Institute, November 25, 2014), www.egmontinstitute.be/beyond-russias-versailles-syndrome/, accessed February 5, 2019.

15 *Russia Military Power* (Washington, DC: Defense Intelligence Agency, June 28, 2017), www.dia.mil/Portals/27/Documents/News/Military%20Power%20Publications/Russia%20Military%20Power%20Report%202017.pdf, accessed October 8, 2018.

16 "Russia Has 'Invincible' Nuclear Weapons," *BBC News*, March 1, 2018, sec. Europe, www.bbc.com/news/world-europe-43239331, accessed January 5, 2019.

17 Ceylan Yeginsu, "Royal Navy Escorts Russian Warship near U.K.," *The New York Times*, December 26, 2017, Web Edition, sec. World, www.nytimes.com/2017/12/26/world/europe/british-navy-russia.html, accessed October 7, 2018.

18 Pavel Seifter, "The Real Danger Isn't Brexit. It's EU Break-Up," *The Guardian*, May 26, 2016, sec. Opinion, www.theguardian.com/commentisfree/2016/may/26/danger-brexit-break-up-eu-europe-russia, accessed October 7, 2018.

19 Stefan Wagstyl and Henry Foy, "Angela Merkel Says Russia Damaging Europe's Security," *Financial Times*, July 7, 2016, www.ft.com/content/b2d16102-4446-11e6-9b66-0712b3873ael, accessed October 7, 2018.

20 Stephanie Pezard et al., *European Relations with Russia: Threat Perceptions, Responses, and Strategies in the Wake of the Ukrainian Crisis* (Santa Monica, CA: RAND Corporation, 2017), X–XI, HQD146843, https://doi.org/10.7249/RR1579, accessed October 7, 2018.

21 Valery Gerasimov, "The Value of Science Is in the Foresight," trans. Robert Coalson, *Military-Industrial Kurier*, February 27, 2013, https://jmc.msu.edu/50th/download/21-conflict.pdf, accessed October 7, 2018.

22 Dimitar Bechev, *Russia in the Balkans*, Conference Report (London: London School of Economics, March 13, 2015), www.lse.ac.uk/LSEE-Research-on-South-Eastern-Europe/Assets/Documents/Events/Conferences-Symposia-Programmes-and-Agendas/2015-Report-Russia-in-the-Balkans-merged-document.pdf, accessed October 8, 2018.

23 James Kirchick, "Russia's Plot against the West," *Politico Europe*, March 17, 2017, www.politico.eu/article/russia-plot-against-the-west-vladimir-putin-donald-trump-europe/, accessed October 7, 2018.

24 Mark Leonard and Nicu Popescu, *A Power Audit of EU-Russia Relations*, Policy Paper (London: European Council on Foreign Relations, 2007), 27, www.ecfr.eu/page/-/ECFR-02_A_POWER_AUDIT_OF_EU-RUSSIA_RELATIONS.pdf, accessed October 8, 2018.

25 Ibid., The project was suspended by the Bulgarian government in December 2011 for environmental reasons.

26 "Supplier Countries," *European Commission*, https://ec.europa.eu/energy/en/topics/imports-and-secure-supplies/supplier-countries, accessed October 7, 2018.

27 Georg Zachmann, "Elements of Europe's Energy Union," Policy Paper, *Bruegel*, September 9, 2014, www.bruegel.org/2014/09/elements-of-europes-energy-union/, accessed October 8, 2018.

28 Sandya Abrar et al., *The Strategic Energy Technology (SET) Plan: At the Heart of Energy Research and Innovation in Europe* (Luxembourg: Publications Office of the European Union, 2017), http://edepot.wur.nl/464074, accessed October 8, 2018.

29 Thilo Hanemann and Daniel H. Rosen, "China Invests in Europe," *Rhodium Group*, June 2012), 3–4, https://rhg.com/wp/content/uploads/2012/06/RHG_ChinaInvestsInEurope_June2012.pdf, accessed November 1, 2018.

30 Andrew Jones, "China to Complete Its Answer to GPS with Beidou Navigation Satellite Launches in March, May," *SpaceNews*, February 28, 2020, https://spacenews.com/china-to-complete-its-answer-to-gps-with-beidou-navigation-satellite-launches-in-march-may/, accessed March 7, 2020; Stephen Clark, "China Launches Beidou Satellite, Aims for Completion of Navigation Network in May," *Spaceflight Now*, March 9, 2020, https://spaceflightnow.com/2020/03/09/china-launches-beidou-satellite-aims-for-completion-of-navigation-network-in-may/, accessed May 5, 2020.

31 Daniel Franklin, "The World in 2018," *The Economist*, 2017, 67.

32 David P. Goldman, "The Chinese Challenge," *Claremont Review of Books*, Spring 2020, https://claremontreviewofbooks.com/the-chinese-challenge/, accessed June 7, 2020.

33 Valbona Zeneli, "Mapping China's Investments in Europe," *The Diplomat*, March 14, 2019, https://thediplomat.com/2019/03/mapping-chinas-investments-in-europe/, accessed January 17, 2020.

34 Julianne Smith and Torrey Taussig, "Europe Needs a China Strategy; Brussels Needs to Shape It," *Brookings Institute* (blog), February 10, 2020, www.brookings.edu/blog/order-from-chaos/2020/02/10/europe-needs-a-china-strategy-brussels-needs-to-shape-it/, accessed May 7, 2020.

35 Helen Raleigh, "The European Union Finally Recognizes China as a Dangerous Rival, without Taking Action," *The Federalist*, March 25, 2019, sec. World Affairs, https://thefederalist.com/2019/03/25/european-union-finally-recognizes-china-dangerous-rival-without-taking-action/, accessed January 4, 2020.

36 Tomasz Berg et al., *V4 Goes Global: Exploring Opportunities and Obstacles in the Visegrad Countries' Cooperation with Brazil, India, China and South Africa*, ed. Patryk Kugiel (Warsaw: Polski Instytut Spraw Międzynarodowych, 2016), 10, www.pism.pl/file/39e4fb60-ca9a-4e77-a3e4-0b4199388f8f, accessed March 7, 2018.

37 Ibid., 40, 43, 48.

38 The, "China's Footprint in Southeast Europe: Constructing the 'Balkan Silk Road,'" *The Corner* (blog), October 11, 2017, http://thecorner.eu/news-europe/chinas-footprint-southeast-europe-constructing-balkan-silk-road/67816/, accessed February 7, 2018.

39 Jakub Jakóbowski, Konrad Popławski, and Marcin Kaczmarski, "The Silk Road: The EU-China Rail Connections–Background, Actors, Interests," trans. Magdalena Klimowicz, *OSW Studies*, no. 72 (February 2018): 16.

40 Gisela Grieger, *China, the 16+1 Format and the EU*, Briefing (Brussels: European Parliamentary Research Service, September 2018), 1, PE 625.173.

41 Lucrezia Poggetti, "China's Charm Offensive in Eastern Europe Challenges EU Cohesion," *The Diplomat*, November 24, 2017, https://thediplomat.

com/2017/11/chinas-charm-offensive-in-eastern-europe-challenges-eu-cohe
sion/, accessed February 5, 2018.

42 *European Parliament Resolution of 16 December 2015 on EU-China Relations*
(Strasbourg: European Parliament, December 16, 2015), P8_TA(2015)0458,
www.europarl.europa.eu/doceo/document/TA-8-2015-0458_EN.html,
accessed November 8, 2017.

43 Jens Bastian, "China Goes to the Balkans," Interview by Francesco Martino,
November 30, 2017, https://medium.com/obc-transeuropa/china-goes-to-
the-balkans-14c7ea0719d4, accessed February 7, 2018.

44 Stuart Lau, "Italy May Be Ready to Open Four Ports to Chinese Investment,"
South China Morning Post, March 19, 2019, sec. News, www.scmp.com/news/
china/diplomacy/article/3002305/italy-may-be-ready-open-four-ports-chi
nese-investment-under, accessed January 7, 2020.

45 "Oettinger Calls for EU Veto on Italy-China Deal," *Euractiv*, March 25, 2019,
sec. EU-China, www.euractiv.com/section/eu-china/news/oettinger-calls-for-
eu-veto-on-italy-china-deal/, accessed December 8, 2019.

46 Frank Sieren, "Sieren's China: The Cracks in the EU's United Trade Front," *DW.
COM*, March 29, 2019, sec. World, www.dw.com/en/sierens-china-the-cracks-
in-the-eus-united-trade-front/a-48122055, accessed December 8, 2019.

47 Yaroslav Trofimov, "Europe's Face-Off with China," *Wall Street Journal*,
February 28, 2020, sec. Life, www.wsj.com/articles/europes-face-off-with-
china-11582905438, accessed April 8, 2020.

48 Andrew Small, "Why Europe Is Getting Tough on China," *Foreign Affairs*,
April 3, 2019, www.foreignaffairs.com/articles/china/2019-04-03/why-europe-
getting-tough-china, accessed November 7, 2019; Angela Stanzel et al., *China's Investment in Influence: The Future of 16+1 Cooperation* (Berlin: European
Council on Foreign Relations, December 14, 2016), https://www.ecfr.eu/
publications/summary/chinas_investment_in_influence_the_future_of_161_
cooperation7204, accessed November 8, 2018.

49 Stephen M. Walt, "Europe's Future Is as China's Enemy," *Foreign Policy*, January 22, 2019, https://foreignpolicy.com/2019/01/22/europes-future-is-as-
chinas-enemy/, accessed November 8, 2018.

50 Vasily Kashin, "Russia and China Take Military Partnership to New Level,"
The Moscow Times, October 23, 2019, sec. News, www.themoscowtimes.com/
2019/10/23/russia-and-china-take-military-partnership-to-new-level-a67852,
accessed January 7, 2020.

51 Ibid.

52 Perry Anderson, "Depicting Europe," *London Review of Books*, September 20, 2007,
www.lrb.co.uk/the-paper/v29/n18/perry-anderson/depicting-europe, accessed
October 8, 2018.

53 Robert Gilpin, *The Challenge of Global Capitalism: The World Economy in the
21st Century* (Princeton, NJ: Princeton University Press, 2000), 9–10, 16.

54 Ibid., 17.

55 Ibid.

56 Ibid., 93.

57 Kendall Breitman and Kevin Cirilli, " 'Unpredictability' on Nukes among Trump
Keys to Muslim Respect," *Bloomberg*, March 23, 2016, www.bloomberg.com/
news/articles/2016-03-23/trump-lays-out-vision-for-gaining-respect-from-
muslim-world, accessed November 8, 2018.

58 Chris Cillizza, "Here's What Was Missing from Donald Trump's Foreign Policy
Speech," *Washington Post*, April 27, 2016, www.washingtonpost.com/news/the-
fix/wp/2016/04/27/the-gauzy-generalities-of-donald-trumps-foreign-policy-
vision/, accessed November 8, 2018.

59 Chris Cillizza, "Donald Trump's Brexit Press Conference Was beyond Bizarre," *The Washington Post*, June 24, 2016, sec. The Fix, www.washingtonpost.com/, accessed October 18, 2018.

60 Donald Trump: 'Brexit Will Be a Great Thing . . . You Were So Smart,' Interview by Michael Gove and Donald Trump, January 16, 2017, www.thetimes.co.uk/article/brexit-will-be-a-great-thing-you-were-so-smart-to-get-out-09gp9z357, accessed October 19, 2018.

61 Jon Henley, "Donald Trump's Europe Tour Leaves Leaders Strangely Shaken," *The Guardian*, May 27, 2017, sec. US News, www.theguardian.com/us-news/2017/may/27/donald-trumps-europe-tour-leaves-leaders-shaken, accessed October 16, 2018.

62 Ben Jacobs, "Donald Trump: Marine Le Pen Is 'Strongest Candidate' in French Election," *The Guardian*, April 21, 2017, sec. US News, www.theguardian.com/us-news/2017/apr/21/donald-trump-marine-le-pen-french-presidential-election, accessed October 17, 2018.

63 Andrew MacAskill, "Trump Hints Retaliation at 'Very Unfair' EU Trade Policies," *Reuters*, January 28, 2018, sec. Business News, https://uk.reuters.com/article/uk-usa-trump-trade-idUKKBN1FH0WK, accessed November 8, 2018.

64 Jacques Pelkmans, *Trade Policy-Making under Irrationality*, CEPS Commentary (Bruges: Centre for European Policy Studies, March 12, 2018), 2, Archive of European Integration, http://aei.pitt.edu/93562/1/JP_TrumpTariffs_0.pdf, accessed January 9, 2019.

65 Agence France-Presse, "EU Says It Would React 'Swiftly' to Any Trump Trade Curbs," *Industry Week*, January 29, 2018, www.industryweek.com/the-economy/article/22025029/eu-says-it-would-react-swiftly-to-any-trump-trade-curbs, accessed November 8, 2018.

66 "EU Official Warn US on Trade: EU Will Hit Back If Needed," *Associated Press News*, February 4, 2018, sec. European Union, https://apnews.com/61bd98695fbc4b3793f4d02d58aafd46, accessed January 8, 2019.

67 Ana Swanson, "Trade Partners Respond in Kind to Tariff Plans," *The New York Times*, March 3, 2018, Print Edition, sec. U.S., www.nytimes.com/2018/03/02/us/politics/trump-tariffs-steel-aluminum.html, accessed November 19, 2018.

68 Andrea Shalal and David Lawder, "As Trump Takes Aim at EU Trade, European Officials Brace for Fight," *Reuters*, February 11, 2020, www.reuters.com/article/us-usa-trade-europe-analysis-idUSKBN2051AK, accessed May 7, 2020.

69 Ibid.

70 Elizabeth Schulze, "How Trump's Criticism of the EU Makes the Region Stronger," *CNBC*, August 14, 2017, sec. Europe News, www.cnbc.com/2017/08/14/how-trumps-criticism-of-the-eu-makes-the-region-stronger.html, accessed December 5, 2018.

71 Silvia Amaro, "'Very Dangerous': Putin, Trump Want to Weaken the European Union, Top Official Says," *CNBC*, May 22, 2019, sec. Politics, www.cnbc.com/2019/05/22/very-dangerous-putin-trump-want-to-weaken-eu-top-official-says.html, accessed December 9, 2019.

72 Ibid.

9 Conclusion

The socioeconomic achievements

The European economy before integration

During the late eighteenth century, Europe began its ascent to the top of the world. The first Industrial Revolution in Britain gradually spread over the Continent, and the first important steps of a second industrial revolution led by Germany occurred in the middle of the nineteenth century. By 1870, Europe was producing 45 percent of the world's total income. The 23 countries of the Western half of the European Continent produced nearly three times more than the United States, Canada, Australia and New Zealand combined. Europe was the world economic leader.

This leading position, however, soon disappeared. In 1913 Europe produced only 27 percent of the world's total income, lagging behind the overseas West: the average per-capita GDP levels in America, Canada, Australia, and New Zealand were already more than 70 percent that of Western Europe. The United States took over the leading role; its average income level reached one-and-a-half times (143 percent) the income level of Western Europe.[1] Before World War II, in 1938, the combined per-capita GDP of the leading West European countries was less than half (47 percent) that of the United States. Income differences within Europe also increased; the south and east of the Continent produced less than half of what the West did.

World War II caused tragic devastation in Europe, killing about 40 million people – 10 percent of the Continent's population – and, together with sharply declining birth rates, caused a population deficit of between 110 and 120 million. It also destroyed a great part of the Continent's infrastructure and productive capacities. By the end of World War II, Austria's and Germany's per-capita national incomes had dropped to less than half; France, Italy, and the Netherlands's per-capita GDPs dropped to somewhat more than half of their prewar levels. The war, in other words, actually fully realized the trend of the previous half-century. In 1945, devastated Europe dropped back sharply to somewhat more than one-third (35 percent) of the American economic level. That was the starting point for European integration.

Economic advantage of integration

Postwar reconstruction and economic development were strongly influenced by integration though other factors, such as the extensive development model

Europe used also played some role. This was based on modern technology imports from America, which also influenced the European economy. The post-war years were not "normal": economic growth in the first two decades was characterized by fast, so-called "reconstruction growth" which led to "economic miracles." Integration, however, became a major factor by increasing trade and investment, enlarging the market, making possible a much larger scale of production, and increasing productivity. Integration thus significantly contributed to the change in trend, which had previously been characterized by the permanent relative decline of Europe compared to the rapidly rising American and Western overseas world. Europe started to elevate again, into the leading group of the world's most advanced regions.

A great number of economists, using various methods, have analyzed the impact and advantages of European Union integration for economic development. Some of them have used the counterfactual method introduced by Robert Fogel in 1964, when he calculated what the American economic development would have been if the US railroad network had not been built.[2] Making absolutely exact measurement is naturally impossible. First of all, some countries joined the integration in 1957, others in 1973, again others in the 1980s, 1995, 2004, 2007 and 2013. In other words, the impacts are different according to each country's time within the EU.

Furthermore, the seventy-year integration process itself had several stages. Although it began during the 1950s–1960s, it took a decade to eliminate tariffs among member countries. Integration became much deeper after the introduction of the Single Market in 1992, and again after the introduction of the common currency at the turn of the millennium. The character of integration somewhat changed again when several economically less-developed, cheap-wage countries joined the Union, first in the 1980s in the south and then in 2004–2007 in the east. A new type of cooperation became possible between the old, advanced and the new, less-developed member countries.

The outcomes of the various calculations are understandably often rather different and contradictory, and there are unsolved questions. However, it seems unquestionable that integration promotes capital accumulation, productivity and economic growth via the acceleration of intra-European trade, macro-economic and institutional stability, all-European financial integration, better resource allocation, easy investment opportunities in other countries and much bigger amount of foreign direct investment, and the reduction of exchange-rate volatility. The building of Europe-wide value chains – huge networks, sometimes throughout dozens of countries – had an especially positive outcome. The various components of a single product are produced across these networks in several different countries, and because each producer delivers large quantities, this system is advantageous for its huge production scale. The common currency led to an additional positive outcome: it stimulated trade.

After these aspects of integration (the Single Market and the common currency) were in place, the Union's common market of 500 million people boasted an average per-person GDP of €25,000 and encapsulated a high-income community that tremendously stimulated internal trade of goods among member countries. In the short period between 2002 and 2018, for example – in spite of the crisis years after 2008 – goods trade among member countries more than doubled (215 percent). The less-developed new member countries from Central Europe increased their trade the most. While Germany and Belgium more than doubled their exports of goods to other EU member countries, Poland and Slovakia increased their exports by more than four times. The bulk of Slovakia's goods exports (86 percent) went to other EU countries. Altogether, member countries' goods trade with each other reached nearly two-thirds (64 percent) of their total trade.[3] Europe is definitely much more integrated than any other major macro-region in the world. In 2006, when globalization was in full swing, intra-trade in the Americas (North and South) was 59.7 percent of countries' total trade and intra-trade in the Asia-Pacific was only 50 percent, while intra-European trade elevated to 76.5 percent of total trade in Europe.

According to some calculations, the per-capita GDP in European countries that have adopted the euro is approximately 2 percent higher than in countries that have not yet adopted the common currency. Others have concluded that per-capita European incomes in the absence of the institutional integration would have been about 10 percent lower on average, compared to countries' per-capita GDPs after their first ten years within the EU. Others estimate that EU membership produces about 0.6 percent to 0.8 percent in additional growth every year.

RAND Europe made some calculations about the not-yet-exploited potential of the Single Market and concluded that the EU's income could grow by an additional $200–290 billion income per year if realized.[4] According to the European Commission, completing the EU digital Single Market could contribute $480 billion per year to Europe's economy.[5] Coordinating armed forces across the member states could save between $3.23–9.7 billion a year on wages alone.[6] Integration has numerous advantages that will lead to better lives for the citizens of the European Union.

Strong evidence proves the highly positive net benefits from EU membership, but with considerable heterogeneity across countries.[7] Analysts have found that per-capita GDP and labor productivity have increased in Ireland, the United Kingdom, Portugal, Spain, Austria, Estonia, Hungary, Latvia, Slovenia, and Lithuania the most, but the effects is smaller (although still positive) in Finland, Sweden, Poland, the Czech Republic and Slovakia. Finally, certain counterfactual calculations have suggested that out of all EU member countries, only Greece experienced a lower per-capita GDP and labor productivity after EU accession than it might have been without it.[8] All in all, the European Union as a whole increased per-capita income in the range of 5 percent, minimum, up to a maximum of 20 percent. These enormous gains are the direct consequence of integration.[9]

Another kind of proof of the advantages integration holds is the extraordinary growth of the founding countries of the European Community. Between 1950 and 1992 (until the introduction of the Single Market), they increased their average per-capita GDP by 363 percent, while Western Europe as a whole increased by only 295 percent. In contrast, the world average was 240 percent; the combined average GDP of the United States, Canada, Australia and New

Zealand increased by 225 percent.[10] In the second half of the twentieth and early twenty-first centuries, integrated Europe – in spite of the interval of international economic recessions in the 1970s–1980s and after 2008 – experienced the best economic prosperity.

The catching-up of less developed countries

After the miraculous postwar reconstruction, Europe enjoyed a great boom period and became more than five times richer. Equally importantly, because the integration process, less-developed countries and regions that joined the European Union accelerated in catching up with the traditionally most developed countries. In 1950, the combined average per-capita GDP of the Mediterranean countries and Ireland reached only half (51.2 percent) of the average GDP level of the rich northwest European countries, but by 2019, they had achieved already three-quarters (75 percent) of that level. When communism collapsed, the average per-capita GDP of the Central European and Baltic countries stood at less than a quarter (23 percent) of the Northwest European countries' average per capita GDP level, but by 2019 it was already more than a third (36.4 percent) of it. The catching-up process gained momentum as a result of the huge direct investments undertaken by more developed member countries and the ensuing market possibilities, as well as through generous EU aid to less developed members.

The trend of catching-up is brand-new in the history of this region; for the previous one hundred and thirty years, the Central European region had consistently been losing its position in the global order and shifting downwards (Table 9.1). This trend changed for first time in one-and-a-half centuries after the turn of the millennium; the region's ability to catch up with the more advanced parts of the Continent occurred as a result of European integration.

Between 1973 and 2014, when all of the most important new integration factors were in place for the northwestern and southern countries, Northwest Europe increased its income level by nearly two times (189 percent), and Spain and Portugal by three and three-and-a-half times, respectively. The Mediterranean countries and Ireland increased their average GDPs by four times (395 percent); and Ireland alone did so by almost eight-times (781 percent). Integration significantly helped the European South to catching up.

Table 9.1 Central Europe GDP per capita in % of Northwestern Europe

Year	Central Europe as % of the West[11]
1870	54
1913	50
1950	48
1990	37
2000	23
2019	36

Table 9.2 Increase of per capita GDP in four European regions, 1913–2016[12]

Year	Northwestern Europe	Mediterranean Europe & Ireland	Central Europe & Baltics	Russia-Turkey-Balkans*
1913	100	100	100	100
1950	138	115	156	142
2013	12,163	16,413	8,471	3,667

The tremendous development within the European Union is especially well documented if – examining a longer time period – we compare the advancement that took place between the first half (1913–1950) and second half (1950–2010s) of the twentieth century. The picture is similar if we compare the EU member countries and the non-EU countries of the eastern European-Turkish-Balkan region.

The table reflects that between 1913 and 1950 all of the European regions had very slow progress – between 15–50 percent – while between 1950 and the early 2010s we witnessed a dramatic breakthrough and advancement. The non-EU countries of the Continent in the Russian-Turkish-Balkan region, however, only experienced rather moderate progress compared to the EU regions: this area saw only half of the progress of the Central European-Baltic region, and only one-third to one-fourth of the advancements that took place in the southern and northwestern regions.

Europe and the United States

The huge gap that existed between Europe and the United States in 1950 is also closing. Around the end of the 2010s, the per-capita GDP was $37,417 in the European Union and $59,531 in the United States. Thus, the EU's income level increased from half to nearly two-thirds (63 percent) of the American one. And while 37 percent might still seem like a large gap, a closer look reveals that it is not actually so big. The difference is mainly the result of just two key factors. Firstly, the average level in Europe elides huge differences among the member countries. About 75 percent of the entire EU's GDP is produced by five western countries, and the contributions of another 12 countries account for 23–24 percent; 10 small and relatively poorer countries together produce only 2–3 percent of the EU's GDP. The mostly new Central European and Balkan countries are far away from being able to compete with America and therefore lower the EU average.

The second main reason is that the Europeans work about 20 percent less than Americans because they have less work hours per week and much longer paid vacations. In the European social market system, the work-hours are roughly one third less. If we count income per hour in France, Germany, Ireland, the Netherlands, Norway, Belgium and Luxembourg, they all have surpassed the US, although their average per-capita income level is still somewhat behind because they work less hours. This disparity means that the value produced in one hour is basically the same in America and the western countries of the EU.

In other words, the decisive productivity level is quite similar. Actually, until 1995, Europe's productivity increased much faster than America's. Between 1950 and 1973, its annual growth was 5.3 percent (in the US, 2.5 percent); between 1973 and 1995, it was 2.4 percent (compared to 1.2 percent in the US). However, around the turn of the millennium (between 1995 and 2006) this trend reversed and the European 1.5 percent increase was surpassed by the American 2.3 percent increase. The United States was stronger in knowledge-based economic sectors. According to certain calculations, the per-capita productivity increase around the turn of the millennium was nevertheless pretty close: 2.1 percent in Europe and 2.2 percent in the United States.[13] Europe's catching-up process strongly depends on what the long-term rate of productivity increase will be in subsequent decades of the twenty-first century.

All in all, the economic output of the northwest European countries became very close to the American level, moreover, three-quarters of European countries are already richer than the United States, among them Ireland, which had hardly surpassed half of the West-European average level when joined the EU. As Barry Eichengreen concluded in his 2007 book *The European Economy Since 1945*, the dramatic transatlantic difference in the quality of life that existed 50 years ago is effectively gone, because in the second half of the twentieth century, the average European's buying power tripled, while working hours fell by a third.

In the 2010s, the European Union, together with countries that are non-members but share some components of integration and are members of the common market – Norway, Switzerland and Iceland – accounted for 25.4 percent of world output compared to the American share of 22.5 percent. In 2018, the European Union produces 16.28 percent of the world's total GDP in comparison to the United States' 15.2 percent; this share is expected to decrease to 13.9 percent by 2024.

The European Single Market is one of the most attractive markets for investors: foreign direct investments in Europe surpassed $5.1 trillion, while the EU's investments in foreign countries total $9.1 trillion – by far the highest amount of domestic and foreign investments in the world. Similarly, the EU belongs to the top traders in the world economy. While member countries' trade with each other is 64 percent of their total trade – this figure varies country-by-country from between 30–90 percent – the EU has about 100 trade agreements with non-EU countries. It contains 80 top-trading partner countries (in contrast to the US's 20 top-trading countries), and has a tremendous advantage – truly the strongest position – in its ability to make trade agreements as a unified entity. In 2018, the EU's exports represented 15.2 percent of global exports, and its imports amounted to 15.1 percent, making it the world's biggest trade player. The United States' share, by comparison, was 8.5 percent.

In the mid-2010s, in spite of the 37 percent difference between the European and American per-capita GDP, the average gross annual income per household was actually the same in the EU and the US: in the EU it was €35,000 (compared to the American €35,000–36,000). The average net annual family income was €24,000 in the EU (compared to the American €24,610).

Modernized structure and the social market system

Economic success is based on the ability to create a thoroughly modernized economy. Parallel with the integration process, the European Union went through robust structural change. While agricultural production soared, the sectoral share of agriculture within the total economy dramatically decreased to 1–3 percent; on average, 1.5 percent. (This figure is similar to the US and Japan, where this share is 1 percent.)

De-industrialization and the service revolution radically changed the shares of these sectors in the total economy as well. The manufacturing industry's share dropped to 11–12 percent in some countries, and in others to 28–30 percent; altogether as an average, the manufacturing industry produced 23.8 percent of the EU's GDP. In the US and Japan, manufacturing accounts for 21 percent and 26 percent of GDP, respectively.

As with modern economies in general, banking and services became dominant in the EU's economy as well. Their combined share was at least 70 percent, but reached 78–79 percent in several countries. On average, these sectors were responsible for producing 74.7 percent of the EU's GDP, compared to 73 percent and 78 percent in Japan and the US, respectively.[14] The European Union's economic structure modernized and became equal to those of the best-developed economies.

The European Union also takes seriously the importance of ensuring free-market competition and does not allow oligopolistic market monopolies. A good example is the merging attempt of two giants, Germany's Siemens and French's Alstom, which attempted to merge their railway activities in 2017. The EU's competition commissioner, Margrethe Vestager, decided that the merger "would have significantly reduced competition" in the high-speed train industry and rejected the merger in February 2019. The EU keeps its market free and competitive.[15] Compared to the United States, where consumers must choose between just two internet service providers, in France, one can chose from five. The American 'free market' became overly oligopolistic. As Thomas Philippon stated in 2019, "The American airline industry has become fully oligopolistic; profits per passenger mile are now about twice as high as in Europe, where low-cost airlines compete aggressively with incumbents."[16] According to his calculations, the average monthly cost of a broadband internet connection was $29 in Italy, $31 in France, and $37 in Germany; the same connection in the US cost $68. Because of sufficient competition, the average European consumer spends about 5–10 percent less per month for the same services.[17]

Another major achievement of the European Union was that its very rapid economic growth was accompanied by a relatively more balanced income distribution: income disparities in the EU are much lower than the world average, as well as lower than those found in America. Although countries' Gini coefficients – the figure that measures income distribution on a scale of 0 to 1, where the higher the number, the higher the inequality – has increased all over the world since the collapse of communism, figures have risen much more moderately in Europe than in other parts of the world. The European Union's aggregate GINI index is 0.31, while the US and Russia both have figures of 0.41, reflecting the much higher levels of income inequality in these countries.

In the European Union, these economic benefits are accompanied by better social well-being and better and cheaper – in several places, free of charge – health and educational services. In several countries, even higher education is tuition-free at public universities on both the B.A. and M.A. levels for students from all EU countries. This is the case in Austria, Sweden, Denmark and Germany. In countries where students have to pay, tuition rates are mostly very low. The yearly fee in France is between €170 and €650; in the Netherlands, between €700–2,100; and in Spain, between €150–3,500. Students from all EU countries can apply for the European Health Insurance Card and enjoy the same type of medical care they receive in their home country. European education continues to become more Europeanized: students spend more time in other EU member countries and feel a stronger sense of European identity.

It is important to consider three main factors – countries' development levels, average per-capita income levels, and health and educational levels – together. One way of measuring and comparing between countries is to use the so-called Human Development Index (HDI). Besides taking GDP into consideration, this index also considers the average health of the population by measuring average lifespan, and factors in average educational level by counting the average number of years spent in school.

The countries and regions of the European Union are far ahead of the world average, and as such they belong to the top regions of the world (Table 9.3). Among the best ten countries ranked by HDI, seven are Northwest European; the United States is 13th. After taking the entire European Union's three regions into account, the United States of America is ahead (920 points compared to 915), although that disparity comes from the US's higher GDP. Life expectancy is lower in America – 79.5 years, compared to the European average of 81 years.

Table 9.3 Human Development Index (HDI), world in 2016[18] (maximum level is 1,000)

World average	717
United States of America	920
Northwestern Europe, average	915
Mediterranean-Irish region, average	881
Central European-Baltic average	856
Russia-Balkans-Turkish average	771
Latin America, average	751
Developing countries average	670
Sub-Saharan Africa average	523

The same is true of education: the average EU citizen spends 17.6 years in school over her/his lifetime, whereas the average in the United States is 16.5 years.[19] It is pretty impressive that, in spite of the EU's somewhat lower GDP level, across the three main regions of the EU – the west, south, and east – the human development index figures are rather near close to that of America's (99, 96 and 93 percent, respectively). These facts clearly show that some extreme left-wing criticism like the following rejects the truth:

> But of a "social Europe" . . . there is as little left as a democratic Europe. . . . The salutary truth is that "the EU is overwhelmingly about the promotion of free markets. Its primary interest group support comes from multinational firms, not least US ones. In short: regnant in this Union is not democracy, and not welfare, but capital. The EU is basically about business."[20]

Although business is indeed a central issue in the European Union, the EU has a version of the social market system (to use the postwar German term). In the 2010s, Japan spent 21.9 percent of its GDP on social expenditures, the United States spent 18.7 percent, Australia 17.8 percent, Iceland and Switzerland 16 percent, Turkey 12.5 percent, Chile 11 percent, and Mexico 7.5 percent. The European Union is far ahead in social spending. The EU member countries' average social spending is roughly about 25–27 percent of their aggregate GDP. The share increased in the early twenty-first century: in 2000, the average social spending in EU countries was 25.7 percent, in 2016, it had already reached 28 percent of the GDP.[21] Differences among member countries are significant. Several countries – Ireland, Latvia, Lithuania, Slovakia and Holland – spend only 14–17 percent of their GDP on welfare expenditures. However, most of the member countries – Germany, Spain, Greece, Slovenia, Poland and Estonia spend between 18 and 25 percent. Other countries – such as Belgium, Finland, Denmark, Sweden, Austria and Italy spend between 26–28 percent. France is at the top, ahead of Denmark and Finland: it spends 31–32 percent of its GDP on social expenditures. On average in the 19 euro-zone countries, the numbers of medical doctors and hospital beds per 1,000 citizens are 3.9 (in the US, 2.6), and 6.2 (in the US, 2.9), respectively.

Social expenditures are financed by state revenue, which mainly comes from taxation. Between 2006 and 2018, direct and indirect tax incomes in France, Finland and Belgium were equal to 43–44 percent of the countries' GDP. In Austria, this number was 40–42 percent, in Germany it was 37–40 percent of GDP, in Hungary 36–38 percent, in Spain and Estonia 32–34 percent, in Slovakia 29–34 percent; in Ireland 22–28 percent; and in Bulgaria 27–28 percent. Overall, the tax payments of the European Union population represented between 33 and 40 percent of GDP.

Besides the social spending of the member states, the EU also support social programs from its budget that account for roughly 1 percent of the EU's aggregate GDP (in 2019 it was equal to €165.8 billion.) The EU's long-term budget for 2014–2020 was €1,082.5 billion. Roughly one-third of it was used to support the agricultural population, and even somewhat more was put towards creating growth and jobs, and towards reducing economic gaps between the EU's various regions and countries. The so-called cohesion fund's budget for 2014–2020 was €74,822,264,412. The greatest part supported 15 countries – Bulgaria, Croatia, Cyprus, the Czech Republic, Estonia, Greece, Hungary, Latvia, Lithuania, Malta, Poland, Portugal, Romania, Slovakia and Slovenia – and assisted their catching-up process.

According to the Eurostat's new figures from 2019, 5.6 percent of the EU citizens still live in very poor conditions, at risk of poverty and social exclusion. The situation is the worst in the Balkans; Bulgaria (almost 20 percent); Greece (almost 16 percent); and Romania (more than 12 percent); followed by Lithuania, Cyprus, Hungary, and Slovakia (more, or about 8 percent); Poland (almost 4 percent); and the Czech Republic (nearly 3 percent). In the Nordic member countries such as Sweden, the Netherlands and Finland, this segment of society is miniscule (between 1.5 and 2.5 percent).[22]

If one considers the impact of European integration on peace, the picture of historic significance becomes clear. For many, this is the most important achievement of the integration process. If counterfactual calculations about the economic impact of integration are uncertain, it seems to be more realistic to imagine postwar Europe in the light of a counterfactual hypothesis. Postwar revenge against Germany – the realization of the European plans (whether French or Russian) to mutilate and paralyze the country – would have led to a repetition of the same mistakes that were made after World War I. If that had occurred, it would have naturally led to a situation in which countries planted the seeds of the revenge of the revenge, thus creating new wars. Reconciliation between France and Germany and the creation of friendly relations and interconnections among countries at last were the most important results of integration. After the terrible, war-ridden first half of the twentieth century, and after a period in which the 200 of the previous 400 years saw major continual warfare on the Continent, European countries integrated and forged close interconnections. As a result, they have lived in peace for the last 75 years; war among the member countries of the European Union has become absolutely unimaginable.

What about the future?

The historical balance sheet of European integration, in spite of various existing weaknesses, unfinished business and unsolved problems, is excellent, and makes the post-World War II history of Europe quite exceptional. Nevertheless, it does not provide any guarantees for the future. Today, lack of understanding and lack of recognition for peoples' real self-interests are often combined with devastating nationalism. All these influences may undermine, halt or even destroy the great historical achievement of integration. The EU's reticence to punish vicious violations of the Union's basic democratic values and the rising anti-integration attacks by some member countries' governments – not to mention the EU's continued financial aid to those same governments – may strengthen nationalist forces and undermine the achievements of integration. An electoral victory of Marine Le Pen in France or the Alternative für Deutschland party in Germany might be enough for destruction. The lack of solidarity and burden sharing during the first part of the severe dual pandemic and economic crises of 2020 was a bad message, but major actions of solidarity and assistance, sharing the burden of the pandemic-generated crisis could significantly strengthen the Union.

Several authors who have written about the European Union end their studies by prophesizing about future possibilities. History, the immediate past and the present, may indeed offer some trends that could give a bit of ground for foreseeing possibilities for further progress towards a multi-speed structure for the European Union. This structure actually already exists in the form of the euro-zone countries, which share a common currency and a quasi-banking union, versus countries that are not part of it. The possibility of coexistence between different groups within the Union that are at different stages of integration is very realistic. Some countries, mentioning the extremes, may decide to move towards federal unification; others may choose just to remain in the free-trade zone. It is also a real possibility that nationalist-populist forces in more countries will also gain ground. In this case, they may deconstruct the entire Community into a simple free-trade zone. Some historians are guessing about the future, but I don't want to join them. I agree with German historian Jürgen Kocka, who stated in *Historians and the Future*: "Life experience and scholarship tell us that history usually enters the future and influences the paths it takes. [But] the possibilities from learning directly from history – in the sense of [Cicero's] *historia magistra vitea* – are very limited."[23] Numberless factors will influence the future of the Union – not only internal ones, but, as this entire book tries to prove, changes in the capitalist world system and the world political order as well. Who could have foreseen, even around the end of 2019, that within a few weeks the COVID-19 pandemic and a new economic crisis would cause such dramatic changes? Historians of the European Union can only document and prove the unparalleled advantages of integration, and point to the existing gaps and shortcomings of integration in order to aid understanding and emphasize the need for corrections and improvements. Thus we can help to show that the best future is an "ever closer union."

Notes

1 In this chapter, I have used some of my previous books connected to this topic: *An Economic History of Twentieth-Century Europe: Economic Regimes from Laissez-Faire to Globalization*, 2nd ed. (Cambridge: Cambridge University Press, 2016); *Economic History of a Divided Europe: Four Diverse Regions in an Integrating Continent* (London: Routledge, 2020); *The Economics and Politics of European Integration: Populism, Nationalism in the World and the History of the EU* (London: Routledge, forthcoming in 2021).

2 Robert William Fogel, *Railroads and American Economic Growth: Essays in Econometric History* (Baltimore, MD: Johns Hopkins Press, 1964).

3 "Intra-EU Trade in Goods–Main Features," *Eurostat*, April 2020, https://ec.europa.eu/eurostat/statistics-explained/index.php?title=Intra-EU_trade_in_goods_-_main_features, accessed May 29, 2020.

4 Marco Hafner, Enora Robin, and Stijn Hoorens, *The Cost of Non-Europe in the Single Market: Free Movement of Goods* (Santa Monica, CA: RAND Corporation, 2014), RR-862-EP, www.rand.org/pubs/research_reports/RR862.html, accessed October 5, 2017.

5 "Shaping Europe's Digital Future," *European Commission*, July 8, 2020, https://ec.europa.eu/digital-single-market/en, accessed July 10, 2020.

6 Stijn Hoorens, "A Closer Europe Is a Better Europe," *US News & World Report*, March 3, 2017, sec. Opinion, www.usnews.com/opinion/world-report/arti cles/2017-03-24/sixty-years-later-european-integration-has-benefited-eu-coun tries, accessed December 5, 2017.

7 This compilation gives some examples of recent research on the topic: "EU Membership – an Overview," *ScienceDirect Topics*, 2020, www.sciencedirect.com/top ics/economics-econometrics-and-finance/eu-membership, accessed July 10, 2020.

8 Kizito Uyi Ehigiamusoe and Hooi Hooi Lean, "Do Economic and Financial Integration Stimulate Economic Growth? A Critical Survey," *Economics*, Discussion Paper, June 15, 2018, https://doi.org/10.5018/economics-ejournal. ja.2019-4, accessed December 1, 2018; Nauro F. Campos, Fabrizio Coricelli, and Luigi Moretti, "Institutional Integration and Economic Growth in Europe," *Journal of Monetary Economics*, no. 103 (August 14, 2018): 88–104, https://doi.org/10.1016/j.jmoneco.2018.08.001, accessed September 27, 2018; Katja Mann, "The EU, a Growth Engine? The Impact of European Integration on Economic Growth in Central Eastern Europe," *FIW Working Paper*, no. 136 (January 2015); Richard Baldwin and Elena Seghezza, "Growth and European Integration: Towards an Empirical Assessment," *CEPR Discussion Papers*, 1996, https://ideas.repec.org/p/cpr/ceprdp/ 1393.html, accessed September 28, 2017; Dan Ben-David, "Equalizing Exchange: Trade Liberalization and Income Convergence," *The Quarterly Journal of Economics* 108, no. 3 (1993): 653–679, https://doi.org/10.2307/2118404, accessed September 23, 2017; Magnus Henrekson, Johan Torstensson, and Rasha Torstensson, "Growth Effects of European Integration," *European Economic Review* 41, no. 8 (August 1997): 1537–1557, https://doi.org/10.1016/S0014-2921(97)00063-9, accessed October 6, 2018; Ali M. Kutan and Taner M. Yigit, "European Integration, Productivity Growth and Real Convergence: Evidence from the New Member States," *Economic Systems* 33, no. 2 (June 1, 2009): 127–137, https://doi.org/10.1016/j.ecosys.2009.03.002, accessed November 5, 2017.

9 The two extremes are presented by Harald Badinger, *Growth Effects of Economic Integration: The Case of the EU Member States (1950–2000)*, IEF Working Paper 40 (Vienna: Research Institute for European Affairs, December 2001); Barry Eichengreen and Andrea Boltho, *The Economic Impact of European Integration*, Discussion Paper No. 6820 (London: Centre for Economic Policy Research, May 2008), www.researchgate.net/publication/4761629_The_Economic_Impact_of_Euro pean_Integration, accessed October 8, 2017.

10 Angus Maddison, *Monitoring the World Economy, 1820–1992* (Paris: Development Centre of the Organisation for Economic Co-operation and Development, 1995).

11 Throughout this section, the calculations up to 1990 are based on Maddison. *The 2000 and 2014 Figures Are Calculated from Pocket World in Figures 2004* (London: Economist Books, 2005); *Pocket World in Figures 2017* (London: Economist Books, 2018). The 2016 figures are based on data from "Countries by Projected GDP per Capita 2016," *Statistics Times*, June 7, 2017, http://statisticstimes.com/ economy/countries-by-projected-gdp-capita.php, accessed October 2, 2017.

12 The 1913 and 1950 figures are based on Maddison, *Monitoring the World Economy, 1820–1992*. The 2013 figures are based on *Pocket World in Figures 2017*.

13 Bart van Ark, Mary O'Mahoney, and Marcel P. Timmer, "The Productivity Gap between Europe and the United States: Trends and Causes," *Journal of Economic Perspectives* 22, no. 1 (March 2008): 25–44, https://doi.org/10.1257/jep.22.1.25, accessed November 8, 2017.
14 *Pocket World in Figures 2017.*
15 Thomas Philippon, "The U.S. Only Pretends to Have Free Markets," *The Atlantic*, October 29, 2019, sec. Ideas, www.theatlantic.com/ideas/archive/2019/10/europe-not-america-home-free-market/600859/, accessed January 28, 2020.
16 Ibid.
17 Ibid.
18 Selim Jahan et al., *Human Development Report 2016: Human Development for Everyone* (New York City: United Nations Development Programme, 2016), https://doi.org/10.18356/ b6186701-en, accessed September 8, 2017.
19 "Number of Expected Years of Education per Person over a Lifetime in the European Union (28 Countries) from 2003 to 2012," *Statista*, March 2015, www.statista.com/statistics/435552/eu-28-expected-years-of-education-over-life time/, accessed October 18, 2017.
20 Perry Anderson, "Depicting Europe," *London Review of Books* 29, no. 18 (September 20, 2007), www.lrb.co.uk/the-paper/v29/n18/perry-anderson/depicting-europe, accessed October 27, 2017.
21 "Social Protection Statistics 2016," *Eurostat*, November 2019, https://ec.europa.eu/eurostat/statistics-explained/index.php/Social_protection_statistics, accessed January 3, 2020.
22 "Social Protection Statistics 2016?," https://www.lrb.co.uk/the-paper/v29/neurostat-news/-/DDN-20200429-1, accessed November 3, 2017.
23 Jürgen Kocka, *Historians and the Future*, The Wittrock Lecture Book Series 1 (Uppsala: Swedish Collegium for Advanced Study, 2020), 26, www.swedish collegium.se/subfolders/Books&Lectures/SCAS_Publications.html, accessed June 3, 2020.

Index

Printed in the United States
By Bookmasters